Gender Inequality at Work

Gender Inequality at Work

Jerry A. Jacobs
editor

SAGE Publications
International Educational and Professional Publisher
Thousand Oaks   London   New Delhi

For information address:

Sage Publications, Inc.
2455 Teller Road
Thousand Oaks, California 91320

SAGE Publications Ltd.
6 Bonhill Street
London EC2A 4PU
United Kingdom

SAGE Publications India Pvt. Ltd.
M-32 Market
Greater Kailash I
New Delhi 110 048 India

Printed in the United States of America

Library of Congress Cataloging-in-Publication Data

Gender inequality at work / edited by Jerry A. Jacobs.
    p. cm. —
    Includes bibliographical references and index.
    ISBN 0-8039-5696-7 (cl). — ISBN 0-8039-5697-5 (pb)
    1. Sex discrimination in employment. I. Jacobs, Jerry A., 1955–   .
HD6060.G46   1995
331.4′133—dc20   94-32845

95 96 97 98 99 10 9 8 7 6 5 4 3 2 1

Sage Production Editor: Diana E. Axelsen

Contents

1

Introduction

JERRY A. JACOBS

I am delighted to bring this fine collection of papers to a wide audience. This volume brings together cutting-edge research by leading scholars in the area of gender inequality. Readers will learn a great deal about gender inequality in earnings, authority, occupational status, and career processes. Why do women earn less than men? Why are men the bosses and women the subordinates? Do occupations decline in status when women enter? These questions and many related ones are addressed here in sophisticated yet accessible chapters.

You will see how gender affects careers in a variety of settings: among screenwriters, managers, civil servants, teachers, and sociologists. You will learn what areas of opportunity have opened up to working women in recent years and what barriers remain. You will learn why women have entered certain occupations in large numbers and what the consequences of feminization can be. You will see many points of agreement among the analysts included here, along with some notable areas of disagreement. The chapters are written in clear and straightforward prose: Every effort has been made to render sophisticated statistics and complex theories in a manner easily understood by the nonspecialist.

This project began as a special issue of the journal, *Work and Occupations*. I was convinced that the articles in that issue were of such high quality and of such broad interest that they should be published as a book. Mitchell Allen of Sage Publications, Inc., agreed. For this volume, seven chapters were added to the five original articles. Just after the *Work and Occupations* special issue appeared, I organized a panel at the Society for the Advancement of Socio-economics meetings at which Jo Anne Preston, Donald Tomaskovic-Devey, Patricia Roos, Rosemary Wright, and I presented papers. Four of the supplemental papers included in this volume stemmed from that meeting. This introductory essay provides an overview of these 12 chapters in the context of contemporary research on gender and equality, and Pamela Stone of Hunter College provides a closing analytical review and assessment of progress in Chapter 14.

The expanded scope of the volume enabled me to include three chapters on each of four topics: compensation, management and authority, career processes and trends, and occupational feminization. I chose these topics because of their importance for working women and because in each of these areas I was able to locate an excellent set of interrelated papers that advanced our understanding of gender inequality.

Each of these areas is fundamental to our understanding of the sex segregation of work and its implications for gender inequality. Earnings are the principal tangible reward that workers take home. The chapters included here provide important new evidence and explanations of the link between the gender gap in earnings and workplace segregation between men and women. Gender differences in authority have garnered increased attention as a new term, *the glass ceiling,* has entered the political vocabulary.

The chapters included here provide rich detail on the contours of managerial authority and indicate the extent to which women have made progress in entering the ranks of management. Gender differences in career processes feature prominently in many explanations of gender inequality. The chapters in this section are fine examples of how careful analyses can specify how gender shapes the trajectory of careers. And, finally, examining the process of feminization should enable us to understand the mechanisms responsible for occupational segregation. The three chapters in this section consider the feminization of sociology, computer work, and teaching as case studies.

In this introductory chapter, I briefly sketch how sex segregation came to be recognized as a linchpin of gender inequality at work. I then briefly review the economic approach to gender inequality and show how a sociological approach has become a necessary complement to the economic perspective. I then discuss each of the four topics examined here. I summarize the chapters in the volume and explain how each builds on established knowledge in each area.

Sex Segregation and Gender Inequality

The segregation of men and women at work refers to the degree to which men and women do different work. Segregation occurs along many dimensions. Men and women work in different sectors of the economy (e.g., government, nonprofit, private sector), in different occupations, and in different industries. The more finely grained the classification system employed, the more segregation is revealed. When researchers employ the job titles used by firms as their unit of analysis, a very high degree of workplace segregation between men and women becomes evident. Workplace segregation is commonly measured by the index of dissimilarity, which indicates the proportion of women who would have to move in order for women to be distributed in the same manner as men. This measure, along with other useful indices, is described in Chapter 10 (see also Jacobs, 1993).

Research on sex segregation at work is scarcely 20 years old. Only a few important pieces of research were conducted before 1974. In 1968, Gross showed that the level of occupational segregation by sex remained remarkably constant throughout the 20th century. Gross's article has become a standard reference in this area, and subsequent research has refined and reconfirmed his basic findings (Jacobs, 1989a), yet before 1974 hardly any researchers pursued the questions raised by Gross.

In 1974, Rosaldo and Lamphere's collection of anthropological papers appeared. It marked a consolidation of interest in gender inequality in its field, focusing on the separation of men and women into different spheres of social life. An interdisciplinary collection edited by Blaxall and Reagan (1976) quickly followed. The Blaxall and Reagan volume identified sex-segregated work roles as an important area of research for students of gender inequality.

Before sex segregation could take center stage in sociology, however, it had to emerge from the shadow of the status attainment framework, which dominated sociological research on inequality during the 1970s. This framework sought to delineate the connections between the occupational status of fathers and sons. Once feminist research questions began to enter sociology, this work was criticized for leaving women out (Acker, 1980). But when women were included, results were puzzling. The status attainment framework was not revealing with respect to gender inequality. The problem was not simply leaving women out of the analysis, but rather the questions asked and the measures used were designed to understand the situations of male breadwinners. Gender inequality is not reducible to social class: Women and men can be in the same social class but have very different gender statuses. Simply put, women—whether they live in rich, middle-class, or poor families—are more economically vulnerable than their male counterparts. A more subtle problem with the status attainment approach was that the measure of occupational success was designed to index the occupational status of men and proved misleading when applied to occupational comparisons of men and women (Jacobs, 1989b; Jacobs & Powell, 1987). These difficulties led researchers interested in better understanding gender inequality to focus on other measures, such as earnings, authority, and sex segregation itself, although some researchers occasionally relapse into reliance on the status attainment framework (Diprete & Grusky, 1990).

By the time the National Academy of Sciences reports on sex segregation at work were released (Reskin, 1984; Treiman & Hartmann, 1981), sex segregation had become recognized as a central component of gender inequality. Chapters in Reskin's volume established themes that continue to be important: the link between sex segregation and earnings inequality, stability and change in the level of sex segregation, the high level of job-level segregation, the processes of career mobility, and the process of occupational feminization.

As sociologists moved away from intergenerational mobility to a focus on the structure of labor markets and the dynamics of career processes, they began to confront economic theories. It would be hard to give an account of the intellectual climate of this period without recognizing the ongoing debate between economic and sociological approaches to labor markets. In the next section I briefly summarize some of the central reservations sociologists have regarding the economic explanation of gender inequality at work.

Gender Inequality and Investments in Skills

Labor economists hold that earnings reflect workers' productivity. Large earnings differences across groups must reflect differences in investments in skills that make one group more productive than another. When confronted with the persistent gender gap in wages, economists look for differences in skills to explain this gap. It must be that women invest less in the acquisition of skills than do men, presumably because they expect to work for fewer years than men and thus have less opportunity to reap the returns on their investments. However, the investment story does not fit the facts.

It may be useful to separate out three different strands of the investment story. The first pertains to the years of schooling of men and women. What is remarkable is that women in the United States throughout the 20th century have remained in school nearly as long as men (England, 1993; Jacobs, 1989b). Women have been more likely than men to finish high school, although men have been more likely to start and finish college. If one focuses on women in the labor market, working women have surpassed men in the number of years of schooling completed.

Women may seek to acquire an education for many reasons. Schooling is not simply an investment in earnings but also represents an investment in a richer and more stimulating life, with a broadened set of interests and the social skills needed to handle life's challenges. Economically, more schooling for women means more than just their expected wages. For example, more schooling for women increases their chances of marrying a better educated and higher-earning husband (although very highly educated women may be less likely to marry) (Goldin, 1992). For whatever reasons, working women have stayed in school as long as men. Thus, in its most commonly understood sense, it is not the case that women's underinvestment in schooling is responsible for the sex gap in earnings we observe.

A second strand of the investment story is that women concentrate in educational specialties that are less economically rewarding than those chosen by men. Economists sometimes refer to this pattern as a difference in educational quality, as if a degree in literature were of lower quality than a degree in engineering. What they mean is that certain fields are more rewarding financially. Part of the sex gap in earnings is due to the specialization of women in different fields than men choose (Jacobs, 1994; U S. Bureau of the Census, 1987). But women's selection of different fields of study itself is difficult to explain as an investment strategy. Why should women specialize in different fields than men choose? The cost of getting a degree in classics is the same as getting one in engineering, in terms of the tuition paid and the "opportunity cost" of lost earnings during schooling. Why not pursue the fields with the highest payoffs?

Again, the economic explanation for these decisions falls short. It has been suggested that women's pursuit of certain typically feminine specialties enables them to maximize their lifetime earnings. Female-dominated fields, it has been argued, have relatively high rewards early in life and a low rate of growth in earnings over time. By pursuing these fields, women earn the most during the period when they are most likely to be working (Polachek, 1978). It is an interesting theory, but it doesn't fit the facts. Female-dominated fields pay less than male-dominated fields, both in starting salary and in subsequent salary growth and promotions (England, Farkas, Kilbourne, & Dou, 1988). Nor has anyone shown convincingly that women's choice of field of study is related to their expected number of years in the labor force. In other words, there is no evidence that women who receive education and nursing degrees in college expect to work fewer years than those who pursue business or engineering degrees. An analysis of a survey of college seniors shows that the expectation of working full-time 10 years after college does not explain women's concentration in different fields of study from their male counterparts (Jacobs & Powell, 1994).

A third strand of the investment story is that individuals accumulate skills on the job. Women have less work experience than men, and it has been shown repeatedly that a significant fraction of the gender gap in earnings is due to the interrupted work experience of women. But this aspect of the investment story is much more complicated, on closer inspection. First, it is not entirely clear why more experience translates into higher wages. Some have argued that seniority rather than higher productivity accounts for a significant part of the experience premium (Abraham & Farber, 1988). Second, low wages contribute to lower labor force attachment among women (Killingsworth & Heckman, 1986). All things being equal, a woman will be more likely to quit working to stay home with a young child if she barely earns enough to pay for child care, whereas a woman with a high-paid professional job will have more incentive to remain in the labor force. Thus the sex differential in experience reflects as well as contributes to the gender gap in wages. Historically, there have been periods when women were barred or strongly discouraged from working after marriage (Goldin, 1990), a practice that has remained common until recently in certain positions in Japan (Brinton, 1993). A third problem with the on-the-job experience story concerns the question of who pays the cost of training, employers or employees. Much economic writing suggests that employees bear the cost of learning general (as opposed to firm-specific) skills, and this would lead to the same prediction as above: Women would invest less in training because they have a shorter period during which to realize the payoffs of this investment (Becker, 1964). But others argue that employers bear the cost of training (Bassi, 1994). Studies have shown that employers invest less in training women (Jacobs, Lukens, & Useem, 1994; Lynch, 1991). Thus, part of the earnings gap attributed to differences in experience may itself reflect gender differences in access to career development opportunities.

In short, the investment story is not sufficient to explain gender inequality at work. This is not to say that skills are irrelevant in the labor market. Skills do matter, and skills can account for some group differences. The gap in earnings between white men and African American men, for example, has much more to do with educational differences than does the gap between women and men. However, to explain the gender gap in wages, we must look beyond skills to other processes at work.

Sex Segregation and Social Control

A brief overview of the sociological approach to employment is outlined in the chapter by Jacobs and Steinberg (Chapter 4, this volume) on "compensating differentials." There we argue that sociologists include context, politics, and culture in their analyses of employment outcomes. Sociologists hold that context matters because labor markets are not perfectly efficient. People do not have perfect information on all alternatives, change is costly, and people become used to their situations (in economic terms, "tastes" are "endogenous").

Politics—both governmental and in the workplace—matter. Governments set the terms of labor market arrangements by regulating hours worked, wages, hiring, and training practices, and benefits. Economists tend to see politics as external mechanisms that potentially undermine the efficiency of labor markets, whereas sociologists see employment systems as inevitably embedded in social life in ways that are sometimes constructive and other times less so. Politics within the workplace matter for morale, retention, and productivity. Culture matters not simply as a reflection of individual tastes. The predominant expectations set for groups of people matter a great deal. Economists often see labor markets as naturally eroding prejudices and other cultural beliefs that are inconsistent with market efficiency. Sociologists, in contrast, tend to see employment systems as adaptable systems that reflect as much as determine the prejudices of the members of a society.

My own research has focused on the question of gender and social control (Jacobs, 1989b). This view points to social forces that restrict women's options before and after they enter the labor market. It is distinctive in stressing the similarities between social pressures exerted before and after women enter the labor market. Whereas economists exclude taste formation from their analysis and insist that individuals bring fixed tastes with them to the marketplace, my research has stressed the instability of behavior over time and the extent to which lines of demarcation between male and female are continually negotiated and must be continually reinforced over time.

In my view, career aspirations are important in determining expectations and preferences. But these aspirations are much less fixed and determinative than is often supposed. In other words, the level of segregation by sex in career aspirations mirrors that found in the labor market. But individuals change career goals with remarkable frequency between male-dominated, sex-neutral, and female-dominated fields. The structure of preferences stays segregated, but individuals move within this segregated structure. Similarly, although the choice of field of study in college is subject to enormous change during the college years, male and female college seniors remain largely as segregated from one another as they were as freshmen. The sex type of college major thus reflects social influences during the college years in addition to initial preferences and career expectations. I document similar patterns of mobility in the labor force as well. A related point is that during periods of change, change is experienced not just by new entrants to the labor market but also by those already at work.

Many of the questions addressed throughout this book are directly related to the issues raised by the social control framework, although the terminology of social control is not always used. The social control thesis raises questions regarding career processes that are addressed in the chapters by Bielby and Bielby (Chapter 8, this volume) and Rosenfeld and Spenner (Chapter 9, this volume). It also raises questions regarding the rates and patterns of change in segregation. If social control forces throughout the life course are responsible for maintaining occupational segregation, then relaxing those controls may affect those already in the labor force, as well as new entrants. The extent to which we have seen a decline in segregation in men's and women's roles at work is a running concern throughout this volume.

The social control thesis is concerned with the access of women to different positions, whether it is jobs, occupations, or positions with authority. It assumes the differential evaluation of male-dominated and female-dominated work. This undervaluation of women's work is where the chapters in this book begin.

The Gender Gap in Wages

Earnings differences between working men and women have been the focus of a great deal of empirical research, not only because of the importance of money. This line of research speaks directly to the issue of whether inequality is meritocratic, whether markets are efficient, and whether our society is fair. Moreover, earnings is an outcome measure easily assessed with available data sets.

What do we know about the gender gap in earnings? The most recent statistics indicate that women working full-time and all year earn three quarters of the take-home pay of their male counterparts. The gender gap in wages has been shrinking, although the interpretation of this change is not settled. Economists emphasize that women's work experience has been growing, whereas sociologists have emphasized changes in the labor market that have reduced men's earnings (compare O'Neil & Polachek, 1993, and Institute for Women's Policy Research, 1993).

Women are paid less than men in large part because they do different work. The problem is thus not readily correctable by legislation calling for equal pay for equal work. Data from the 1990 Census indicate that more than half of women would have to change occupations before women would be distributed in the same manner as men (Reskin, 1994). Occupational data capture only a portion of the true level of segregation at work. When segregation is estimated across jobs rather than occupations, approximately 70% of women would have to move before complete integration with men would be achieved.

The significance of sex segregation has been challenged because occupational segregation explains "only" one fifth to one third of the sex gap in wages. Adding industry-level segregation increases the total due to workplace segregation to about two fifths of the gender gap in wages (Sorensen, 1989). However, adding job-level data captures a very substantial proportion of the gender gap in wages. In fact, the weakness of occupational segregation is in fact more a matter of measurement limitations than a weakness in the underlying concept.

The comparison between occupations and jobs is the starting point for Tomaskovic-Devey's chapter (Chapter 2, this volume). He shows that job-level data capture more of the gender gap in wages than do occupational data. Ever since Bielby and Baron (1984) showed that sex segregation measured across job titles within firms is extremely high, students of gender inequality have recognized the importance of job-level studies.

Yet Bielby and Baron could not link their job-level data to individuals' earnings. Tomaskovic-Devey's study delivers the findings on the earnings consequences of job-level segregation, findings that have been anticipated for a decade. His analysis of North Carolina survey data shows that job-level segregation explains nearly half of the sex gap in wages. Occupational measures, in contrast, explain one third of the gap. Further, more than one fifth of the sex gap in wages is due to other job-level factors, many of which are indirectly related to the sex composition of the job. Specific jobs in particular firms—rather than occupations within broadly defined industries—are key contributors to gender inequality.

Tomaskovic-Devey's research, along with other recent studies (Petersen & Morgan, 1993), leaves little doubt that jobs in which women predominate pay less than jobs traditionally performed by men. But why does women's work pay less? Steinberg's work on the sex bias of job evaluation systems (Chapter 3, this volume) seeks to identify the mechanisms responsible for the undervaluation of women's work. Steinberg delves into the mechanics of job evaluation systems that are commonly used to administer wages in large organizations. She shows that job attributes defined nearly a half-century ago continue to bias wage systems against women's work. By exploring the technical underpinnings of the Hay system, a leading proprietary job evaluation system, she shows how important aspects of technical, clerical, and service jobs become invisible in terms of the allocation of financial rewards. Several of her examples are especially telling. She notes that because the Hay system's definition of Human Relations Know-How is skewed toward managerial responsibilities rather than client contact, Hay consultants rate the human relations skills of prison guards, who have quasi-managerial authority, higher than those of nurses. Using data from the state of Minnesota and other sources, Steinberg demonstrates just how much these assumptions cost women.

Many justifications have been offered as explanations for the low wages paid to female-dominated occupations. Sometimes it seems as if a minor industry has arisen devoted to setting up and knocking down the latest rationalization for paying women less. One of these ideas, the notion of compensating differentials, is the topic of the chapter by Jacobs and Steinberg (Chapter 4, this volume). Economists have suggested that women earn less in part because men work in dangerous, dirty, strenuous, and otherwise distasteful jobs. The results of the analysis do not support this conclusion, even when extreme working conditions and clusters of job attributes are considered. The study draws on data on a wide range of job attributes culled from *The New York State Comparable Pay Study* (Steinberg, Haignere, Possin, Chertos, & Treiman, 1985). The chapter also reviews the distinctive elements of a sociological approach to labor markets.

Gender and Managerial Authority

The second section of this book examines the gender gap in authority. The glass ceiling has become a familiar term for the idea that women continue to face barriers in making their way up the corporate hierarchy. One of the key obstacles to women's advancement is that the higher one climbs on the corporate ladder, the more likely one is to have subordinates. Our society remains quite resistant to the notion of women having authority, although important changes have occurred in this area over the last 20 years.

The gender gap in authority has been studied less than the gender gap in earnings, because data on authority relations at work are rarely available. The available data are often limited in scope, typically including a simple question about supervisors and subordinates. The first prominent study of the gender gap in wages treated managerial authority as a dummy variable: Either one had a position of authority or not (Wolf & Fligstein, 1979). Yet detailed studies of workplace relations reveal a wide spectrum of managerial discretion. Some managers control budgets, scheduling, and policies, in addition to having the authority to hire and fire subordinates. Other managers have much more limited power.

The chapter by Reskin and Ross (Chapter 5, this volume) employs such data to provide an unprecedented examination of the contours of gender inequality in authority. In an analysis of data collected in 1982 in Illinois, Reskin and Ross consider whether women exercise as much authority on the job as men do. The authors demonstrate that men led women in 15 of 21 types of responsibility. Multivariate analyses show that even after productivity-related measures and tenure were controlled, women garnered less authority than men and earned less than men with similar standing in their organizations. Reskin and Ross show that women remain well behind their male counterparts in enjoying the rewards of management.

Boyd, Mulvihill, and Myles (Chapter 7, this volume) cover some of the same terrain, using data for Canada. Linking their analysis to the growth of a postindustrial economy, they suggest that women do not gain access to authority as a result of the expansion of service-sector jobs. As was the case with Reskin and Ross, their chapter is remarkable for the richness of the data. The Boyd et al. chapter is unique because it includes information on the sex composition of subordinates. They document what many have suspected: Women supervise other women and rarely exercise authority over men.

But the gender gap in authority needs to be put in perspective. One must recognize the dramatic increase in representation among managers. Women's representation among managers in the United States soared from 17% in 1970 to 40% in 1988. Women's substantial representation among managers is likely to continue if college enrollment data are any indication. In 1990, 46.7% of undergraduate business degree recipients were women. My chapter on women managers (Chapter 6, this volume) asks whether this dramatic transformation in the ranks of managers is real or whether it is a smoke screen designed to thwart reporting requirements of the Equal Employment Opportunity Commission (EEOC). The chapter documents that the sex gap in earnings among managers narrowed somewhat during this period, evidence that is consistent with the conclusion that women are not simply getting managerial titles but are indeed making progress into the ranks of middle management. The study also draws on data from the General Social Survey on authority, attitudes, and values of male and female managers. Thus an historical view suggests significant expansion in opportunities for women in the ranks of American managers during the 1970s and 1980s.

Career Dynamics and Trends

The next section includes chapters on career processes and a study of recent trends in opportunities for women. The increasing availability of data sets that follow individuals over time has led to increasing interest in career processes. Yet theoretical progress in this area has been limited. Many women experience career interruptions, and much debate has focused on assessing the impact of these disruptions on women's earnings. But a broader analysis of career development has been slow in coming.

As I mentioned above in the discussion of social control, most theories assume substantial continuity in careers. The basic metaphor that dominates the analysis of careers is that of tracking. One must get on track early and stay on track, because it becomes increasingly difficult, if not impossible, to switch at a later date. Early life experiences are assumed to predict later ones, and inequality is assumed to grow as a result of cumulative disadvantage. However, women's careers are not as orderly as this model implies. Moreover, the U.S. employment system is more flexible than those in many other countries, and the tracking system is less tightly structured. To what extent can we account for the sex segregation of work in terms of the tracking metaphor?

Rachel Rosenfeld and Kenneth Spenner (Chapter 9, this volume) consider this question by examining moves between male-dominated and female-dominated fields in a representative sample of 2,500 young women. Most theories assume that women who pursue work in traditionally female jobs are different in terms of family commitments and career orientation from those who pursue male-dominated jobs. Yet a series of studies has documented remarkable movement between male-dominated and female-dominated jobs, suggesting that the two types of workers are not as distinct as many assume. Fully 86% of young women changed the sex type of their occupation at least once in the 13 years following high school, findings that match earlier results quite closely (Jacobs, 1989b; Rosenfeld, 1983). Rosenfeld and Spenner examine detailed life history data and employ sophisticated event-history techniques to ask what factors facilitate such moves. The authors extend previous research by showing that moves between male- and female-dominated fields have little to do with family considerations, although some moves are related to women's career aspirations, educational credentials, and preferences for higher salaries. These results show that sex segregation is not simply a product of the investments and tastes women bring with them to the labor market. Rather sex segregation is reinforced by a system of social control that is reproduced throughout the careers of working men and women. Rosenfeld and Spenner conclude by suggesting that a typology of career moves is needed to explain individual mobility across sex-typed boundaries.

Many aspects of gender inequality—such as earnings—grow over the course of careers. However, other aspects are less tied to age. The sex segregation of occupations in the United States is not higher for older women than for younger women, and during the 1970s women in all age groups moved into previously male-dominated fields. Specifying which aspects of inequality grow with time and which are stable is an important question. A related issue is identifying the contexts in which inequality grows with age and labor market experience and those in which it is more stable over time. This is the question addressed in Chapter 8 (this volume). William and Denise Bielby explore the market for television screenwriters by analyzing a large data set on earnings and mobility that spans the 1980s. The study documents a sizable and persistent gender gap in earnings among screenwriters, which occurs outside formal organizational structures, as screenwriters usually act as independent subcontractors. The authors maintain that this earnings gap results from the ambiguous nature of judging creative personnel, such as script writers. In such circumstances, "social similarity, in general, and gender stereotypes, in particular, are likely to influence decisions." This is a case of continuous, rather than cumulative, disadvantage over the course of writers' careers. Bielby and Bielby conclude by noting modest improvements in the relative standing of recent cohorts of women screenwriters.

How does sex segregation in the United States compare to that observed in other countries? Are the same trends in evidence throughout the world, or perhaps throughout the industrialized world? Or is the United States unique?

My chapter with Suet T. Lim (Chapter 10, this volume) explores trends in occupational and industrial sex segregation in 56 countries. This chapter is based on highly aggregated data, yet makes the case that detailed and broad measures of segregation tend to move in the same direction over time. The evidence indicates that sex segregation declined slightly between 1960 and 1980 in many countries. This trend is even more uniform when the growth of segregated fields is controlled. In other words, the *compositional* changes in occupations and industries are generally moving toward more integration, even though this trend is cancelled in some countries by higher growth rates of segregated fields. A multivariate analysis indicates that these trends are not related to modernization indices.

Feminization, Resegregation, and Ghettoization

The last section of this volume considers explanations for occupational feminization. How do occupations become dominated by women? What are the consequences for earnings, status, and careers? One of the most intriguing lines of inquiry in the area of women and work has been devoted to explaining the cases where occupations change their sex composition. The logic of inquiry is appealing: By focusing on fields that switch from being male-dominated to female-dominated, perhaps we will be able to see how occupations become labeled as appropriate for one sex or the other. There is also a disturbing aspect to the questions raised in these studies. Whereas statistical analyses of segregation see women's entry into previously male-dominated fields as an unqualified advance, this line of inquiry explores whether such advances are less than they seem. Do women receive rewards equal to their male counterparts? Will the status of the occupation diminish once women enter? In short, are the gains of women short-lived or illusory, to be undercut by a process of ghettoization or resegregation?

Roos and Jones (Chapter 11, this volume) consider the case of sociology, which they note is increasingly recruiting women to its ranks, although academic positions are far from being dominated by women. They draw on the influential Reskin and Roos (1990) model, which holds that the status of an occupation is often beginning to decline before women are permitted to enter in large numbers. Roos and Jones document many facets of the decline in academic sociology, including declining federal support for sociological research, declining job prospects, and declining earnings. Roos and Jones contend that these factors contributed to a decline in the numbers of young men aspiring to be sociologists. They also note that for the first time, academic departments of sociology sought out women as a result of the cultural changes and direct pressure brought about by feminists.

Wright and Jacobs (Chapter 12, this volume) challenge the Reskin and Roos model as applied to the case of computer workers. Women entered computer work in large numbers of the last 2 decades, yet Wright and Jacobs show that the earnings of computer workers are not in decline relative to their counterparts in the labor force. Their study is based on a panel of computer workers interviewed by the National Science Foundation four times between 1982 and 1989. Further, they maintain that men do not leave computer work in response to women's entry. In this way, the feminization of an occupation, at least in recent years, has not resulted in male flight, paralleling the flight of whites from neighborhoods following the entry of African Americans.

Preston (Chapter 13, this volume) addresses many of the same issues in the context of the feminization of teaching in the 19th century. She considers how feminization limited the professionalization of teaching. Preston shows how jobs in Massachusetts were constructed so that there was no overlap in titles between men and women, despite the fact that both served as classroom teachers. Male grammar school teachers were called grammar masters, writing masters, submasters, and ushers, whereas women were called head assistants and assistants. Even the male ushers, the lowest rank in the male hierarchy, earned double the amount of the top female salary and nearly three times the female average. Preston argues that teachers' autonomy in the classroom and their control over their profession were limited because the work was performed by women.

It is fashionable in some circles to criticize "politically correct feminists" for their narrow-minded dogmatism. Readers turning here for ammunition to support this view will be disappointed, for there is no party line in this collection. Indeed, there is vigorous disagreement on a number of issues. My chapter on women in management (Jacobs, Chapter 6, this volume) stresses the progress made over the last 20 years, whereas the chapters by Reskin and Ross (Chapter 5, this volume), and Boyd and her colleagues (Chapter 7, this volume) emphasize the remaining disparities between men and women in the realm of authority. Roos and Jones (Chapter 11, this volume) approach the nature of occupational feminization differently than do Wright and Jacobs (Chapter 12, this volume). Tomaskovic-Devey (Chapter 2, this volume) insists on the need to analyze job-level data, whereas Jacobs and Lim (Chapter 10, this volume) analyze highly aggregated occupation and industry data in their broadly international chapter.

Taken together, this work suggests an active research frontier. These chapters make progress in specifying mechanisms responsible for continued gender stratification and in indicating conditions under which such inequality is attenuated. This volume leaves me optimistic that much progress is being made toward an interweaving of social, political, economic, and organizational explanations for stability and change in gender stratification.

There is both diversity and commonality in mode of inquiry and subject matter. The chapters are quantitative and qualitative, historical and contemporary, structural and cultural. Represented are case studies and analyses of national data sets, academic reports and policy-oriented material. Readers will find much common ground as well. The chapters focus on explaining change over time, both in the lives of individual women and in the opportunities they face, following C. Wright Mills' (1959) dictum that sociologists should address the intersection of biography and history. Some of the chapters follow individuals over their lives and careers. Others follow an occupation or profession over time. A couple of chapters employ the traditional cross-sectional design, but even these are set in an historical context and address the basic historical questions of how much change we have seen in opportunities for women and how much distance remains between our current state of affairs and complete gender equality. This collection covers a broad terrain and reflects the vitality and diversity of current sociological research on gender inequality.

I am well aware that many topics have been left out. Race, ethnicity, and international comparisons all receive less attention than they deserve. Fortunately, a number of researchers have examined issues of race, ethnicity, and gender (Andersen & Collins, 1992; Bean & Tienda, 1987; Collins, 1990; Jones, 1985; King, 1992; McGuire & Reskin, 1993; Ortiz, 1994; Reskin, 1994; Tomaskovic-Devey, 1993; Yamanaka & McClelland, 1994; Zinn & Dill, 1994). The Memphis State Center for Research on Women has compiled an excellent bibliography of materials on race and gender.

The cross-national literature on gender inequality remains relatively small (Blau & Kahn, 1992; Gornick & Jacobs, 1994; Rosenfeld & Kalleberg, 1990; Treiman & Roos, 1983). Policy issues, including part-time and other flexible employment policies, child care, the double shift, sexual harassment in the workplace, and others, also are underrepresented in this volume (but see Gutek, 1985; Hochschild, 1989; Hyde & Essex, 1991; Kahne, 1985; Kammerman & Kahn, 1991; Spalter-Roth & Hartmann, 1990; Tilly, 1990). The publications of the Institute for Women's Policy Research in Washington, D.C., are an excellent starting place for those interested in an analysis of a progressive policy agenda. Yet given the remarkable vitality of research in this area, it is simply not possible to represent the full range of quality research under way. I decided it would be best to offer depth on those issues that are covered. I would hope this volume will be judged by the excellent research included here rather than the many important topics that are left out.

I would like to thank three journals for granting permission to reprint the following articles. The chapter entitled "Gender, Power, and Postindustrialism" is a revised version of an article with the same title first printed in the *Canadian Review of Sociology and Anthropology,* Volume 28, Number 4. The chapter entitled "Women's Entry into Management" first appeared as an article with the same title in *Administrative Science Quarterly,* Volume 37, Number 2. The chapter entitled "Male Flight from Computer Work: A New Look at Occupational Resegregation and Ghettoization" first appeared in the *American Sociological Review,* Volume 59, Number 4.

I would like to thank all the contributors for the excellent (and prompt) contributions and Andrew Abbott for suggesting the *Work and Occupa-*

I would like to thank all the contributors for the excellent (and prompt) contributions and Andrew Abbott for suggesting the *Work and Occupations* special issue. I finished work on this project during my stay as a Visiting Scholar at the Russell Sage Foundation. I want to thank Eric Wanner and the staff at Russell Sage for this opportunity to work in such a supportive and stimulating setting. This book is dedicated to my daughter, Elizabeth, in the hope that her career options will be many and her hurdles no greater than those of the boys she plays with in her day-care class.

References

Abraham, K. G., & Farber, H. S. (1988). Returns to seniority in union and nonunion jobs: A new look at the evidence. *Industrial and Labor Relations Review, 42*, 3-19.

Acker, J. (1980). Women and stratification: A review of recent literature. *Contemporary Sociology, 9*(1), 25-35.

Andersen, M. L., & Collins, P. H. (1992). *Race, class and gender: An anthology.* Belmont, CA: Wadsworth.

Bassi, L. J. (1994). Workplace education for hourly workers. *Journal of Policy Analysis and Management, 13*(1), 55-74.

Bean, F. D., & Tienda, M. (1987). *The Hispanic population of the United States.* New York: Russell Sage Foundation.

Becker, G. (1964). *Human capital.* New York: Columbia University Press.

Bielby, W. T., & Baron, J. N. (1984). A woman's place is with other women: Sex segregation in the workplace. In B. Reskin (Ed.), *Sex segregation in the workplace: Trends, explanations, remedies* (pp. 27-55). Washington, DC: National Academy Press.

Blau, F. D., & Kahn, L. M. (1992). The gender earnings gap: Learning from international comparisons. *The American Economic Review, 82*, 533-538.

Blaxall, M., & Reagan, B. (Eds.). (1976). *Women and the workplace: The implications of occupational segregation.* Chicago: University of Chicago Press.

Brinton, M. C. (1993). *Women and the economic miracle: Gender and work in post-war Japan.* Berkeley: University of California Press.

Collins, P. H. (1990). *Black feminist thought: Knowledge, consciousness, and the politics of empowerment.* Boston: Unwin Hyman.

Diprete, T. A., & Grusky, D. B. (1990). Structure and trend in the process of stratification for American men and women. *American Journal of Sociology, 96*, 107-143.

England, P. (1993). *Comparable worth: Theories and evidence.* New York: Aldine deGruyter.

England, P., Farkas, G., Kilbourne, B., & Dou, T. (1988). Explaining occupational sex segregation and wages: Findings from a fixed effects model. *American Sociological Review, 53*(4), 544-588.

Goldin, C. (1990). *Explaining the gender gap: An economic history of American women.* Oxford: Oxford University Press.

Goldin, C. (1992). *The meaning of college in the lives of American women: The past one-hundred years* (Working Paper No. 4099). Cambridge, MA: National Bureau of Economic Research.

Gornick, J., & Jacobs, J. A. (1994). *A cross-national analysis of the wages of part-time workers: Evidence from the United States, the United Kingdom, Canada, and Australia* (Working paper No. 56). New York: Russell Sage Foundation.

Gross, E. (1968). Plus ça change... ? The sexual structure of occupations over time. *Social Problems, 16,* 198-208.

Gutek, B. (1985). *Sex and the workplace.* San Francisco: Jossey-Bass.

Hochschild, A. (1989). *The second shift.* Berkeley: University of California Press.

Hyde, J. S., & Essex, M. J. (Eds.). (1991). *Parental leave and child care: Setting a research and policy agenda.* Philadelphia: Temple University Press.

Institute for Women's Policy Research. (1993). *The wage gap: Women's and men's earnings* (Briefing Paper). Washington, DC: Author.

Jacobs, J. A. (1989a). Long-term trends in occupational segregation by sex. *American Journal of Sociology, 95*(1), 160-173.

Jacobs, J. A. (1989b). *Revolving doors: Sex segregation and women's careers.* Stanford, CA: Stanford University Press.

Jacobs, J. A. (1993). Theoretical and measurement issues in the study of sex segregation in the workplace. *European Sociological Review, 9*(3), 325-330.

Jacobs, J. A. (1994, August). *The sex typing of academic specialties: Trends among college and graduate degree recipients during the 1980s.* Paper presented at the American Sociological Association Meetings, Los Angeles.

Jacobs, J. A., Lukens, M., & Useem, M. (1994, March). *The structure of job training in U.S. firms: Evidence from the national organizations study.* Paper presented at the Eastern Sociological Society Meetings, Baltimore, MD.

Jacobs, J. A., & Powell, B. (1987). *On comparing the social standing of men and women.* Unpublished manuscript, Department of Sociology, University of Pennsylvania.

Jacobs, J. A., & Powell, B. (1994). *Gender, work expectations and college majors.* Unpublished manuscript, Department of Sociology, University of Pennsylvania.

Jones, J. (1985). *Labor of love, labor of sorrow.* New York: Vintage.

Kahne, H. (1985). *Reconceiving part-time work: New perspectives for older workers and women.* Totowa, NJ: Rowman and Allanheld.

Kammerman, S. B., & Kahn, A. J. (1991). *Child care, parental leave and the under 3s: Policy innovation in Europe.* New York: Auburn House.

Killingsworth, M., & Heckman, J. (1986). Female labor supply: A survey. In O. Ashenfelter & R. Layard (Eds.), *Handbook of labor economics* (Vol. 1, pp. 103-204). New York: Elsevier.

King, M. C. (1992). Occupational segregation by race and gender, 1940-1980. *Monthly Labor Review, 115,* 30-37.

Lynch, L. M. (1991). The role of off-the-job vs. on-the-job training for the mobility of women workers. *American Economic Review, 81*(2), 151-156.

McGuire, G. M., & Reskin, B. F. (1993). Authority hierarchies at work: The impacts of race and sex. *Gender and Society, 7*(4), 487-506.

Mill, C. W. (1959). *The sociological imagination.* New York: Oxford University Press.

O'Neil, J., & Polachek, S. (1993). Why the gender gap in wages narrowed in the 1980s. *Journal of Labor Economics, 11*(Part 1), 205-228.

Polachek, S. (1978). Sex differences in college major. *Industrial and Labor Relations Review, 31*(4), 498-508.

Reskin, B. F. (Ed.). (1984). *Sex segregation in the workplace: Trends, explanations, remedies.* Washington, DC: National Academy Press.

Reskin, B. F. (1994, January). *Segregating workers: Occupational differences by race, ethnicity, and sex.* Paper presented at the Annual Meetings of the Industrial Relations Research Association, Boston.

Reskin, B. F., & Roos, P. A. (1990). *Job queues: Explaining women's inroads into male occupations.* Philadelphia: Temple University Press.

Rosaldo, M. Z., & Lamphere, L. (1974). *Woman, culture and society.* Stanford, CA: Stanford University Press.

Rosenfeld, R. (1983). Sex segregation and sectors. *American Sociological Review, 48*(5), 637-656.

Rosenfeld, R. A., & Kalleberg, A. L. (1990). A cross-national comparison of the gender gap in income. *American Journal of Sociology, 96,* 69-106.

Sorensen, E. (1989). Measuring the effect of occupational sex and race composition on earnings. In R. T. Michael, H. I. Hartmann, & B. O'Farrell (Eds.), *Pay equity: Empirical inquiries* (pp. 49-69). Washington, DC: National Academy Press.

Spalter-Roth, R. M., & Hartmann, H. I. (1990). *Unnecessary losses: Costs to Americans of the lack of family and medical leave.* Washington, DC: Institute for Women's Policy Research.

Steinberg, R., Haignere, L., Possin, C., Chertos, C., & Treiman, D. (1985). *The New York state comparable pay study: Final report.* Albany, NY: Center for Women in Government.

Tilly, C. (1990). *Short hours, short shrift: Causes and consequences of part-time work.* Washington, DC: Economic Policy Institute.

Tomaskovic-Devey, D. (1993). *Gender and racial inequality at work: The sources and consequences of job segregation.* Ithaca, NY: ILR Press.

Treiman, D. J., & Hartmann, H. I. (1981). *Women, work and wages.* Washington, DC: National Academy Press.

Treiman, D. J., & Roos, P. A. (1983). Sex and earnings in industrial society: A nine-nation comparison. *American Journal of Sociology, 89,* 612-650.

U. S. Bureau of the Census. (1987). Male-female differences in work experience, occupation, and earnings: 1984. *Current Population Report* Series P-70, No. 10. Washington, DC: U.S. Government Printing Office.

Wolf, W. C., & Fligstein, N. (1979). Sex and authority in the workplace. The causes of sexual inequality. *American Sociological Review, 44,* 235-252.

Yamanaka, K., & McClelland, K. (1994). Earning the model-minority image: Diverse strategies of economic adaptation by Asian-American women. *Ethnic and Racial Studies, 17*(1), 79-114.

Zinn, M. B., & Dill, B. T. (1994). *Race, class and gender: An anthology.* Philadelphia: Temple University Press.

PART I

Gender and Compensation

2

Sex Composition and Gendered Earnings Inequality

A Comparison of Job and Occupational Models

DONALD TOMASKOVIC-DEVEY

It is well-established that both male and female earnings tend to fall as female employment in an occupation or job rises. Sex composition has come to represent the dominant (but certainly not exclusive) explanation of the male-female earnings gap in the sociological literature (see Marini, 1989, for a fairly complete review of competing explanations). The evidence supporting this statement has been based upon both national studies of occupational sex composition (e.g., England, Farkas, Kilbourne, & Dou, 1988; Parcel, 1989; Sorensen, 1989a, 1989b) and organizational studies of job sex composition (e.g., Baron & Newman, 1990; Bridges & Nelson, 1989; Jacobs & Steinberg, 1990). The occupational sex composition approach has used occupational data to measure sex composition as well as employment-related skill and power characteristics. The organizational case study approach, although often having access to indicators of job-level sex composition and occasionally of skill and power, is

AUTHOR'S NOTE: This chapter has benefited from the generous comments of Jerry Jacobs, Paula England, and Pamela Stone. The chapter was originally presented at the 1993 annual meeting of the Society for the Advancement of Socio-economics. Please contact the author at Department of Sociology, North Carolina State University, Raleigh, NC 27695-8107, (919) 737-3291 or DON_TOMASKOVIC-DEVEY@NCSU.EDU.

inherently limited in terms of generalizability. This criticism is particularly apt in that most organizational studies have relied on public sector
organizational data (Filer, 1990).

Because occupational data are available in most surveys of adults, and
in all employment-oriented surveys, the use of occupational measures of
sex composition has been convenient. The use of occupational sex composition to predict earnings and to explain male-female earnings inequality has also been empirically powerful, even in the face of extraordinary
statistical controls (e.g., England et al., 1988). One potential problem
with the use of occupational measures of sex composition is that the
theoretical interpretation of effects on earnings is not clear. Is there some
national occupational sex-typing process that sets wage rates? Few social
scientists would argue that this is a dominant process in the United
States. Wage rates, with few exceptions, are set in local labor markets and
are attached to jobs within firms. More compelling are explanations that
the observed effects of occupational sex composition on earnings reflect
processes that operate at the job level (Reskin, 1993). The two dominant
processes discussed in most work on this subject are that women are
hired into less desirable jobs and that once a job becomes associated with
women, it is devalued in the organizational context. This suggests that in
most research, the observed effect of the percentage of women in the job
on earnings reflects both a status composition process in which typically
female work is organizationally devalued and a status closure or discrimination process in which women are denied access to more skilled or
more powerful jobs.

Many researchers have tried to isolate the status composition process
by statistically controlling for job skill and power characteristics. Comparable worth lawsuits and analogous research does this directly by
measuring job sex (and often race) composition and a series of job skill
attributes (for a review see England, 1992; for a research example, see
Jacobs & Steinberg, 1990). In studies that use occupational sex composition, this same goal has been approached through the use of occupational
skill and aptitude measures from the *Dictionary of Occupational Titles*
(DOT) and other sources (e.g., England et al., 1988; Filer, 1989; Parcel,
1989; Sorensen, 1989a, 1989b).

This chapter directly compares job- and occupation-based measures of
sex composition and job skill and power in earnings models for a representative sample of North Carolina jobs. It is the working hypothesis of
this chapter that the use of occupational measures of sex composition and
skill and power—compared to job measures, which are theoretically

more appropriate—leads to increased measurement error. This error, in turn, tends to result in statistical underestimates of the magnitude of the sex composition effect in determining wages. At the same time, relatively weak measures of sex composition may exaggerate the effects on earnings of better measured individual characteristics such as education, experience, tenure, and even sex. Because sex composition is already the dominant explanation of gender wage inequality in the sociological literature, this hypothesis should be particularly challenging to those who propose human capital or other meritocratic or rational-choice, job attainment-based accounts.

How much measurement error is introduced when we use national estimates of occupational sex composition rather than measures of jobs within establishments? The work of Bielby and Baron (1984, 1986) suggests that job-level segregation within firms may be quite a bit higher than estimated occupational segregation measures. Using the index of dissimilarity, Bielby and Baron (1986) estimated that job-level sex segregation was 93.4 (where 100 would indicate complete segregation for all jobs and 0 complete integration) for a diverse, but not random, sample of California establishments in the late 1960s.[1] Using three-digit detailed occupational codes, they reported that an occupation- rather than job-based index of dissimilarity for their sample was only 75.1. Substantively, the job-level measure suggests near total sex segregation in employment in 1970, whereas the occupational measures suggest high, but nowhere near complete, segregation. A recent article examining job-level sex composition data from U.S. Department of Labor, Area Wage Surveys (for 1972 through 1983), reaches a similar conclusion. Petersen and Morgan (in press) report that although 90% of detailed occupations in their survey data were sex integrated, only 10.5% of jobs within establishments were sex integrated (see also Reskin, 1993).

The survey data used in this study contain employee-provided information on the gender and race composition of their jobs.[2] Sex segregation is quite high in this sample. About 77% of women (or men) would have to change jobs in order to achieve complete integration.[3] Because the gender composition of national occupations is not directly descriptive of the North Carolina economy (the occupational and gender distributions are different) and we do not have a sample large enough to compute an occupation-based index of dissimilarity for the state, we cannot use the index of dissimilarity to compare occupational and job segregation within this sample. We can compare occupational and job-based measures directly, as they describe the status segregation of the North Caro-

Table 2.1 Comparisons of Actual Job and National Occupational Sex Segregation for the North Carolina Sample of Employees

	Percent Female	
	National Occupation	*Actual Job*
All employees	49.13	52.39
Males	27.92	8.36
Females	65.43	88.33

lina labor force. Table 2.1 describes segregation based on job and occupation measures in the North Carolina sample. We can see that the average man in North Carolina is in an *occupation* that is nationally 27% female, but he holds a job that is only 8% female. The average woman is in an occupation 65% female, but a job that is 88% female.[4] Sex segregation is dramatically underestimated when measured at the occupational rather than the job level.[5]

Because we have good reason to suspect that aggregate occupational measures substantially underestimate the actual degree of segregation, their use in models predicting income probably attenuates estimates of the effects of sex segregation on wages. Almost all general population studies (for the exception, see Filer, 1989) find that the percentage of women in the job is associated with lower earnings for both males and females, even with extensive job skill and human capital controls; the use of aggregate occupational measures of gender composition most likely attenuates these estimates. Thus we can expect that the actual effect of the gender composition of jobs on earnings is higher than that in the reported literature. Sorensen's (1989b) estimate that 20% of the gender gap in pay is a function of the percentage of women in the job is likely to be a substantial underestimate. Even the higher estimate of 40% reported by Treiman and Hartmann (1981) is likely to underestimate the actual effects of gender composition on earnings in the general population, because it also relies on studies using occupational rather than job measures.[6]

In addition, because national studies have generally used occupational rather than job measures of job skill and power, it is likely that the contributions of job characteristics to gender wage inequality has been underestimated as well. The measurement error introduced by using national aggregate skill estimates (i.e., DOT) instead of job-level estimates most likely has attenuated the effects of job characteristics on wages for reasons similar to those discussed for the percentage of women in the job. Because gender wage gap models are often interested in testing competing explanations for gender earnings inequality, including one focused on job skill and power exclusionary practices, the use of occupational measures of job sex composition and job power or skill is particularly problematic. If these occupational measures are less accurately taken than the human capital measures they are often compared to, models will be misspecified. More important, this misspecification can lead to incorrect conclusions. This might happen if human capital or labor supply effects are overestimated in empirical models because of poor measures of the competing job composition or job power explanations.

Building a Theoretical Model

This chapter will examine the consequences of using job versus occupational measures of both sex composition and job power in models designed to explain gender inequality in earnings. We need to explicitly conceptualize the earnings process before we proceed. Earnings are assumed to be primarily attached to employment positions, secondarily to the people who fill those positions. Gender earnings inequality, like earnings inequality generally, reflects two basic social processes. The first is the organizational process that leads to variations in job quality and job earnings. The second is the allocation of individuals to jobs and inequalities in compensation within jobs that reflect individual (rather than job) characteristics. This allocation process can include both meritocratic (i.e., human capital based) and social closure (i.e., discriminatory) activity.

The organizational process that leads to job earnings inequality can be conceptualized as being driven by three main social forces: organizational resources, job power, and the status composition of jobs. Organizational resources represent the size of the earnings pie to be distributed within the organization (Hodson, 1983; Tomaskovic-Devey, 1989). Job power and status composition processes determine how that pie gets sliced within workplaces (Kalleberg, Wallace, & Althauser, 1981; Tomaskovic-Devey, 1993b).

The allocation process can be described as a job status attainment process within labor markets.[7] It is here that human capital, race, gender, and other individual credentials and attributes influence the flow of information about jobs; application decisions; and employers', supervisors', and coworkers' reactions to job applications and candidates for promotions or raises. It is during this job status attainment process that individual, gender-linked, and other inequalities are distributed. The proximate causes of gender inequality are selection processes that use gender, rather than some other attribute (such as education, experience, or race), as a screening device. Women tend to end up in jobs that are disadvantaged in terms of their status composition, job power, and skill attributes. Males often end up in relatively advantaged jobs. Why? The mainstream explanation of human capital differences is often assumed to be at least part of the answer. Status-based social closure, in which employers and advantaged employees try to monopolize access to the most desirable jobs, is probably at least as important (Tomaskovic-Devey, 1993b).

Human capital explanations suggest that gender differences in job placement arise from individual differences in productivity acquired through education, labor force experience, and job tenure (Becker, 1957). The assumption is that the labor market is relatively efficient in sorting individuals into jobs that are commensurate with human capital characteristics. Although human capital explanations of gender inequality have proved to be limited (Cain, 1986; Tomaskovic-Devey, 1993a), they have a strong track record of providing useful insight into the job allocation process more generally. It is hard to argue that education, training, and experience are not linked to job requirements.[8]

The second theoretical explanation of gendered status attainment processes focuses on exclusionary social closure processes. The notion of social closure can be traced to Weber (1968), but has its fullest contemporary treatments in Parkin (1979) and Murray (1988). In general, status groups create and preserve their identity and advantages by reserving certain opportunities for members of the group. Exclusionary practices reserve the best positions and most desirable opportunities for members of more powerful status groups. An important implication of the social closure argument is that advantaged white male employees are conceptualized to benefit from, and so to struggle for, exclusionary practices (Tomaskovic-Devey, 1993b). Thus social closure includes conventional notions of discrimination but makes explicit the hypothesis that advantaged employees, as well as employers, create and enforce exclusionary practices.

A well-known organizational closure argument is associated with dual economy theory (Edwards, 1979; O'Connor, 1973), as well as neoclassical economic theory's discussion of "tastes" for discrimination (Becker,

1957). In general, the argument is that high-resource organizations (i.e., large firms in oligopolistic sectors of the economy) can afford to employ higher-paid white male labor. Women and African Americans are systematically denied access to the most favorable employment organizations. In both the dual labor market and neoclassical traditions, discriminatory behavior by employers is seen to stem from the preservation of white and male privilege. Employers respond to pressures from advantaged employees or their own discriminatory preferences when they refuse to hire women or minority employees.

The parallel job closure argument is that more highly skilled and otherwise advantaged jobs are reserved for white males (Bonacich, 1972, 1976; Cockburn, 1988; Edwards, 1979; Halaby, 1979; Marshal, 1974; Walby, 1986). Again the general argument is that employers discriminate in hiring, generally with encouragement from white male employees, allocating women and minorities to lower-skilled jobs than they might be able to perform.[9]

The data analysis that follows cannot distinguish the degree to which pressures for exclusionary practices, at either the organizational or job level, come from employers or advantaged employees. The use of the social closure language is important, however, in that it makes explicit the theoretical explanation that exclusionary practices fostered by advantaged workers and employers create observed patterns of organizational and job segmentation. Simple notions of unreflective employer discrimination based on prejudices are not sufficient. Social closure arguments are about active practices that produce and preserve advantages.

The status composition hypothesis is that jobs that are disproportionately female or male become stereotyped, and the work process itself begins to reflect the social value of the master status of typical incumbents (see Acker & Van Houten, 1974; Bielby & Baron, 1985; Caplow, 1954, pp. 230-247; Treiman & Hartman, 1981). This is not an argument about discrimination against individuals but against jobs. The argument is that jobs and organizational structure may be fundamentally influenced by gender (Acker, 1990; Cockburn, 1988; Tomaskovic-Devey, 1993b; Walby, 1986).[10]

Data, Models, and Variables

This chapter uses data collected in the North Carolina Employment and Health Survey (NCEHS) in 1989. The NCEHS is a random-sample survey of employed North Carolinians age 18 and over. The response rate for this telephone survey was 72%, and comparisons of sex, race, age, occupation, and industry composition with Current Population Survey data for North Carolina show that the sample data are representative of the North Carolina labor force (Tomaskovic-Devey, 1993b).[11]

Most comparable worth studies use language that refers to productivity or skills in describing job content. Studies by England (1992), Acker (1987, 1990), and Bose and Spitze (1987) demonstrate that the definition of what is compensable skill is intimately tied up with the power of the job in the context of the organization. Many sociologists see jobs as not only about skill in production but also about power struggles over control of the organization (e.g., Kalleberg et al., 1981). That job characteristics are typically evaluated as embodying varying levels of skill required to do the job is undeniable. The actual organization of jobs is not, however, the unambiguous product of efficiency considerations; it represents the outcome of organizational and class politics. Steinberg (1990) and Cockburn (1988), among others, provide compelling arguments that the very definition and evaluation of skill may be influenced by the gender of typical job incumbents. I have elected to describe these characteristics as job power because it is both consistent with the case study record and current sociological theory about workplace inequality.

We will start with the typical analytic strategy of comparable worth-type models. Earnings within a single firm are conceptualized as a function of job power- or skill-related characteristics and the percentages of minorities and women in the job. Although studies vary in their approach, the general functional form of the model is

$$w_j = b_0 + b_1 J_j + b_2 PF_j + b_3 PM + u_j \qquad 2.1$$

where the subscript j indicates the set of jobs, w is the job's hourly (often starting) wage, J is a vector of job characteristics, PF and PM are the percentages of females and minorities in the job, and u is a random error term.

In order to extend this organizational model to a general population of jobs with identifiable incumbents, we modify Equation 2.1 to take into account the potential impact of individual variation in skills, productivity, or organizational value, and we extend the model to include interfirm as well as intrafirm wage variation. Recognizing that there are important regional differences in earnings, previous studies have added a vector of regional control variables, as well (e.g., Sorensen 1989a, 1989b; Parcel, 1989). These typically have included U.S. regions and some measure of city size. Because the data used in this study are for a single state, only city size is used in the models. The new model can be written in the following manner:

$$w_{ij} = b_0 + b_1 J_{ij} + b_2 PF_j + b_3 PM_j + b_4 HC_i + \\ b_5 OR_{ij} + b_6 F_i + b_7 M_i + u_i \qquad 2.2$$

where subscript ij indicates the set of individuals in the sample of jobs, i is attributes of individuals, and j is attributes of jobs; HC is a vector of human capital attributes; OR is a vector of firm and regional characteristics; F is 1 if the respondent is female; M is 1 if the respondent is minority; and the other terms are defined as above. Equation 2.2 implies that wage variation across jobs is a function of job-related characteristics, firm characteristics, individual skill-related characteristics, the race and gender composition of the job, and the race and sex of the individual in the job. The model is substantively similar to pay equity-type models in that it assumes a single process that sets wages for all jobs. It diverges from pay equity-type models in that it accounts for the additional variation in wages attributable to individual characteristics, differences in firm resources, and regional labor markets. It is anticipated that the coefficients for percentage of females (and percentage of minorities) will be negative and those coefficients will represent the source of the pay gap that is attributable to job status composition. The coefficients associated with the vector of human capital traits represent the sources of the pay gaps associated with human capital investments. The coefficients associated with the vector of job characteristics will represent the sources of the pay gaps associated with job-based social closure. The coefficients associated with the vector of organizational characteristics will represent the sources of the pay gaps associated with organizational-based social closure, as well as regional earnings processes.[12]

Previous research has tended to focus on wages rather than earnings in order to control for differences in male and female labor supply. This approach is also consistent with microeconomic accounts of the employment relation as essentially a spot market. The focus on wages is quite conservative, however, because there are demand-side limits on full-time employment stemming from the creation of gendered part-time work. In this chapter we replace wages with a measure of monthly earnings attached to an individual in a job (ME_{ij}) and model hours as an additional term in the regression equation to be estimated ($b_8 H_{ij}$). Because it is the goal of this chapter to directly compare job and occupational models of the gender earnings gap, Equation 2.2 is further modified to reflect parallel job and organizational approaches to measuring job status composition and job power. Equations 2.3 and 2.4 represent the job and occupational models that will be compared in this chapter. All terms are defined as above, except the subscript o (denoting occupation measures) has been added to Equation 2.4 for the sex and race composition variables and to the vector of job characteristics.[13] Equation 2.4 will be estimated with the subset of available variables that most nearly matches those available in prominent studies that have used occupational data in the past (e.g., England et al., 1988; Parcel, 1989; Sorensen, 1989a, 1989b).

$$ME_{ij} = b_0 + b_1J_{ij} + b_2PF_j + b_3PM_j + b_4HC_i + \\ b_5OR_{ij} + b_6F_i + b_7M_i + b_8H_{ij} + u_{ij} \qquad 2.3$$

$$MEij = b_0 + b_1J_o + b_2PF_o + b_3PM_o + b_4HC_i + \\ b_5OR_{ij} + b_6F_i + b_7M_i + b_8H_{ij} + u_{ij} \qquad 2.4$$

All of these models assume that the variables on the right-hand side of the equation are equally exogenous to the earnings determination process. To the extent that this is false—and the gender and race composition of jobs is an important determinant of other job characteristics—models that control for job characteristics will tend to underestimate the impact of gender and race composition on earnings (Cain, 1986). In path analytic terms, these models will produce only the direct effects of race and gender composition, obscuring the indirect effects. There is good evidence that gender and race composition influence the organization of work, not just wages (Acker & Van Houten, 1974; Glass, 1990; Reskin, 1988; Tomaskovic-Devey, 1993b; Walby, 1986). Thus the models are developed by sequentially adding the human capital, organizational and regional, job or occupational, and hours variables to an initial model containing only the gender and race composition of the job or occupation. This allows us to produce upper and lower estimates of the contribution of the gender and race composition to earnings.

Regressions take untransformed monthly earnings as the dependent variable.[14] In most studies of earnings inequality, the natural logarithm of earnings is analyzed. This practice helps compensate for the skewness of most earnings distributions. Unfortunately, this practice also removes much of the gender inequality to be explained. Figures 2.1 and 2.2, using the data from this study, demonstrate that the logged earnings distribu-

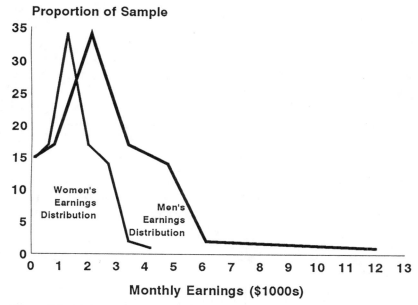

Figure 2.1. Male and Female Monthly Earnings Distributions

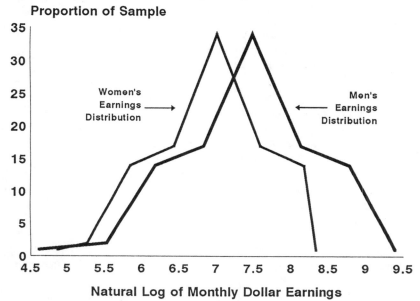

Figure 2.2. Male and Female Monthly Natural Log Earnings Distributions

tion implies much less gender inequality than does the actual earnings distribution. In fact, women on average earn 62% of male monthly earnings in this sample, but 94% of logged earnings. Logging has the effect of reducing the size of the right tail of the income distribution. It is precisely the exclusion of women and typically female jobs from the right tail of the income distribution that is hypothesized to create male-female earnings inequality. There are strong theoretical reasons not to take the log of earnings if your goal is to explain group earnings inequalities (Hodson, 1985). This chapter examines untransformed monthly earnings.[15]

Percentages of females and minorities in the job are measured as discussed above.[16] National percentages of females and minorities in the occupation in 1989 were taken from *Employment and Earnings* (U.S. Department of Labor, 1990) and matched to three-digit occupational codes.

Years of education, experience, experience squared, and years of tenure with current employer are the indicators of individual human capital. Years of experience is measured as age minus 5, minus years of education, minus tenure with current employer, minus .25 for each reported spell of prolonged unemployment. In addition, experience is deflated by estimates of workforce interruption by sex and age groups, based on figures reported by the U.S. Department of Commerce (1987). It is well-known that most age-based measures of experience overstate the labor market experience of women, because absences from the labor force for childbirth and household responsibilities are missed. Without these deflators, the women in this sample have on average slightly more experience than men. After deflating, women have on average almost 2 years less experience than men, much closer to estimates of actual male-female experience differences. This procedure eliminates the average known male/female measurement error in age-based experience measures and allows us to get better estimates of average wage differences.

A variable measuring size of place taps common urban/rural differences in labor market organization. This variable, also used by Sorensen (1989b), is included in both the job and organizational models. Organizational and industry characteristics are used to model possible inter-firm variations in wages that reflect differences in firm resources (Curran & Tomaskovic-Devey, 1992; Hodson, 1983; Kalleberg et al., 1981; Tomaskovic-Devey, 1989). Measures used to model firm variations in resources include dummy variables for 12 industrial sectors, establishment size, and national versus local firms. Previous research on the gender and race composition of jobs has either failed to model firm variation (e.g., England et al., 1988) or used industrial characteristics and an estimate of establishment size (e.g., Sorensen 1989b). Following Sorensen (1989a, 1989b) only industry characteristics and establishment size will be included in the occupational model. Although the measures in this study represent an improvement over past research, they are incomplete and may be measured with more error than other variables in the analyses (Parcel, Kaufman, & Jolly, 1991). It seems reasonable to assume that some variation in earnings associated with firm resources is not captured by these measures. If this measurement error is associated with sex or race, this will lead to some tendency to underestimate firm characteristic effects on earnings inequality.

Job characteristics include whether the job is directly supervised, the degree of supervisory authority, job task complexity, closeness of supervision, union membership, job-required credentials, prior experience requirements, and the weeks necessary to learn to do the job well (measured as its natural logarithm). This is an unusually broad range of measured job characteristics that can be expected to influence earnings somewhat independently of the gender composition of the job. It is hypothesized that these characteristics represent potentially superior measures to the DOT occupation codes generally employed in similar models (e.g., England et al., 1988; Sorensen, 1989a, 1989b), because they are measured directly at the job level.[17]

The available measures of occupational characteristics all come from the DOT and were matched to the sample data by three-digit occupational and industry codes. Seventeen occupational training and skill aptitude variables were coded. Unlike the job variables most of these variables do not have specific job power interpretations. Instead, they can be thought of as indicators of required occupational skills. The first three DOT variables are the degree of activity with data, people, and things. These are followed with measures of general educational development and specific vocational preparation, referring to job-required training and experience and educational preparation, respectively. In addition, the DOT provides measures of required occupational aptitude or ability for 12 traits; intelligence, verbal, numerical, spatial activity, form perception, clerical perception, motor coordination, finger dexterity, manual dexterity, eye-hand-foot coordination, color discrimination, and physical demands. These occupational variables will only enter the occupational model described in Equation 2.4. In addition, the union variable will be included in Equations 2.3 and 2.4, because it has been used in prior occupationally based studies of gender composition.

Findings

In pay equity studies all job characteristics are seen as legitimate sources of pay variation, whereas the effects of the percentage of females and blacks are the indicators of institutionalized discrimination to be remedied. Because these studies make the unreasonable assumption that job characteristics are not themselves the result of the gender and race composition of jobs, they undoubtedly underestimate the contribution of gender and race segregation at the job level to earnings inequality.

Appendix tables (A1 through A3) report the regression estimates that are used to compute the consequences of using occupation- and job-based measures of sex composition to understand the gender gap in earnings. Table A2 presents six job models and Table A3 six occupational models. Although readers may be interested in these regression results, this chapter will not focus on them. Instead, I will use these results to estimate the consequences of sex composition for gender earnings inequality.

The procedure for arriving at these estimates is quite simple. Men in our sample are in jobs that average 8.06% female. Women are in jobs that average 87.93% female. Thus women are on average in jobs that are held by 79.87% more females than males. By multiplying this difference by the coefficient for the percentage of females in the job in each equation in Table A2, we get an estimate of the contribution of job gender composition to the pay gap, controlling for other variables in the model. The procedure is identical for the percentage of females in the occupation in Table A3, except that we use the difference between the percentage of females in men's occupations (27.24%) and the percentage of females in women's occupations (65.72%). Women are in occupations that average 38.48% more female than do men's occupations in this sample.[18]

Table 2.2 presents the results of this exercise.[19] From Model 1 in Table 2.2 we see that the percentage of females in the job is associated with 84% of the monthly earnings gap between men and women. Using the percentage of females in the occupation, the corresponding proportion is only 23%. With only percentage of minorities statistically controlled, we can see that the percentage of females in the job has a much stronger

Table 2.2 Decomposing the Gender Gap in Earnings Associated With the Sex Composition of the Job and Occupation

	Job Model			Occupation Model		
	Dollar Value	Percent of Earnings Gap	Source Table and Model[a]	Dollar Value	Percent of Earnings Gap	Source Table and Model[a]
Monthly earnings gap	809.30	100	Table A1	793.00	100	Table A1
Association of sex composition with earnings:		Job Sex Composition			Occupational Sex Composition	
Net of percent black	679.72	84	Table A2 Model 1	182.44	23	Table A3 Model 1
Net of 1 with additional control for human capital	665.35	82	Table A2 Model 2	342.47	43	Table A3 Model 2
Net of 2 with additional control for organizational and regional characteristics	604.62	75	Table A2 Model 3	279.50	35	Table A3 Model 3
Net of 3 with additional controls for job or occupation characteristics	432.92	53	Table A2 Model 4	315.22	40	Table A3 Model 4
Net of 5 with additional control for hours of work	373.81	46	Table A2 Model 5	261.04	33	Table A3 Model 5

NOTE: a. Source tables and models are in Appendix.

absolute association with the gender wage gap than does the percentage of females in the occupation.[20]

Model 2 controls for human capital characteristics. This slightly reduces the impact of job sex composition (to 82%) on the gender monthly earnings gap. Controlling for human capital actually increases the proportion of the pay gap associated with occupational sex composition (to 43%). Model 3 adds controls for organizational and regional characteristics. Job sex composition's contribution to the earnings pay gap is now estimated to be 75%, a drop of 7%. Occupational sex composition's contribution to the gender earnings gap is less than half the job estimate at 35%. Once job characteristics are controlled, job sex composition is associated with 53% of the gender earnings gap. The contribution of occupational sex composition increases to 40% after DOT control variables are added to the model. Finally, after hours of work are added to the model, job sex composition remains associated with 46% of the pay gap, but occupational sex composition is associated with only 33%.

Across all comparisons, job sex composition accounts for a much larger proportion of the pay gap than does occupational sex composition. As in previous studies, occupational sex composition has a substantial effect upon job earnings. The comparison to job sex composition shows quite clearly that occupational measures understate the actual effect of gender segregation upon earnings inequality. Depending on your preferred theoretical model, gender job segregation in this sample explains between 82% and 46% of the monthly gender earnings gap.[21] Occupational composition explains between 43% and 23% of the earnings gap.

The comparison of nested models suggests an additional disturbing aspect of using occupational sex composition measures. If human capital, organizational, and job power and skill measures represent competing explanations to a status composition explanation, then adding them to the models should reduce or not change the effect of the percentage of females on the earnings gap.[22] This happens in all job models but only in the occupational models where organizational/regional characteristics and hours are entered. When human capital and job power are controlled, the occupational sex composition effect is strengthened. This suggests that some of the substantial measurement error involved in using occupational sex composition measures actually suppresses the earnings effects until that error variance can be absorbed by other variables. In the job models, the introduction of alternative explanations behaves as theoretically expected. Each new block of variables reduces the estimated consequence of sex composition upon gender earnings.

We now have fairly strong evidence that the use of occupational measures of job sex composition seriously underestimates the actual consequences of job segregation for gender earnings inequality. That is, we learned what we expected, that measurement error attenuates observed relationships in this case. Does the use of occupational measures effect substantive conclusions? If not, then occupational measures are reasonable proxies for job measures, when job measures are unavailable. If substantive conclusions are measurement dependent, then the use of occupational measures is more troubling.

Table 2.3 decomposes the gender earnings gap into its constituent parts for the pay equity-type model, providing theoretically distinct sets of explanations. This is accomplished in the same manner as in Table 2.2, except that it is done for all coefficients in the model. The average male-female difference for each variable in the model is multiplied by the estimated regression coefficient for that variable, and then the variable specific estimates of contributions to the gender pay gap are summed within the three categories of human capital indicators, firm indicators, and job characteristics.[23] These decompositions are based on final models (5) in Tables A2 and A3. These include all theoretical variables except individual gender. Gender is represented in these decompositions as the unexplained residual in the last row of Table 2.3. One can see from the appendix tables that this residual is nonsignificant in the job model but significant in the occupational model. That is, the job model explains all significant gender earnings inequality, but the occupational model leaves a substantial portion of the pay gap unaccounted for.

In the job model, sex composition is the most important source of the gender pay gap (46%), followed by job characteristics (22%), hours (14%), organizational and regional characteristics (8%), human capital (3%), and percentage of minorities in the job (1%). The occupational model also ranks sex composition as most important (33%), followed by hours (19%), organizational and regional characteristics (7%), the percentage of minorities in the occupation and human capital (6% each), and finally, occupational skill characteristics (2%).

The use of occupational measures produces substantively different findings than the use of job measures. Occupational measures imply that human capital effects are stronger than they actually are and that the gender sorting of men and women into desirable and undesirable jobs is much weaker than it probably is. Although the use of occupational measures introduces substantial measurement error into our estimates of the consequences of job sex composition, the use of DOT measures of job

Table 2.3 Decomposing the Gender Gap in Earnings Associated With the Sex Composition of the Job and Occupation and Other Groups of Variables

	Job Model Table A2, Model 5		Occupation Model Table A3, Model 5	
	Earnings Pay Gap	Proportion of Gap	Earnings Pay Gap	Proportion of Gap
Total	809.30	100%	793.00	100%
Percent female	373.89	46%	261.03	33%
Percent black	6.78	1%	44.06	6%
Human capital	26.61	3%	46.97	6%
Organizational and regional characteristics	63.24	8%	57.66	7%
Job or occupational characteristics	175.82	22%	17.82	2%
Hours	113.46	14%	152.88	19%
Unexplained	49.50	6%	212.59	27%

NOTE: All results are calculated by first taking the gender difference for each explanatory variable (i.e., the male mean minus the female mean) than multiplying it by the corresponding regression coefficient in Model 5 of Tables A2 and A3 (see Appendix) and then summing the result within each vector of variables.

skill and power introduces much more error into attempts to estimate job-characteristic contributions to earnings inequality. This can be seen quite clearly by looking at the proportion of the explained earnings gap for the job and occupational models. The percentage of females in the job accounts for 46% of the gap, whereas the percentage of females in the occupation accounts for 33%. These seem similar in their relative contribution. Job characteristics, on the other hand, account for 22% of the job model's explained earnings gap, whereas the parallel occupational measures account for a meager 2% of the explained gap in the occupational models. A secondary consequence of this measurement error is that in the occupational model, estimates of contribution of human capital, percentage of minorities in the job, and hours to the gender pay gap are all inflated.

Conclusions

The use of job-level measures of sex composition and job power and skill are theoretically appropriate if you conceptualize the earnings process to be primarily determined by a job-level process of organizational rewards and individual allocation. It is my contention that most of the U.S. labor market works in this way.[24] Thus for the United States at least, job-level measures of sex composition and job power and skill are theoretically more appropriate than occupational measures.

If, however, occupational characteristics and job characteristics are nearly identical, the use of occupational measures as proxies for job measures would be quite desirable because of their ready availability and lower data collection costs. Evidence presented in this chapter (see also Bielby & Baron, 1986; Petersen & Morgan, in press) suggests that occupational measures of sex segregation provide considerable underestimates of actual sex segregation in the workplace.

This chapter shows quite clearly that the use of occupational measures of sex composition consistently underestimate the impact of sex segregation upon the earnings inequality process. If one conceptualizes sex segregation to represent the allocation of women into less desirable jobs and the devaluing of jobs filled primarily by women, then the job measure of sex composition suggests that these dual segregation processes (one allocative and the other valuative) account for fully 75% of the gender earnings gap in this sample. The comparable occupational estimate is less than half as large (35%).

Because the use of occupational sex composition measures is often accompanied with occupational estimates of job skills, substantive conclusions about the sources of gender inequality may be misleading as well. One key finding is that the *Dictionary of Occupational Titles* provides very poor indicators of the job power sources of gender earning inequality. This does not mean that these occupational skill measures do not predict earnings variation. Many of the DOT variables are significant in Table A3, and their joint contribution to the model is significant as well. They do not provide as powerful a contribution to the earnings models as do direct job power measures (compare the incremental F

statistics and changes in explained variance in Tables A2 and A3). Most fundamentally, they do not measure the job traits that are fundamental to the sorting of men and women into different jobs. Women are not a low-skill or low-aptitude labor force. They are hired into low-training-time, low-complexity jobs. This sorting process is not primarily about individual skill or work capacity; it is primarily about gaining access to powerful and desirable job characteristics.

The use of occupational skill measures from the DOT leads us to overestimate both the contribution of gender composition and human capital explanations to the gender earnings gap.

What is to be done? Occupational measures of sex composition should be used with caution. Comparisons of sex composition explanations with all other explanations will be underestimates but will not produce grossly misleading substantive interpretations. This avenue is not particularly exciting, however, because we already have a fairly strong consensus in both sociology and economics that sex composition matters. Our disagreements revolve around how it matters. To resolve these disagreements, and not be misled by measurement error, requires equally adequate measures of all theoretical constructs.

This suggests that the organizational case study approach will continue to be fruitful. Filer's (1990) criticism that almost all of these have been in the state sector should be treated seriously, and every attempt should be made to explore the sex segregation process in private sector firms. The case study route is likely to lead to strong tests of organizational (i.e., status composition) theories of sex segregation.[25] It is less likely to provide strong insights into the job status attainment process within a labor market, except perhaps for studies of intrafirm career mobility. For these attainment or allocative theories, which include new home economics, human capital, organizational segmentation, and job closure/discrimination approaches, additional general population data similar to that explored in this chapter would seem most appropriate.

It is tempting to call for national labor force studies that include questions on the respondents' job characteristics and job sex (and race) composition. Although much could be learned from such studies, similar studies on smaller geographic areas would probably be as useful. National studies would offer better global estimates of the relative contribution of status composition, job closure, organizational segmentation, and human capital explanations. If, however, we suspect that most earnings are set at the organizational job level in local labor markets, then we should also expect that the relative contribution of these theorized processes should vary from place to place and over time as a function of the local relations of production. Those relations can be expected to reflect previous class, gender, and race conflict, as well as regionally distinct organizational patterns.

This study is based on a regional sample. Even a single state might be too broad if the gender segregation process is hypothesized to differ by region. Other aspects of the earnings process, particularly returns to skill and organizational membership, do vary within North Carolina depending on local relations of production (Curran & Tomaskovic-Devey, 1992). These regional effects were explored in preliminary models for this chapter but did not effect the gender earnings gap. Some previous research has found that sex segregation tends to be higher in rural areas (McPherson & Smith-Lovin, 1986; Rogers & Gudy, 1981; Tomaskovic-Devey, 1993b). Where sex segregation is lower, one might hypothesize that other mechanisms for creating gender inequality (such as direct wage differentials or human capital differentials) might become more important. This would be consistent with the social closure argument advanced in this chapter (see also Reskin, 1988). On the other hand, in places where political mobilization, either by working class or feminist organizations, directly challenges wage inequalities, then we might expect that even in the presence of high sex segregation at the job level we might find lower gender earnings inequality. This, of course, is the goal of organizational-level comparable worth lawsuits. If typically female jobs are more likely to be low paying, then working-class movements that raise the minimum wage will by definition reduce the effect of gender composition upon the wage gap. Bettio (1988) reports that this is actually what happened in Italy when working-class organizations negotiated wage contracts to reduce inequalities between high- and low-priced labor.

How we measure sex composition matters. The use of occupational measures of sex composition produces substantial underestimates of both the degree of sex segregation and its consequences for gender earnings inequality. The use of DOT measures instead of direct job measures of skill and power leads to extraordinary underestimates of the degree to which men and women are allocated into unequal jobs. This in turn potentially leads to substantively misleading conclusions about the relative importance of competing explanations as to the sources of gender earnings inequality.

Table A1 Measurement and Means by Gender and Model for All Variables

	Job Models		Occupation Models	
	Males	Females	Males	Females
N	302	341	—	—
Monthly earnings	2116.77	1307.47	2113.50	1320.50
Percent job female	8.06	87.93	—	—
Percent occupation female	—	—	27.24	65.72
Percent job minority	20.52	23.42	—	—
Percent occupation minority	—	—	9.73	11.69
Education (years)	13.31	13.14	13.22	13.18
Firm tenure (years)	7.61	7.63	7.66	7.90
Experience[a] (years)	10.08	7.68	10.55	7.33
Experience squared	214.36	120.59	230.11	115.31
Autonomous[b]	.08	.06	—	—
Supervisory authority[c]	1.69	1.11	—	—
Job complexity[d]	8.31	7.92	—	—
Closeness of supervision[e]	5.94	6.15	—	—
Union member (yes = 1)	.10	.08	.10	.09
Job required credential[f]	5.88	5.37	—	—
Prior experience required (yes = 1)	.75	.62	—	—
Weeks to learn job[g]	3.51	2.56	—	—
DOTDATA:[h] Involvement with data	—	—	3.86	3.77
DOTPEOPLE:[h] Involvement with people	—	—	6.53	6.21
DOTTHING:[h] Involvement with things	—	—	4.99	6.58
DOTGED:[i] General educational development	—	—	3.41	2.88
DOTSVP:[j] Specific vocational preparation	—	—	3.94	3.45
APTITUDES				
DOTG: Intelligence[k]	—	—	2.29	2.17
DOTV: Verbal[k]	—	—	2.20	1.90
DOTN: Numerical[k]	—	—	2.91	2.78
DOTS: Spatial[k]	—	—	2.81	2.72
DOTP: Form perception[k]	—	—	2.85	2.80
DOTQ: Clerical perception[k]	—	—	3.14	2.86
DOTK: Motor coordination[k]	—	—	2.89	2.77
DOTF: Finger dexterity[k]	—	—	2.89	2.80
DOTM: Manual dexterity[k]	—	—	2.67	2.60
DOTE: Eye-hand-foot coordination[k]	—	—	3.26	2.14
DOTC: Color discrimination[k]	—	—	3.50	3.38

Table A1 (Continued)

	Job Models		Occupation Models	
	Males	Females	Males	Females
DOTPHY: Physical demands[l]	—	—	1.42	1.19
Establishment size[m]	3.95	3.89	3.98	3.94
SECTOR:				
Extractive	.017	.003	.018	.003
Construction	.109	.015	.109	.015
Manufacturing	.295	.282	.276	.278
Transportation/utility	.066	.015	.073	.020
Wholesale trade	.046	.018	.055	.018
Retail trade	.119	.173	.124	.164
Business services	.073	.135	.080	.135
Personal services	.026	.021	.029	.023
Social services	.103	.279	.109	.287
Public administration	.146	.059	.127	.057

NOTE: The sample size for the occupation models is somewhat reduced because residual occupational (e.g., fabricators, not elsewhere classified) and industry (e.g., miscellaneous fabricated metal products) categories do not have DOT codes.

a. Experience is measured as age minus education, minus 6, minus current firm tenure, minus .25 for each reported spell of unemployment. In addition, following U.S. Department of Commerce (1987) guidelines, all experience measures are deflated to take into account average male and female workforce interruptions. The deflators for men are: age less than 29 = .977, age 30 to 45 = .947, age 46 and over = .991. The deflators for women are: age less than 29 = .947, age 30 to 45 = .834, age 46 and over = .773.

b. Coded 1 if does not report to supervisor.

c. Six-item scale (reliability = .90) made up of questions about presence and degree of supervisory and managerial authority.

d. Four-item scale (reliability = .54) made up of questions about task variety, routinization, repetitiveness, and standardization.

e. Four-item scale (reliability = .64) made up of questions about discriminating freedom, work pace discretion, closeness of supervision, and task autonomy.

f. What level of formal education do you think is needed for a person to do your job? None, some grade school, complete grade school, some high school, high school, trade school or apprenticeship, some college, junior college degree, 4-year degree, specialized 4-year degree, graduate degree.

g. How long (coded in weeks) would it take a qualified new person to learn to do your job reasonably well?

h. The People, Data and Things DOT codes range from 0 = a great deal to 9 = no involvement.

i. General educational development typically required for the job ranges from 0 = none to 7 = advanced degree.

j. Specific vocational preparation in training time typically required to learn to do the job ranges from 0 = no training to 9 = 10 years or more.

k. The aptitude scales range from 0 = high to 5 = none required aptitude.

l. The physical demand scale ranges from 0 = light to 5 = heavy physical demands.

m. About how many people work for your organization at the location where you work? I mean all types of workers in all departments? Response categories: less than 10; 10 to 25; 26 to 50; 51 to 100; 101 to 500; 501 to 1,000; 1,001 to 10,000; more than 10,000.

Table A2 Job Model (Equation 2.3) Monthly Earnings Regressed on the Variables ($N = 643$)

Model	1	2	3	4	5	6
Percent job female	−8.51	−8.33	−7.57	−5.42	−4.68	−2.22
	(.92)	(.78)	(.82)	(.80)	(.79)	(1.52)
Percent job minority	−5.88	−3.92	−5.35	−2.15	−2.33	−1.77
	(1.35)	(1.15)	(1.15)	(1.11)	(1.08)	(1.26)
Education	—	198.89	181.91	68.95	73.12	73.02
		(14.96)	(16.20)	(19.91)	(19.42)	(19.39)
Firm tenure	—	47.30	43.58	32.82	33.29	33.11
		(4.63)	(4.59)	(4.44)	(4.33)	(4.33)
Experience	—	48.58	44.66	35.08	31.57	31.36
		(8.58)	(8.34)	(7.79)	(7.61)	(7.60)
Experience squared	—	−1.07	−.92	−.80	−.65	−.66
		(.26)	(.25)	(.24)	(.23)	(.23)
Establishment size	—	—	90.88	82.06	81.38	75.94
			(19.86)	(18.78)	(29.40)	(18.31)
National firm	—	—	247.81	252.18	262.85	255.32
(yes = 1)			(94.54)	(87.85)	(85.65)	(85.69)
Industry sector						
Extractive	—	—	386.50	575.09	508.75	525.44
			(361.23)	(337.34)	(329.02)	(328.66)
Construction	—	—	231.96	91.81	125.41	138.95
			(178.53)	(167.24)	(167.23)	(163.07)
Manufacturing	—	—	80.50	179.08	150.49	167.78
			(128.23)	(120.34)	(117.40)	(117.55)
Transport/utility	—	—	804.57	860.67	837.88	834.33
			(203.15)	(189.18)	(184.46)	(184.22)
Wholesale trade	—	—	151.75	164.56	134.22	152.74
			(217.19)	(202.72)	(197.67)	(197.53)
Retail trade	—	—	−74.39	−19.09	33.81	46.54
			(142.35)	(133.58)	(130.53)	(130.57)
Business services	—	—	355.40	349.21	364.69	381.51
			(151.47)	(141.60)	(138.04)	(138.16)
Personal services	—	—	214.26	229.24	220.37	250.67
			(243.83)	(227.83)	(222.08)	(222.22)
Social services	—	—	37.02	−94.90	−29.61	−4.49
			(131.73)	(124.22)	(121.61)	(122.12)

Table A2 (Continued)

Model	1	2	3	4	5	6
(Public administration reference category)						
Place size	—	—	70.67	84.42	81.38	84.96
			(32.24)	(30.16)	(29.40)	(29.41)
Autonomous	—	—	—	199.23	208.07	204.09
(yes = 1)				(127.15)	(123.95)	(123.02)
Task complexity	—	—	—	45.67	36.85	38.36
				(21.78)	(21.29)	(21.26)
Closeness of supervision	—	—	—	−35.85	−34.86	−33.24
				(17.77)	(17.32)	(17.32)
Supervisory authority	—	—	—	61.72	43.37	46.28
				(17.28)	(17.14)	(17.17)
Union (yes = 1)	—	—	—	192.06	202.00	199.04
				(113.46)	(110.60)	(110.44)
Required credential	—	—	—	81.99	72.48	70.18
				(18.53)	(18.14)	(18.14)
Prior experience	—	—	—	22.37	5.26	6.23
(yes = 1)				(73.44)	(71.64)	(71.52)
Weeks training (ln)	—	—	—	106.49	88.21	83.59
				(28.57)	(18.14)	(28.08)
Hours	—	—	—	—	19.67	19.17
					(3.41)	(3.41)
Female	—	—	—	—	—	−257.87
(yes = 1)						(135.48)
Minority	—	—	—	—	—	−74.67
(yes = 1)						(94.71)
Intercept	2246.41	−1047.53	−1461.67	−1268.01	−1950.65	−1924.02
Adjusted r^2	.139	.393	.451	.530	.553	.555
Incremental F	53.17	67.65	6.63	14.18	33.33	2.08
Significance of F	.000	.000	.000	.000	.000	.125

NOTE: The table provides regression coefficients, with standard errors in parentheses.

Table A3 Occupation Model (Equation 2.4) of Monthly Earnings Regressed on the Variables ($N = 617$)

Model	1	2	3	4	5	6
Percent occupation female	−4.74 (1.38)	−8.89 (1.23)	−7.26 (1.33)	−8.19 (1.51)	−6.78 (1.44)	−3.15 (1.01)
Percent occupation black	−63.91 (7.74)	−29.65 (7.36)	−34.31 (7.51)	−27.39 (8.20)	−22.47 (7.80)	−21.10 (7.72)
Education	—	202.36 (16.96)	184.84 (18.13)	158.68 (18.78)	142.69 (17.90)	129.68 (17.73)
Firm tenure	—	49.71 (4.77)	43.95 (4.77)	42.86 (4.80)	41.01 (4.56)	38.99 (4.49)
Experience	—	60.30 (8.91)	57.12 (8.65)	53.24 (8.56)	45.06 (8.17)	42.87 (8.02)
Experience squared	—	−1.20 (.27)	−1.09 (.26)	−1.07 (.26)	−.83 (.25)	−.88 (.24)
Establishment size	—	—	78.52 (20.89)	77.33 (20.73)	67.16 (19.68)	68.23 (19.30)
Industry sector						
Extractive	—	—	465.50 (376.42)	345.32 (377.50)	278.81 (357.79)	278.00 (350.78)
Construction	—	—	119.87 (199.98)	123.94 (207.19)	134.57 (196.32)	163.52 (192.77)
Manufacturing	—	—	17.01 (139.14)	52.41 (148.90)	74.53 (141.11)	167.76 (140.36)
Transport/utility	—	—	803.57 (206.39)	910.02 (209.97)	916.11 (198.95)	922.79 (195.49)
Wholesale trade	—	—	161.97 (225.67)	258.93 (225.32)	208.45 (213.58)	185.31 (209.38)
Retail trade	—	—	−254.37 (155.34)	−187.63 (157.72)	−73.73 (150.09)	−00.26 (148.22)
Business services	—	—	256.22 (161.87)	236.18 (162.82)	263.39 (154.31)	336.81 (152.40)
Personal services	—	—	−27.73 (250.63)	−6.22 (249.54)	68.39 (236.62)	141.25 (232.42)
Social services	—	—	−30.76 (141.77)	−77.68 (146.02)	17.89 (138.83)	91.21 (137.13)

Table A3 (Continued)

Model	1	2	3	4	5	6
(Public Administration reference category)						
Place size	—	—	41.36	52.16	52.76	68.07
			(33.58)	(33.03)	(31.29)	(30.98)
Union member	—	—	—	27.97	69.67	62.63
(yes = 1)				(124.88)	(118.44)	(116.09)
DOTDATA	—	—	—	−43.15	−40.43	−37.92
				(27.05)	(25.63)	(25.22)
DOTPEOPLE	—	—	—	1.18	9.20	1.68
				(23.03)	(21.84)	(21.47)
DOTTHINGS	—	—	—	36.93	35.89	31.17
				(18.31)	(17.35)	(17.03)
DOTGED	—	—	—	19.93	28.31	19.99
				(30.11)	(28.55)	(28.02)
DOTSVP	—	—	—	52.63	51.43	50.90
				(17.84)	(16.90)	(16.60)
DOTG	—	—	—	29.97	26.86	34.07
				(51.37)	(48.68)	(47.74)
DOTV	—	—	—	−64.95	−62.61	−73.63
				(34.44)	(32.63)	(32.05)
DOTN	—	—	—	−70.62	−74.35	−66.16
				(40.84)	(38.70)	(37.99)
DOTS	—	—	—	90.72	76.24	66.01
				(37.47)	(35.55)	(34.91)
DOTP	—	—	—	−92.14	−104.29	−94.69
				(47.53)	(45.06)	(44.20)
DOTQ	—	—	—	84.24	99.55	91.75
				(40.25)	(38.18)	(37.45)
DOTK	—	—	—	27.93	23.43	33.31
				(77.48)	(73.42)	(71.9)
DOTF	—	—	—	−.78	28.95	25.90
				(79.20)	(75.64)	(74.13)
DOTM	—	—	—	29.59	1.21	−19.20
				(56.47)	(53.61)	(52.72)
DOTE	—	—	—	−59.21	−51.57	−46.73
				(31.49)	(29.86)	(29.29)
DOTC	—	—	—	35.48	20.48	14.84
				(25.02)	(23.72)	(23.33)

(Continued)

Table A3 (Continued)

Model	1	2	3	4	5	6
DOTPHY	—	—	—	172.22 (53.89)	132.02 (51.30)	103.78 (50.54)
Hours	—	—	—	—	29.25 (3.57)	26.21 (3.55)
Female (yes = 1)	—	—	—	—	—	–412.67 (86.48)
Minority (yes = 1)	—	—	—	—	—	–176.95 (87.45)
Intercept	2595.63	–959.46	–1147.49	–1429.69	–2447.06	–1963.62
Adjusted r^2	.135	.374	.439	.455	.511	.530
Incremental F	49.06	59.68	5.72	2.95	67.13	12.98
Significance of F	.000	.000	.000	.000	.000	.000

NOTE: The table provides regression coefficients, with standard errors in parentheses.

Notes

1. The index of dissimilarity can be interpreted as the proportion in either group who would have to change jobs in order to achieve an equal distribution.

2. This was done with three questions. The first question asked how many people in the employment establishment had the same job title as the respondent. Following Bielby and Baron (1984, 1985, 1986), the question focused on job title rather than same general duties or tasks, because it is the proliferation of titles that seems to enhance segregation in larger firms. Once we knew how many people were in the job, we followed up by asking how many of that total were white and how many were male. Question wording and interviewer instructions, as well as evidence of reliability in the measurement of job gender and race composition, are discussed in detail in Tomaskovic-Devey (1993a, 1993b). Although this chapter focuses on job sex composition, data on job race composition were collected as well. Substantive analyses of race composition are discussed in more detail in Tomaskovic-Devey (1993a, 1993b). Job and occupational race composition are included in the analyses that follow but are not the central focus of this chapter.

3. The sex segregation levels are quite a bit lower than those reported by Bielby and Baron (1986) for 20 years earlier. Importantly, Jacobs (1989a) reports a 15.2% drop in occupational sex segregation between 1970 and 1986. The level of sex segregation at the job level in North Carolina in 1989 is 17.8% less than the 1969 level reported for California. Although the Bielby and Baron (1984) sample is not, strictly speaking, comparable to this

one, being both nonrandom and from California (not North Carolina), it is reassuring that the only two general sample job-level sex segregation measures currently available seem to parallel the occupational sex segregation trends toward more gender integration of jobs over the last 2 decades (Jacobs, 1989a, 1989b; see also Beller, 1984).

4. For this sample, the average black is in an occupation that nationally is only 14% black. They are in jobs, however, that average 54% black. The race composition figures for whites are more comparable at the job and national occupation levels, despite the fact that the black labor force is twice as large proportionally in North Carolina as it is across the nation.

5. The simple correlation between the percentage of females in the job and the corresponding occupational measure for this sample is .62. This suggests that the use of a national occupational estimate of job sex composition, although empirically associated with job sex composition, is not the same thing.

6. The standard practice of using national occupational aggregates probably produces even more substantial underestimates of racial segregation than of sex segregation, because race (unlike sex) distribution is spatially uneven. Even if nearly all the building custodians in the rural South are black, very few rural North building custodians can be any race but white. National aggregates might make many highly segregated occupations look quite integrated because of this spatial variation in racial distribution.

7. The words *job* and *labor market* are used deliberately to signify the differences from a traditional status attainment approach that treats the employment attainment processes as *occupational* and *societal*.

8. It is not necessary to accept the human capital argument—that employers compensate productivity—to use and interpret human capital variables. The working assumption of this research is that employers typically use past employment and educational credentials as screening devices to make educated guesses about future productivity and trainability, and also as sorting mechanisms to order the queue of job applicants. Although not discussed at length, the empirical models show quite clearly that the effects of human capital variables on the earnings distribution are largely mediated through access to jobs of more or less skill and power.

9. The theory of statistical discrimination (Arrow, 1973a, 1973b; Bielby & Baron, 1986; Phelps, 1972) argues that employers discriminate against minorities and women based on perceived differences in training costs. It is a theory of job skill-based social closure. It differs from the social closure-based approach advanced in this chapter in several respects. Most important for current purposes, the theory of statistical discrimination sees the source of discrimination in employers' attempts to preserve their profit advantages. The theory of social closure sees the sources of discrimination in employers' and advantaged employees' attempts to preserve their material and status advantages. There is ample historical and contemporary evidence that both employers and advantaged employees are actors in workplace discrimination (Cohn, 1985; Tomaskovic-Devey, 1993b; Walby, 1986; Williams, 1987; Wilson, 1977). In addition, in a recent article I have found strong evidence that job gender composition and sex segregation are more consistent with a social closure account than they are with a statistical discrimination account (Tomaskovic-Devey, 1992).

10. Although this chapter focuses on gender wage inequality, the same basic processes also operate to produce racial inequality (see Baron & Newman, 1990; Semyonov & Lewin-Epstein, 1989 [for Israel]). It does seem to be the case, however, that racial job composition is a less powerful source of earnings inequality than is gender job composition (Tomaskovic-Devey, 1993a, 1993b).

11. The analyses that follow are weighted to represent a random sample of jobs. The original sampling protocol required that at Stage 1 we take a random sample of households. Within households, we took a random sample of employed adults and interviewed them about their primary jobs, yielding a random sample of employed adults. To overcome any sampling bias introduced by the oversampling of one-worker households, each observation is weighted relative to total household employment size. The sampling weight $= j/J$ where j is the number of jobs in the household and J is the average number of jobs across all households.

12. Previous research has shown that organizational and regional factors are not dramatic sources of gender earnings inequality. For this reason in the analyses to follow the vectors of both organizational and regional variables will be examined together.

13. This chapter will examine only pooled models estimated across the entire sample of jobs and individuals. Separate models within gender categories can also be estimated. Such models generate information on gender differences in earnings rates of return for the explanatory variables. Such an exercise would detract from the comparison in this chapter, but it can be found in Tomaskovic-Devey (1993a).

14. Respondents were asked to report their monthly job earnings from wages, tips, bonuses, and overtime, but they were allowed to respond in either hourly, weekly, biweekly, monthly, or yearly earnings units in order to increase the reliability of their reports. Respondents were also asked their normal hours of work per week and weeks per year. All earnings units were standardized to monthly earnings.

15. See Tomaskovic-Devey (1993a) for a comparison of the two approaches.

16. In this chapter, the percentage of blacks and percentage of minorities, and the words *black* and *minority,* are used interchangeably. Strictly speaking, they are not the same, but almost all minorities in North Carolina are black. In our sample, 96% of minorities are black, 2% are Native Americans, and 1% are Hispanics and Asians.

17. The job skill measures are all derived from self-reports of employees. This procedure has some advantages and disadvantages for the project at hand. Relative to the DOT or some other secondary source of occupational characteristics, the self-reports are much more likely to capture the actual job-level experience, rather than some more aggregate and so more error-prone occupational measure (Glass, 1990). In addition, the range of job-skill dimensions explored through self-reports is much broader than that available in any secondary source. On the other hand, there may be measurement distortion introduced by self-reports rather than some more objective on-site job evaluation. If this were the case, the distortion would have to be seriously correlated with race or sex to affect the conclusions of this chapter. Bielby and Bielby (1988) and Smith (1979) suggest that, at least for sex, this is unlikely to be a source of bias. In a large study of New York State government jobs, Jacobs and Steinberg (1990) report that self-reports of job attributes were very highly associated with managers' ratings.

18. The formulas for these decompositions are:

$$\beta \text{ Percent Female } (\chi \text{ Percent Female}_{male} - \chi \text{ Percent Female}_{female})$$

and

$$\beta \text{ Percent Black } (\chi \text{ Percent Black}_{white} - \chi \text{ Percent Black}_{blacks}),$$

where β is the estimated regression coefficient from the appropriate model and χ is the mean value for that variable for the subsample in the subscript.

19. The job and occupational models have slightly different dollar values in the total gender earnings gap because the occupational models have slightly more missing data than the job models.

20. In the only other general population estimate of the zero order effect of job sex composition upon the earnings pay gap, Petersen and Morgan (in press) estimate that 83% of the wage gap in their sample is tied to job sex composition.

21. I am assuming that all theoretical models would treat human capital as exogenous to the job wage setting process, but that organization, job power, and hours may be conceptualized by some researchers as tied to the gendered construction of employment relations. Thus the most conservative reading of this data is from Model 5 in Appendix Table A2, and the most (i.e., totally) gendered reading is from Model 2.

22. The sex composition effect would be reduced if the competing explanations actually operated as alternative mechanisms that produced observed gender earnings inequality. There would be no change if the theoretical explanations of gender earnings inequality for human capital, organizational resources, and job power were incorrect.

23. The general formula is $\Sigma_i \, [\beta X_{ij} \, (\chi_{ij\,male} - \chi_{ij\,female})]$ or $\Sigma_i \, [\beta X_{ij} \, (\chi_{ij\,white} - \chi_{ij\,black})]$ where X_{ij} refers to ith variables within the j vector of variables, and χ refers to the mean values of all Xs for the subsample. For example, the human capital vector of variables includes education, experience, experience squared, and employer tenure.

24. This is not necessarily the case in more centralized economies such as Australia or Italy. In economies where wage rates are set by national collective bargaining or administrative decision making, the measurement distance between occupation and job can be expected to be much smaller. This conceptualization of labor market processes is developed in more detail in Tomaskovic-Devey (1993b). Even in the United States, some societal forces, such as state regulation and cultural stereotyping of certain highly gendered occupations such as nursing or secretarial work, may influence wage setting to some extent.

25. Of course, the general population study with job-level measures reported here also suggests that sex composition wage-setting processes are powerful in the private sector.

References

Acker, J. (1987). Sex bias in job evaluation: A comparable worth issue. In C. Bose & G. Spitze (Eds.), *Ingredients for women's employment policy* (pp. 183-196). Albany: State University of New York Press.

Acker, J. (1990). Hierarchies, jobs and bodies: A theory of gendered organizations. *Gender & Society, 4,* 139-158.

Acker, J., & Van Houten, D. R. (1974). Differential recruitment and control: The sex structuring of organizations. *Administrative Science Quarterly, 19,* 152-164.

Arrow, K. (1973a). Some mathematical models of race in the labor market. In A. Pascal (Ed.), *Racial discrimination in economic life* (pp. 83-102). Lexington, MA: D. C. Heath.

Arrow, K. (1973b). The theory of discrimination. In O. Ashenfelter (Ed.), *Discrimination in labor markets* (pp. 3-33). Princeton, NJ: Princeton University Press.

Baron, J. N., & Newman, A. E. (1990). For what it's worth: Organizations, occupations and the value of work done by women and non-whites. *American Sociological Review, 55,* 155-175.

Becker, G. S. (1957). *The economics of discrimination.* Chicago: The University of Chicago Press.

Beller, A. (1984). Trends in occupational segregation by sex, 1960-1981. In B. F. Reskin (Ed.), *Sex segregation in the workplace: Trends, explanations, remedies* (pp. 11-26). Washington, DC: National Academy Press.

Bettio, F. (1988). *The sexual division of labour: The Italian case.* Oxford: Clarendon.

Bielby, W. T., & Baron, J. N. (1984). A woman's place is with other women: Sex segregation within organizations. In B. F. Reskin (Ed.), *Sex segregation in the workplace: Trends, explanations, remedies* (pp. 27-55). Washington, DC: National Academy Press.

Bielby, W. T., & Baron, J. N. (1985). Organizational barriers to gender equality: Sex segregation of jobs and opportunities. In A. S. Rossi (Ed.), *Gender and the life course* (pp. 233-251). Hawthorne, NY: Aldine.

Bielby, W. T., & Baron, J. N. (1986). Men and women at work: Sex segregation and statistical discrimination. *American Journal of Sociology, 91,* 759-799.

Bielby, D. D., & Bielby, W. T. (1988). She works hard for her money: Household responsibilities and the allocation of work effort. *American Journal of Sociology, 91,* 759-799.

Bonacich, E. (1972). A theory of ethnic antagonism: The split labor market. *American Sociological Review, 37,* 547-559.

Bonacich, E. (1976). Advanced capitalism and black/white race relations in the United States: A split labor market view. *American Sociological Review, 41,* 34-51.

Bose, C., & Spitze, G. (1987). *Ingredients for women's employment policy.* Albany: SUNY Press.

Bridges, W. P., & Nelson, R. L. (1989). Markets in hierarchies: Organizational and market influences on gender inequality in a state pay system. *American Journal of Sociology, 95,* 616-659.

Cain, G. G. (1986). The economic analysis of labor market discrimination: A survey. In O. Ashenfelter & R. Layard (Eds.), *Handbook of labor economics* (pp. 693-785). Amsterdam: North-Holland.

Caplow, T. (1954). *The sociology of work.* New York: McGraw-Hill.

Cockburn, C. (1988). *Machinery of dominance: Women, men and technical know-how.* Boston: Northeastern University Press.

Cohn, S. (1985). *The process of occupational sex-typing.* Philadelphia: Temple University Press.

Curran, S., & Tomaskovic-Devey, D. (1992). Uneven development in North Carolina? Job quality differences between local and nonlocal firms. *Rural Sociology, 57,* 123-146.

Edwards, R. (1979). *Contested terrain.* New York: Basic Books.

England, P. (1992). *Comparable worth: Theories and evidence.* New York: Aldine deGruyter.

England, P., Farkas, G., Kilbourne, B. S., & Dou, T. (1988). Explaining occupational sex segregation and wages: Findings from a model with fixed effects. *American Sociological Review, 53,* 544-558.

Filer, R. K. (1989). Occupational segregation, compensating differentials, and comparable worth. In R. T. Michael, H. I. Hartmann, & B. O'Farrell. *Pay equity: Empirical inquiries* (pp. 153-170). Washington, DC: National Academy Press.

Filer, R. K. (1990). Compensating differentials and the male-female wage gap: A comment. *Social Forces, 69,* 469-473.

Glass, J. (1990). The impact of occupational segregation on working conditions. *Social Forces, 68,* 779-796.

Halaby, C. N. (1979). Job-specific sex differences in organizational reward attainment: Wage discrimination vs. rank segregation. *Social Forces, 58,* 108-127.

Hodson, R. (1983). *Workers' earnings and corporate economic structure.* New York: Academic Press.

Hodson, R. (1985). Some considerations concerning the functional form of earnings. *Social Science Quarterly, 14,* 374-394.

Jacobs, J. A. (1989a). Long-term trends in occupational segregation by sex. *American Journal of Sociology, 95,* 160-173.

Jacobs, J. A. (1989b). *Revolving doors: Sex segregation and women's careers.* Stanford, CA: Stanford University Press.

Jacobs, J. A., & Steinberg, R. J. (1990). Compensating differentials and the male-female wage gap: Evidence from the New York State Comparable Worth Study. *Social Forces, 69,* 439-468.

Kalleberg, A. L., Wallace, M., & Althauser, R. P. (1981). Economic segregation, worker power, and income inequality. *American Journal of Sociology, 87,* 651-683.

Marini, M. M. (1989). Sex differences in earnings in the United States. *Annual Review of Sociology, 15,* 348-380.

Marshal, R. (1974). The economics of racial discrimination: A survey. *Journal of Economic Literature, 12,* 849-871.

McPherson, J. M., & Smith-Lovin, L. (1986). Sex segregation in voluntary associations. *American Sociological Review, 51,* 61-71.

Murray, R. (1988). *Social closure: The theory of monopolization and exclusion.* New York: Oxford University Press.

O'Connor, J. (1973). *The fiscal crisis of the state.* New York: St. Martin's Press.

Parcel, T. L. (1989). Comparable worth, occupational labor markets and occupational earnings: Results from the 1980 Census. In R. T. Michael, H. Hartmann, & B. O'Farrell (Eds.), *Pay equity: Empirical inquiries* (pp. 134-152). Washington, DC: National Academy Press.

Parcel, T. L., Kaufman, R. L., & Jolly, L. (1991). Going up the ladder: Multiplicity sampling to create linked macro-to-micro organizational samples. *Sociological Methodology, 21,* 43-79.

Parkin, F. (1979). *Marxism and class theory: A bourgeois critique.* New York: Columbia University Press.

Petersen, T., & Morgan, L. (in press). Separate and unequal: Occupation-establishment segregation and the gender wage gap. *American Journal of Sociology.*

Phelps, E. S. (1972). The statistical theory of racism and sexism. *American Economic Review, 62,* 659-666.

Reskin, B. F. (1988). Bringing the men back in: Sex differentiation and the devaluation of women's work. *Gender and Society, 2,* 58-81.

Reskin, B. F. (1993). Sex segregation in the workplace. *Annual Review of Sociology, 19,* 241-270.

Rogers, D. L., & Gudy, W. J. (1981). Community structure and occupational segregation, 1960 and 1970. *Rural Sociology, 46,* 263-281.

Semyonov, M., & Lewin-Epstein, N. (1989). Segregation and competition in occupational labor markets. *Social Forces, 68,* 379-396.

Smith, R. (1979). Compensating wage differentials and public policy: A review. *Industrial and Labor Relations Review, 32,* 339-359.

Sorensen, E. (1989a). The crowding hypothesis and comparable worth. *The Journal of Human Resources, 25,* 55-89.

Sorensen, E. (1989b). Measuring the effect of occupational sex and race composition on earnings. In R. T. Michael, H. Hartmann, & B. O'Farrell (Eds.), *Pay equity: Empirical inquiries* (pp. 49-70). Washington, DC: National Academy Press.

Steinberg, R. J. (1990). The social construction of skill: Gender, power and comparable worth. *Work and Occupations, 17,* 449-463.

Tomaskovic-Devey, D. (1989, August). *Organizational stratification and the size of the pie: Environmental constraints on organizational income streams.* Paper presented at Annual Meeting of American Sociological Association, San Francisco.

Tomaskovic-Devey, D. (1992, August). *How come everybody looks like me?: The sources of job level sex and race segregation.* Paper presented at Annual Meeting of the American Sociological Association, Cincinnati, OH.

Tomaskovic-Devey, D. (1993a). The gender and race composition of jobs and the male/female, white/black pay gaps. *Social Forces, 72,* 999-1029.

Tomaskovic-Devey, D. (1993b). *Gender and race inequality at work: The sources and consequences of job segregation.* Ithaca NY: ILR Press.

Treiman, D. J., & Hartmann, H. I. (Eds.). (1981). *Women, work and wages: Equal pay for jobs of equal value.* Washington, DC: National Academy Press.

U.S. Department of Commerce, Bureau of the Census. (1987). Male-female differences in work experience, occupation and earnings: 1984. *Current Population Reports* (p. 7010). Washington, DC: U.S. Government Printing Office.

U.S. Department of Labor. (1990). Employed civilians by detailed occupation, sex, race and Hispanic origin (Table 22). *Employment and Earnings, 37,* 183-188.

Walby, S. (1986). *Patriarchy at work.* Minneapolis: University of Minnesota Press.

Weber, M. (1968). *Economy and society* (F. Roth & C. Wittich, Eds.). New York: Bedminster.

Williams, B. (1987). *Black workers in an industrial suburb: The struggle against discrimination.* New Brunswick, NJ: Rutgers University Press.

Wilson, W. J. (1977). *The declining significance of race.* Chicago: University of Chicago Press.

3

Gendered Instructions

Cultural Lag and Gender Bias
in the Hay System of Job Evaluation

RONNIE J. STEINBERG

The labor market is not gender neutral. Gender influences job content, the structure of authority and control, access to jobs, training opportunities, and mobility channels. It informs ideologies that legitimate workplace arrangements and employer choices, and it even shapes what is noticed about jobs and the people who fill them (Acker, 1989; Beechey, 1988; Beechey & Perkins, 1987; Cockburn, 1983; Game & Pringle, 1983; Scott, 1986). Assumptions about gender saturate the structure of compensation. According to historian Alice Kessler-Harris (1990), "Wages . . . suggest a set of gendered instructions that speak to men and women and to the relations between them" (p. 2).

Job evaluation systems are one set of organizational practices that introduce cultural assumptions about men and women into the labor market. Systems of job evaluation are social documents constructed in particular historical contexts (Steinberg, 1990). Assumptions about what

AUTHOR'S NOTE: This research was funded by the Ontario Nurses Association. I gratefully acknowledge the statistical assistance of Mary Lou King of the Ontario Nurses Association in the analysis of the Minnesota data. Special thanks go to Jerry A. Jacobs for his help in shaping the direction of this chapter. Michael Ames offered helpful comments on an earlier draft.

57

is valuable job content embedded in these systems remain invisible and unquestioned as long as they stay consistent with widely held cultural beliefs (Remick, 1981). Even after conceptions about gender have changed, job evaluation systems of earlier eras may transport outdated criteria into the new labor market contexts.

This chapter examines gender bias in the Hay Guide Chart-Profile Method, perhaps the most widely used and copied system of job evaluation. Many of the shortcomings of the Hay system are shared by other commonly used evaluation systems. In this chapter, I reach two conclusions. First, the Hay system continues to reflect gender bias that was endemic during its inception in the 1940s and 1950s when the wages paid to women's jobs were lowered systematically and explicitly because they were performed by women. By continuing to apply remarkably similar factor definitions and factor weights today, the Hay system perpetuates discrimination against women in the wage structure.

Second, the illusion of gender neutrality obscures a system geared to reproducing existing inequalities and biased toward executive functions. By cleansing the system of all direct references to gender or the gender division of labor, it appears to "objectively" value jobs solely as a function of universal criteria. On further examination, however, we find that the Hay system evaluates all jobs in terms of a set of operational definitions of job content that were developed to capture complexity specifically for executive, administrative, and managerial work. It fails to adequately valorize or even recognize distinctive job content characteristics associated with nonmanagerial work, especially work performed predominantly by women. Instead, it only recognizes differences in job complexity that can be reduced to positions on hierarchically constructed organizational charts.

The chapter first links the development of the Hay system to broader cultural assumptions about appropriate allocation of wages by gender and by occupation. Because Edward Hay was an academic as well as an entrepreneur, he chronicled the evolution and rationale for his system in a set of articles published over the period of a decade. These essays cover the values, orientation, and structure of the early system in sufficient detail to make possible comparisons with contemporary versions of the system. The chapter then demonstrates the continuity of the basic structure and values of the Hay system over almost half of a century. The final section examines an actual application of the Hay system to determine whether there is a gender effect in evaluation outcomes. The data are drawn from public sector jobs in the state of Minnesota. Regardless of the factor examined, a strong male bias emerges, in which managerial jobs are consistently found to be more complex than nonmanagerial jobs.

Gendered Wages and Job Evaluation Historically

Throughout the 19th and 20th centuries, the wage structure was reflective of "an abiding tension between a market that is said to distinguish between workers' skills, education, and commitment . . . and a set of social constructs that values sexual difference in various ways" (Kessler-Harris, 1990, pp. 3-4). Men's wages reflected not only what they were worth but also their status as breadwinners for a family. By contrast, women's wages were viewed merely as a supplement to the wages of other family members. As Kessler-Harris (1990) concluded, "The nineteenth century fight for a family wage was . . . simultaneously a fight for a social order in which men could support families and receive the services of women, and women, dependent on men, could stay out of the labor force" (p. 9). Both labor and management continued to agree with these assumptions in the 20th century. As far back as the 1920s, historians have documented separate pay scales by gender, with the least skilled male worker earning more than the most skilled female worker (Schatz, 1983, p. 32). The persistence of the wage gap over the 20th century attests to the strength of these views of sex roles and to their institutionalization in a two-tiered wage structure. Women were paid a wage enabling family subsidy (and not self-sufficiency), independent of what a job was "worth."

Such assumptions and ideologies are embedded in the job evaluation systems that rationalize and legitimate the wage structure. Job evaluation systems can be traced back over 100 years to the U.S. Civil Service Commission in 1871 or to Frederick Taylor in 1881 (Treiman, 1979, p. 1). Their use in the private sector became widespread during World War II, "prompted by decisions of the National [U.S.] War Labor Board permitting wage increases only for the purpose of correcting demonstrated 'inequities' in wage structures" (Treiman, 1979, p. 1; see also Baron, Dobbin, & Jennings, 1986; Baron, Jennings, & Dobbin, 1988). Today's systems of job evaluation were thus developed at a time when hiring advertisements said, "Help Wanted—Male" or "Help Wanted—Female."

Modifications of these systems have been largely cosmetic. As a result, 50-year-old wage policies constrain current wage-setting practices. For example, one study of the gender effects of compensation practices in California state government employment found that the 1986 salaries were affected by gender bias embedded in the job evaluation system then in place, which had been implemented in 1931. The salary and classification study on which the system was based "explicitly lowered salaries for female-dominated jobs" (Kim, 1989, p. 39).

Many early job evaluation textbooks overtly recommended procedures that would maintain customary low wages for historically female work. One expert reported in 1937 that

> the conferees noted with approval that most occupations in their companies were filled respectively by men or by women throughout. The conference favored the segregation of men's jobs and women's jobs for valuation purposes. The representatives held that men's jobs should be valued with reference to market rates for similar types of men's work, and women's jobs should be valued with reference to market rates for similar types of women's work. (Riegel, 1937, p. 21)

In a recent review of these earlier job evaluation texts, Taylor (1989) concludes that

> the historical record shows that overt sex discrimination was, in the not distant past, an integral part of personnel practice. Employers routinely placed men and women in sex-typed job classes and assigned lower pay rates to women than men, regardless of the similarities of their work. (pp. 25-26)

It is widely acknowledged that early job evaluation systems chose factors and factor weights to best reproduce, rationalize, and legitimate an existing wage hierarchy, including lower wages for historically female work (Beatty & Beatty, 1984; Remick, 1981; Treiman, 1979). Schwab (1985) has remarked that

> job evaluation is typically validated against a wage criterion (Schwab, 1980a, Treiman and Hartmann, 1981). That is, the acceptability of job evaluation results are initially determined by the correspondence between the job hierarchy produced by the valuation system and some existing distribution of wages for those jobs. (pp. 41-42)

Because women's work was especially low paying at the time of the development of these systems, this method for constructing job evaluation systems assured that the characteristics differentially associated with historically female jobs would not be treated as valuable job content. Hidden from view within evaluation systems were assumptions about the value of work as a function of the gender of the typical incumbent. Thus these systems institutionalized the taken-for-granted reality of the late 1940s and 1950s of women workers as secondary workers in low-wage jobs. The tension between market and gender noted above was obscured, although decidedly maintained.

Early job evaluation systems also carry an indirect gender effect in the types of jobs for which they were designed. Job evaluation systems were first developed largely in manufacturing contexts during World War II and then again during the U.S. Korean War, primarily in defense-related manufacturing industries where wage freezes were in effect (Patton & Littlefield, 1957; Shils, 1972). Systems also were developed to capture managerial positions in administrative contexts, most notably the Hay system. In their review of the most widely used job evaluation systems, including Hay, Treiman and Hartmann (1981) recognize the lack of fit between the categories of work on which job evaluation systems were developed and the types of technical and service-provision jobs characteristic of the contemporary labor market. These early systems failed to capture the complexity of technical and service work, limiting their usefulness as reliable instruments for gender-neutral job evaluation. Thus three features of traditional job evaluation account for its simultaneous appearance of gender neutrality and profoundly gendered character: the structure and values of the labor market at the time of its development, the use of the existing wage structure as the criterion for establishing factors and factor weights, and the types of work settings evaluated. The sources of gender bias identified in traditional job evaluation systems used today are the residue of these features.[1]

Managerial Bias in the Hay System: Development and Continuity

Managerial Bias

Although many have written about the managerial bias in the Hay system, its historical roots have not been systematically investigated (Acker, 1989; Burton, 1987; Treiman, 1979; Werwie, 1987). Certainly, there is considerable evidence in the articles written by Hay and others to attest to its managerial orientation at the time of its development. Writing in 1951, Hay and an associate, Dale Purves, introduced the personnel manager to a new method of job evaluation distinctively developed for use on managerial, higher-level professional, and executive jobs. They contended that job evaluation procedures used to evaluate these kinds of jobs needed to be different from those used to evaluate "simpler" jobs. Although the job components, broadly defined, were the same for both categories,

> the mental application requirements consist of choices, and are easily determined, but are circumscribed through established standards and supervision. . . . But as we go up the ladder in job complexity and importance, the tangibility decreases, and the evaluating yardsticks are called upon to measure quantities for which they were not designed. . . . The emphasis shifts from doing and following to thinking and delegating; from following mapped out courses to mapping out the courses. It becomes increasingly difficult to measure leadership components by followership criteria. . . . The difference in degree between low- and high-level job elements is so great that it amounts to a difference in kind. (Hay & Purves, 1951, pp. 163-164)

This quotation provides an excellent statement of the assumptions that went into the construction of the Hay system of job evaluation and that continue to influence it today. Note the strong assumption that complexity and the bureaucratic/organizational hierarchy are synonymous: High-level jobs are "complex" and "important"; low-level jobs are "simple" and "circumscribed." In other words, these two categories of jobs are not just different; rather, complexity is defined precisely and only in terms of one category of jobs—high-level managerial/executive jobs. Other jobs are, by definition, simple. The difference between high-level and low-level jobs is asserted to be a "difference in kind." Throughout their article, the definition of a high-level job is clear: It involves supervision, formal organizational responsibility, and a management title. Accordingly, a low-level job means the absence of formal supervision (i.e., hiring, firing, scheduling, formal organizational responsibility, and a management title).

Following the logic of this view of job complexity, as one moves up the hierarchy there is a shift from doing to thinking and from following to leading. These assumptions are presented as so obvious—so taken for granted—that no further explanation is necessary. I suggest and will illustrate below that treating the organizational dimensions of job complexity and responsibility as the only dimension of complexity and responsibility severely limits the full evaluation of nonmanagerial jobs.

Although, on average, managerial work involves complex skills and responsibilities, so do many nonmanagerial jobs, such that, were we to expand the range of dimensions of complexity and responsibility, we would find reasonable equivalence in skills, effort, and responsibilities among many managerial and nonmanagerial job classes.

The managerial bias in the development of the Hay system is further evidenced in the assumption by Hay and Purves (1951) that the job and the incumbent are indistinguishable for managerial jobs but not for non-managers.

> The essential difference between high-level and low-level jobs is the difference between conception, creation and direction *vs.* execution. Since the job is to a large extent made by the man, it is to be expected that good men will change the nature and extent of any jobs they may hold. (p. 164, emphasis in original).

In a later work, Hay and Purves (1953) state,

> It is immaterial who is in the low-level job, so long as he is properly qualified to do it. But at high levels, the job is largely built around the man. Low-level jobs are usually designed to be done "one best way." In . . . a high-level job, there is no "one best way" to do it. (p. 244)

These early statements in support of the profile method of job evaluation are full of problematic assumptions:

1. Managers are high-level employees who perform the most complex and responsible jobs in an organization.
2. Nonmanagers are low-level employees engaged in simple work of limited complexity with limited responsibilities.
3. Complexity is measured unidimensionally as organizational complexity.
4. Only managers think, whereas nonmanagers do.
5. Responsibility is defined as formal or ultimate responsibility and not as practical or actual responsibility.
6. People in low-level jobs are interchangeable, whereas people in high-level jobs are unique.

It is possible to see first-hand the consequences of these assumptions in the discussion of the "profile" of a typist according to the three job dimensions isolated in this system of job evaluation:

"What are we paying a typist for—knowledge, mental application or accountability?" Certainly we are not paying very much for the mental application . . .
for she is not called upon to use her head very much in making decisions; or
in planning, policy making, or in creativeness. She is doing exactly as she is
told with almost no room for a choice. Nor are we paying much for accountability. . . . About the only error that she could make is putting down the
wrong thing on paper. What about the requirement for knowledge? . . . Not
only must she be able to type but she must also be fluent in reading and
understanding the language. After that comes the training in typing and finally
the short time required to learn the duties of her job. . . . The typist is being
paid primarily for *knowledge.* (Hay & Purves, 1951, p. 166)

By contrast, the profile for administrative or managerial jobs involves
less emphasis on knowledge and more on mental application and accountability (Hay & Purves, 1951, pp. 167-168). A later article is exclusively concerned with describing the parameters of the high-level job in
terms of its functions. The manager must design his organization, make
and interpret policy, and plan, direct, and control his operations. He may
also specialize—indeed, he may even be an expert with no organization
under him. But, in this case, he will still be evaluated as having a
high-level job, largely because of his position in the organizational hierarchy. Again, the focus of that article is clear: It is possible to describe
and analyze managerial work and to measure all other jobs in terms of the
presence or absence of characteristics found in managerial work.

The problem is not that the Hay system recognizes differences in
complexity between managerial and nonmanagerial work but that location in the organizational hierarchy is the primary dimension of job
complexity used to differentiate jobs. The consequence of this decision is
to artificially define nonmanagerial work as being of lower complexity
than managerial work, regardless of its job content, and to compress
almost all nonmanagerial work into a few categories at lower factor
levels. In the next section, we examine the consequences of these rules in
the evaluation of actual jobs.

The distinctive managerial perspective embodied in the Hay Guide
Chart-Profile Method is spelled out more explicitly in later articles, as is
the self-interested motives for introducing managerially driven systems:

Bargaining over wages is a familiar part of the economic scene. But who is
there to fight for better salaries for corporate executives? . . . Little formal
attention is given to the salary problems of the executive. . . . In recent years,

a method of evaluating high level jobs has been developed which uses management thinking. Called the Guide Chart-Profile Method, . . . it . . . was devised to explain the reasons for suggested job evaluation salary standards—to show management how to evaluate high level jobs by thinking of them in management terms. . . . We have seen that the Guide Chart-Profile Method was designed for a specific purpose—evaluating managerial and technical jobs in order to get equitable salary standards. (Hay, 1958, pp. 63-65, 71-72)

Thus, by 1958, the job evaluation system associated with Hay was developed specifically for the evaluation of managerial jobs. It brought a managerial perspective to the definition of the major dimensions of job content. As discussed more fully below, this managerial bias has a pronounced gender effect, both because managerial and administrative jobs have been disproportionately male and because the types of jobs typically held by women involve job content that is not captured in evaluation systems conceptualized in terms of the organizational hierarchy.

Continuity

Bellak's (1982) article (still routinely distributed by the Hay group) presents the parameters of the Hay system. It acknowledges the link between the Hay job evaluation system developed in the 1950s and the basic system in use today: "Over the years since 1951, the fundamental principles of the Guide Chart-Profile Method have remained intact although there have been many refinements in language and application" (p. 5). This emphasis on the stability of the system is routinely used by compensation consulting firms as a strong selling point of their systems. However, with a concern for pay equity in the 1980s, what was once a desirable feature has become a point of contention.

The continuity in the approach can be observed both with respect to process and structure—that is, the factors and factor weights.[2] Given the constraints of this article, I discuss only the continuities in the structure of the system.

Three basic Guide Charts—Know-How, Problem-Solving, and Accountability—were "devised [in the 1950s] to explain the reasons for suggested job and salary standards—to show management how to evaluate high level jobs by thinking about them in management terms" (Hay, 1958, p. 65). A fourth Guide Chart—Working Conditions—was developed later, ostensibly in reaction to union pressure in the evaluation of manufacturing and other blue-collar jobs. Working conditions are typically given little weight, and this scale is used infrequently upon request (Bellak, 1984).

All of the information examined below on the Hay Guide Chart-Profile Method of Job Evaluation is drawn from public records. Versions of the Hay Guide Charts are culled from published articles, final reports of pay equity studies, or reports prepared for litigation before a pay equity tribunal in Ontario, Canada. Data on job evaluations were obtained from the Minnesota Department of Personnel.

When examining the three major factors of the Hay system, the similarity between the description of the factors in Hay (1958) and in Bellak (1982) is striking. Table 3.1 presents the definitions of Know-How, Problem-Solving, and Accountability as offered in Hay (1958) and in Bellak (1982). Although the definitions in Bellak are somewhat more elaborate, the ideas about what constitutes valuable work and about the differentiation of factor levels remain essentially intact. Know-How continues to define skills in terms of technical skill, managerial skills, and the skills involved in working with other people. Problem-Solving encompasses the creative application of these skills or the thinking associated with a job. It is defined in terms of the environment and the difficulty of the thinking. Accountability is measured along three dimensions: freedom, impact, and size.

Fortunately, Edward Hay offered the basic format of the Hay subfactor levels in a 1958 article, so it is possible to compare subfactor definitions more specifically to contemporary Hay Guide Charts available in the public record. Indeed, as Tables 3.2 through 3.4 illustrate, when subfactor-level definitions for four versions of the Hay system are compared, the continuity is even more striking.[3] In the Know-How Guide Chart, the only modification was to move Organizational Know-How from the top levels of a Technical Know-How dimension to create a third dimension to the factor. Interestingly, this modification has the effect of actually increasing the weight given to Managerial Know-How, as it is quite rare for jobs that score high on Organizational Know-How to score low on Technical Know-How.[4]

The definitions of Managerial Know-How are quite consistent across the contemporary systems. Note that Hay consultants are provided with internal memos that offer several variants of language that can be used in constructing this subfactor. The variations are usually on the basis of the size and complexity of the organizational hierarchy. The expansion of levels usually occurs at the top. If the chief executive officer (CEO) represents the highest level, then there must be enough additional levels

Table 3.1 Comparison of Factor and Subfactor Definitions for Hay Guide Chart-Profile Method 1958 and 1982

Factor/Subfactor	Hay (1958)	Bellak (1982)
Know-How	"Each position must be thought of as requiring a specific kind of job know-how. . . . In addition to the specialized technical kinds of know-how required, skill in human relations is important in high-level policy-making jobs. Administrative knowledge is also necessary in jobs which have managerial responsibilities. . . . [The] guide chart for know-how . . . combines scales for these three kinds of skill and knowledge."	The sum total of every kind of capability or skill, however acquired, needed for acceptable job performance. Its three dimensions are requirements for: • Practical procedures, specialized techniques and knowledge within occupational fields, commercial functions, and professional and scientific disciplines. • Integrating and harmonizing simultaneous achievement of diversified function within managerial situation occurring in operating, technical, support, or administrative fields. This involves, in some combination, skills in planning, organizing, executing, controlling, and evaluating and may be exercised consultatively (about management) as well as executively. • Active, practicing person-to-person skills in work with other people.
Problem-Solving	"Thinking is always done in a specific environment which allows a particular degree of latitude. . . . [The] problem-solving chart [combines] the two scales of environment and thinking."	The original self-starting use of Know-How required by the job to identify, define, and resolve problems. "You think with what you know." This is true of even the most creative work. The raw material of any thinking is knowledge of facts, principles, and means. For that reason, Problem-Solving is treated as a percentage of Know-How. Problem-Solving has two dimensions:

Table 3.1 (Continued)

Factor/Subfactor	Hay (1958)	Bellak (1982)
		• The environment in which thinking takes place
		• The challenge presented by the thinking to be done
Accountability	"There is one more important job element—the actions which must be taken. . . . The actions taken may be considered according to 1. The amount of freedom. 2. The strength of the impact. 3. The size of the area affected. These three aspects of action may be described as accountability for performance. The job holder is accountable for taking the necessary actions and thus accomplishing the aims of management."	The answerability for action and for the consequences thereof. It is the measured effect of the job on end results of the organization. It has three dimensions in the following order of importance: • Freedom to act—the extent of personal, procedural, or systematic guidance or control of actions in relation to the primary emphasis of the job • Job impact on end results—the extent to which the job can directly affect actions necessary to produce result within its primary emphasis • Magnitude—the portion of the total organization encompassed by the primary emphasis of the job. This is usually, but not necessarily, reflected by the annual revenue or expense dollars associated with the area in which the job has its primary emphasis.

of Organizational Know-How to encompass the multiple levels of management under the CEO. By contrast, regardless of the complexity and variety of nonmanagerial jobs, nonmanagerial factor levels remain the

(Text continued on page 72)

Table 3.2 Comparison of Know-How Definitions—Guide Chart Categories

Subfactor	Hay (1958)	Bellak (1982)	Treiman (1979)	Hubbard & Revo-Cohen (1989)
Technical Know-How	A. Basic B. Elementary vocational C. Vocational D. Advanced vocational E. Specialized technical F. Seasoned-specialized—technical G. Specialized—technical mastery H. Intermediate managerial I. Administrative managerial J. General managerial	A. Basic B. Elementary vocational C. Vocational D. Advanced vocational E. Basic technical—specialized F. Seasoned technical—specialized G. Technical—specialized mastery H. Professional mastery	A. Primary B. Elementary vocational C. Vocational D. Advanced vocational E. Basic specialized F. Seasoned specialized G. Specialized mastery H. Professional mastery	A. Primary B. Elementary vocational C. Vocational D. Advanced vocational E. Basic specialized F. Seasoned specialized G. Specialized mastery
Managerial Know-How	NA[a]	1. None or minimal 2. Related 3. Diverse 4. —[b]	I. None or minimal II. Intermediate III. Broad IV. Comprehensive V. Total	I. Limited II. Intermediate III. Broad IV. Comprehensive
Human Relations Know-How	1. Normal courtesy and effectiveness. 2. Understanding and motivation of people is an important, but not an overriding, consideration. 3. Skills in selecting, developing, organizing, and/or motivating people are overriding.	NA[b]	1. Ordinary courtesy and effectiveness in dealing with others. 2. Understanding, influencing, and/or servicing people are important but not critical considerations. 3. Alternative or combined skills in understanding, selecting, developing, and motivating people are important in the highest degree.	1. Ordinary courtesy and effectiveness in dealing with others. 2. Understanding, influencing, and/or serving people are important considerations. 3. Alternative or combined skills in understanding, selecting, developing, and motivating people are important in the highest degree.

a. Not available. In Hay (1958), managerial know-how was embedded as the most complex levels of Technical Know-How. Its separation into a separate subfactor (with varying levels depending on the size and organization complexity of the firm) actually increases the number of points and the weight given to scope of managerial responsibility.

b. Not available. Bellak (1982) presents only the lower sections of the Guide Chart-Profile Method because it is a proprietary system.

Table 3.3 Comparison of Problem-Solving Definitions—Guide Chart Categories

Subfactor	Hay (1958)	Bellak (1982)	Treiman (1979)
Thinking Guidance		A. Strict routine B. Routine C. Semiroutine D. Standardized E. Clearly defined F. Broadly defined G. Generally defined H. Abstractly defined	A. Strict routine B. Routine C. Semiroutine D. Standardized E. Clearly defined F. Broadly defined G. Generally defined H. Abstractly defined
	A. Strict routine B. Routine C. Semiroutine D. Standardized E. Directed F. Generally directed G. Guided H. Generally guided		
Thinking Challenge	1. Stable: Conditions covering jobs are inherently stable or repetitive, and are characterized by general absence of original problem-solving 2. Normal: Conditions covering job call for improvisation or adaptation to meet changing situations of manufacture, market, and the like 3. Uncharted: Path-finding in novel, nonrecurring, or swiftly changing situation in which the approach to the objective is not fully defined	1. Repetitive: Identical situations requiring solution by *simple* choice of learned things[a] 2. Patterned: Similar situations requiring solution by *discriminating* choice of learned things[a] 3. Interpolative: Differing situations requiring search for solutions within area of learned things 4. Adaptive: Variable situations requiring analytic, interpretive, and/or constructing thinking 5. NA[b]	1. Repetitive: Identical situations requiring solution by *simple* choice of learned things[a] 2. Patterned: Similar situations requiring solution by *discriminating* choice of learned things[a] 3. Interpolative: Differing situations requiring search for solutions within area of learned things 4. Adaptive: Variable situations requiring analytic, interpretive, and/or constructing thinking 5. Uncharted: Novel or nonrecurring path-finding situations requiring the development of new concepts and imaginative approaches

a. Emphasis added.
b. Not available. Bellak (1982) does not provide complete information because the Guide Chart-Profile Method is a proprietary system.

Table 3.4 Comparison of Accountability Definitions—Guide Chart Categories

Subfactor	Hay (1958)	Bellak (1982)	Treiman (1979)
Freedom to Act	A. Standardized B. General regulated C. Operational direction D. Oriented direction E. Top management, guidance F. Presidential guidance	A. Prescribed B. Controlled C. Standardized D. Generally regulated E. Directed F. Oriented directed G. Broad guidance H. Strategic guidance	A. Prescribed B. Controlled C. Standardized D. Generally regulated E. Directed F. Oriented directed G. Broad guidance H. Strategic guidance I. Governor/chief justice
Magnitude	1. Small or indeterminate 2. Medium 3. Large 4. Very large	1. Very small or indeterminate 2. Small 3. Medium 4. NA[a]	1. Very small or indeterminate 2. Small 3. Medium 4. Large 5. Very large
Impact	1. Remote: Positions that provide informational or custodial services used by others[b] 2. Indirect: Occurs when counsel or advice is provided 3. Shared: Participation with others in making decisions 4. Primary: Independent decision where there is little sharing of accountability with others	1. Remote: Information, recording, or *incidental* services for use by others in relation to some important end result[c] 2. Contributory interpretive, advisory, or facilitating services for use by others in taking action 3. Shared: Participating with others (except own subordinates or superiors) within organizational unit in taking action 4. Primary: Controlling impact on end results, where shared accountability with others is subordinate	1. Remote: informational, recording, or *routine* services for use by others in taking action[c] 2. Contributory interpretive, advisory, or facilitating services for use by others in taking action 3. Shared: Participating with others (except own subordinates or superiors) within *or outside* the organizational units in taking action[c] 4. Primary: Controlling impact on end results, where shared accountability with others is subordinate

a. Not available. Bellak (1982) does not provide complete information because the Guide Chart-Profile Method is a proprietary system.

b. Guide Chart definitions elaborated in Hay (1958, p. 69).

c. Emphasis added.

71

same and compressed.[5] The language defining Human Relations Know-How has changed hardly at all in the past 33 years, with the assumption that working with subordinates is more complex than working with clients remaining intact.

In the Problem-Solving Guide Charts, there have been minor word changes in the Thinking Guidance dimension (e.g., "directed" has been changed to "clearly defined" and "generally directed" to "broadly defined"). Another modest change in the Thinking Challenge dimension is the division in half of the bottom two levels, so that a three-level subfactor now has five levels. The basic differentiation, however, remains intact, with the highest "uncharted" level using almost the same descriptive language.

The same is true of the Accountability Guide Chart. Along the first subfactor, Freedom to Act, two lower levels have been added, presumably to allow for the evaluation of low-level jobs with little organizational autonomy. One level has been added to the Magnitude subfactor, differentiating small and indeterminate. This subfactor also can expand or contract depending on the complexity and the size of a firm and its fiscal parameters. The Impact dimension has remained virtually identical since the late 1950s.

There has been remarkable continuity in the structure of the Hay system over the past 3 decades. This raises many problems about potential gender bias. Because job evaluation systems are socially constructed, they carry assumptions that were prevalent at the time of their development. The Hay Guide Chart-Profile Method emerged at a time when women were regarded as secondary workers and when even equal pay for equal work was not yet a widespread legal standard. It carries forward a set of values and a wage structure characteristic of that time period, when it was almost universally believed that a woman's wage was not the same thing as a man's wage. It was developed for the evaluation of executive and managerial jobs and not for use in evaluating historically female jobs. Because of this orientation, the Hay system evaluates all jobs in terms of management and administrative functions, even when this perspective treats the content of a job class as invisible or as being of lower complexity. It effectively ends up collapsing nonmanagerial jobs into a few undifferentiated factor levels while differentiating more finely among managerial and administrative jobs.

Unlike the example above of the California compensation system, the Hay system did not need to be explicit about the secondary position of women in the labor market. It could embed such assumptions in its broad factor definitions and in its evaluation process, with negative consequences for women's wages. Specifically, the construction of a system based on the wage structure at a specific historical moment in time ensures that, at later points in time, the wage structure is reproduced because the job content differentially found in historically female jobs is not treated as valuable. The next section examines more directly the impact of this system on the differential evaluation of male jobs and on the invisibility of women's work.

Gender Bias in the Hay System: The Effect of Managerial Bias

Thus far, we have demonstrated that there is continuity in the factors and factor-level definitions in the Hay Guide Charts over the almost half-century during which they have been put to use. We have also shown strong evidence that the system was developed to evaluate professional, managerial, and executive job classes. Although this represents the introduction of cultural assumptions of the 1940s and 1950s into the contemporary labor market—what we might consider to be a cultural lag—does it constitute gender bias?

Assessing job evaluation systems from a contemporary standpoint, Remick (1979) and Treiman (1979) note the tendency of job evaluation systems to measure and assign points on the basis of job characteristics found in historically male work (Werwie, 1987, p. 103). This bias is embedded in the definition of factors so that as the factor moves from less complex (or responsible) to more complex (or responsible), the jobs assigned to levels move from female-dominated to male-dominated. Similarly, bias is revealed in the tendency, within factors, to more finely differentiate levels of complexity (or responsibility) in male jobs than in female jobs. To assess gender bias in the structure of the Hay system, it is necessary to demonstrate both how the factors measure as valuable the skills, responsibilities, effort, and undesirable working conditions differentially found in male work *and* the ways in which job content found in historically female work is treated as invisible, unskilled, and less responsible. In this section, I illustrate both aspects of gender bias in the Hay system, which assigns greater value to job content differentially found in male jobs.

The findings are based on several assessments of the Hay system (Acker, 1987, 1989; Burton, 1987; Haignere & Steinberg, 1985; Treiman, 1979; Werwie, 1987), on statistical analyses of results of job evaluations conducted using the Hay system in the state of Minnesota, and on information on the content of the job of registered nurse collected from focus groups of registered nurses in four Ontario, Canada, hospitals. Information on registered nurses is supplemented by secondary sources (Benner, 1984; College of Nurses of Ontario, 1989; Growe, 1991; Melosh, 1982; Reverby, 1987).

An assessment of the subfactor definitions and levels and their application on a set of jobs makes visible the specific ways in which bias toward capturing job content of managerial work dominates the system. Because managerial jobs have historically been designed for and disproportionately held by men, this constitutes an evaluation bias in favor of historically male jobs.[6]

The standard Hay system is composed of four Guide Charts that contain 11 subfactors—3 for Know-How, 3 for Accountability, 2 for Problem Solving, and 3 for Working Conditions—among which I have found managerial bias is expressed outright in the definitions of 5 of the most heavily weighted subfactors—Managerial Know-How, Human Relations Know-How, Freedom to Act, Magnitude, and Impact—and expressed indirectly in three others—Technical Know-How, Thinking Challenge, and Thinking Environment. I restrict the analysis here to managerial bias in 3 subfactors: Human Relations Know-How (HRKH), Freedom to Act (FTA), and Technical Know-How (TKH). I select these because, unlike Organizational Know-How, Magnitude, and Impact, these subfactor-level definitions are less explicitly written in terms of organizational scope or job hierarchy. I also select them over Thinking Challenge and Thinking Environment because the points gained as a result of FTA and TKH are partly derivative from and highly correlated with points received on other subfactors. Furthermore, the Working Conditions subfactors are not biased in favor of managerial work, although they are male biased. A complete analysis of male bias in each Hay Guide Chart factor is found in Steinberg (1991).

Human Relations Know-How (HRKH)

There are four ways in which the HRKH subfactor carries a male bias:

1. It combines different types of human relations skills, one of which is double counted because it has already been measured under Managerial Know-How.
2. It arbitrarily defines supervisory skills as more complex than client-oriented skills.
3. It defines supervision in ways that differentially exclude the forms of supervision typical of female-dominated work.
4. It fails to differentiate adequately among levels of nonsupervisory human relations skills.

It both advantages managerial and supervisory work and disadvantages service-oriented jobs.

Table 3.2 lists the standard subfactor-level definitions for HRKH. HRKH provides for three levels of differentiation, with the top level defined in terms of supervisory capabilities—"motivating . . . and developing people." As constructed, this subfactor allows, primarily, for the differentiation between supervisory and nonsupervisory jobs (between Level 3 and Levels 2 and 1) and, secondarily, for the differentiation between client-oriented and non-client-oriented jobs (between Levels 1 and 2). The implicit assumptions about complexity are that supervising employees involves more complex use of skills, such as communicating, motivating, influencing, understanding, listening, and teaching, than does working with clients or patients. The system offers no documentation about actual job content to support this assumption. Burton (1987) has questioned this assumption in asking whether supervising employees involves skill or the exertion of organizational power (pp. 90-91). She also suggests that women work up and across organizational hierarchies, whereas men work down the hierarchy. Acker (1989) reports that the Oregon Legislative Task Force overseeing a comparable worth study of public employment was similarly critical of the lack of differentiation and narrow dimensions found in HRKH, as well as of overreliance on notions of the formal organization hierarchy. Earlier, Acker (1987) writes,

> Deciding who was or was not a supervisor was important for the emergent ranking. . . . The evaluation team, with the help of the consultants, developed rules to deal with this complexity. . . . The secretary who supervises 15 to 20 workers is seen simply as a lead worker. . . . Many [nonsupervisory jobs with supervisory functions] are female-dominated and adding some extra points

for supervision may be one of the sources of scores that show that these jobs have been undervalued. (p. 85)

Furthermore, by combining into one subfactor those human relations skills necessary for working with clients and those necessary for supervision, the Hay system cancels out the relative impact that nonmanagerial human relations skills can have on total points for nonmanagerial jobs. If, by definition, all managerial jobs receive the highest score on this factor, there is no way that a nonmanagerial job can be assessed as involving more complex human relations skills. But consider, for example, the registered nurse, who must negotiate with recalcitrant patients about life-sustaining medication or who must work regularly with dying patients who have no hope of recovery.

Moreover, when client-oriented skills and supervision skills are combined, human services jobs that involve both aspects of human relations only receive points for one skill dimension (Steinberg, 1990). So, for example, a registered nurse administrative supervisor receives fewer points than he or she would if the Hay system included two separate subfactors on Human Relations skills, one for supervision and a second for client-oriented skills. The inclusion of supervisory skills in HRKH also involves double counting of skills because supervisory responsibility is included as part of the definition of Managerial Know-How.

Hay consultants in Oregon appeared to be aware of the consequences of constructing HRKH to combine supervisory and client-oriented skills and to treat the former as more complex. They proved to be the biggest opponents to a proposed modification of the system by task force feminists, arguing that it "would result in a higher value placed on human relations relative to managerial skills." They viewed HRKH as a "subscale of Managerial Know-How," regardless of the commonsense meaning of the term, and they feared that modification "might change the rank order of some jobs." Their second objection to a revaluation of service provision work was that it would "decrease the point spread between managerial and non-managerial jobs," which would cause "even more difficulties in recruiting and keeping good managers" (Acker, 1987, pp. 189-190).

Examining the evaluation of 1,441 job titles in the state of Minnesota, I found noteworthy differences in evaluation scores by gender of job. For female-dominated jobs, 16.2% score at Level 1, 45.5% score at Level 2, and 38.3% score at Level 3. By contrast, for male-dominated jobs, the percentages are 13.6, 30.3, and 56.1 for Levels 1, 2, and 3, respectively.

The definition of supervisor clearly carries a gender effect, as does the artificial definitional ceiling that prohibits service provision skills from scoring at the highest level.

Freedom to Act (FTA)

FTA is defined in terms of extent of supervisory review at the lower levels of the scale and as scope of managerial direction at the upper ends of the scale. This is a classic representation of employee autonomy from the standpoint of the top of the organization. However, by defining autonomy only in terms of formal review relationships, this subfactor renders invisible the frequent actions taken by employees to autonomously carry out highly responsible tasks and functions—especially in human services contexts when time pressure is often significant. For example, the registered nurse informs the physician that a medical emergency warrants his or her intervention. In an emergency situation, the nurse will often begin medical procedures in anticipation of what she or he knows the doctor will order or because the doctor has placed a standing order allowing for autonomous intervention with legal protection. Under the Hay system, because human services workers are formally supervised, the supervisor receives credit (in points and in money) for the responsibilities actually carried out by his or her subordinate. In this case, the physician has formal, final responsibility for medical decisions, and all positions below him or her are treated as operating with little autonomy.

The concept of formal responsibility inflates the work performed by supervisors and diminishes the work performed by subordinates. It obscures the practical responsibility and autonomy of nonmanagerial employees, understating the extent to which incumbents of nonmanagerial jobs have control over the main goal of their jobs. It overstates the amount of supervision that supervisors engage in, especially when subordinates are performing their jobs competently (Burton, 1987, p. 92). Acker (1989) also observed an explicit reliance on the organizational chart in carrying out evaluations of actual jobs, based on the assumption that "supervisors ought to have more points than those beneath them, and fewer points than those above them in the hierarchy" (p. 89). Acker concludes that the assumption of "congruence between responsibility, job complexity, and hierarchical position" works to the disadvantage of differentially female nonmanagerial jobs: "Tasks delegated to a secretary by a manager will not raise her hierarchical level because such tasks are still his responsibility, even though she has the practical responsibility to see that they are done" (p. 220).

The descriptions for each level of FTA are ambiguous and open to subjective judgments in their application. What differentiates "constant . . . supervision" from "very close supervision" or from "close supervision"? The top four levels of this subfactor are more clearly specified but only in reference to the scope of the organization managed, which theoretically is a proxy for autonomy. We can begin to understand what is meant by these words through a review of actual evaluations of job classes on FTA in the state of Minnesota: 99% of the 1,441 jobs with at least one incumbent are evaluated on FTA at Levels B and F (A is lowest and G is highest).

Table 3.5 lists a sample of representative jobs from a variety of job categories evaluated at Levels A through C. Fewer than 20 of the 1,441 job classes were scored at Level A, and these were disproportionately female-dominated. Job classes that score at Level A equate male jobs such as mail handler with female jobs such as child care center aide and entry-level clerk typist and stenographer. It is unclear why child care center aide and clerk stenographer require "very close supervision" as compared to "close supervision," especially in comparison to male jobs scoring at Level B, such as meat cutter, baker, and automobile driver. Do the job descriptions calculate the amount or percentage of time directly supervised or the number or types of instructions and work routines? In this instance, basing autonomy only on formal organizational review creates false differentiations that are not based on careful assessment of actual differences in work routines and extent of instruction and review.

Similarly, no rationale is offered for the decision to score licensed practical nurse, child care center assistant, supervisors of word processing centers, and dining hall managers at the same level of autonomy as athletic equipment manager, meat cutter, and groundskeeper. The autonomy and responsibility of working with sick clients is equated with the autonomy and responsibility of cutting meat. Handling children is equivalent to handling equipment. Performing at the highest level of clerk stenographer is at the same level of autonomy and responsibility as driving an automobile or baking. At Level C, coordinating a child care center is equivalent in autonomy and responsibility to that assigned an electrician, plumber, or heavy equipment operator.

Most notably, what these evaluations do reveal is that supervisors of what are considered low autonomy positions are scored on FTA on the basis of the *assumed* low autonomy of the positions they supervise.

Table 3.5 Representative Job Classes Evaluated on Freedom to Act/Accountability Subfactor, State of Minnesota

Subfactor Level	Female	Male	Balanced
A	Child Care Center Aide Clerk I Clerk Typist I Clerk Stenographer I Data Entry Operator Food Service Worker Laboratory Attendant A Laundry Worker	Mail Handler Traffic Recorder	Service Worker Inserting Machine Operator

B	Licensed Practical Nurse 1
	Licensed Practical Nurse 2[a]
	Physical Therapy Aide B
	Switchboard Operator
	Word Processing Operator
	Word Processing Center—
	  Supervisor B[b]
	Account Clerk
	Clerks 2-4[a]
	Clerk Stenographers 2-4[a]
	Clerk Stenographer 4
	  Supervisor[a]
	Office Services Supervisor 1
	Child Care Center Assistant
	Dining Hall Manager
	Human Services Technician—
	  Senior
	Dental Assistant
	Sewing Machine Operator
	Medical Records Clerk
		Athletic Equipment Manager
		Meat Cutter
		Materials Transfer Driver
		Labor—Trades and Equip-
		  ment
		Laboratory Attendant 2
		Baker
		Barber
		Automobile Driver
		Highway Maintenance Manager
		General Maintenance Worker
		Groundskeeper
		Groundskeeper—Intermediate[a]
		Groundskeeper—Senior[a]
		Chief Cook
			Stores Clerk
			Recreation Pro-
			  gram Assistant
			Admissions/Gift
			  Shop Clerk
			First Aid Services
			  Assistant
			Audio-Visual
			  Technician

C	Registered Nurse
	Social Worker
	Legal Secretary
	Legal Secretary, Senior[a]
	Legal Secretary, Senior
	  Supervisor[a]
	Public Health Sanitarian 1
	Animal Health Specialist
	Accounting Technician
	Account Clerk—Senior
	Typing Services Coordinator
	Child Care Center Coordinator
		Zookeeper
		Electrician
		Mason
		Painter
		Plumber
		Roofer
		Heavy Equipment Mechanic
		Heavy Equipment Operator
		Building Maintenance Lead
		  Worker
		Bridge Worker
		Electrician Lead[a]
		Electrician Supervisor[a]
		Architect Drafting Technician
		Stores Clerk—Senior
			Auditor
			Bacteriologist 1
			Behavior Analyst 1
			EDP Programmer

a. Balanced class.
b. A lot of supervisors of positions found in Level D.

Specifically, supervisors or coordinators of employees or a program are scored one step higher than the level of autonomy of the employees they supervise or coordinate. Thus the lower the evaluation on FTA assigned to a group of employees, the lower the level assigned to the supervisor of those employees or the manager of the program in which they work. So, for example, the child care center coordinator scores at a low level on FTA because the child care aide scores even lower.

The impact of this score compression is especially marked for managerial-level nursing positions. At least three levels of nursing supervisors are included in one level of FTA. This includes the registered nurse senior, the registered nurse principal, the registered nurse supervisor, the registered nurse administrator supervisor, and the director of nursing.[7] By contrast, managerial positions in engineering job series are not as compressed. By imposing bureaucratic/administrative conceptions of autonomy on the provision of services and clinical care, the Hay system treats as invisible the extensive independence of action and initiative required of hands-on work. For example, the administrative distinction between the short run and the long run is less applicable in human services settings. Indeed, imposing it as the basis of differentiating levels of complexity and responsibility can obscure autonomy and responsibility in clinical and service provision settings, resulting in misjudgments in scoring. Often, of necessity, human service jobs must act "in the short run," or else patients will die or suffer serious consequences. In addition, following a set of general professional standards as those found in the Standards of Nursing Practice is not the same application of procedures, practices, or precedents typical of jobs in bureaucratic settings. Scoring administrator and director levels of nursing work at Level D of a subfactor that spans from A to H suggests that the image of nursing held by the Hay group is of work with limited autonomy and regular supervisory review of results, even including the Director of Nursing.

This general rating principle results in lower scores for female-dominated job classes. Of all male-dominated jobs in Minnesota state government, 70.1% are scored at Levels D and E, compared with only 48% of female-dominated titles. By contrast, three times as many (19.9%) of female jobs score at Levels A or B as male-dominated jobs (5.3%).

The male bias observed in FTA involves several aspects of its construction: its heavy reliance on the formal organizational chart as the operational definition of what constitutes autonomous work; its devaluation of the autonomy involved in direct clinical and service provision work; its tendency to evaluate supervisory and managerial positions in reference to the jobs supervised; compression of career ladders in female-dominated groups of jobs; and its reliance on only half of the defined levels to evaluate 97% of all job classes. Several dimensions of job autonomy are not acknowledged, and those that are, are not insufficiently differentiated and artificially compressed.

Technical Know-How (TKH)

When operationalized, TKH, like FTA, follows the general rule that a supervisory job should score higher than but close to the position supervised. In addition, for TKH, knowledge gained through work and other experience is given less recognition than formal and institutionally gained occupational knowledge and general credentials. Even women's formal knowledge, such as typing skills learned at school, is trivialized (Burton 1987, p. 89).

Given the ambiguous wording of the definitions of subfactor levels of TKH, it is necessary to ground their meaning in their application and impact. Table 3.6 lists examples of jobs ranked at different levels with the TKH subfactor. Some interesting patterns emerge. Few jobs score at Level A. At the lower end of the continuum on TKH are those male-dominated jobs that require no educational prerequisites or prior experience, such as the ability to drive a car, to learn tasks associated with sorting or delivering mail, or to do maintenance, custodial, or security work. Female-dominated jobs scored as equivalent include entry-level clerical, food service, and child care workers. Some of these jobs carry educational prerequisites. Others, such as food service and child care, carry strong associations with roles that women are assumed to perform in the home—in other words, it is assumed that these jobs are unskilled. Invisible and unrecognized are the organizational knowledge and language skills of clerical workers, the technical knowledge of food preparation in institutional settings, and the psychological knowledge and skills associated with child care work.

In my review of evaluations conducted in the state of Minnesota, I found clustering of jobs within a career ladder. This finding is consistent with an evaluation procedure that was followed by the state of Massachusetts in applying a Hay system. According to Department of Personnel Administration staff members, the descriptions from each career ladder or job series were considered at the same time, beginning with the

Table 3.6 Representative Job Classes Evaluated on Technical Know-How
Subfactor, State of Minnesota

Subfactor Points	Male	Female
A	Mail Handler	Laboratory Attendant
B	Automobile Driver Building & Grounds Worker Delivery Van Driver General Maintenance Worker Groundskeeper Security Guard	Child Care Center Aide Clerk 1 and 2 Data Entry Operator, Lead, and Senior Dictaphone Operator Food Service Worker Interpretive Guide Parks Worker Switchboard Operator Work Therapy Technician

C	Automotive Technician
	Baker
	Barber
	Building Services Manager
	Engineering Aide
	General Repair Worker
	Highway Maintenance Worker
	Meat Cutter
	Office Machine Repair
	   Supervisor
	Painter
	Plasterer
	Stores Clerk Chief
		Administrative Secretary
		Account Clerk Supervisor
		Beauty Operator
		Cashier
		Child Care Center Coordinator
		Clerk Stenographer
		Dental Assistant
		Health Program Aide
		Special Education Program
		   Assistant
		Human Rights Aide
		Legal Secretary
		Licensed Practical Nurse
		Medical Claims Technician
		Physical Therapy Assistant

D	Heavy Equipment Operator
	Plumber
	Architectural Drafting
	   Technician 2 and 3
	Automotive Mechanic
	Bridge Worker
	Cabinet Maker
	Driver Improvement Specialist
	Electrician
	Senior Engineering Aide
	Land Surveyor
	Machinist
	Public Health Sanitarian
	Radio Technician
		Dental Hygienist
		Legal Secretary Senior Supervisor
		Income Maintenance Program
		   Analyst
		Senior Legal Secretary
		Medical Laboratory Technician
		Registered Nurse
		Recreation Therapist Coordinator
		Social Worker

Table 3.6 (Continued)

Subfactor Points	Male	Female
E[b]	Physical Plant Director Attorney 1[a] Boiler Inspector 2 Business Manager Economic Policy Analyst EDP Programmer/Analyst Elevator Inspector Senior Engineer Financial Institution Examiner Geologist Health Services Analyst[a] Psychologist Public Health Sanitarian 3 and 4 Systems Analyst Welfare Specialists[a]	Nutritionist Occupational Therapist Physical Therapist Assistant to Chief Executive Officer Child Health Program Supervisor Clinical Nurse Specialist Dietitian 1 Health Educator Library/Information Research Services Specialist Personnel Director 1 and 2 Registered Nurse Supervisor
F	Dentist Attorney 2 and 3[a] (12) Directors (Programs, Labs, 12 Divisions) Pollution Control Scientist Assistant Commissioner[c] Assistant Director titles[d] Chief Executive Officer Education Finance Supervisor Education Specialist[a] Engineer Administrative titles Central Payroll Director Industrial Hygienist Plant Management Director Staff Physician[a] Transportation Director titles	Personnel Director 3 and 5 Public Health Nursing Director

a. Balanced class.
b. A lot of supervisors of positions found in Level D.
c. Three balanced: one male and two female titles; one title at Level G.
d. Six of 15 titles at Level E.

highest job in the ladder and working backward to the lowest (Haignere & Steinberg, 1985, p. 26). Thus the points for TKH are not simply based on the actual technical requirements of the job but on where a job falls within a job series and where the top, or the bottom, of that series falls on the organization chart as a whole.

One important reason why evaluating a job in terms of its position in a series carries a gender effect is that the disproportionate number of top management and professional jobs are held by men. If these top management and professional jobs score at the top levels of a subfactor, then, simply as an artifact of the evaluation process, even the bottom jobs in these series will score at high sublevels, regardless of job content and technical skills.

The use of these shortcuts in job evaluation can be seen with respect to the education barrier in scores for TKH. It appears that a job cannot score at Level E or above on TKH unless it requires a college degree. As a result of this rule, all secretarial and clerical positions *must* score at Level D or below, regardless of the actual technical, communication, organizational, and human relations skills associated with the job. This barrier has a similar effect on other female-dominated technical jobs that require 2- and 3-year vocational degrees. Note in Table 3.6 that the medical laboratory technician and the registered nurse both score at Level D, whereas the physical therapist and health educator score at Level E.

The impact of supervision on scores for TKH can be seen for all jobs evaluated in the state of Minnesota. Recall that all jobs that supervise automatically score at Level 3 of HRKH. Only one job class ranked as low as Level C for TKH was scored as supervisory on HRKH. The overlap between the managerial and technical factors is even more striking. All of the jobs scoring at Level D or below on TKH were rated at the bottom level of the managerial scale (MKH), indicating no need for knowledge of managerial skills. At the higher levels of TKH, a much greater percentage of job titles score high on HRKH, and by Level F of TKH, almost all jobs are at least at Level 2 for MKH (and at Level 3 for HRKH). Of the 180 jobs scoring at least at Level 2 of MKH, 166, or 92.2% score at Level F on TKH.

A related point is that the interrelationships between the ostensibly independent subfactors results in the inflation of managerial positions. The intercorrelations of three of the Hay subfactors—Know-How, Problem-Solving, and Accountability—range from 0.97 to 0.99 for Minnesota and 0.94 to 0.98 for Philadelphia (data not shown). Because these subfactors are so highly interrelated, giving greater weight to one or another of them would not significantly affect gender bias. Under these circumstances, gender bias is largely a function of the subfactor definitions. Once the definitions are made more inclusive, it would be possible to shift the weighting to more adequately recognize the value of acknowledged job content.[8]

The gender effect of evaluations on TKH in the state of Minnesota is clear. Whereas few male or female jobs score at Levels A or B, 26.8% of female-dominated jobs score at Level C, compared to 9.3% of male jobs. By contrast, over one third (36.6%) of all male-dominated job classes score at Level F, compared with only 18.4% of female-dominated job classes.

As the data drawn from the state of Minnesota and other analyses indicate, the definitions of each of the three subfactors were constructed in ways that capture male-dominated work better than historically female work. HRKH, FTA, and TKH are oriented to treat supervisory and managerial work as more complex. Secondarily, TKH defines professional work requiring a college degree as more complex than professional work requiring vocational degrees and on-the-job experience. Evaluations rely heavily on formal hierarchical relationships. This is reflected in the clustering and compression observed in actual evaluation scores. It also accords with direct observations of evaluations by Acker (1989) in Oregon and interviews about the evaluation process conducted by Burton (1987) in Australia and Haignere and Steinberg (1985) in Massachusetts.

Conclusion

The Hay system has not kept pace with changes in the nature of work and in the character and diversity of organizational forms since the 1940s and 1950s. It has failed to modify its definitions of skills to encompass the technological and knowledge changes that have taken place in many nonmanagerial jobs. The system crafted by Edward Hay and Dale Purves between 1946 and 1958 remains essentially intact. Its power and stability rest precisely in the ability of the system to carry from one organization to another a set of values that sustains high managerial wages even in the face of organizational and technological changes that might undercut this traditional wage structure.

These findings are consistent with research on organizational practices and structural arrangements, research that points to the social and economic context at the time of development as a critical determinant of its contemporary character (Baron, 1991; Bielby & Baron, 1987; Stinchcombe, 1965). For example, reflecting on almost a decade of research on the "organizational factors" that "influence the way jobs are defined, evaluated, and staffed," Baron (1991) concludes that once practices and policies are in place, "organizations exhibit inertia" (p. 135). This inertia is sustained in the absence of conditions that facilitate change (such as external pressure and likelihood of internal collective action) and in the presence of interests that seek to maintain the status quo. Viewing organizations as, in part, "arenas in which social relations, political contests, and cultural forces shape the enterprise," Baron acknowledges that a powerful in-group seeking to "institutionalize its privileged position" could do so by treating choices made by those in power as the inevitable product of rational and efficient responses to legitimate bureaucratic practices and to market forces (pp. 136-137).

The Hay Guide Chart-Profile Method of Job Evaluation is one example of an institutional practice that sustains the status quo while masking managerial control of the premises. It was developed initially to evaluate professional, managerial, and executive work. It was justified by Hay in the personnel journals as a system that would "fight for better salaries for corporate executives" (Hay, 1958, p. 63). It accomplishes this objective by treating location in the formal bureaucratic organizational hierarchy as the underlying standard of job complexity against which all other work is assessed. As a result, all nonmanagerial, nonprofessional work is treated as less complex, less responsible, and less onerous. Yet the Hay system is sold as a universal system of evaluation with the capability of evaluating all job content. Thus the Hay evaluation system protects the interests of those in positions of organizational power precisely because it gives the appearance of universality, neutrality, and objectivity.

But the findings that emerged from this assessment of the historical roots and contemporary consequences of the Hay system go beyond an analysis of organizational inertia and simple in-group/out-group interest group politics in two respects. First, job evaluation systems, such as the Hay system, are typically brought into an organization by management to rationalize a wage structure that has, for some reason, become misaligned (Treiman, 1979). For instance, in one metropolitan Toronto hospital I examined as part of my role as an expert witness in one Ontario

Pay Equity Tribunal proceeding, I found that hospital management had chosen an evaluation system and implemented it in such a way as to successfully reestablish historical wage relationships between managerial and allied health professional jobs that had been distorted by market forces. Specifically, the shortage of registered nurses, physiotherapists, respiratory therapists, and others drove up their salaries relative to health administrators. One major objective of the job evaluation exercise was to raise the wages of administrators relative to the health professionals.

Thus the introduction of off-the-shelf systems of job evaluation like the Hay system does not necessarily represent organizational inertia even as it structures wage relationships on the basis of outdated cultural values and economic assumptions. Instead, by undertaking a job evaluation exercise, organizational leadership appears to be instituting a new set of organizational practices, although, in fact, they are introducing a set of economic and cultural relationships that have their roots in the post-World War II cultural context and wage structure.

Second, and perhaps more important, organizational practices and structural arrangements are gendered. Even though the Hay Guide Chart-Profile Method does not refer to male jobs or female jobs or to male employees and female employees, its structure and subfactor definitions and the actual evaluation of jobs that results from its application cannot be fully understood without reference to its roots in the post-World War II reinstitutionalization of the gender division of labor. It is a powerful tool maintaining not only managerial power but white male power.

As Joan Acker (1989, 1990) has noted, the construction of a job implies a gender division of labor and a particular relationship between home life and work life. Definitions of job complexity build these invisible assumptions into the formal evaluation of jobs. And, Acker correctly concludes, the power of these systems derives in no small measure from their appearance of gender neutrality.

It is a problem, then, when sociological explanations of gender-based labor market discrimination ignore the significance of gender relations and gender ideologies as determinants of labor market outcomes. In reaching this conclusion, I find myself in agreement with William Bielby (1991), who, in assessing his research, concludes "that gender ideologies are a strong, semiautonomous force shaping segregation and other manifestations of socioeconomic inequality" (p. 109). Even as women enter managerial work, they enter a job designed for privileged white men whose wives perform unpaid work in the home. And despite all of the attention that is paid to women who enter managerial work, the overwhelming majority of women engaged in paid employment continue to work in nonmanagerial jobs.

As Cockburn (1991) recognizes in her study of four British work sites in which male leadership actively sought to integrate women into their organizations, "there is active resistance by men. They generate *institutional* impediments to stall women's advance in organizations" (p. 215, emphasis in original). Systems of job evaluation that structure compensation practices are a critical institutional impediment to women's labor market equality. Although it is no longer acceptable to speak of women as working for pin money, it is still acceptable to use systems of job evaluation that build such assumptions into their conception of job complexity. Future research on labor markets needs to recognize cultural and ideological sources of discrimination along with a concern with economic forces and power relations. To do so, it is necessary to expose both the historical roots and the gendered character of seemingly innocuous organizational practices.

Notes

1. Sources of gender bias are summarized by Treiman (1979), Treiman and Hartmann (1981), Remick (1984a, 1984b), Steinberg and Haignere (1987), Pay Equity Commission (1989), and Steinberg (1990).

2. A third characteristic of the original Hay job evaluation system—namely, the process by which jobs are evaluated—has remained essentially intact in current evaluation exercises. Detailed description of these features and its continuity is beyond the scope of this chapter. Note merely that the Hay system was developed as a factor comparison system. It was designed to locate the complexity of one job along a dimension of job content relative to another job based on (a) images of content drawn from the personal knowledge of the evaluator and (b) broad job descriptions that have the effect of grounding factor-level definitions in organizational context. This approach makes it quite easy to incorporate gender stereotypes in the evaluation process. Today, the system continues to rely on "the rigorous use of pooled judgment" and the slotting of jobs relative to each other on the basis of broad and ambiguous definitions of job content. Two procedures that check specific evaluation—the use of a "profile" and "sore thumbing"—reintroduce sex stereotypes, knowledge about wages, and beliefs about the appropriate location of a job in the overall organizational hierarchy into the job evaluation process. Discussion of the process of evaluating jobs using the Hay system by Treiman (1979, pp. 26-27), Acker (1989, pp. 61-68) and Burton (1987, chap. 2) and Bellak's (1982) discussion of the system in general (p. 4) make clear the continuity in this area (for a complete discussion of these issues, see Steinberg, 1991).

3. These tables include two additional contemporary Guide Charts, as the definitions provided in the Bellak (1982) article are incomplete because of the proprietary character of the system. These two additional systems, used in the state of Idaho and the city of Philadelphia, indicate the similarity of systems used in different geographical areas and in different employment contexts.

4. In the system reported by Treiman (1979) and in Philadelphia, an eighth level measuring Professional Mastery was added.

5. Ironically, Hay consultants have introduced additional levels at the bottom of several subfactors in several pay equity studies they conducted in the past decade. Certain basic historically male jobs, such as laborer and custodian, are graded below Level A on technical skill, for example. The effect is to improve the relative positions of historically female nonmanagerial jobs to historically male nonmanagerial jobs while protecting the distance between managerial and nonmanagerial jobs in general.

6. Demonstrating the gendered character of managerial work is beyond the scope of this chapter. However, although women have made impressive gains in entering managerial work between 1980 and 1990 (Jacobs, 1992), I have argued elsewhere that managerial work is male work for four reasons (Steinberg, 1991). First, until 1980, managerial work was overwhelmingly male-dominated. It certainly was male-dominated at the time of the development of the Hay system. Second, managerial work is culturally associated with both men and women and with stereotypes of masculinity. Third, as Acker (1989) has developed, gender neutrality of hierarchy is itself a power resource enabling the continuation of male dominance in work organizations. Fourth, women have moved into managerial positions that are consistent with gendered assumptions about the appropriate division of labor, such as relatively lower paying positions in hospital and public sector administration.

7. These ratings are not unique to Minnesota. In South Dakota, staff nurse, charge nurse, registered nurse supervisor, and director of nursing all scored at Level D on FTA. In Philadelphia, for which only points are available, nursing supervisor-ambulatory care appears to have scored at Level D for FTA. Even in a pay equity study in Oregon, only registered nurse assistant director and director of nursing scored at Level E on FTA. By contrast, staff registered nurse, charge nurse, assistant nurse manager, nurse manager A, and nurse manager B all ranked at Level D.

8. Although the correlations between the Working Conditions subfactors and the other three Hay system subfactors are small and negative, shifting the distribution of weights in the direction of working conditions would only improve the relative position of male operational jobs relative to male managerial jobs (for a full examination of the gender bias in weights in the Hay system, see Steinberg, 1991).

References

Acker, J. (1987). Sex bias in job evaluation: A comparable worth issue. In C. Bose & G. Spitze (Eds.), *Ingredients for women's employment policy* (pp. 183-196). Albany: State University of New York Press.

Acker, J. (1989). *Doing comparable worth.* Philadelphia: Temple University Press.

Acker, J. (1990). Hierarchies, jobs, bodies: A theory of gendered organizations. *Gender & Society, 4,* 139-158.

Baron, J. (1991). Organizational evidence of ascription in labor markets. In R. R. Cornwall & P. V. Wunnava (Eds.), *New approaches to economic and social analyses of discrimination* (pp. 113-143). New York: Praeger.

Baron, J., Dobbin, F., & Jennings, P. D. (1986). War and peace: The evolution of modern personnel administration in U.S. industry. *American Journal of Sociology, 92,* 350-383.

Baron, J., Jennings, P. D., & Dobbin, F. (1988). Mission control? The development of personnel systems in U.S. industry. *American Sociological Review, 53,* 497-514.

Beatty, R., & Beatty, J. (1984). Some problems in contemporary job evaluation. In H. Remick, (Ed.), *Comparable worth and wage discrimination* (pp. 59-78). Philadelphia: Temple University Press.

Beechey, V. (1988). Rethinking the definition of work. In J. Jenson, E. Hagen, & C. Reddy (Eds.), *Feminization of the labour force* (pp. 45-62). Cambridge: Polity.

Beechey, V., & Perkins, T. (1987). *A matter of hours: Women, part-time work and the labour market.* Minneapolis: University of Minnesota Press.

Bellak, A. (1982). The Hay Guide Chart-Profile Method of Job Evaluation. In M. Rock (Ed.), *Handbook of wage and salary administration* (2nd ed., reprint). New York: McGraw-Hill.

Bellak, A. (1984). Comparable worth: A practitioner's view. In U.S. Commission on Civil Rights (Ed.), *Comparable worth: Issue for the 80's* (Vol. 1, pp. 75-82). Washington, DC: U.S. Government Printing Office.

Benner, P. (1984). *From novice to expert: Excellence and power in clinical nursing practice.* Menlo Park, CA: Addison-Wesley.

Bielby, W. (1991). The structure and process of sex segregation. In R. R. Cornwall & P. V. Wunnava (Eds.), *New approaches to economic and social analyses of discrimination* (pp. 97-112). New York: Praeger.

Bielby, W., & Baron, J. (1987). Undoing discrimination: Job integration and comparable worth. In C. Bose & G. Spitze (Eds.), *Ingredients for women's employment policy* (pp. 211-229). Albany: State University of New York Press.

Burton, C. (1987). *Women's worth: Pay equity and job evaluation in Australia.* Canberra: Australian Government Publishing Service.

Cockburn, C. (1983). *Brothers.* London: Pluto Press.

Cockburn, C. (1991). *In the way of women: Men's resistance to sex equality in organizations.* Ithaca, NY: ILR Press.

College of Nurses of Ontario. (1989). *Standards of nursing practice for registered nurses and registered nursing assistants.* Toronto: Author.

Game, A., & Pringle, R. (1983). *Gender at work.* Sydney, Australia: Allen & Unwin.

Growe, S. J. (1991). *Who cares: The crisis in Canadian nursing.* Toronto: McLelland & Stewart.

Haignere, L., & Steinberg, R. (1985). *Review of Massachusetts statewide classification and compensation system for achieving comparable worth.* Albany, NY: Center for Women in Government.

Hay, E. (1958). Setting salary standard for executive jobs. *Personnel, 36*(1), 63-72.

Hay, E., & Purves, D. (1951). The profile method of high-level job evaluation. *Personnel, 28*(2), 162-170.

Hay, E., & Purves, D. (1953). The analysis and description of high-level jobs. *Personnel, 29*(4), 344-354.

Hubbard and Revo-Cohen, Inc. (1989). *Draft final report to the city of Philadelphia Mayor's Commission for Women*. Philadelphia: Office of the Mayor.

Jacobs, J. A. (1992). Women's entry into management: Trends in earnings, authority, and values among salaried managers. *Administrative Science Quarterly, 37,* 282-301.

Kessler-Harris, A. (1990). *A woman's wage: Historical meanings and social consequences.* Lexington: University of Kentucky Press.

Kim, M. (1989). Gender bias in compensation structures: A case study of its historical basis. *Journal of Social Issues, 45*(4), 39-50.

Melosh, B. (1982). *The physician's hand.* Philadelphia: Temple University Press.

Patton, J. A., & Littlefield, C. L. (1957). *Job evaluation: Text and cases.* Homewood, IL: Irwin.

Pay Equity Commission. (1989). *How to do pay equity comparisons* (Pay Equity Implementation Series, No. 9). Toronto: Author.

Remick, H. (1979). Strategies for creating sound, bias free job evaluation plans. In Industrial Relations Counselors (Ed.), *Job evaluation and EEO: The emerging issues* (pp. 85-112). New York: Industrial Relations Counselors, Inc.

Remick, H. (1981). The comparable worth controversy. *Public Personnel Management, 10,* 371-383.

Remick, H. (1984a). Dilemmas of implementation: The case of nursing. In H. Remick (Ed.), *Comparable worth and wage discrimination* (pp. 90-98). Philadelphia: Temple University Press.

Remick, H. (1984b). Major issues in *a priori* applications. In H. Remick (Ed.), *Comparable worth and wage discrimination* (pp. 99-117). Philadelphia: Temple University Press.

Reverby, S. (1987). *Ordered to care: The dilemma of American nursing, 1850-1945.* Cambridge: Cambridge University Press.

Riegel, J. W. (1937). *Wage determination.* Ann Arbor, MI: Bureau of Industrial Relations.

Schatz, R. (1983). *The electrical workers: A history of labor at General Electric and Westinghouse, 1923-1960.* Urbana: University of Illinois Press.

Schwab, D. (1985). Job evaluation research and research needs. In H. Hartmann (Ed.), *Comparable worth: New directions for research* (pp. 37-52). Washington, DC: National Academy Press.

Scott, J. (1986). Gender: A useful category of historical analysis. *American Historical Review, 91*(5), 1053-75.

Shils, E. (1972). Developing a perspective on job measurement. In M. Rock (Ed.), *Handbook of wage and salary administration* (pp. 3-18). New York: McGraw-Hill.

Steinberg, R. (1990). The social construction of skill: Gender, power and comparable worth. *Work and Occupations, 17*(4), 449-482.

Steinberg, R. (1991). *Report concerning the proposed testimony of Dr. Ronnie Steinberg concerning the appropriateness of the Hay Guide Chart-Profile Method for use at St. Michael's Hospital.* Unpublished manuscript, Department of Sociology, Temple University, Philadelphia.

Steinberg, R., & Haignere, L. (1987). Equitable compensation: Methodological criteria for comparable worth. In C. Bose & G. Spitze (Eds.), *Ingredients for women's employment policy* (pp. 157-182). Albany: State University of New York Press.

Stinchcombe, A. (1965). Social structure and organizations. In J. G. March (Ed.), *Handbook of organizations* (pp. 142-193). Chicago: Rand McNally.

Taylor, S. (1989). The case for comparable worth. *Journal of Social Issues, 45*(4), 23-37.

Treiman, D. (1979). *Job evaluation: An analytic review.* Washington, DC: National Research Council, National Academy of Sciences.

Treiman, D., & Hartmann, H. (1981). *Women, work and wages: Equal pay for jobs of equal value.* Washington, DC: National Academy Press.

Werwie, D. (1987). *Sex and pay in the federal government: Using job evaluation systems to implement comparable worth.* New York: Greenwood.

4

Further Evidence on Compensating Differentials and the Gender Gap in Wages

JERRY A. JACOBS
RONNIE J. STEINBERG

One explanation for the sex gap in wages is that women choose to work in jobs that are pleasant, safe, and comfortable. If men are paid a premium for working in dirty, noisy, or dangerous jobs, then part of the sex gap in wages may reflect men's rewards for performing more hazardous, onerous, or distasteful work. In other words, women garner a higher proportion of their overall compensation package in amenities, including such intangibles as pleasant working conditions, whereas men take home larger paychecks.

Extra pay for working in undesirable settings or performing unpleasant tasks is referred to by economists as a compensating differential. This means that the differential in pay between two jobs reflects an offsetting difference in the nonmonetary aspects of employment. One receives higher pay if the job is less desirable—other things, such as educational requirements, being equal. This idea is quite central to labor economics (Rosen, 1986) and dates back at least as far as Adam Smith (1776/1976).

Yet, despite the prominence accorded to the compensating differentials thesis in economic theory, there is actually little empirical support for it. In an earlier article (Jacobs & Steinberg, 1990), we tested this notion with detailed data on a wide range of working conditions. Our results indicated that little of the sex gap in earnings is due to undesirable working conditions. There are several reasons for this finding. First, undesirable working conditions are not the exclusive preserve of blue-collar, male-dominated jobs. Jobs in which women predominate also are characterized by a number of undesirable working conditions. Second, undesirable working conditions are not consistently associated with higher wages. Wages in positions with undesirable working conditions are often lower than wages in more attractive jobs.

And third, specific undesirable working conditions, such as strenuous physical activity, were found to actually lower the wages of a job, net of its other characteristics. Even when compensating differentials were observed, they were small in magnitude compared with other factors influencing pay. We also summarized the results of eight other comparable worth studies that found little support for the idea that sex differences in working conditions explain the wage gap between male-dominated and female-dominated jobs.

In this study, we further explore this question by considering other models of the relationship between working conditions and wages under circumstances in which the undesirable working conditions are extreme or where there are clusters of undesirable job attributes. Perhaps it is not undesirable working conditions per se that have a positive effect on wages, but rather undesirable working conditions that are of central significance to the character of the job. By conducting a further exploration of the compensating differentials perspective, we provide a more rigorous test of this theory and its role, if any, in explaining the sex gap in earnings.

Most studies consider each working condition separately. The functional form of the regression equations estimated in such studies assumes that each working condition has a separate, additive effect on earnings. Moreover, studies have generally assumed the relationships are linear (with respect to the log of earnings). Thus, the first increment of unpleasantness has an equal effect to the last increment's impact.

Yet it is probably more realistic to assume that it is only extreme conditions that require extra rewards. Take the case of shift differentials, which are common in nursing compensation practices. The frequent need for employees to stay an hour late for shift changes may not be sufficient to justify extra pay, but regularly requiring employees to work the night shift may warrant a shift differential. Thus, nurses are paid 10% to 15% more if they work at night or on the weekends, compared to working during the day (personal communication, Noelle Andrews, 1993). Similarly, driving a truck may involve some risk of injury or accident, but it is a risk many take for granted, as it is similar to the risk people take driving their car to the grocery store. However, cleaning windows on skyscrapers involves risks that fewer people are willing to take, and thus may produce a wage premium. Or, to provide a final example, nurses' exposure to needle sticks that may result in hepatitis or AIDS infection may be perceived as so risky that extra pay is necessary as an incentive to produce a sufficient supply of nurses (Clever & Omenn, 1988; Zoloth & Stellman, 1987). We examine this first issue—whether workers exposed to extremely undesirable working conditions receive higher wages—by an analysis of the potential curvilinearity in the relationship between wages and working conditions.

The second issue we address is whether clusters of undesirable job attributes combine to produce higher wages. As our analysis will show, job attributes often come in clusters. Lumberjacks, for example, work outside, often in cold conditions, and are faced with a risk of injury from falling limbs. The combination of these job characteristics may warrant a wage premium, whereas any one of these factors might not. We assess for the first time whether combinations of undesirable working conditions are associated with a wage premium.

The next section briefly summarizes a sociological approach to employment systems. Because we do not abide by the compensating differentials analysis of labor markets, we offer an alternative sociological perspective. In this section, we also highlight differences between sociological and economic perspectives. We then review the evidence relating to the compensating differentials thesis. Next, we explore the issue of gender differences in work-related preferences. Finally, we turn to data analysis from *The New York State Comparable Pay Study* (Steinberg, Haignere, Possin, Chertos, & Treiman, 1985).

A Sociological Approach to Work

Sociologists approach the study of work somewhat differently than do economists. Although sociologists often use the same data sets as economists and often discuss economic approaches in great detail (e.g., England, 1992), sociologists continue to differ from economists in their emphasis on context, politics, and culture.

Whereas economic theory in the abstract focuses on the intersection between supply and demand, in practice labor market economics has to a remarkable extent become the analysis of labor supply. The theory of labor economics holds that the labor market is efficient and consequently that differences in earnings among workers are due to differences in skills and preferences. In other words, differences in earnings are a function of choices individuals make prior to entering the labor market. Most labor economists hold to this position, even in the face of contrary data (Madden, 1984). Demand-side factors are occasionally invoked— for example, to explain the growth in earnings inequality in recent years (e.g., Goldin & Margo, 1992). But the demand side of the labor market is rarely if ever used as an explanation for earning differences between groups. In other words, most labor economists believe that discrimination, in the sense of firms paying one group less than another equally productive group, does not exist or, if it does, it will not exist for long.

Sociologists, particularly those studying gender, race, ethnic, and other inequalities, assume that many actors in the economy discriminate among groups to various degrees and that some fraction of group differences may be accounted for by labor market discrimination. Several have examined directly how sex segregation and unequal rewards between men and women grow directly out of production strategies and employer decision making (Acker, 1989; Baron & Newman, 1989; Bielby & Baron, 1987; Cockburn, 1991; Cohn, 1985; Milkman, 1987; Reskin, 1988; Smith, 1984; Tomaskovic-Devey, 1993). Sociologists have proposed many explanations for how discrimination can persist despite market pressures that in theory should erode such distinctions. These explanations include the interdependence of workers, the prevalence of long-term employment relationships, skills that are often specific to particular firms and groups of workers, and the insularity of many firms and many workers from market pressures, among others (Jacobs, 1989). Recent studies have identified the role of managerial power (Cohn, 1985; Milkman, 1987), male power (Acker, 1989; Cockburn, 1991; Reskin, 1988), institutional inertia (Baron, Jennings, & Dobbin, 1988; Baron & Newman, 1988), and gendered institutions (Burton, 1991; Steinberg, 1991) in maintaining segregation and unequal rewards. For example, Bielby and Baron (1987) conclude that statistical discrimination does operate in the labor market, but that it is neither as rational nor as efficient as economists believe. They found that for some jobs, physical demands were listed as a rationale for hiring men, yet detailed job analyses revealed that there were few actual demands for the use of physical strength. These factors reduce the extent to which employers can easily substitute low-wage workers for otherwise equivalent high-wage workers, a substitution that is at the root of the economic model of efficient labor markets. But discrimination is only one aspect of sociologists' focus on the demand side of the labor market.

Sociologists who study employment systems consider both the decisions of individuals and the context in which work is conducted (for programmatic statements, see Baron & Bielby, 1980; Block, 1990; Kalleberg & Berg, 1987; Kalleberg & Sorensen, 1979). The economics of labor markets is based on an analogy to an auction, where an item is sold to the highest bidder. Yet the social context of work is usually more complex than one would find in a spot-market situation, which is characterized by a once and for all transaction principally based on price and not quality. Relations at work are typically enduring quality matters, and motivation must be elicited. Thus employment systems emerge, and rules are developed for selecting, training, evaluating, motivating, promoting, and jettisoning workers. A set of procedures that "work" become formal policies, and these serve as precedents for subsequent conflicts over fairness and legitimacy. These systems develop their own logics and histories, some recorded, others simply understood.

Power relations also enter into the construction and maintenance of these employment systems. Once in place, group interests become attached to these systems and they tend to remain in place until such time as either economic constraints make their continuation infeasible or group pressure undermines the legitimacy of such systems and renders them too costly—in terms of employee morale—to continue. For example, job evaluation systems began to be used widely during and after World War II (Baron et al., 1988). They remained intact until the late 1970s and early 1980s, when the demand for equal pay for work of comparable worth gained political visibility. Advocates of reform linked the source of wage differentials between historically male and historically female jobs to job evaluation procedures; even without referring to men or women, these procedures incorporated a cultural bias about the value of work that ensured significant wage advantages to jobs historically occupied by men (Remick, 1979; Treiman, 1979). Yet, as Acker's (1989) in-depth account of the Oregon Pay Equity initiative reveals, the gender bias in compensation practices largely remained intact, resulting in the maintenance of wage differentials between historically male and historically female jobs. Despite the efforts of feminist reformers, the old system and the inequality it produced were relegitimated, and some incumbents of the lowest-paid female jobs received modest pay adjustments. Thus, as gender bias is uncovered, wage hierarchies are reproduced and relegitimated. Proponents have proved powerful enough to put pay equity on the political map, but not powerful enough to achieve the goals of this reform (Steinberg, 1991).

Economists have recently attempted to tap some of this complex social reality with the concept of implicit contracts, but (a) this has principally been applied only to a limited range of work-related issues, such as the length of employment and the trajectory of wages over the life course (Rosen, 1985); and (b) we are not persuaded that these economic models provide a persuasive account of the origins or dynamics of workplace practices. These extensions of economic theory continue to rely on the individualist social-psychological assumptions underlying the rest of economic theory.

Sociologists believe that structural and cultural context matters in part because an individual's productivity inheres in the job setting as much as in the person. Many historically specific social factors structure the work relationship, including geographic location, organization, occupation, and even individual job attributes.

As the examples cited above indicate, sociologists have devoted a great deal of attention to organizational factors that influence career dynamics and the distribution of rewards (for example, Baron, 1984; Baron & Cook, 1992). Labor contracts and career experiences in large firms with highly differentiated internal employment systems operate very differently from those found in small firms. Recruitment patterns, screening procedures, earnings, benefits, the degree of formalization, and many other key aspects of work differ dramatically across employment settings. Economists, of course, have noticed differences in earnings across firms and industries (Krueger & Summers, 1987). These interindustry differences cannot be dismissed as simply due to the self-selection of more productive workers into higher-paying sectors. Yet this finding has not resulted in a shift in the basic premises of economic theory. Despite contrary empirical evidence, economists tend to downplay the role of market structure in determining outcomes for workers.

Occupations represent another facet of the work situation that has a significant bearing on work outcomes. Occupations often have their own internal stratification systems, and some occupations are more closed than others. As both Milkman (1987) and Strober (1984) have demonstrated, employers decide the sex type of an occupation based on labor costs and then use stereotypes about gender norms to legitimate their practices and obscure their underlying motives. Sociologists often study gender inequality within particular occupations. Indeed, this volume includes five such chapters. Sociologists tend to pay much more attention to particular occupations than do economists (but see Hochner, Granrose, Goode, Simon, & Appelbaum, 1988, for a notable exception).

Even occupations represent overly broad aggregations, as far as many sociologists are concerned. This attention to the basic building block of the employment system—the individual job— stems in large part from Bielby and Baron's striking finding (1984) that jobs are far more segregated by sex than are occupations or industries. Although there is a great deal of interest in the job as the unit of analysis, research has been slowed by the paucity of available data, especially at the level of the firm. Our study (along with the Tomaskovic-Devey chapter in this volume) is one of the few academic reports analyzing gender inequality conducted at the job level.

Sociologists tend to see employment relations as reflecting power relations, as well as pure market forces. Wages are not simply set by workers' accepting what is offered; they are contested both individually and collectively. The most obvious form involves collective bargaining between unions and management, which influences not only the wages of a company's workers but also wages in firms seeking to avoid unionization. Professional associations have often played the same role. Perhaps less recognized is the fact that administered wage systems also are replete with political influence. Large firms in the United States and elsewhere have developed compensation policies, such as the one discussed above for the state of Oregon, that are designed to promote internal equity as well as external competitiveness. These systems are subject to political influence in many ways: the selection of factors to be used, the weights assigned to the factors, and the application of the system to many nonbenchmark jobs. All of these involve political decisions that affect how people are paid (see Steinberg, this volume). And initiatives to modify such systems have often been stymied by many obstacles, technical and political.

A final area of difference between sociologists and economists is in the significance accorded to and the treatment of culture. Economists take preferences as given. Sociologists view preferences as partly what individuals bring to social situations and partly how individuals adapt to preexisting expectations. Economists take preferences as fixed, whereas sociologists recognize that preferences often change in response to experiences in the workplace, the influence of friends and family, and changing values and mores in society (Jacobs, 1989; Kohn & Schooler, 1983).

Sociologists maintain that culture often lags behind other types of social change and can constrain contemporary actors in ways not acknowledged by economists. Thus preferences and the choices individuals make based on preferences do not emerge in a vacuum. They are, in no small part, the product of the prevailing distribution of opportunities in the labor market and of individuals' realistic perceptions of their options.

Gender interacts with context, politics, and culture in many ways. Women are disadvantaged in their structural position (that is, access to good jobs), in their political leverage to argue for higher pay, and in the cultural resources needed to make claims for higher rewards. Acker's study (1989) documents these disadvantages in remarkable detail. We believe these categories—context, politics, and culture—capture much of the voluminous sociological literature on gender inequality in the workplace, a claim that we can only put forth here, as we do not have space sufficient to thoroughly document these claims in this chapter.

The sociological model of the labor market we have just outlined posits that compensating differentials are the exception and not the rule. Jobs with undesirable working conditions are unlikely to be concentrated in the most favorable organizational and occupational contexts, are unlikely to be located in politically powerful positions, and are unlikely to have access to the cultural resources needed to maximize their earnings. If a wage premium were found to be related to undesirable features of a job, according to the sociological perspective on the labor market, it would most likely be due to the unique structural, political, and cultural resources of particular groups of workers.

Studies of Compensating Differentials

The notion of compensating differentials has been applied to diverse workplace amenities and disadvantages, including the risk of injury and death (Hwang, Reed, & Hubbard, 1992; Olson, 1981), the risk of losing one's job (Hamermesh & Wolfe, 1990), retirement benefits (Allen, Clark, & Sumner, 1986), and shift work (Kostiuk, 1990). Other studies include a range of job attributes in a single analysis (Barry, 1987; Duncan & Holmlund, 1983; Reed & Holleman, 1988; Filer, 1985, 1989). The results of these investigations often contradict the compensating differentials logic: Jobs with undesirable attributes frequently pay less than those with more attractive features (Brown, 1980; Rosen, 1986; Smith, 1979).

Several recent studies affirm the compensating differentials thesis (Duncan & Holmlund, 1983; Hwang et al., 1992; see Rosen, 1986, for a review and discussion). These studies follow individuals over time to see if changes in pay are offset by changes in working conditions. These studies show that when people change jobs, they typically do not move to less attractive jobs without some supplemental compensation. In other words, some workers move to more attractive jobs at a cut in pay, whereas others move to more remunerative but otherwise less attractive jobs. Yet this reseach does not show that the pay disparities between jobs are equalized by the presence or absence of amenities. Heroic assumptions regarding the efficiency of markets are necessary to reach such a conclusion, and it is such assumptions that are themselves at issue.[1]

Compensating Differentials and Workers' Preferences

How do workers' preferences relate to the issue of compensating differentials? From an economic standpoint, the existence of a compensating differential requires substantial agreement on the undesirability of a given job attribute. Moreover, that attribute must be important enough to lead some people to avoid taking the job as a result of it. If there were substantial heterogeneity of preferences with respect to a particular set of job attributes, then that aspect of a job would be unlikely to produce a wage premium. Consider a hypothetical example. Let's say some people prefer office jobs whereas others prefer to work outdoors. If there were an adequate supply of both types of workers, then neither office jobs nor outdoor work would require an extra wage premium to entice workers (above and beyond whatever training might be needed). Thus, in order to produce a compensating differential, there must be wide agreement that a given job attribute is undesirable, and it must be sufficiently salient that people would be discouraged from taking a job because of it. Examples of job attributes considered candidates for supplemental pay include night work, dirty work, risky work, high-stress jobs, and physically fatiguing labor. Some individuals may be more inclined than others to accept such working conditions. Weston (1990), for example, found that male construction workers often work without their safety gear as a sign of courage and toughness, constructing masculinity in the act of risk taking. However, these undesirable working conditions are theorized to require extra wages only if they make it difficult to attract sufficient numbers of qualified individuals to fill these jobs.

How do these considerations relate to gender differences in preferences? If women and men preferred different types of jobs, then neither men nor women would be expected to receive a premium for doing the type of work they prefer. For example, if women prefer to sew and men prefer to chop wood, then neither sewing nor wood cutting would pay extra unless there were excessive demand for one type of activity over the other. Because unemployment rates for men and women are quite similar, we don't believe that men are paid more because the types of work they prefer are in more demand than women's work.

There would be a sex-linked wage premium, however, if neither men nor women liked to chop wood, and if only men were willing to do so. In this case, both groups seek to avoid a given activity, but one group is more willing to engage in it in exchange for extra wages. Another way of making this point is that men and women find the same types of work distasteful, but that men are more willing to put up with distasteful work in exchange for higher wages. In essence, this logic assumes that men place a greater emphasis on making money, and women place a greater emphasis on working in pleasant conditions.

This assumption, however, does not receive significant empirical support. Survey data suggest that working women rank income as high as men do on a list of factors for choosing a job (as reviewed in Jacobs & Steinberg, 1990; see also Jacobs, 1992). This type of analysis has been applied to explaining the relatively low pay of workers in the nonprofit sector, which is predominantly staffed by women (see Steinberg & Jacobs, 1994). It has been suggested that nonprofit workers are willing to accept lower wages because they place such a high value on working in a socially beneficial setting. In this case, workers trade off a positive amenity—socially redeeming work—in return for wages. Here again, this explanation falls short for a number of reasons. First, the conclusion is inferred from discounting other explanations, rather than on the basis of direct evidence (see, for example, Preston, 1989). Second, in order to account for the concentration of women in the nonprofit sector, this argument would have to assume that women are less interested in money than men. As we noted above, survey evidence is generally inconsistent with this thesis.

Third, the preferences explanation in general assumes more stability in preferences than actually exists. Data on career aspirations show substantial inconsistency between individuals' preferences and jobs actually pursued—one study found that occupational aspirations poorly predicted occupational behavior 10 years later (Jacobs, 1989). Fourth, this approach ignores the feedback between opportunity and preferences. Preferences are not attributes that spring into individuals' heads at one moment and remain fixed forever. Rather, they are actively shaped and reshaped throughout prelabor market and labor market years by many factors and contingencies, a good many of which emerge out of labor market experience (Gerson, 1985; Schultz, 1990). Those who work in historically female jobs and, by extension, in historically female sectors typically do not "choose" to work for lower wages but are constrained to accept jobs characterized by a wage structure that is gendered and that devalues the feminine (Reskin & Padavic, 1994).

Thus there are good reasons to be skeptical of the compensating differentials logic and its applicability to the gender gap in wages. Let us now turn to empirical data to see if the proposed specifications of the compensating differentials model improve the fit between predictions and results.

Data and Methods

In this chapter, we focus on the determinants of the wage structure of jobs by examining those attributes of a job title that affect its salary grade. In the New York State Civil Service system, the job title is the appropriate unit of analysis. Like most other public sector employers, and many large private sector firms that rely on some form of job evaluation for salary setting, New York State bases its compensation policies exclusively on the job, not the individual. Individual salaries are a strict function of the job title and seniority. Every employee in a given grade level is accorded the same increment, strictly dependent on years of service. There are no merit raises or other elements of discretion in the setting of salaries. Thus the determinants of the compensation of each job title are the determinants of the compensation of its incumbents. Consequently, in this context, there is no confounding of the attributes of individuals and the rewards allocated to the position.

To obtain information on job content, Steinberg et al. (1985) sampled all employees in each job title with under 20 incumbents; in titles with more than 20 incumbents, at least 20 incumbents were sampled. For female-dominated and disproportionately minority job titles, up to 150 incumbents were sampled. The sampling procedure and rationale is described in detail in Steinberg et al. (1985). In all, *The New York State Comparable Pay Study* surveyed 25,852 incumbents in New York State Civil Service jobs to rate the characteristics of 2,582 job titles.

Employees rated the attributes of their own jobs. Pretest results indicate that employee responses correlate highly with those of supervisors (Steinberg et al., 1985). Incumbent responses for each job title were averaged. (For some variables, the percentage responding in a particular way was used.) This averaging process produces highly reliable measures for each job title. For this analysis, we limited our job sample to 1,605 job titles with four or more incumbents in order to have a stable measure of percentage female.

Eighty content characteristics were collected for each job title. The items were designed deliberately to capture the widest possible range of the work actually done in the New York State system. Every effort was made to measure as completely as possible the range of content of both female-dominated and male-dominated positions, correcting for gender bias in the array of job-content information collected. The specific measures were drawn from (and went beyond) 20 prior job-content surveys used primarily by compensation consulting firms. The survey was refined in a pretest of 1,862 respondents. (A more detailed discussion of the survey instrument, rationale for items, and pilot test is available in Steinberg et al., 1985, Chapters 3 and 4.)

Fourteen scales were constructed to tap the main dimensions of job characteristics and to avoid problems of multicolinearity. The 14 scales were derived through a factor analysis of the 80 job characteristic measures. The reliability measures of the factors are unusually and uniformly high (Steinberg et al., 1985, Chapter 7). Working conditions was one of the factors. As we are interested in a more detailed examination of working conditions, we disaggregate this factor for the present analysis. In addition, we include 10 additional job-content variables that were not included in the 14 factors. Table 4.1 lists the variables used in the analysis.

Our study predicts the salary grade of job titles from the attributes of these jobs in a multiple regression framework. The dependent variable in the analysis is the salary grade of the job title. As noted above, in the New York State Civil Service, wages are strictly a function of salary grade and seniority.

We included in our analysis controls for management and supervisory responsibility, education and experience requirements, and other indicators of job skills. Specific variables include: management/supervision,

Table 4.1 List of Variables Selected From the New York State Comparable Pay Study

---

A. Salary, Sex, and Race Composition

---

1. MSG or Mean Salary Grade, which is the dependent variable for this analysis

2. PFEM or Percentage Female, which allows a direct test of the effect of sex composition of a job on its salary grade

3. PM or Percentage Minority, which allows for a direct test for potential wage discrimination based on minority incumbency

---

B. Working Conditions Measures

---

1. An Unfavorable Working Conditions Index, based on six questions, including:

    2. Hot or cold

    3. Cleaning others' dirt

    4. Fumes

    5. Loud noise

    6. Strenuous physical activity

    7. Risk of injury

8. Contact with Difficult Clients: a composite index based on four questions: the seriousness of client problems; dealing with emotionally troubled clients; the number of patients or inmates served; and handling sick or injured clients

9. Communication with the Public: a composite index based on four questions: answering questions or complaints from the public; dealing with upset clients or public; and dealing with nonagency personnel

10. Stress: a composite index based on six questions: feeling rushed; conflicting demands; telling people what they don't want to hear; feeling pressure to meet deadlines; the need to learn skills just to keep up; and having to make quick decisions

11. Job Autonomy: a composite index based on three questions: freedom to decide how to complete the assigned tasks; the order of tasks; and the speed of work

12. Working with sick patients

13. Repetition (doing the same thing over and over)

14. Unexpected problems

15. Close supervision (being told what to do)

(Continued)

Table 4.1 (Continued)

C. Job Content and Educational Control Variables

---

1. Management/supervision: a composite index based on 11 questions: level of supervision; numbers supervised; prevention of wasting time; hiring and firing responsibility; scope of planning responsibility; estimation of training needs; substitute for boss in supervision; settling job disputes; finding replacements for no-shows; setting operating practices; keeping employees informed of work policies

2. Education required for position

3. Data entry requirements: a composite index of three questions: entering data; editing data; verifying data

4. Group facilitation: a composite index of three questions: planning meetings/workshops; leading meetings/workshops; giving speeches

5. Computer programming: a composite index of four questions: writing original programs; doing systems programming; using packaged programs; doing systems design

6. Fiscal responsibility: a composite index of three questions: propose money for agency/facility; spend money within budget; propose budget for unit

7. Consequence of error: a composite index of two questions: mistake hurt good name of agency; mistake hurt good name of unit

8. Time effort: a composite index of two questions: working overtime without compensation; working weekends without compensation

9. Dealing with information

10. Writing complexity

11. Experience requirements for position

12. Physical coordination

13. Filing responsibility

14. Responsibility for equipment

---

data entry requirements, group facilitation, computer programming, fiscal responsibility, consequence of error, time effort, physical coordination, responsibility for equipment, dealing with information, writing complexity, and responsibility for filing.

We present descriptive statistics for the Working Conditions Index but employ its six components in the multivariate analysis. These measures encompass the standard questions about hazards and bad physical conditions that have been used in most research on compensating differentials: strenuous physical activity, fumes, risk of injury, working in hot or cold conditions, working near loud noise, and cleaning others' dirt.

Variables (8) through (15) in Table 4.1 tap other undesirable job attributes that have rarely been included in an analysis of compensating differentials. Measures (8) through (11)—contact with difficult clients, job stress, lack of autonomy, and communication with the public—are factors that combine variables. Single-variable measures are used for working with sick patients, repetition, unexpected problems, and close supervision. We consider each measure to capture an aspect of work that could reasonably be regarded as undesirable.

Those who work with difficult clients (such as convicted criminals, troubled youth, individuals with drug or alcohol problems) or those who work with dying patients experience job burnout because of the nature of their work. Nurses, for example, have extremely high turnover rates as a result of the high stress levels associated with this work (Roberts, 1989). Similarly, many jobs involve time pressures, conflicting role demands, and interpersonal communication about undesirable topics. In the Oregon pay equity initiative, the Comparable Worth Task Force added a job factor to its job evaluation system to encompass these job features because of the widely held view among Oregon employees that these job characteristics were undesirable (Acker, 1989). We use a similar rationale for including communication with the public as an undesirable working condition. New York State employees interviewed often complained of the difficulty of dealing with public clients (such as workmen's compensation claimants, unemployed workers, and other distressed citizens seeking government relief and claiming extenuating circumstances) who were often angry and upset (Steinberg et al., 1985).

As noted above, excessive repetition is a feature of work which is often included on lists of undesirable job attributes. Unexpected problems is perhaps the most ambiguous measure on our list, in that one would expect this job attribute to be associated with challenging jobs with diverse responsibilities. Yet New York State employees often complained of this job feature, suggesting that it might be tapping the classic concern of industrial sociologists about the lack of control over one's job (Blauner, 1964). Thus, our approach was to add these measures of undesirable job attributes to the ones conventionally used so as to include any available measure that might be regarded as undesirable by "the marginal employee" in our test of the compensating differentials hypothesis.

The sex and race composition of job titles is an independent variable of particular interest. In several analyses, we contrast female-dominated jobs with white male-dominated jobs. For the purposes of this analysis, white male-dominated titles are defined as those in which 90% of the incumbents are white and male. Steinberg et al. (1985) found that the proportion minority in a job title had a relatively small, yet discernible, negative effect on the salary grade of the title. Therefore, in order to select a set of job titles unlikely to be affected by gender or race composition, 90% white and male was set as the cutoff point. There are 533 New York State job titles that met these criteria. Female-dominated positions are defined as those in which 67.2% of incumbents are women. This figure is 40% above the proportion of women among all New York State employees, which is 48.4 percent (Steinberg et al., 1985). A total of 297 jobs fell into this category.

Although public sector wage-setting practices may not seem the most appropriate economic context in which to test propositions about the workings of the labor market, we maintain that this setting represents a fair test of the compensating differentials thesis. Government agencies, although lacking external competition, nonetheless have scarce resources and attempt to allocate them so as to deliver services cost-effectively, within political and fiscal constraints (Kelman, 1987). Given this motivation, there is every reason to keep compensation as low as is consistent with adequate staffing and motivation. Data indicate that compensation practices in the public sector are sensitive to wage levels of what are called "key job titles" in the local labor market (Bridges & Nelson, 1988; Remick, Ginorio, & Brtiz, 1987). Further, one out of every five employed women and one out of every six employed men work in the public sector (U.S. Department of Labor, 1983, p. 71). The importance of the public sector and the size of this case study (it is a case employing approximately 170,000 individuals) make it a case of considerable interest. Finally, we believe that testing the compensating differentials hypothesis within one large organization has certain advantages over using national survey data, because we are able to remove the confounding effects on wages of organizational variables (Baron & Bielby, 1980; Berheide & Steinberg, 1989).

We coded extreme cases in two ways: those falling into the top 10% of the distribution, and those falling into the top 5% of the distribution, for each working condition measure. In some cases, the variables were not normally distributed and the top code includes more than 10% of the cases. The results we obtained for these two measures were quite similar, although the patterns for the top 10% measures were somewhat more consistent across models. We consequently report results for the extremes of the distribution with data on the top 10% of the cases.

We coded multiple working conditions scores by adding up the number of undesirable working conditions using the top 10% measure just described. We only included the eight measures found to have a statistically significant effect on earnings: hot or cold, cleaning others' dirt, sick patients, loud noise, strenuous work, repetition, risk of injury, and close supervision. Thus, the multiple conditions scores range from 0 to 8.

Results

Distribution of Job Attributes by Sex Type of Job

Table 4.2 reports the percentage of male-dominated and female-dominated jobs that fell in the top 10% of the distribution for each of 14 job characteristics, along with a composite working conditions factor. Male-dominated jobs were more likely to involve extreme cases of undesirable working conditions than were female-dominated jobs. The sex differences in extreme measures were consistent with the sex differences in the means for all of the variables we considered.

If a broad range of working conditions is investigated, many undesirable working conditions will surface in female-dominated jobs, as well. Male-dominated jobs were more likely to involve hot or cold conditions and exposure to fumes or to require physically strenuous work. Incumbents in these positions were more likely to report that their jobs were stressful, that work required communication with the public, and that they encountered unexpected problems. Female-dominated jobs were more likely to involve cleaning other people's dirt and exposure to loud noise. Women's work involved more encounters with difficult clients and sick patients. Workers in female-dominated jobs reported less autonomy, more repetition, and more supervision. Clearly, many of these working conditions apply to some jobs and not others. Janitorial jobs involve cleaning others' dirt, whereas hospital jobs involve contact with sick patients. How many of these conditions are present in the same jobs? Table 4.3 summarizes how male-dominated and female-dominated jobs stack up in terms of multiple working conditions. For each job, we calculated the number of undesirable attributes that fell in the top 10% of the distribution for that variable. Male-dominated jobs averaged 2.46 extreme working conditions, compared with 2.12 for female-dominated jobs. This difference is statistically significant, but it is perhaps not as

Table 4.2 Means and Standard Errors for Working Conditions and Other Job Characteristics, by Sex Type of Job Title

		White Male Jobs (90%+ White Male) (n = 533)	Female Jobs (67.2%+ Female) (n = 297)
Working Conditions Variables		Percent with High Scores[a] (Top 10%)	Percent with High Scores[a] (Top 10%)
F2*	Unfavorable working conditions (Index)	15.76* (1.58)	5.72 (1.35)
MI25	Hot or cold	20.08* (1.74)	0.67 (0.48)
MI26	Fumes	13.32* (1.47)	8.42 (1.61)
MI27	Cleaning others' dirt	8.44* (1.21)	13.13 (1.96)
PI31	Percent loud noise	15.38* (1.56)	21.21 (2.38)
MI32	Strenuous physical activity	13.88* (1.50)	9.09 (1.67)
MI37	Risk of injury	13.88* (1.50)	6.40 (1.42)
F3	Difficult clients	3.38* (7.83)	18.52 (2.26)
F4	Communications with the public	19.89* (1.73)	7.07 (1.49)
F10	Stress	49.34* (2.17)	35.70 (2.78)
F11	Autonomy	16.51* (1.61)	5.05 (1.27)
MI28	Working with sick patients	4.13* (0.86)	21.21 (2.38)
MI33	Repetition	6.94* (1.10)	17.85 (2.23)
MI94	Unexpected problems	13.70 (1.49)	9.43 (1.69)
MI102	Close supervision	9.94 (1.30)	13.47 (1.98)

NOTE: Numbers in parentheses are standard errors. The acronyms used here (F13, MI40, and so on) correspond to those used in *The New York State Comparable Pay Study* (Steinberg et al., 1985).
a. The top 10% of distribution of each variable.
*$p < .05$.

Table 4.3 Distribution of Multiple Working Conditions

Working Conditions Variables	White Male Jobs (90%+ White Male) (n = 533) Percent with High Scores (Top 10%)	Female Jobs (67.2%+ Female) (n = 297) Percent with High Scores (Top 10%)
Number of unfavorable working conditions, top 10%	2.46* (0.04)	2.12 (0.09)
Number of unfavorable working conditions, top 5%	1.98* (0.06)	1.67 (0.08)
Number of extreme working conditions		
0	8.26%	22.90%
1	23.45%	30.64%
2	21.39%	20.88%
3	19.89%	12.12%
4	14.82%	9.43%
5+	12.20%	4.04%

NOTE: Numbers in parentheses are standard errors.
*$p < .05$.

large as some might expect. When the analysis is limited to the top 5% of the distribution of working conditions, the results are generally the same as those presented here.

However, differences do emerge when examining the range of working conditions. Of the 533 male-dominated jobs, only 8.3% had no extreme working conditions, as compared with 22.9% of female-dominated jobs. At the other extreme, almost 15% of male-dominated jobs involve four or more extreme working conditions, and over 12% involve five or more, as compared with 9.4% and 4.0% respectively for female-dominated jobs. Some of this discrepancy may be due to the greater percentage of male jobs that reported the highest levels of job stress.

Effect of Extreme Working Conditions

Regression equations that estimate the impact of extreme working conditions on wages are presented in Table 4.4. The first model repro-

Table 4.4 Regression Analysis: Predicting Mean Salary Grade From Job Requirements, Job Content, Extreme Working Conditions, and Sex Composition

Variable		*Model 1* *b*	*Model 2* *b*	*Model 3* *b*
Intercept		4.77***	−0.34	5.03***
		(0.77)	(0.60)	(0.80)
F1	Management/supervision	4.27***	4.59***	4.46***
		(0.38)	(0.40)	(0.38)
F5	Education required	12.08***	12.60***	12.09***
		(0.43)	(0.44)	(0.44)
F12	Consequences of error	1.88***	2.10***	1.61***
		(0.48)	(0.51)	(0.48)
F13	Time effort	1.51**	0.92	1.58**
		(0.53)	(0.56)	(0.53)
Information		4.78***	4.94***	4.95***
		(0.71)	(0.75)	(0.71)
Writing		5.42***	6.82***	5.13***
		(0.76)	(0.77)	(0.76)
MI40	Experience required	7.63***	8.29***	7.57***
		(0.33)	(0.34)	(0.33)
MI74	Filing (combined 74 & 54)	−1.45**	−1.97**	−1.09*
		(0.51)	(0.53)	(0.51)
PI96	Responsible for equipment	0.72***	1.11***	0.63***
		(0.17)	(0.17)	(0.17)
MI25	Hot or cold	−1.56*		−2.32**
		(0.53)		(0.71)
MI27	Cleaning others' dirt	−2.87***		−3.55***
		(0.57)		(0.82)
MI28	Handling sick patients	4.71***		4.45***
		(0.48)		(0.80)
PI31	Loud noise	−1.33**		−1.53***
		(0.42)		(.47)
MI32	Strenuous physical activity	−3.15***		−4.63**
		(0.60)		(0.75)

(Continued)

duces the results we presented in an earlier article (Jacobs & Steinberg, 1990). This model represents the standard for the analysis of working conditions. Each variable is considered to have separate and additive effects on earnings. Moreover, each variable is considered to have an incremental effect throughout its distribution.

Table 4.4 (Continued)

Variable		Model 1 b	Model 2 b	Model 3 b
MI33	Repetition	−2.48***		−2.67***
		(0.48)		(0.62)
MI37	Risk of injury	−1.34***		−1.21*
		(0.41)		(0.51)
MI102	Close supervision	−1.44*		−1.62*
		(0.57)		(0.70)
Top 10% Measures				
MI25	Hot or cold		−0.57*	0.68*
			(0.25)	(0.32)
MI27	Cleaning others' dirt		−1.15***	0.44
			(0.25)	(0.35)
MI28	Handling sick patients		1.46***	0.24
			(0.24)	(0.40)
PI31	Loud noise		0.57**	0.28
			(0.15)	(0.17)
MI32	Strenuous physical activity		−0.46***	0.95***
			(0.26)	(0.32)
MI33	Repetition		−0.85***	0.32
			(0.23)	(0.28)
MI37	Risk of injury		−0.57***	0.21
			(0.24)	(0.28)
MI102	Close supervision		−0.57*	0.02
			(0.23)	(0.27)
PFEM	Proportion women	−2.56***	−1.75***	−2.53***
		(0.25)	(0.25)	(0.25)
R^2		.897	.883	.900

NOTE: Numbers in parentheses are standard errors. The acronyms used here (F13, MI40, and so on) correspond to those used in *The New York State Comparable Pay Study* (Steinberg et al., 1985).
*$p < .05$; **$p < .01$; ***$p < .001$.

Perhaps the most notable result in Model 1 is that most of the working conditions measures have *negative* effects on earnings. Recall that the compensating differentials logic holds that workers receive a wage premium for working in jobs with undesirable attributes. These results indicate the opposite: workers suffer a wage penalty for working in unattractive jobs. It should also be noted that, even after productivity-related-measures and working conditions are controlled, female-dominated jobs continue to pay less than male-dominated jobs.

Model 2 estimates the effect of extreme working conditions, controlling for productivity-related measures. With one exception, these results are consistent with those found in Model 1 and run counter to the compensating differentials thesis. The exception is for loud noise, which changes from a negative to a positive coefficient. All other things being equal, the presence of extreme working conditions typically results in lower pay for a job. In six of the eight cases, extreme working conditions lowered wages.

Model 3 tests the curvilinearity by including both a continuous measure of each working condition and a dummy variable representing an extreme level of this attribute. The results are especially interesting in that they provide limited evidence in support of the notion that the effects of working conditions on earnings is curvilinear. The signs on all the measures of extreme working conditions are positive. In only two cases, however, are the results statistically significant. These results indicate that wages are lower in jobs with undesirable working conditions, but that this wage penalty is sometimes offset when the working conditions reach extremely undesirable levels. The results also indicate that despite the small effect of extreme working conditions on the wages of some jobs, the percentage of women in a job continues to exert a strong negative impact on wages. The coefficient for a job's percentage female is virtually the same in Model 3, compared with Model 1. In other words, these models indicate that the impact of the sex type of a job on wages continues to be strong, independent of other content characteristics. Thus, the sex gap in wages persists, whether or not we take into account the effect of extreme working conditions.

Effect of Multiple Working Conditions

Table 4.5 presents a series of models designed to assess whether the presence of multiple instances of extreme working conditions are associated with a wage bonus or penalty. Model 1 is the baseline model, presented for the purposes of comparison. Model 2 estimates the impact of additional working conditions measures on earnings. Dummy variables were constructed to represent one working condition, two working conditions, and so on through five or more working conditions. The reference category in the analysis is no adverse working conditions. The

Table 4.5 Regression Analysis: Predicting Mean Salary Grade From Job
Requirements, Job Content, Multiple Working Conditions, and
Sex Composition

Variable		Model 1 b	Model 2 b	Model 3 b
Intercept		4.77***	−2.66***	5.13***
		(0.77)	(0.60)	(0.80)
F1	Management/supervision	4.27***	4.96***	4.27***
		(0.38)	(0.40)	(0.38)
F5	Education required	12.08***	14.02***	12.08***
		(0.43)	(0.44)	(0.43)
F12	Consequences of error	1.88***	2.60***	1.50**
		(0.48)	(0.53)	(0.50)
F13	Time effort	1.51**	0.92	1.38*
		(0.53)	(0.58)	(0.54)
Information		4.78***	5.52***	4.70***
		(0.71)	(0.77)	(0.71)
Writing		5.42***	7.78***	5.39***
		(0.76)	(0.78)	(0.76)
MI40	Experience required	7.63***	8.48***	7.61***
		(0.33)	(0.35)	(0.33)
MI74	Filing (combined 74 & 54)	−1.45**	−1.16**	−1.42**
		(0.51)	(0.54)	(0.51)
PI96	Responsible for equipment	0.72***	1.25***	0.66***
		(0.17)	(0.18)	(0.17)
MI25	Hot or cold	−1.56*		−1.64**
		(0.53)		(0.53)
MI27	Cleaning others' dirt	−2.87***		−3.15***
		(0.57)		(0.58)
MI28	Handling sick patients	4.71***		4.51***
		(0.48)		(0.49)
PI31	Loud noise	−1.33**		−1.41***
		(0.42)		(.42)
MI32	Strenuous physical activity	−3.15***		−3.48***
		(0.60)		(0.60)
MI33	Repetition	−2.48***		−2.61***
		(0.48)		(0.48)
MI37	Risk of injury	−1.34***		−1.47***
		(0.41)		(0.42)
MI102	Close supervision	−1.44*		−1.58**
		(0.57)		(0.57)

(Continued)

Table 4.5 (Continued)

Variable	Model 1 b	Model 2 b	Model 3 b
1 extreme working condition		0.05	0.23
		(0.27)	(0.25)
2 extreme working conditions		−0.18	0.28
		(0.27)	(0.25)
3 extreme working conditions		−0.71*	−0.04
		(.29)	(0.27)
4 extreme working conditions		−0.46	0.74*
		(0.32)	(0.30)
5+ extreme working conditions		−0.97**	0.87*
		(0.32)	(.34)
PFEM Proportion women	−2.56***	−1.08***	−2.63***
	(0.25)	(0.25)	(0.25)
R^2	.897	.875	.898

NOTE: Numbers in parentheses are standard errors. Extreme cases represent the top 10% of the distribution. The acronyms used here (F13, MI40, and so on) correspond to those used in *The New York State Comparable Pay Study* (Steinberg et al., 1985).
$*p < .05; **p < .01; ***p < .001$.

results in Model 2 indicate that the presence of multiple undesirable working conditions lowers wages. These results, taken by themselves, do not support the compensating differentials logic.

Model 3, however, considers the impact of extreme working conditions, controlling for the continuous measures of working conditions. Here we do we see evidence supporting the compensating differentials perspective. In particular, those jobs with four or five undesirable working conditions are paid more than those with three or fewer such attributes.

Note, however, that the sex gap in wages does not diminish in Model 3 as a result of the observed curvilinear relationships. The net effect of a job's percentage female on its earnings is virtually unchanged between Models 1 and 3. The reason for this finding is that the benefits obtained by the combination of multiple working conditions are not sufficient to offset the cost incurred by each individual working condition. In essence, it is not really that multiple job conditions produce a wage premium so much as that they somewhat reduce the wage penalty associated with individual working conditions. And, ironically, this specification results in a slightly higher penalty associated with most of the individual job attributes.

Structure, Politics, Culture, Gender, and Wages

Women have had more difficulty than men in translating their skills, experience, and job characteristics into wages. This is not only because women have not achieved equal access to the best jobs in the best organizations, but also because the work in which they are concentrated is undervalued relative to its productive contribution to the work organization. It is also because turnover is viewed as more acceptable in women's jobs than in men's jobs, because women have less power in the politics of wage negotiations in both union and nonunion settings (Acker, 1989; Milkman, 1987), and because women's jobs do not fit neatly into well-established frameworks for evaluating and valuing jobs, developed over many years for historically male work.

Job attributes that are worthy of compensation and characterize women's work are often invisible, just as skills women bring to the workplace are invisible (Steinberg, 1990). This lack of recognition of the characteristics differentially found in historically female jobs extends to the undesirable working conditions found in these jobs. These working conditions are often not captured in standard surveys of work attributes. Women find it more difficult to make a case that these attributes deserve compensation because they do not fit the standard male model of what constitutes an undesirable working condition. The results of this analysis and of our previous study suggest that both men and women find it difficult to make a successful claim that the working conditions in their jobs require extra pay. But the problem is even more difficult for women, because the working conditions found in their jobs—stress, exposure to illness, and so on—differ from the standard categories.

Even when considering the same facet of work, women have more difficulty in making a case that the attributes of their jobs should qualify for compensation. Thus, when people think of risky work, they think of window washers on skyscrapers, of coal miners, of oil-rig operators. They do not typically think of nurses, of dental hygienists, of hospital aides. Consider, for example, what Remick (1984) has labeled male dirt and female dirt. Male dirt is associated with construction work, gardening, and other parks and grounds-related activities, and with infrastructure work involving sewage treatment, boiler rooms, and the like. Female dirt—working with incontinent patients, with blood and other bodily wastes—in hospitals and nursing homes remains invisible, perhaps because of the emphasis placed on maintaining sterile conditions in these contexts. Thus jobs involving female dirt receive neither recognition nor remuneration for working around blood and human waste and for maintaining sterile conditions despite them.

These cultural difficulties are compounded by women's political disadvantages, specifically the underrepresentation of women in unions and in the wage-setting echelons of corporate decision making. As both Acker (1989) and Milkman (1987) illustrate in their case studies, union women's demands were mediated by the priorities of the male membership and leadership. If women could not translate their gender-based demands into class-based demands, they were unable to gain union support for their claims. In nonunion settings, the low wages of women are maintained in part because they have few, if any, institutional channels through which to mobilize their claims. To cite one specific problem, high turnover associated with their jobs does not result in the wage increases for women that it does for men. According to the logic of the compensating differentials hypothesis, working conditions are supposed to influence wages because they influence labor supply. If the job were not worth the trouble, people would leave. But not for women's jobs: In these jobs, high turnover does not result in increased wages. Instead, women are seen as less committed employees, who therefore may be more easily substituted for one another.

This emphasis on political, cultural, and institutional forces in wage setting is consistent with the notion that extreme cases of working conditions may sometimes produce wage premiums. As we maintained in an earlier article (Jacobs & Steinberg, 1990), workers' efforts to receive supplemental compensation for working in undesirable conditions involves a process of conflict in a context of unequal power. Where workers are able to claim that they work under a set of extremely undesirable working conditions, they may be able to translate this claim into a wage premium. Yet, as our results suggest, the undesirable working conditions must be extreme and multiple. Even here, the wage premiums are modest in size. The mechanism producing the wage effect is different from that posited by the compensating differentials thesis, but the results are the same.

Conclusions

The results of this analysis indicate that working conditions do not account for the sex gap in wages. Our analysis shows that male-dominated jobs are more likely to have extreme working conditions and multiple working conditions. Moreover, there is some limited evidence that extreme and multiple working conditions are positively compensated. More specifically, our results show that the wage cost associated with undesirable working conditions is somewhat offset in cases of extreme working conditions and in cases of multiple working conditions. However, these differences do not account for the sex gap in wages. These results are consistent with a political, cultural, and institutional view of labor markets. Further refinements in this alternative view of labor markets are in order.

Appendix:
Job Content and Educational Control Variables

		White Male Jobs (90%+ White Male) (n = 533)	Female Jobs (67.2%+ Female) (n = 297)
		Mean	Mean
F1	Management/supervision	.49	.34
		(.010)	(.012)
F5	Educational requirements	.52	.42
		(.009)	(.012)
F6	Data entry	.37	.42
		(.013)	(.018)
F7	Group facilitation	.34	.20
		(.010)	(.013)
F8	Computer programming	.14	.06
		(.008)	(.006)
F9	Fiscal responsibility	.24	.11
		(.009)	(.007)
F12	Consequences of error	.70	.54
		(.006)	(.010)

(Continued)

Appendix *(Continued)*

		White Male Jobs (90%+ White Male) (n = 533)	Female Jobs (67.2%+ Female) (n = 297)
		Mean	Mean
F13	Time effort	.18 (.008)	.07 (.005)
	Information	.55 (.006)	.40 (.008)
	Writing	.50 (.007)	.37 (.008)
MI40	Experience required	.56 (.011)	.27 (.011)
MI44	Physical coordination	.34 (.014)	.49 (.020)
MI74	Filing (combined 74 & 54)	.51 (.008)	.59 (.009)
MI96	Responsible for equipment	.58 (.011)	.42 (.014)
Other Variables:			
MSG	Mean salary grade	19.66 (.289)	12.12 (.354)
PFEM	Proportion women	.03 (.002)	.85 (.006)

NOTE: The acronyms used here (F13, MI40, and so on) correspond to those used in *The New York State Comparable Pay Study* (Steinberg et al., 1985).

Note

1. To us it is curious that economists don't seem to realize that the selectivity argument undermines the claim of an equalizing market. How do some jobs attract better workers than others? Because they are more attractive. But that is precisely what critics are trying to prove: that some jobs are more desirable than others with the same skill requirements. This differential is required in order to generate the selectivity that the economists then use to refute claims of interjob differentials. In other words, selectivity assumes that some jobs are more attractive than others, and some employers are thus in a better position to select from a larger pool of workers than others. The less desirable jobs would have to pay extra to get the identical worker, but they don't.

References

Acker, J. (1989). *Doing comparable worth: Gender, class and pay equity.* Philadelphia: Temple University Press.

Allen, S. G., Clark, R. L., & Sumner, D. A. (1986). Postretirement adjustments of pension benefits. *Journal of Human Resources, 21*(1), 118-137.

Baron, J. N. (1984). Organizational perspectives on stratification. *Annual Review of Sociology, 10,* 37-69.

Baron, J., & Bielby, W. T. (1980). Bringing the firms back in: Stratification, segmentation, and the organization of work. *American Sociological Review, 45,* 737-756.

Baron, J. N., & Cook, K. S. (1992). Process and outcome: Perspectives on the distribution of rewards in organizations. *Administrative Science Quarterly, 37*(2), 191-198.

Baron, J. N., Jennings, P. D., & Dobbin, F. R. (1988). Mission control? The development of personnel systems in U. S. industry. *American Sociological Review, 53,* 497-514.

Baron, J. N., & Newman, A. E. (1989). Pay the man: Effects of demographic composition on prescribed wage rates in the California Civil Service. In R. Michael, H. Hartmann, & B. O'Farrell (Eds.), *Pay equity: Empirical inquiries* (pp. 107-130). Washington, DC: National Academy Press.

Barry, J. (1987). Compensatory wages for women production workers at risk. In A. H. Stromberg, L. Larwood, & B. Gutek (Eds.), *Women and work: An annual review* (pp. 69-91). Beverly Hills, CA: Sage.

Berheide, C., & Steinberg, R. (1989). *Wage differentials by gender and race: Job content, structure and value bias as sources of pay inequities.* Unpublished manuscript, Skidmore College. [Revision of a paper presented to the American Sociological Association, August 1987.]

Bielby, W. T., & Baron, J. N. (1984). A woman's place is with other women: Sex segregation within organizations. In B. Reskin (Ed.), *Sex segregation in the workplace: Trends, explanations, remedies* (pp. 27-55). Washington, DC: National Academy Press.

Bielby, W. T., & Baron, J. N. (1987). Undoing discrimination: Job integration and comparable worth. In C. Bose & G. Spitze (Eds.), *Ingredients for women's employment policy* (pp. 211-229). Albany: State University of New York Press.

Blauner, R. (1964). *Alienation and freedom.* Chicago: University of Chicago Press.

Block, F. (1990). *Post-industrial possibilities: A critique of economic discourse.* Berkeley: University of California Press.

Bridges, W. P., & Nelson, R. L. (1988). Markets in hierarchies: Organizational and market influences on gender inequality in a state pay system. *American Journal of Sociology, 95,* 616-658.

Brown, C. (1980). Equalizing differences in the labor market. *Quarterly Journal of Economics, 94,* 113-134.

Burton, C. (1991). *The promise and the price: The struggle for equal opportunity in women's employment.* Sydney: Allyn & Unwin.

Clever, L. H., & Omenn, G. S. (1988). Hazards for health care workers. *Annual Review of Public Health, 9,* 273-303.

Cockburn, C. (1991). *In the way of women: Men's resistance to sex equality in organizations.* Ithaca, NY: ILR Press.

Cohn, S. (1985). *The process of occupational sex typing: The feminization of clerical labor in Great Britain.* Philadelphia: Temple University Press.

Duncan, G. J., & Holmlund, B. (1983). Was Adam Smith right, after all? Another test of the theory of compensating wage differentials. *Journal of Labor Economics, 1,* 366-379.

England, P. (1992). *Comparable worth: Theories and evidence.* New York: Aldine de-Gruyter.

Filer, R. (1985). Male-female wage differences: The importance of compensating differentials. *Industrial and Labor Relations Review, 38*(3), 426-437.

Filer, R. (1989). Occupational segregation, compensating differentials, and comparable worth. In R. T. Michael, H. I. Hartmann, & B. O'Farrell (Eds.), *Pay equity: Empirical inquiries* (pp. 153-171). Washington, DC: National Academy Press.

Gerson, J. (1985). *Hard choices: How women decide about work, career and motherhood.* Berkeley: University of California Press.

Goldin, C., & Margo, R. (1992). The great compression: The wage structure in the United States at mid-century. *Quarterly Journal of Economics, 107,* 1-34.

Hamermesh, D. S., & Wolfe, J. R. (1990). Compensating wage differentials and the duration of wage loss. *Journal of Labor Economics, 8*(1, Part 2), 175-197.

Hochner, A., Granrose, C., Goode, J., Simon, E., & Appelbaum, E. (1988). *Job saving strategies: Worker buyouts and QWL.* Kalamazoo, MI: W. E. Upjohn.

Hwang, H., Reed, W. R., & Hubbard, C. (1992). Compensating wage differentials and unmeasured productivity. *Journal of Political Economy, 100*(4), 835-858.

Jacobs, J. A. (1989). *Revolving doors: Sex segregation and women's careers.* Stanford, CA: Stanford University Press.

Jacobs, J. A. (1992). Women's entry into management: Trends in earnings, authority, and values among salaried managers. *Administrative Science Quarterly, 37*(2), 282-302.

Jacobs, J. A., & Steinberg, R. (1990). Compensating differentials and the male-female wage gap: Evidence from the New York state pay equity study. *Social Forces, 69*(2), 439-468.

Kalleberg, A., & Berg, I. (1987). *Work and industry: Structures, markets and processes.* New York: Plenum.

Kalleberg, A. L., & Sorensen, A. B. (1979). The sociology of labor markets. *Annual Review of Sociology, 5,* 351-379.

Kelman, S. (1987). *Making public policy: A hopeful view of American government.* New York: Basic Books.

Kohn, M. L., & Schooler, C. (1983). *Work and personality.* Norwood, NJ: Ablex.

Kostiuk, P. F. (1990). Compensating differentials for shift work. *Journal of Political Economy, 98*(5, Part 1), 1054-1075.

Krueger, A. B., & Summers, L. H. (1987). Reflections on the inter-industry wage structure. In K. Land & J. S. Leonard (Eds.), *Unemployment and the structure of labor markets* (pp. 18-47). New York: Basil Blackwell.

Madden, J. F. (1984). The persistence of pay differential: The economics of sex discrimination. In L. Larwood, A. H. Stromberg, & B. A. Gutek (Eds.), *Women and work: An annual review* (Vol. 1, pp. 76-114). Beverly Hills, CA: Sage.

Milkman, R. (1987). *Gender at work.* Urbana: University of Illinois Press.

Olson, C. A. (1981). An analysis of wage differentials received by workers on dangerous jobs. *Journal of Human Resources, 16*(2), 167-185.

Preston, A. (1989). The nonprofit worker in a for-profit world. *Journal of Labor Economics, 7,* 438-463.

Reed, W. R., & Holleman, J. (1988). *Do women prefer women's work?* (Working Paper 88-02). College Station: Department of Economics, Texas A&M University.

Remick, H. (1979). Strategies for creating sound bias-free job evaluation systems. In *Job evaluation and EEO: The emerging issues* (pp. 85-112). New York: Industrial Relations Counselors.

Remick, H. (1984). Major issues in a priori applications. In H. Remick (Ed.), *Comparable worth and wage discrimination: Technical possibilities and political realities* (pp. 99-117). Philadelphia: Temple University Press.

Remick, H., Ginorio, A. B., & Brtiz, P. (1987). A case study in Washington State. In National Committee on Pay Equity (Ed.), *Pay equity: An issue of race, ethnicity and sex* (pp. 109-147). Washington, DC: National Committee on Pay Equity.

Reskin, B. (1988). Bringing the men back in: Sex differentiation and the devaluation of women's work. *Gender and Society, 2,* 58-81.

Reskin, B., & Padavic, I. (1994). *Women and men at work.* Thousand Oaks, CA: Pine Forge Press.

Roberts, M. (1989). *Commonwealth Fund report on the nursing shortage* (Draft Final Report). Boston: Commonwealth Fund.

Rosen, S. (1985). Implicit contracts: A survey. *Journal of Economic Literature, 23*(3), 1144-1175.

Rosen, S. (1986). The theory of equalizing differences. In O. Ashenfelter & R. Layard (Eds.), *Handbook of labor economics* (pp. 641-692). New York: Elsevier.

Schultz, V. (1990). Telling stories about women and work: Judicial interpretations of sex segregation in the workplace in Title VII cases raising the lack of interest argument. *Harvard Law Review, 103,* 1749-1843.

Smith, A. (1976). *An inquiry into the nature and causes of the wealth of nations* (E. Cannan, Ed). Chicago: University of Chicago Press. (Original work published 1776)

Smith, J. (1984). The paradox of women's poverty: Wage earning women and economic transformation. *Signs, 19,* 291-310.

Smith, R. (1979). Compensating wage differentials and public policy: A review. *Industrial and Labor Relations Review, 32*(3), 339-352.

Steinberg, R. J. (1990). The social construction of skill. *Work and Occupations, 17,* 449-482.

Steinberg, R. J. (1991). Job evaluation and managerial control: the politics of technique and the techniques of politics. In J. Fudge & P. McDermott (Eds.), *Just wages: A feminist assessment of pay equity* (pp. 193-218). Toronto: University of Toronto Press.

Steinberg, R., Haignere, L., Possin, C., Chertos, C., & Treiman, D. (1985). *The New York state comparable pay study: Final report.* Albany, NY: Center for Women in Government.

Steinberg, R., & Jacobs, J. A. (1994). Pay equity in nonprofit organizations: Making women's work visible. In T. Odendahl & M. O'Neill (Eds.), *Women and power in the nonprofit sector* (pp. 79-120). San Francisco: Jossey-Bass.

Strober, M. H. (1984). Toward a general theory of occupational sex segregation: The case of public school teaching. In B. Reskin (Ed.), *Sex segregation in the workplace: Trends, explanations, remedies* (pp. 144-156). Washington, DC: National Academy Press.

Tomaskovic-Devey, D. (1993). *Gender and racial inequality at work: The sources and consequences of job segregation.* Ithaca, NY: ILR Press.

Treiman, D. J. (1979). *Job evaluation: An analytic review.* Washington, DC: National Academy of Sciences.

U.S. Department of Labor, Women's Bureau. (1983). *Time of change: 1983 handbook on women workers* (Bulletin 298). Washington, DC: U.S. Government Printing Office.

Weston, K. (1990). Production as means, production as metaphor: Women's struggle to enter the trades. In F. Ginsburg & A. L. Tsing (Eds.), *Uncertain terms: Negotiating gender in American culture* (pp. 137-151). Boston: Beacon Press.

Zoloth, S., & Stellman, H. (1987). Hazards of healing: Occupational health and safety in hospitals. In A. Stromberg, L. Larwook, & B. Gutek (Eds.), *Women and work: An annual review* (Vol. 3, pp. 45-65). Beverly Hills, CA: Sage.

PART II

Women and Authority

5

Jobs, Authority, and Earnings Among Managers

The Continuing Significance of Sex

BARBARA F. RESKIN
CATHERINE E. ROSS

Historically, employers have limited women's chances to exercise power. For example, the majority of office firms surveyed by the U.S. Women's Bureau in 1940 barred women from positions of authority (Goldin, 1990). Over the next 30 years, women's share of occupations classified by the Bureau of the Census as managers and administrators rose slowly: from one in nine to one in six.[1] However, during the 1970s, women posted unprecedented gains in management occupations, and in 1980 and 1990, respectively, they claimed 30% and 40% of the jobs the Census Bureau classified as managerial, executive, and administrative (U.S. Bureau of the Census, 1984; U.S. Bureau of Labor Statistics, 1991). Yet the business press describes barriers that women managers still face (Fierman, 1990; Fisher, 1987; Hymowitz & Schellhardt, 1986; Konrad, 1990). Indeed, the incorporation into popular speech of the phrase "glass ceil-

AUTHORS' NOTE: We thank Joe Spaeth for the use of these data. Data collection was funded by the Department of Sociology and the Research Board of the University of Illinois, Urbana. We are grateful to Marianne Ferber, Lowell L. Hargens, James R. Kluegel, Jerry A. Jacobs, Patricia Martin, Gail McGuire, Patricia A. Roos, and anonymous reviewers for their helpful comments on a previous version of this chapter.

ing" (Hymowitz & Schellhardt, 1986) points to a widespread feeling that invisible barriers separate women from top jobs and genuine authority.

This chapter investigates whether women's substantial share of census-designated managerial jobs signals commensurate access to organizational authority and the monetary rewards that such authority brings men (Wright & Perrone, 1977). In other words, we explore whether equity in access to workplace authority and in returns to authority have accompanied women's progress toward representational parity with men in census managerial occupations.

Theoretical perspectives on women's exclusion from management predict conflicting answers to this question. On one hand, if women have been denied authority because they lacked the qualifications or because employers stereotyped them as lacking necessary personality traits, then recent changes in women's education and work experience, combined with campaigns to rebut stereotypes, should have enhanced their access to authority and its rewards. On the other hand, if employers have denied women authority in order to preserve men's power and privileges, there is less reason to be optimistic that women's growing share of managerial jobs has brought an equitable distribution of authority (see Reskin, 1988). Below, we review these explanations and describe the evidence of sex differences in authority and its rewards. Then, after discussing our methods, we present results showing sex differences in access to authority and the determinants of these differences.

The human capital and status attainment approaches that predominated a decade ago assume that workplace rewards—including authority—were allocated unequally because of women's deficiency in necessary qualifications or relevant experience (Hill, 1980; Wolf & Fligstein, 1979). But the experience gap between the sexes has shrunk. By the mid-1980s, women claimed over one third of bachelor's degrees and one quarter of the master's degrees in business (U.S. National Center for Educational Statistics, 1987). Women's and men's college majors have become more similar, as have their occupational aspirations (Jacobs, 1989; Wilson & Boldizar, 1990).

Others, such as Goldin (1990), have stressed employers' concerns over sex differences in labor force commitment. Goldin argued that after World War I, white-collar firms created promotion ladders (internal labor markets) to reduce costly turnover. However, employers assumed that women's primary attachment to their future families would limit their work time. Thus corporate bureaucracies established promotion ladders to retain male workers (Baron & Bielby, 1986; Edwards, 1979; Hartmann, 1987), while relegating women to dead-end jobs that lacked a path to authority.[2] However, by 1980, women's labor force participation showed more continuity (Reskin & Hartmann, in press), and as women displayed stronger attachment to the labor force and the number of women willing to settle for clerical jobs declined, justifying their relegation to dead-end jobs became harder.

A third explanation emphasizes the effect of employers' attitudes: the tendency to stereotype women as irrational or harboring other traits that ill-suit them for management (Davis, 1975; Larwood, Gutek, & Gattiker, 1984; Powell, 1988; Reskin & Hartmann, 1986) or employers' preference—especially in situations involving uncertainty—for the predictability they ascribed to persons similar to themselves (Kanter, 1977).[3] But the entry of thousands of women into managerial occupations during the 1970s should have weakened stereotypes about women's ill-suitedness for management, undermining their ability to deny women access to authority.

In sum, to the extent that real or perceived sex differences were major factors in women's near exclusion from organizational authority, declining sex disparities in education, turnover, and experience, as well as employers' increased contact with women managers, should have eroded employers' economic motives for denying women authority.

In contrast to this sanguine view are those who doubt women's ability to rapidly close the authority gap. Some contend that male employers deny women authority in order to preserve men's monopoly on organizational power (Acker, 1990). Moreover, men's ability to change the rules when necessary to preserve their advantage (Reskin, 1988) means that the uneven distribution of authority will not disappear easily. Others stress the institutionalized barriers and organizational inertia that slow down any movement toward equality (Baron & Bielby, 1986). Bergmann (1986) linked men's dominant status with institutional barriers, arguing that the "segregation code" codified in many firms' personnel policies prohibits the sexes from interacting as equals, bars women from supervising men, and reserves "training slots" for upper-level jobs for men (p. 114). To the extent that men's desire to preserve their monopoly on authority contributes to women's authority deficits, women's recent increased representation in census managerial occupations should not bring authority. Indeed, women's growing presence in management might reinforce men's impulse to monopolize organizational power. This line of reasoning implies that even organizations that have granted women managerial titles and supervisory status will not reward them equitably for exercising authority.

Sex Differences in Access to Authority

Data mostly collected before women's dramatic inroads into managerial occupations document an authority gap that consigned women to the lowest levels of management (Boyd, Mulvihill, & Myles, Chapter 7, this volume; Churchill, 1977; Halaby, 1979; Harlan & Weiss, 1981; Jacobs, Chapter 6, this volume; Roos, 1981; Spaeth, 1985). Analyses of 1960 data for utility-firm managers showed that women were disadvantaged in rank and were paid less than men in the same rank (Halaby, 1979). According to 1975 data for Wisconsin high school graduates in their late 30s (Wolf & Fligstein, 1979), men were more likely to have authority to hire, fire, set pay, and supervise subordinates' work. Men surveyed in the late 1970s showed an advantage on authority over subordinates' pay or promotions (Hill, 1980). Women in a 1981 sample of workers had fewer subordinates, less discretion, and less monetary and organizational control than men had (Spaeth, 1985). Comparing General Social Survey data for 1972-1979 and 1980-1989, Jacobs (Chapter 6, this volume) found a slight decline in the small sex gap in managers' likelihood of supervising subordinates but no change in the larger disparity in level in the chain of command as measured by the likelihood that one's subordinates had supervisees.[4]

Sex Differences in Managers' Earnings and in Income Returns to Authority

Research also reveals unequal rewards for authority for women and men. Among census-designated managers, the median income of women who worked full-time year-round in 1980 was 56.3% of that of men (U.S. Bureau of the Census, 1984; Table 281).[5] Some of this difference is due to the sexes' different distributions across managerial occupations, but in no detailed managerial occupation had women achieved earnings parity with men. In 1981, women managers' share of men's median weekly earnings ranged from 57% for sales managers to 72% for restaurant, cafeteria, and bar managers (Rytina, 1982, Table 1). Both rank and job segregation contributed to the wage gap among utility managers in 1960 (Halaby, 1979)—women managers were ghettoized in certain areas, such as operations, and in lower ranks than men. However, the same jobs paid men more than women (Halaby, 1979), and among respondents in 1974 to 1977 General Social Surveys, male workers received greater returns than women for having high positions in supervisory hierarchies (Ward & Mueller, 1985). Spaeth (1985) found that male workers' payoff for controlling monetary resources was double that of females, net of education and experience. Finally, Jacobs's (Chapter 6, this volume) comparison of 1969 census data and 1987 Current Population Survey data revealed that, net of education, the wage gap among managers had shrunk between the late 1960s and 1980s, but that taking into account hours and weeks worked, age, broad industry, and specific managerial occupation did not eliminate the effect of sex on managers' earnings. However, Jacobs's supplementary analyses of pooled General Social Survey data for the 1980s revealed no evidence that men received a greater payoff for supervising subordinates than did women.

In sum, the research reviewed above documents some form of an authority gap through the 1970s when management was still largely reserved for men, but several issues remain unresolved. First, we do not know how women managers fare in access to authority after pressures in the late 1970s spurred employers to open managerial jobs to women. Has women's substantial representation in management occupations brought them commensurate decision-making authority? Second, past research used gross indicators of authority. For example, Spaeth's (1985) measure of authority ignored differences in type of input, the distribution of access to authority was highly skewed, and Spaeth did not test for sex differences in the returns to authority. Finally, few studies have compared the sexes' financial returns to authority, so we cannot assess the degree to which contemporary employers universally reward managers for exercising organizational authority.

To answer these questions, this chapter uses 1982 data for managers employed in a wide array of occupations to address three questions. First, did a sexual division of labor allocate women and men managers to different kinds of work? Second, did managers' sex affect their decision making authority, net of their education, experience, nominal organizational rank, and work setting? Third, did managers' sex affect their earnings, beyond the effects of their background characteristics, work setting, managerial level, and authority? The answers to these descriptive questions about why women's workplace achievements do not match those of men have important theoretical implications for sex-based strati-fication. Increasingly, both sexes derive their social and economic stat-uses through their employment, so organizational actions mediate or generate inequality between the sexes. The continuing significance of sex in post-1980 organizational reward systems will point to the survival of institutional barriers, as well as men's continuing ability to monopo-lize authority.

Method

Data

Our data are for a representative sample of Illinois managers employed at least 20 hours per week in 1982. A survey research organization and students enrolled in a research practicum collected the data through tele-phone interviews. For residents of Chicago, interviewers used random-digit dialing; elsewhere, they randomly selected respondents from tele-phone directories (for additional details, see Spaeth, 1985).

Because our interest lies in comparing women and men who do mana-gerial work, we focus on the 222 respondents who described themselves as holding a "management position." Many of these self-declared man-agers held occupations not classified as executive, administrative, and managerial by the Census Bureau. Of the 280 occupations whose titles in 1980 included the term *manager,* the Census Bureau classified fewer than half as executive, administrative, or managerial (U.S. Bureau of the Census, 1980), assigning to less prestigious occupational categories mil-lions of persons who consider themselves managers and are so viewed by their employers.[6] But non-census designated managers nonetheless do managerial work. For example, four fifths of our self-reported manag-ers had supervisees, the same as census-designated managers (Jacobs, 1992), and all but three contributed to some organizational decision. Limiting our sample to persons in occupations that the 1980 Census classified as managerial would have restricted our findings to workers in upper-status occupations and professions and excluded the millions of managers in clerical, sales, precision-production, service, and farming occupations. Because we sought to assess the authority gap among all managers, we rejected the Census Bureau's managerial designation as a definition of managerial work.

Like data in other studies of sex and authority, our data have limitations: They are for a single state and include only 222 managers.[7] However, we know of no data set for a random sample of managers that provides such a detailed picture of the sexual division of authority among managers and thus allows researchers to gauge its causes and its consequences on earnings.

Variables

Education and Experience

The human capital school asserts the importance of education and experience for explaining women's underrepresentation in managerial authority, and studies confirm that education affects workers' chances (particularly men's) of attaining authority or their rewards for authority (Cannings, 1988; Halaby, 1979; Hill, 1980; Jacobs, 1992; Wolf & Fligstein, 1979). We measure education in years of school completed, with graduate and professional degrees coded as 18. Researchers have also found that tenure positively affects access to authority (Halaby, 1979; Hill, 1980; Wolf & Fligstein, 1979). Experience with one's current employer ought to be particularly important for acquiring authority on that job, so we measure experience as years in the 1982 job.

Census Occupational Classification

To learn whether working in an occupation classified by the Census Bureau as managerial enhanced respondents' authority, we created a binary variable distinguishing workers whose occupations the 1980 Census classified as managerial (coded 1). Because the Census tends to reserve its official managerial classification for upper-status occupations, this variable serves as a proxy for occupational prestige.[8]

Type of Employer

How women fare relative to their male counterparts depends partly on whether they work for public or private establishments or are self-employed. Public employment sometimes proves more egalitarian: Women in sex-atypical occupations are overrepresented in government employment, and the wage gap among federal employees is smaller than in the private sector (Markham, Harlan, & Hackett, 1987). Self-employment does not bring women the same rewards as men, but women who own their businesses and some who work in family firms escape employer-imposed mobility barriers (Loscocco & Robinson, 1991). And, of course, self-employment should bring substantially more authority.[9] To allow for the effects of type of employment, we constructed dummy variables for three employment situations—government, private, or employed by oneself or in a family business. The category nonprofit organizations was excluded.

Organizational Characteristics

Organizational size sets limits on organizational rewards systems (e.g., the length of authority chains; see also Jacobs, Chapter 6, this volume) and affects how equitably employers treat the sexes (Baron, 1984). For example, Bielby and Baron (1984) found the most sex segregation in very small and very large firms; although Baron, Mittman, and Newman (1991) reported that sex segregation declined more slowly in large than in small public agencies. The data on organizations' size are in intervals, so we used the midpoint of the interval to measure size. Predominantly female work settings appear to provide more opportunities for women (Shaeffer & Lynton, 1979). To allow for this possibility, we included the percentage of women in respondents' detailed (census three-digit) occupation in 1980.

Race

We included race to control for factors that track people of color out of positions of authority (Kluegel, 1978). Our dichotomy is coded 0 for nonwhites and 1 for whites.

Authority

We measured sex differences in several manifestations of authority, including managerial level, supervisory status, number of direct supervisees, whether direct supervisees had subordinates, total number of direct and indirect supervisees, sex of top subordinate, form of authority over top subordinate, and involvement in decisions in 17 organizational arenas. Appendix A describes the measure of authority used in the regression analyses.

Earnings

Earnings include wages and salary earned in 1981, in thousands of dollars. The 30% of respondents who gave their earnings in intervals rather than reporting exact earnings were assigned the intervals' midpoints.

Results: Sex Differences in Managerial Authority

Managerial Jobs and Workers' Sex

Our data revealed an extreme sexual division of labor that we describe in detail so that readers can appreciate how differently organizations use female and male managers. First, male and female managers tended to work for different kinds of employers. Women were almost twice as likely as men to hold governmental jobs (23.5% vs. 12.3%) but only 60% as likely to be self-employed or work in family businesses (18.5% compared to 31.5%). The data offer tentative evidence that female managers specialized in support services, whereas male managers specialized in revenue-generating activities: Women with extraorganizational duties were significantly more likely than such men to be involved in public relations, a feminizing specialty. One that women are entering in large numbers (Reskin & Roos, 1990), and women managers spent more time than did men providing professional services to others, whereas men devoted almost twice as much of their time to sales as did women. These differences have implications for each sex's ability to develop managerial skills or use their jobs as stepping-stones to future positions (Dipboye, 1987).

This sexual division of labor was compounded by men's greater access to authority. Managers' sex was strongly related to their level in the managerial hierarchy: The odds of reaching top or upper management were more than half again as great for men as women (56.1% vs. 35.8%). Moreover, although equal proportions of the sexes—about one fifth—had no supervisees, men—probably because of their higher placement in their organization's hierarchy—were twice as likely as women to have supervisees who themselves supervised other workers (35.2% vs. 17.3%). Given men's concentration in the upper echelons, it is not surprising that significantly more persons were directly or indirectly responsible to male than to female managers (37.3% vs. 11.3%).

A sexual division of labor also emerged in the sex of managers' supervisees. Three quarters of the managers' top subordinates were the same sex as the managers (77% for the female managers and 76% for the male managers), replicating findings for Canadian managers (Boyd et al., Chapter 7, this volume). These results are consistent with employers' adherence to the norm against women exercising authority over men and with the fact that segregation creates opportunities for women to supervise other women.

Women and men managers tended to play different roles with respect to their supervisees. Slightly but not significantly more women than men usually decided what their top subordinate should do (52% vs. 47%) and how they should do it (30% vs. 22%). This difference stems from differences in female and male managers' position in the supervisory hierarchy and their likelihood of having female subordinates. Whereas low-level managers expect to monitor subordinates closely, high-level managers reportedly try to avoid close supervision. Indeed, Jackall (1988) claimed that middle and top managers dislike giving subordinates detailed instructions. A high-level manager explained, "If I tell someone what to do [and he fails] . . . I lose any right I have to chew his ass out. . . . This is why a lot of bosses don't give explicit directions. They just give a statement of objectives." Almost 30% of the women worked in administrative support occupations where they presumably scheduled and closely supervised mostly female clerical workers. The association between sex and managers' authority over their top subordinate dropped slightly when we controlled for the sex of managers' top subordinate, but in general managers granted more autonomy to male subordinates.

Another measure of managers' authority over their most responsible subordinates—how often they usually checked their work—showed the opposite pattern, with men checking their top subordinates' work more frequently than women (17% vs. 8% did so frequently; one quarter of the men but half of the women checked only rarely). This significant zero-order relationship with sex ($r = .21$) runs counter to the stereotype that women bosses hold a tighter rein. However, as Kanter (1977) cautioned, sex differences may stem from differences in organizational positions. Presumably, the tasks that higher-level managers assign their most responsible subordinates are more complex and hence require more supervision, whereas those assigned by lower-level managers are more routinized. Given the associations between managerial level and sex and between the workers' sex and their tasks, managerial level could explain the association between sex and closeness of supervision. Our data support this interpretation: Managers higher in the chain of command, who were disproportionately male, checked subordinates more closely than did lower-level managers, and all managers checked more closely on male than female subordinates—presumably because male and female subordinates did different kinds of work. Controlling for the sex of managers' top subordinates and for whether those subordinates supervised others reduced the effect of managers' sex to a nonsignificant $r = .08$. Thus what appeared to be a sex difference in managers' behavior resulted from differences in the sexes' organizational rank and the sex of their top subordinates.

Sex Differences in Decision-Making Authority

We also examined the association between managers' sex and their decision-making power in 17 realms (see Table 5.1) and explored the reasons for that association. The sexes differed both in the number of arenas in which they were involved in decision making and in whether their involvement was to provide information, recommend actions, or make decisions. Although the sex difference in average number of arenas of involvement was statistically insignificant, men made some kind of input into more arenas than did women (see columns 1 and 2 of Table 5.1). It was in the realm of final decision making in which substantial sex differences emerged. Women made final decisions in an average of 2.8 arenas, compared to men's 4.6. As the third and fourth column in Table 5.1 indicate, 27% of the female managers lacked final say in a single arena, compared to 17% of the men, and men were twice as likely as women to have final say in at least 5 (40% vs. 20%) or at least 10 realms (15% vs. 7%).

Because the survey asked respondents about their decision-making role in 17 arenas (see Table 5.2), we can see for which decisions the authority gap was greatest. We grouped these 17 decisions into four categories identified by a factor analysis: *goals and organization* in managers' own unit, *personnel* in managers' unit, *budget and spending* in managers' unit, and *matters related to other units.* Men were more likely than women to decide issues in all 17 arenas, and 12 of these sex differences were statistically significant. Men's advantage over women was largest in decisions related to personnel. Of the 115 men and 64 women who had any supervisees, 79% of the men and 58% of the women had the

Table 5.1 Number of Arenas in Which Manager Had Any Input and Made Final Decisions, by Sex (in percentages)

Number of Arenas	Any Input		Final Decision	
	Women	*Men*	*Women*	*Men*
None	1.2	1.4	27.2	16.8
1	3.7	1.4	28.4	14.7
2	6.5	9.1	6.2	13.3
3	4.9	4.2	12.3	8.4
4	7.4	5.6	4.9	7.0
5	12.3	5.6	3.7	4.9
6 to 10	38.3	34.3	9.8	23.2
11 to 15	24.6	31.5	7.4	11.2
16+	1.2	7.0	—	0.7
Total[a]	100.1	100.1	99.9	100.2
N	81	143	81	143

a. Percentages do not equal 100 because of rounding error.

last word on at least one personnel matter. The sexes differed least in decisions about scheduling supervisees' work—the personnel decision both female and male managers were most likely to make—and in transferring supervisees—the least common personnel decision. In short, the authority gap was greatest for the bread-and-butter decisions of hiring, firing, and authorizing promotions and raises. Women were usually advisers; men called the shots.

Men's significant advantage over women in the likelihood of having the final say in decisions involving their own unit's organization and goals stemmed from their moderately greater involvement in shaping their units' goals. Only about one quarter of the managers exercised final authority in decisions concerning other units, but the sexes differed significantly in their likelihood of making such decisions. Only 16% of women had final say in any decisions affecting other units, compared to 30% of the men. This confinement of female managers' authority to their own unit reflects men's higher levels in managerial hierarchies. High-level managers' authority extends beyond their own unit, and men were more likely than women to hold high-level posts. In fact, managerial level was associated with the chance to make final decisions in each of

Table 5.2 Percentage Making Final Decisions, by Organizational Arena and Sex

Organizational Arena	Women	Men
Goals and organization in own unit	49.4	60.8*
Setting goals for unit	38.3	51.8*
Work unit organization	43.2	53.9
Personnel in own unit	45.7	63.6*
Hiring supervisees	23.5	39.9*
Scheduling supervisees	37.2	48.2*
Promoting supervisees	13.6	30.8*
Raising supervisees' wages	12.4	32.9*
Transferring supervisees	7.4	21.0*
Firing supervisees	22.2	40.6*
Budget and spending in own unit	25.9	35.0
Largest monetary decision in last year	19.8	28.3
Size of unit's budget	6.4	13.6*
How unit's budget is spent	16.9	19.4
Other units	17.3	30.8*
Establishing/closing other units	6.2	16.8*
Evaluating other units	6.3	10.5
Allocating resources in other units	7.4	18.2*
Setting pay in other units	2.5	9.8*
Setting rules in other units	11.1	12.6
Setting budget in other units	4.9	11.2*
N	81	143

*Sex difference is statistically significant at .05 level.

the four broad categories, and the correlations were stronger for men (from .42 to .48) than women (from .28 to .46). Finally, just over 30% of the managers had ultimate authority over their unit's budget. Although men were more likely than women to make final budgetary decisions for their own units, the small number of managers who made budgetary decisions precludes a large sex difference, and the sex difference was not significant.

These findings indicate marked sex differences in organizational power. Attaining a high level in the managerial hierarchy more often brought men than women the right to make decisions. Male managers' more extensive authority is reflected in the span of their decision making authority—the number of arenas in which managers had any input and especially the number of arenas in which they made final decisions.

Explaining the Authority Gap

The authority gap can stem from differences in the education and experience the sexes bring to their jobs, employers' propensity to assign female and male managers to different jobs, or organizations' failure to entrust female managers with as much authority as they give equally qualified men in similar jobs. We assessed these possibilities by regressing the number of arenas in which managers made final decisions on managers' education, firm tenure, hours worked, race, sex, self-employment and private employer (as compared to government employer), organizational size, occupational percentage of females, census-designated managerial occupation, managerial level, and position in the supervisory hierarchy. Appendix B shows the intercorrelations among the variables in the regressions in Tables 5.3 and 5.4.

As Table 5.3 indicates, managers' human capital and performance contributed to their organizational authority, although the effect of firm experience was negative, contrary to human capital theory, even in an equation with only human capital variables (not shown). Education's zero-order association with authority ($r = .21$) disappeared in the regression equation, indicating that education operated by enhancing managers' access to authority-conferring jobs. As expected, being self-employed significantly increased the breadth of managers' decisive authority. The organizational variables dominated the authority attainment process. Most important for broadening the reach of managers' final-decision authority was their position in their organization's managerial hierarchy and its chain of command. The significant net effect of holding an occupation the Census classified as managerial reflects the greater organizational authority available to managers in the high-status occupations the Census designated as managerial.

Net of other variables, the more female the census occupation in which managers worked, the more extensive their authority.[10] However, we must bear in mind that 8 of the 17 decisions in our measure involve either the organization of work or personnel decisions in managers' own units, so the breadth of managers' authority in predominantly female occupations probably reflects the organizational isolation of heavily female

Table 5.3 Regression for Number of Arenas of Final Decision Making

	b (SE)	beta
Sex (male = 1)	1.034** (.496)	.141
Race (white = 1)	.292 (.770)	.020
Education	.003 (.078)	.002
Firm tenure	−.050** (.019)	−.139
Hours	.047** (.018)	.148
Self-employed	1.127* (.664)	.142
Private employer	.200 (.501)	.028
Organization size	.000 (.000)	.056
Managerial level	1.227** (.221)	.384
Supervisory authority	1.578** (.289)	.309
Occupational percentage female	2.303** (.900)	.179
Census-designated managerial occupation	1.551** (.421)	.203
Constant	−6.263**	
R^2	.455**	
N	221	

*Statistically significant at .10.
**Statistically significant at .05.

occupations and the positive effect of such isolation on the number of areas in which managers exercise final say. Net of several characteristics of work and managers' organizational position, men made significantly more final decisions than did women. In other words, the effect of sex was not simply the result of sex differences in human capital and organizational factors; after taking those into account, sex remained statistically significant.

Male managers may wield more authority than females both because women are lower in the chain of command and because similar ranks confer less authority on women. To determine whether organizations better rewarded men than women for making decisions and for positional authority, we added sex interactions to the equation that allowed the effects of the authority predictors to vary for women and men. However, none was significant, indicating that none of the independent variables yielded significantly greater returns for men or women (results not shown in Table 5.3). Thus female managers' decision-making authority fell short of men's, not because they received less authority for the same qualifications and positions but because they were lower in managerial hierarchies, occupied truncated supervisory chains, were less likely to hold occupations the Census classified as managerial, were less likely to be self-employed, worked slightly fewer hours per week than men (despite their greater likelihood of working in a female-dominated occupation)—and because they were female.

Sex Differences in Managers' Earnings

We turn now to whether the sexes' earnings returns to authority were equitable. Among the managers we studied, women averaged 53.8% of what men made in 1981 ($17,448 vs. $32,445). For sampled managers employed full-time, the *annual* earnings ratio was .576, a value in line with the ratio of .608 for median *weekly* earnings for a national sample of managers employed full-time (U.S. Bureau of Labor Statistics, 1982). Potential contributors to the earnings gap include sex disparities in inputs (women managers averaged 4 fewer years of firm experience and worked 6 fewer hours per week than men), women's concentration in predominantly female (and hence lower paid) occupations, women's depressed rank in managerial hierarchies, their more limited span of authority, the effect of sex itself, and any higher payoffs for men for these factors. To assess the relative importance of these factors, we examined the effects on salary of education, firm tenure, hours worked, type of employer, occupational sex composition, census-designated managerial occupation, managerial level, supervisory authority, decision making authority, and sex. To allow for declining returns to tenure, we estimated an equation with tenure squared as well as tenure, but the former did not significantly improve our ability to predict earnings, so we report equations with just the nontransformed measure.

Equation 1 of Table 5.4 shows the effects of managers' human capital inputs and their sex on their 1981 wages or salary (coded in thousands of dollars). Education, firm experience, hours worked, and sex all signifi-

Table 5.4 Regression for Salaries

	Equation 1		Equation 2		Equation 3	
	b (SE)	beta	b (SE)	beta	b (SE)	beta
Sex (male = 1)	12.774** (2.486)	.343	10.487** (2.448)	.282	−.669 (4.072)	−.018
Race (white = 1)	.713 (4.743)	.010	−.143 (4.676)	−.002	−1.092 (4.582)	−.015
Education	1.519** (.478)	.205	1.056** (.479)	.143	.981** (.468)	.133
Firm tenure	.320** (.118)	.176	.303** (.117)	.167	.301*** (.114)	.165
Hours	.205** (.106)	.126	.127 (.108)	.078	.124 (.105)	.076
Private employer (= 1)			5.094 (3.069)	.141	−.797 (3.878)	−.022
Self-employed (= 1)			2.845 (4.086)	.071	5.825 (4.072)	.144
Organization size			.000 (.000)	.066	.000 (.000)	.075
Census-designated managerial occupation (= 1)			6.885** (2.657)	.177	6.644** (2.586)	.171
Managerial level			2.534 (1.438)	.156	2.332** (1.401)	.144
Supervisory authority			1.330 (1.871)	.051	1.558 (1.822)	.060
Final-decision authority			.200 (.418)	.039	−1.334* (.683)	−.263
Sex × Private Employer					11.198** (4.576)	.299
Sex × Final-Decision Authority					1.972** (.722)	.379
Constant	−15.491		−17.713*		−9.535	
R^2	.240**		.309**		.347**	
N	191					

*Statistically significant at .10.
**Statistically significant at .05.

cantly affected managers' earnings in the expected direction. Equation 2, which adds information about managers' employer, their organizational position, and their decision-making authority, retains these significant effects, except for hours. Each additional year of education raised managers' earnings by $1,056, and each year of firm tenure added $303 to their annual pay. Each rung on the managerial ladder was worth an additional $2,534, and working in a census-designated managerial occupation brought an extra $6,885. Pursuing a more female occupation did not significantly reduce managers' earnings; we do not include this variable in the equation in Table 5.4 because of its strong correlation with managers' sex ($r = .66$).

Other researchers have found that men do better than women at translating positional authority into earnings, perhaps, according to Roos (1981), because they are higher in managerial hierarchies. However, being male remained an asset for managers even after we controlled for managerial level, supervisory authority, and final-decision authority: Men outearned women with the same levels of education and experience, type of employer, and managerial rank by $10,487 a year.

Another possible contribution to the earnings gap is a higher payoff for men for any of the factors increasing earnings. To find out whether the returns for any variables in Equation 2 were greater for men than women, we tested—one at a time—interactions for sex and each possible determinant of income. Equation 3 includes the only two significant sex interactions: private sector employment and number of final decisions.[11]

Private Sector Employer

Equation 3 indicates that the nonsignificant main effect of working for a private employer in Equation 2 masked a nonsignificant negative effect for women and a significant positive one for men. At the average level of all other variables in the equation, male managers employed in private companies earned $33,362 in 1981; female managers earned $23,033.[12] In contrast, women managers who worked in government or in their own or a family business did almost as well as men, consistent with our expectations.

Final Decisions

The significant interaction between sex and number of final decision areas in Equation 3 means that each additional arena in which men made final decisions brought them an extra $638 in 1981 dollars.[13] The negative coefficient for the main effect of number of final decisions—which approached significance (alpha = .052)—indicates that each additional final decision arena cost women over $1,334. Of the 12 female managers who made final decisions in at least 5 arenas, 6 managed workers in health, clerical support, or education, and 1 supervised production. The remaining 5 were self-employed: an insurance salesperson, a home-based child care provider, an educational administrator, and 2 sales proprietors. The low incomes of the last 2 suggest they ran home-based businesses or worked in pyramid-sales operations, and their large numbers of final decisions (5 to 12) probably reflect the small scale of their operations. In contrast, the majority of the 51 male managers who made final decisions in five or more arenas were professionals or worked in finance, personnel and labor relations, marketing, public relations, production, construction, transportation, or sales. Over half of the men in sales were self-employed, but they ran larger establishments than did self-employed women (businesses run by the female managers averaged 16 employees compared to 794 for businesses run by the self-employed men). Thus the negative earnings effect of number of final decisions for women probably reflects two factors: first, employed women's segregation in administrative support jobs that did not reward making decisions, and second, the small scale of self-employed women's operations in which final decisions are a dime a dozen and their payoff is not much higher.

Conclusion

Women's increased access to managerial jobs is beyond dispute, but the sexes' more equitable representation in managerial jobs has not eliminated the significance of gender in the distribution of organizational authority and the monetary rewards that authority traditionally brings. Women managers were concentrated near the bottom of chains of command; they tended to supervise workers of their own sex, consistent with conventions that women should not supervise men; they were substantially less likely than men to exercise decision-making authority; and their involvement in decision making was largely confined to offering input into decisions that men made.

The sex gap in access to authority exacerbated an earnings gap between male and female managers. Both male and female managers' salaries rose with education and experience, managerial level, and a census-designated managerial occupation, but men earned $10,487 more than women with the same values on these variables. Furthermore, exercising decision-making authority paid off for men but reduced women's pay, because of the contexts in which they exercised authority. That women did not derive the same rate of return as men for making decisions exacerbated the earnings gap between equally qualified male and female managers.

These data were collected almost 20 years after the 1963 Equal Pay Act mandated equal pay for equal work and Title VII of the 1964 Civil Rights Act outlawed sex discrimination in employment, and 10 years after a presidential executive order required federal contractors to practice affirmative action in hiring and promoting women. Yet in 1982— well after female managers had become commonplace—the organizations that employed our sample of managers disproportionately denied women genuine authority; even the few women who had secured broad decision-making power did not realize financial gain from that achievement. The similarity of these findings to those for data collected over 20 years ago (Halaby, 1979) is striking: Before and after the feminization of managerial work and federal antidiscrimination regulations, women managers' near exclusion from high-ranking jobs ensured men's substantial earnings advantage while minimizing the role of unequal returns to managerial authority.

What do our results suggest about the authority gap, in light of women's unprecedented inroads into managerial jobs in the 1970s and 1980s? They imply that the barriers to managerial titles are more easily breached than those to final authority. A survey of women vice presidents conducted in the same year as our data were collected confirms this inference. The survey organization had to cut its initial sample of over 2,000 women to fewer than 800 because many, despite their titles, worked at relatively low levels (Dipboye, 1987, p. 132). Employers had two incentives to open managerial occupations to women. The first was the same reason they created mobility ladders to management posts for men earlier in this century: to reduce costly turnover. By the 1970s, employers' increased dependence on women prompted them to promote more women to retain their firm-specific human capital. The second incentive was to avoid the appearance of sex discrimination with its risk of sanctions. In the early 1970s, the Equal Employment Opportunity Commission targeted banking and insurance (industries that subsequently gave jobs to tens of thousands of women in management), and 5 years later, the Office of Federal Contract Compliance Programs announced that it would view women's underrepresentation in the broad occupational category manager as prima facie evidence of discrimination (Reskin & Roos, 1990, p. 54). Moreover, during the 1970s, the Equal

Employment Opportunities Commission monitored the numbers of female and minority employees in management in many firms in order to encourage women's and minorities' employment as managers. However, various observers (including the oversight hearings of the Senate Banking Committee) concluded that some employers inflated their statistics by assigning women to managerial job titles without giving them commensurate responsibilities and rewards (Jacobs, Chapter 6, this volume; Miller, 1980; Reskin & Roos, 1990).[14]

Yielding to economic and regulatory agency pressures to increase women's share of management jobs without equalizing authority and its rewards has not substantially altered the gender hierarchy in work organizations and has helped to maintain the managerial wage gap. Although women have made revolutionary gains in access to managerial titles, our findings suggest that the desegregation of managerial occupations has not signaled the decline of sex discrimination in the allocation of workplace authority.

Appendix A

Authority Measures

Managerial level refers to position in the managerial hierarchy, with lower-level management coded 1, middle management 2, upper-level management 3, and top management 4.

Supervisory authority is coded 0 if respondent (R) had no supervisees, 1 if R had supervisees who did not supervise others, and 2 if R's supervisees supervised others.

Total number of subordinates is the number of subordinates reporting directly to R plus the number reporting to R's subordinates.

Authority over most responsible subordinate is coded 1 if manager decides what top subordinates should do and how they should do it, 2 if manager and subordinates decide jointly, and 3 if subordinates decide.

Decision authority is based on manager's involvement in 17 arenas in which final decisions are made: how R's work unit is organized; R's unit's goals; hiring, promoting, firing, transferring, and scheduling subordinates; raising their pay; size of R's unit's budget; how that budget is spent; R's largest monetary decision in the last year; establishing or closing other units, allocating resources to other units, setting other units' budgets; designing procedures to evaluate workers in other units; setting work rules for other units; and setting pay in other units. These 17 arenas fall into four categories (see Table 5.4), which we identified through factor analyses: unit goals and decisions, personnel matters within managers' own unit, unit budget and spending, and matters in other units.

Appendix B

Intercorrelations Among Variables

	2	3	4	5	6	7	8	9	10	11	12	13	14
1. Sex	.05	.20*	.27*	.07	.14*	−.03	.09	−.66*	.09	.23*	.14*	.21*	.42*
2. Education		−.21*	.07	−.15*	−.13*	.04	.11*	.01	.18*	.07	.24*	.16*	.21*
3. Experience			.07	.09	.23*	−.08	−.15*	−.21*	.04	.24*	−.07	.06	.34*
4. Hours				.08	.24*	−.16*	−.12*	−.35*	.08	.30*	.18*	.32*	.25*
5. White					.11*	−.00	−.22*	.02	−.07	.17*	.01	.09	.03
6. Self-employed						.69*	−.26*	−.20*	−.20*	.51*	−.18*	.21*	.06
7. Private employer							.19*	−.25*	.21*	−.25*	.15*	−.06	.07
8. Employer size								−.03	.06	−.37*	.05	−.11*	.06
9. Occupational percentage female									−.10	−.28*	−.18*	−.15*	−.32*
10. Census-designated occupation										.14*	.30*	.33*	.31*
11. Managerial level											.18*	.53*	.31*
12. Supervisory authority												.43*	.26*
13. Decision authority													.30*
14. Earnings													

*Statistically significant at the .05 level.

Final decision authority is a scale that gives respondent 1 point for making final decisions in up to 17 decision arenas.

Census-designated managerial occupation is coded 1 if occupation's reported occupation was included in the broad occupational category "executive, administrative, and managerial" in the 1980 Census (detailed occupational codes 003-037); others are coded 0.

Notes

1. This ratio applies to the occupational classification scheme of the 1970 Census. If 1970 respondents had been coded according to the 1980 scheme (which changed the title of the broad classification to "executives, administrators and managers"), the proportion of females would have been 18.5%.

2. Of course, employers encouraged discontinuous labor force participation by consigning women to jobs that did not reward seniority; indeed, some ensured turnover through rules that required women to quit when they married (Cohn, 1985; Goldin, 1990).

3. Scholars recognize other economic reasons why employers might deny women positions of authority, including the fear that objections from workers, customers, or peers will reduce output, cost them business, or bring ostracism (Reskin & Roos, 1990).

4. For similar findings for Canada, see Boyd et al. (1991).

5. By 1990, this ratio had risen to 65.4% for wage and salary workers (U.S. Bureau of Labor Statistics, 1991).

6. For example, the Census classified branch managers as executives, administrators, or managers if they worked in the banking industry but consigned all other branch managers to the broad occupational category of technical, sales, and administrative support.

7. Of course, statistical tests take into account sample size: Coefficients must be sizable to reject the possibility that they stemmed from sampling error.

8. We omitted from the equations a direct measure of occupational prestige—the SEI—because of its high correlation with education, a theoretically more relevant variable.

9. Another way to control for the effect of self-employment is to exclude the self-employed from the analyses. Regression analyses that were run without the self-employed yielded results (not shown) substantially the same as those we report. We included the self-employed because they represent an important expression of sex segregation in managerial work.

10. Given the zero-order correlations between occupational sex composition and managers' sex, supervisory authority, and managerial level—all of which have moderate to strong independent effects on breadth of final-decision authority—failure to take into account these variables would underestimate the effect of occupational sex composition (see Jaffee, 1989).

11. None of the other sex interactions was statistically reliable at the .05 level for a one-tailed test.

12. We arrived at these values by first solving for the y intercept when we set all control variables equal to their means and then predicting salary for male and female managers in private firms. For men, $y = 25.778 - .669$ (sex = 1) $- 1.754$ (private employer = 1) $+ 9.998$ (sex*private employer = 1); for women, $y = 25.778 - .669$ (sex = 0) $- 1.754$ (private employer = 1) $+ 9.998$ (sex*private employer = 0).

13. To determine the effect of making each additional final decision on men's earnings, we added the coefficient for final-decision making (-1.334) to the coefficient for the sex by decision interaction (1.972).

14. The creation of almost 4.5 million new managerial jobs in the 1970s fostered opening more managerial jobs to women.

References

Acker, J. (1990). Hierarchies, jobs, bodies: A theory of gendered organization. *Gender & Society, 4,* 139-158.

Baron, J. N. (1984). Organizational perspectives on stratification. *Annual Review of Sociology, 10,* 37-69.

Baron, J. N., & Bielby, W. T. (1986). The proliferation of job titles in organizations. *Administrative Science Quarterly, 31,* 561-585.

Baron, J. N., Mittman, B. S., & Newman, A. S. (1991). Targets of opportunity: Organizational and environmental determinants of gender integration with the California Civil Service, 1979-85. *American Journal of Sociology, 96,* 1362-1401.

Bergmann, B. (1986). *The economic emergence of women.* New York: Basic Books.

Bielby, W. T., & Baron, J. N. (1984). A woman's place is with other women: Sex segregation within organizations. In B. F. Reskin (Ed.), *Sex segregation on the job: Trends, explanations, remedies* (pp. 27-55). Washington, DC: National Academy Press.

Cannings, K. (1988). The earnings of female and male middle managers. *Journal of Human Resources, 23,* 35-56.

Churchill, N. C. (1977). Analyzing and modeling human resource flows. In R. G. Shaeffer (Ed.), *Monitoring the human resource system* (Rep. No. 719, pp. 20-29). New York: Conference Board.

Cohn, S. (1985). *The process of occupational sex-typing: The feminization of clerical labor in Great Britain.* Philadelphia: Temple University Press.

Davis, N. Z. (1975). Women on top. In N. Z. Davis (Ed.), *Society and culture in early modern France* (pp. 124-151). Stanford, CA: Stanford University Press.

Dipboye, R. L. (1987). Problems and progress of women in management. In K. S. Koziara, M. H. Moskow, & L. D. Tanner (Eds.), *Working women: Past, present and future* (pp. 118-153). Washington, DC: Bureau of National Affairs.

Edwards, R. (1979). *Contested terrain.* New York: Basic Books.

Fierman, J. (1990, July 30). Why women still don't hit the top. *Fortune,* pp. 40, 42, 46, 50, 54, 58, 62.

Fisher, A. B. (1987, August 3). Where women are succeeding. *Fortune,* pp. 78-86.

Goldin, C. (1990). *Understanding the gender gap.* New York: Oxford University Press.

Halaby, C. N. (1979). Job specific sex differences in organizational reward attainment: Wage discrimination vs. rank segregation. *Social Forces, 58,* 108-127.

Harlan, A., & Weiss, C. (1981). *Moving up: Women in managerial careers* (Working Paper No. 86). Wellesley, MA: Wellesley College Center for Research on Women.

Hartmann, H. I. (1987). Internal labor markets and gender: A case study of promotions. In C. Brown & J. Peckman (Eds.), *Gender in the workplace* (pp. 59-105). Washington, DC: Brookings Institution.

Hill, M. (1980). Authority at work: How men and women differ. In G. J. Duncan & J. Morgan (Eds.), *Five thousand American families* (Vol. 8, pp. 107-146). Ann Arbor: University of Michigan Press.

Hymowitz, C., & Schellhardt, T. D. (1986, March 24). The glass ceiling: Why women can't seem to break the invisible barrier that blocks them from top jobs. *Wall Street Journal* [Special Report on the Corporate Woman], Sec. 4, pp. 1D, 4D, 5D.

Jackall, R. (1988). *Moral mazes.* New York: Oxford University Press.

Jacobs, J. A. (1989). *Revolving doors.* Stanford, CA: Stanford University Press.

Jaffee, D. (1989). Gender inequality in workplace autonomy and authority. *Social Science Quarterly, 70,* 375-390.

Kanter, R. M. (1977). *Men and women of the corporation.* New York: Basic Books.

Kluegel, J. R. (1978). The causes and cost of racial exclusion from job authority. *American Sociological Review, 43,* 285-301.

Konrad, W. (1990, August 6). Welcome to the woman-friendly company. *Business Week,* pp. 48-55.

Larwood, L., Gutek, B., & Gattiker, U. E. (1984). Perspectives on institutional discrimination and resistance to change. *Group and Organization Studies, 9,* 333-352.

Loscocco, K. A., & Robinson, J. (1991). Barriers to women's small-business success in the United States. *Gender & Society, 5,* 511-532.

Markham, W. T., Harlan, S. L., & Hackett, E. J. (1987). Promotion opportunity in organizations. *Research in Personnel and Human Resource Management, 5,* 223-287.

Miller, A. R. (1980). Occupational statistics and labor force analysis. *Proceedings of the American Statistical Association: Social Statistics,* pp. 108-115.

Powell, G. (1988). *Men and women in management.* Newbury Park, CA: Sage.

Reskin, B. F. (1988). Bringing the men back in: Sex differentiation and the devaluation of women's work. *Gender & Society, 2*(1), 58-81.

Reskin, B. F., & Hartmann, H. I. (1986). *Women's work, men's work: Sex segregation on the job.* Washington, DC: National Academy Press.

Reskin, B. F., & Hartmann, H. I. (in press). Job segregation: Trends and prospects. In S. Harlan & R. J. Steinberg (Eds.), *Women's careers: Research and strategies for change.* Philadelphia: Temple University Press.

Reskin, B. F., & Roos, P. A. (1990). *Job queues, gender queues: Explaining women's inroads into male occupations.* Philadelphia: Temple University Press.

Roos, P. A. (1981). Sex stratification in the workplace: Male-female differences in economic returns to occupation. *Social Science Research, 10,* 195-224.

Rytina, N. F. (1982, April). Earnings of men and women: A look at specific occupations. *Monthly Labor Review,* pp. 25-31.

Shaeffer, R. G., & Lynton, E. F. (1979). *Corporate experiences in improving women's job opportunities.* New York: Conference Board.

Spaeth, J. L. (1985). Job power and earnings. *American Sociological Review, 50,* 603-617.

U.S. Bureau of Labor Statistics. (1982, January). *Employment and earnings.* Washington, DC: U.S. Department of Labor.

U.S. Bureau of Labor Statistics. (1991, January). *Employment and earnings.* Washington, DC: U.S. Department of Labor.

U.S. Bureau of the Census. (1980, July). *1980 census of population: Alphabetical index of industries and occupations* (1st ed.). Washington, DC: U.S. Government Printing Office.

U.S. Bureau of the Census. (1984). *1984 census of population: Occupation by industry* (PC80-2-7C). Washington, DC: U.S. Government Printing Office.

U.S. National Center for Education Statistics. (1987). *Digest of educational statistics.* Washington, DC: U.S. Government Printing Office.

Ward, K. B., & Mueller, C. W. (1985). Sex differences in earnings: The effects of industrial sector, authority hierarchy, and human-capital variables. *Work and Occupations, 12,* 437-463.

Wilson, K. L., & Boldizar, J. P. (1990). Gender segregation in higher education. *Sociology of Education, 63,* 62-74.

Wolf, W. C., & Fligstein, N. D. (1979). Sex and authority in the workplace: The causes of sexual inequality. *American Sociological Review, 44,* 235-252.

Wright, E. O., & Perrone, L. (1977). Marxist class categories and income inequality. *American Sociological Review, 42,* 32-55.

6

Women's Entry Into Management

Trends in Earnings, Authority, and Values Among Salaried Managers

JERRY A. JACOBS

The increasing representation of women among the ranks of managers in organizations in the United States is perhaps the most dramatic shift in the sex composition of an occupation since clerical work became a female-dominated field in the late 19th century. In 1970, census data indicated that one in six American managers was a woman; today more than two in five are women. Far more women are managers than are lawyers, doctors, architects, computer specialists, engineers, and natural scientists combined, even though women have entered each of these fields in large numbers in recent years. The surge in the number of women managers accounts for fully one quarter of the decline in occupational sex segregation since 1970.[1] Yet much recent data indicate the continued paucity of women among senior-level managers. The expres-

AUTHOR'S NOTE: This chapter was prompted by discussions with Vicki Smith and Claudia Goldin. The author gratefully acknowledges the comments and suggestions of several anonymous reviewers as well as James N. Baron, Michael Foster, Saul Hoffman, Robin Leidner, Marshall Meyer, David Neumark, Werner von der Ohe, Brian Powell, Samuel H. Preston, Barbara Reskin, Vicki Smith, Michael Useem, and Rosemary Wright. Reprinted from "Women's Entry into Management: Trends in Earnings, Authority, and Values among Salaried Managers," by Jerry A. Jacobs, published in *Administrative Science Quarterly 372*, 282-301 by permission of the *Administrative Science Quarterly*. ©1992.

sion "the glass ceiling" has become a familiar term for describing the invisible but powerful barriers to advancement for women executives (e.g., Garland, 1991).

Recent surveys confirm the near complete absence of women from top managerial positions. *Fortune Magazine* recently surveyed 799 of the largest U.S. industrial and service companies and found that only 19 of the 4,012 (less than half of 1%) highest paid officers and directors were women (Fierman, 1990). Of the next echelon of managers, 5% were women. Another survey, by the *Catalyst* organization, found that less than 3% of the top executives in *Fortune 500* companies were women (Ball, 1991).

Research on recent M.B.A. recipients yields a more favorable reading of women's gains than do the studies of top executives. Olson and Frieze's (1987) review of the literature on the earnings of male and female M.B.A. holders reports that although many of these studies found little or no gender difference in starting salaries, studies that followed business graduates for a longer period after graduation were more likely to show a significant gender gap in earnings.

A great deal of research has documented the difficulties women have faced in advancing through the ranks of managers. Studies of corporations and other settings have shown that women are far less likely to attain positions of authority within organizations than their male counterparts (Boyd & Mulvihill, 1990; Freeman, 1990; Kanter, 1977; Powell, 1988; Reskin & Ross, 1992; Wolf & Fligstein, 1979). A recent international review of the sexual division of labor in the workplace maintains that the generalization "men control, women obey" continues to hold (Bradley, 1989, p. 1). In light of this pattern of evidence regarding the barriers to the progress of women managers, many specialists in the area of women's opportunities are understandably skeptical when presented with census data showing the remarkable entry of women into management and wonder whether these women are really managers in anything other than title. Here, I attempt to determine whether the growth of women managers is real or is the result of artificial reclassification of women without a corresponding real change in earnings or authority.

Skeptical Interpretations of Women's Entry Into Management

Has women's representation among the ranks of managers increased from 18% to 40%, as national survey data indicate? After extensive discussions of these trends with students, colleagues, and specialists, I have concluded that the principal skepticisms of these data can be grouped into three arguments. First, this trend may simply be capturing the artificial reclassification of women into managerial positions to avoid difficulties with the Equal Employment Opportunities Commission (EEOC). Second, these data may paper over an underlying process of resegregation, that is, selected managerial specialties become female dominated while the preponderance of management remains a male bastion. Third, these trends may reflect a general inflation of organizational titles. I refer to these as the glorified secretary, the resegregation, and the title inflation hypotheses.

Glorified-Secretary Hypothesis. Equal Employment Opportunity (EEO) regulations require all firms with over 100 employees and federal contractors with over 50 employees to file an EEO-1 report indicating the number of workers at each level in the firm, and the sex, race, and ethnic composition of its employees. Because the EEO reporting categories are quite broad, employers are able to classify may individuals with little authority as managers.[2] Smith and Welch (1984) reported that there was a rapid increase in the proportion of employees classified as managers during the early years of EEO filing requirements. Miller (1980, p. 109) noticed the rapid rise in the representation of women in management and suggested that "there has been considerable retitling of positions in some large organizations: Under the impetus of affirmative action the administrative secretary has become the administrative assistant or the business administrator and is therefore now classified as a managerial worker." The first hypothesis, then, is that firms responded to external pressures cosmetically, in the designation of positions rather than in the substance of their behavior.

(It is possible that before women's rapid acquisition of managerial titles, many women had a great deal of responsibility with no formal recognition. The distribution of supervisory titles to many formerly subordinate women may have been a belated recognition of their real contributions.)

Resegregation Hypothesis. The resegregation thesis is most effectively developed by Reskin and Roos (1990) in their analysis of the feminization of a dozen occupations. They find that the entry of women into previously male-dominated fields neither represents true desegregation nor generates the gains in earnings and other rewards that might have been expected. In general, the status of these occupations was declining even before women entered; men were already leaving or joining in diminishing numbers; often technological change was lowering the skill requirements of the positions; and salaries and advancement opportunities were declining even before women entered. Reskin and Roos found that an erosion of the status of the occupation preceded women's entry but was reinforced by the feminization of the occupation.

Bird's (1990) study of bank branch managers provides an example of this process of resegregation. She found that the growth of employment in banking during the 1970s, pressure from the EEOC, and the availability of highly educated young women interested in the field led to a rapid influx of women into bank management. Yet women's gains were concentrated among lower-level management, particularly as branch managers, whose authority was already in decline. Bird (1990, p. 164) concludes that "Retail banking, particularly branch management, has become a female ghetto for many women whose chances to advance depend on the opportunity to get experience in other areas of banking." If the case of bank branch managers were typical, women's gains in income and authority would not be commensurate with their increased representation among managers.

Title-Inflation Hypothesis. A final skeptical interpretation of the apparent entry of women into management is that it simply reflects the general proliferation of managerial titles. The scores of vice presidents at financial institutions is a familiar example of this tendency. This view holds that the entry of women into management coincided with a dissemination of managerial titles to positions without significant status or authority. However, the extensive downsizing by corporations during the 1980s may have reversed the trend in the growth of middle management (Pfeffer & Baron, 1988; Smith, 1990), and, consequently, this hypothesis may be more plausible for the 1970s than the 1980s.

Data on trends in earnings and authority can help us to ascertain the underlying trends for women and men in the broad ranks of management, not just the few top positions. What specific implication do these hypotheses hold for changes in pay and authority? First, if the entry of women into management were simply a ploy by firms to circumvent reporting requirements, as the glorified-secretary thesis holds, then the sex gap in earnings and authority among managers would have expanded over the last 20 years. This is true because adding large numbers of women to the lowest ranks of management would depress the average wage of women managers without substantially changing the position of male managers. Thus, among managers, the sex gap in earnings would have grown if this skeptical reading of recent changes is correct. The same reasoning would predict a growing sex gap in authority. (If women had previously been confined to the very bottom rungs of management, then there would have been no change in their position relative to men with the addition of many glorified secretaries.) The resegregation hypothesis similarly predicts no improvement in the position of women managers relative to men. Finally, the title inflation hypothesis implies that the earnings and authority of all managers have fallen relative to the earnings of other workers. Again, among managers women would not have been expected to gain.

Social Change and Organizational Theory

The entry of women into management no doubt had its impetus from developments outside organizations—the rise of the women's movement, the passage of equal opportunity legislation, the rapid rise in women's pursuit of M.B.A. degrees. The question here is how organizations responded to these developments. Relatively few theories provide a basis for understanding the degree of organizational resistance against women or the circumstances in which this resistance might change. For example, Acker's (1990) analysis of gender inequality within institutions does not offer specific predictions about when such inequality would be expected to be high and when it might be expected to decline. Other researchers have examined variation across a set of organizations in order to identify which are more likely to respond to environmental pressure for change (e.g., Baron, Mittman, & Newman, 1991; Bridges & Nelson, 1989). The problem here is a bit different: to explain the average response of organizations to the influx of women into management.

One theory that predicts the direction of organizational response was advanced by Kanter (1977), who argued that women gain political strength and social support networks as they increase their representation within organizations. Her theory incorporates both political and social-psychological elements on the effect of proportions on the opportunities available to women and minorities. She has argued that minority groups were especially vulnerable when their numbers were small, with token women representing the extreme case. Small numbers meant fewer political allies, fewer mentors and role models, and more visibility yet, paradoxically, a greater chance to become viewed stereotypically. She argued that each of these difficulties would tend to be mitigated as the proportions of the minority group climbed within the organization. Thus, from Kanter's analysis we may derive the hypothesis that increasing representation of women in the ranks of management can be expected to increase their chances of advancement along with the attendant financial rewards and authority (see also Pfeffer & Davis-Blake, 1987). I refer to this as the strength-in-numbers hypothesis.

An alternative prediction derives from an opposite view of the impact of proportions on discrimination. Blalock (1967) has maintained that resistance to minority groups increases as their numbers increase. Blalock reached this conclusion after studying residential segregation between whites and African Americans, yet the underlying logic can be applied to gender conflict in organizational settings (Pfeffer & Davis-Blake, 1987). The Blalockian prediction, then, would be that the relative position of female managers would decline as their numbers increase. I will refer to this as the resistance-to-threats hypothesis.

The Blalockian resistance-to-threats hypothesis leads to the same predictions as the several skeptical hypotheses outlined above, whereas Kanter's strength-in-numbers thesis would be consistent with a narrowing of the gap in earnings and authority between male and female managers. These theories can also be tested by examining variation across firms. Although I lack firm-level data, I did conduct tests of industry and occupations to determine whether the progress of women was greatest (or smallest) in areas where they entered in the largest numbers. Each of the predictions could be specified in two forms, one predicting the gross changes observed and another predicting the net size of sex differences after productivity-related measures are controlled. The results address both forms of these predictions.

Methods

Data. A nationally representative sample of 127,125 respondents to the 1970 Census were assigned 1980 occupation and industry codes in conjunction with the 1980 Census (Priebe, 1985; see also Treiman, Bielby, & Cheng, 1988). This double coding enabled me to compare these data with those for 1988, using the same (1980 Census) definition of management. The sample was restricted to those who worked at least 26 weeks and at least 30 hours per week in 1969. For 1970, the sample yielded 8,158 managers, including 1,463 women (17.9%).

Data for 1988 were obtained from the March 1988 Current Population Survey (CPS), a survey of 117,849 individuals. For 1988, the same restrictions of hours and weeks worked produced a sample of 7,039 managers, including 3,084 women (43.9%). Because women were disproportionately represented in the March 1988 CPS data, this 43.9% does not represent the proportion of women managers in the labor force. The 39.3% of managers who were women, reported above, reflects the weighted annual average of women in management based on the U.S. Department of Labor's January 1989 *Employment and Earnings* data. These two data sets were merged in order to create a pooled cross-sectional time series (with two time points).

Census occupational classifications are often quite broadly defined, with management occupations proving particularly difficult to specify. Census experts have repeatedly tried to refine the definition of managers, with limited success. The largest group of managers in 1988—nearly half of all managers—remains "managers, not elsewhere classified."

Employees defined as managers should have positions of authority within organizations and in general should have at least a limited degree of supervisory responsibility. It should be noted, however, that the staff members of executives in line positions are typically also included as managerial-level employees. The particulars of managerial authority vary, sometimes including responsibility for hiring, firing, and promoting, controlling budgets, setting goals, and developing, recommending, and monitoring policies and procedures. Unfortunately, the census question regarding a respondent's occupation does not probe respondents on whether they actually have supervisory authority. To check the validity of the census data on managers, additional data on supervisory responsibility were obtained from the General Social Survey (GSS).

A major obstacle that confounds precise estimates of labor force time trends is the fact that occupational classifications change with every decennial census. Several changes in the definition of managers between the 1970 and 1980 U. S. Censuses should be noted. First, proprietors are now excluded, a change that significantly enhances the earnings position of managers. Second, management-related occupations—such as accountants, auditors, underwriters, and other financial officers—are defined as managers in the 1980 Census definitions, whereas in 1970 they had been classified as professionals. In the empirical analysis, I consider whether using a narrower definition of management that excludes management-related occupations yields the same results as the broader definition. Another important point to note about the current definition of management is that clerical supervisors are excluded from management. Although in principle this exclusion should resolve the glorified secretary question, it nonetheless may be the case that women clerical supervisors misreport themselves as managers. As discussed below, the analysis circumvents the complications posed by the changing definition of management by using a special subsample from the 1970 Census that used 1980 Census titles, along with supplemental analyses using GSS data that employed the 1970 Census titles throughout the 1970s and 1980s.

The earnings measure used is the total annual wage and salary earnings of the individual. It should be noted that the sex gap in earnings is somewhat larger for annual, as compared with hourly, earnings. In the multivariate analysis, the log of earnings is the dependent variable. This measure is conventional in analyses of earnings because it corrects for nonlinear earnings effects and it is easy to interpret in terms of percentage change in earnings. The earnings pertain to the previous year, so that the 1988 data include information on 1987 earnings, and the 1970 data include information on 1969 earnings. Self-employed individuals, as well as those with zero or negative earnings, are excluded from the analysis.

In 1988, 2.6% of managers earned $99,999 or more, the top amount allowed in the coding scheme. The overwhelming majority of these were men. These individuals on average earned considerably more than $99,999, and consequently this figure was adjusted upward to correct for the bias imposed by this top-coding procedure.[3] Data on each individual's sex, years of school completed, hours and weeks worked, and industry were analyzed. Potential labor force experience was estimated as age minus years of schooling completed minus 6. The lack of direct data on experience is an unfortunate limitation of this analysis.

Additional data were obtained from the General Social Survey (GSS), a survey of individuals conducted annually from 1972 through 1989. The GSS data represent a pooled cross-sectional time series with 16 time points (in 1979 and 1981 surveys were not conducted). These data are repeated cross-sections, not panel data following individuals over time. Whereas the larger CPS sample provides more reliable estimates of time trends, the GSS data are of interest because of the broader range of questions included. First, a set of questions on supervisory and subordinate status enabled me to examine sex differences and trends in this basic characteristic of management. I considered whether women were as likely to supervise as men, whether the gap in supervisory authority grew or shrank between the 1970s and 1980s, and whether sex differences in authority help to explain the sex gap in wages. Because these data do not include information on the sex of bosses and subordinates, however, I was unable to test the findings of Boyd and Mulvihill (1990) and Reskin and Ross (1992), who reported that most women managers supervise female subordinates.

A second set of questions in the GSS data pertain to work-related attitudes. Respondents were asked whether they would continue to work, even if they could afford not to. Later, they were asked to rank five aspects of work: high income, job security, short hours, chances for advancement, and meaningful work. I examined sex differences and trends in these variables and explored their impact on the sex gap in wages. The questions were worded as follows:

Do you have a supervisor on your job to whom you are directly responsible? If yes, does that person have a supervisor on the job to whom he is directly responsible?

In your job, do you supervise anyone who is directly responsible to you? If yes, do any of those persons supervise anyone else?

If you were to get enough money to live as comfortably as you would like for the rest of your life, would you continue to work or would you stop working?

Would you please look at this card and tell me which *one* thing on this list you would *most* prefer in a job? Which comes *next?* Which is *third* most important? Which is *fourth* most important? The items listed on the card were High Income; No danger of being fired; Working hours are short, lots of free time; Chances for advancement; and Work important and gives a feeling of accomplishment.

Two additional points concerning the GSS data should be noted. First, the GSS data were coded with the 1970 Census definition of management, and thus provide data on an 18-year period with the 1970 codes, whereas the CPS-census comparison represents an 18-year comparison with 1980 Census codes. Second, GSS data have only a small number of African American managers ($N = 112$, or 4.5%). Consequently, the issue of trends in the earnings of African American managers is not addressed with these data.

I examine trends in sex segregation within management across occupation and industry classifications with the standard index of dissimilarity (D), and the P* measure, introduced by Lieberson (1980) and previously employed by Jacobs (1989b). P* indicates the probability that a random coworker in one's occupation is of the opposite sex. Unlike the index of segregation, P* is influenced by the relative size of different groups and reflects more closely the way changes in segregation are experienced. The P* measure will be of assistance in assessing the strength-in-numbers and resistance-to-threats hypotheses.

Results

CPS Trends

Table 6.1 presents mean earnings data for all salaried managers with earnings in 1987 and 1969, and earnings figures by educational level for full-time, full-year managers. In nominal terms, women's wages rose 3.5-fold during this 18-year period, whereas male managers' wages rose 3.2-fold. In real terms, this represented only slight progress for the men, because according to the U. S. Bureau of the Census (1989), prices increased 3.1-fold between 1969 and 1987; women managers' real earnings rose 13%.

Although not central to our concerns here, it is nonetheless interesting to note that the earnings ratio of managers to other employees narrowed during this period. Relative to other full-time, full-year working men, male managers earned 1.45 times as much in 1969 and 1.44 times as much in 1987. Female managers earned 1.32 times the average of other working women in 1969 and 1.37 times as much in 1987. This finding provides little support for the view that managerial title inflation decreased the standing of managers relative to other groups in the labor force. Declines in these ratios might be viewed by Pfeffer and Davis-Blake (1987) as evidence of a decline in status resulting from the entry of women into the occupation.

Women's earnings as a fraction of men's increased from 54.5% to 59.8% over this 18-year period. For full-time, full-year managers, the sex ratio of earnings rose from 56.9% to 61.1. These results indicate that the growth of women in management was not entirely artifactual: The sex gap in wages did not grow, but, instead, narrowed by a modest amount. Yet the sex gap in wages among managers remained quite large in 1987 and even slightly exceeded that in the labor force as a whole. In 1987, women working full-time, full-year earned 64.6% of their male counterparts (as estimated from the CPS data), compared to the 61.1 ratio among managers.

It is likely that a more comprehensive measure of work rewards that included stock options, golden parachutes, pensions, and other perks

Table 6.1 Annual Earnings of Managers, by Sex, Full-Time Full-Year Status, and Education, 1969 and 1987

Median Annual Earnings	Total	Full-Time, Full-Year				
		Total	≤ High School Graduate	Some College	College Graduate	Post-Graduate
1969						
Female	$ 6,000	$ 6,600	$ 6,000	$ 7,000	$ 8,000	$11,000
Male	$11,000	$11,600	$10,000	$11,000	$14,000	$16,000
Female/Male	54.5%	56.9%	60.0%	63.6%	57.1%	68.8%
1987						
Female	$20,935	$22,000	$15,400	$20,000	$21,100	$26,000
Male	$35,000	$36,000	$26,000	$30,000	$33,500	$41,000
Female/Male	59.8%	61.1%	59.2%	67.7%	62.9%	63.4%

NOTE: Full-time, full-year means over 50 weeks per year and over 35 hours per week. Data are from the March 1988 CPS and the 1970 U.S. Census.

would show even larger sex differences among managers (see also Abowd, 1991; Jencks, Perman, & Rainwater, 1988). A related consideration is that the highly skewed pattern of earnings among managers allows for a larger sex gap in earnings within this group.

The educational breakdown provided in Table 6.1 for full-time, full-year workers indicates that part of the sex gap in wages among managers is attributable to hours and weeks worked and educational levels. Yet the sex gap in wages among full-time workers remains dramatic, even after educational levels are controlled.

The analysis presented in Table 6.1 was repeated with a narrower definition of management occupations. This analysis excluded management-related occupations—such as accountants—from the analysis. The pattern of results, however, is very much the same, both in terms of the male-female differentials and trends over time.

I analyzed data on changes in occupation and industry distribution between 1969 and 1987. The results indicate a slight decline in occupational sex segregation among managers, with the index of segregation dropping from 17.9 to 17.0. More notable was the decline in industrial segregation, which fell from 27.3 to 20.8 measured across nine broad industrial groupings. These data do not support the notion that the ranks of management experienced a process of resegregation, in the sense of specialties becoming increasingly segregated by sex.

Also of note are the dramatic changes in the chances of sharing an occupation with a woman manager. For men, the probability of sharing an occupation with a woman increased from 13.6% in 1969 to 40.5% in 1987. In other words, male managers have not been able to resegregate their work to reestablish the distance from women managers evident 20 years ago. During the same period, women managers moved from being relatively isolated minorities to a situation in which they are almost as likely to share an occupation with a woman as with a man. Women managers' chances of sharing an occupation with another woman, only 16.4% in 1969, increased markedly to 45.7% by 1987. These measures are significant for the Kanter and Blalockian hypotheses, because they pertain to the experience of change in segregation as seen by men and women. These contact indicators suggest that women may be beginning to experience strength in numbers, and they also suggest that male managers have failed to respond to the threat of women's entrance by effectively resegregating managerial specialties.

Analyses not reported here show that the attributes of male and female managers changed in the interim (summary statistics available from the author.) Women managers trail their male counterparts in education and hours and weeks worked. In each of these areas the differences remained of comparable magnitude during the 1969-1987 period. The mean differences are smaller than those observed at the extremes, as there is less variation among women on these measures than among men. The infusion of younger women into management lowered the average age of women managers from 44 to 38, whereas male managers' average age declined by just over 1 year. In the more recent period, then, the age differential may explain a portion of the wage differential, the reverse of the situation in 1970.

A multivariate analysis of changes in earnings is presented in Table 6.2. This is a pooled cross-sectional analysis in which data from the 1970 Census and the 1988 CPS are analyzed together, with a term to capture changes in earnings levels between the 2 years.

The analysis focuses on sex differences in earnings and the time trend in women's earnings relative to men's. The log of annual earnings is the dependent variable. The results reported are restricted to white males and females because of the limited number of cases for African Americans. Comparisons with the patterns observed for African American managers are discussed when there are sufficient data.

Table 6.2 Determinants of Wages of Male and Female Managers

Variable	Model 1	Model 2	Model 3†	Model 4†
Intercept	2.426*	−0.042*	0.052	−0.026
	(.008)	(.045)	(.046)	(.047)
Female	−0.676*	−0.525*	−0.471*	−0.459*
	(.019)	(.017)	(.017)	(.017)
Year	1.091*	0.951*	0.954*	0.953*
	(.012)	(.011)	(.011)	(.011)
Female*Year	0.175*	0.193*	0.173*	0.169*
	(.024)	(.021)	(.021)	(.021)
Education		0.084*	0.086*	0.087*
		(.002)	(.002)	(.002)
Hours worked:				
30–34				
35–39		0.072*	0.070*	0.072*
		(.028)	(.028)	(.028)
40		0.108*	0.100*	0.104*
		(.024)	(.024)	(.024)
41–48		0.182*	0.177*	0.174*
		(.026)	(.025)	(.025)
49–59		0.235*	0.234*	0.223*
		(.026)	(.026)	(.026)
60+		0.205*	0.222*	0.211*
		(.028)	(.027)	(.028)
Weeks worked:				
26–39				
40–47		0.310*	0.308*	0.310*
		(.034)	(.033)	(.033)
48–49		0.458*	0.450*	0.451**
		(.036)	(.034)	(.035)
50–52		0.626*	0.597*	0.599*
		(.027)	(.026)	(.026)
Experience (potential)		0.044*	0.044*	0.042*
		(.001)	(.001)	(.001)
Experience^2/100 (potential)		−0.069*	−0.067*	−0.064*
		(.003)	(.003)	(.003)
Adjusted R^2	0.160	0.376	0.397	0.407

NOTE: Standard errors are in parentheses. N of cases is 13,575. The dependent variable is log of wages. †Model 3 adds controls for 7 broad industry dummy variables and Model 4 adds controls for 12 detailed occupational dummy variables (see text for details). Coefficients available from the author.
*$p < .001$; **$p < .05$.

The baseline equation includes whether individuals are female, a time trend (Year), and a Year*Sex interaction term. Other variables are gradually added in order to explain the sex gap in wages. Once these additional variables are controlled, the resultant sex gap in wages should be smaller than the initial gap.

The first model presented in Table 6.2 indicates that there has been a positive trend in wages for women managers relative to men between 1969 and 1987. This conclusion is substantiated by the positive coefficient on the Year*Female interaction term. Net of the overall trend toward higher wages between 1969 and 1987, women's wages improved relative to men's. Nonetheless, women in 1987 remained lower paid than their male counterparts. The relative position of women in 1987 can be ascertained by adding together the female coefficient with the Year*Female interaction term. Because there is a large negative coefficient associated with being a female and a small positive interaction term, women in 1987 remained at a net disadvantage compared with men.

Model 2 adds controls for education, hours worked, weeks worked, and age to the analysis. The unexplained sex gap in wages declines by a modest amount in this equation, but the positive trend in women's wages relative to men's remains unchanged. This result is significant in that it indicates that the positive time trend for women managers is not principally due to their changing attributes. I tested for a positive time trend in returns to education and did not find such a pattern among these managers.

Model 3 adds controls for industry. The industrial controls consisted of seven dummy variables: retail sales, wholesale trade, utilities, consumer services, business services, social services, and public administration. The reference category was a combination of manufacturing, mining, and construction. Farming was excluded from the analysis.

Model 4 adds detailed occupational controls within the managerial titles. The occuational controls consisted of 12 dummy variables: public officials, personnel managers, financial managers, administrators of protective services, purchasing managers, public relations managers, educational administrators, health administrators, property managers, postmasters, funeral directors, and managers not elsewhere classified. Management-related occupations was the reference category. The addition of these measures explains a modest fraction of the sex gap in earnings among managers. Overall, 32.1% of the gender differential is explained in this analysis, with the majority (22.3%) due to education, hours and weeks worked, and experience differentials.

Results not shown repeat the earnings analysis with a narrower definition of management. As has been noted, the patterns of results for the narrower definition of management closely match those obtained on the broader set of managerial titles. In all, these results support the view that the large increase in female representation has not resulted in a growing gap in earnings between male and female managers.

A further bit of evidence for the positive trend in women's relative wages is that the unexplained gap in earnings declined between 1969 and 1987. In 1969, only 29.1% of the sex gap in earnings could be explained by the variables included in Table 6.2; by 1987, the same variables explained 44.7% of gap. Thus not only has the size of the sex differential diminished, but the residual that may be attributed to discrimination has become attenuated. Thus the evidence points in the direction of Kanter's strength-in-numbers view and against the predictions of the other three hypotheses. Tests of selection bias indicate that the positive time trend cannot be explained by changes in the process of selection of women into management. I computed probabilities of employment in management for the entire GSS sample with a logistic regression equation and reestimated the wage equations including this measure of selectivity. Although this measure is often significant, it does not significantly affect the gender and time trend coefficients in the wage equations.

An additional analysis (not shown) sought to ascertain whether women have narrowed the earnings gap more quickly in certain industries and occupations than others. I tested a series of industry by gender by time interaction terms, which indicate whether the time trend for women in any industry or occupation differed from the baseline trend observed for the sample as a whole. None of the interaction terms were statistically significant. This evidence is at odds with both the Kanter strength-in-numbers and the Blalock's resistance-to-threats hypotheses, which respectively predict differences to be positively or negatively associated with the increased concentration of women. These tests may be weak because they were applied to industries and occupations and not firms; nonetheless, the failure of any of the large number of interaction tests to be significant does indicate a striking uniformity in the pattern of change for women managers.

In other analyses not shown, African American managers earned less than white managers, and there was no statistically significant evidence of a narrowing of this differential for African American men. The Year*Black coefficient was positive, but not significant. However, the earnings trends for African American women closely matched those found for white women. The control variables included in this analysis explain a larger proportion of race difference in earnings than is evident for the sex gap, principally because of the larger educational differentials between African American and white managers.

GSS Trends, Values, and Attitudes

Gender Differences in Supervisory Status

Table 6.3 presents the responses of managers to questions regarding their supervisory status. Women are slightly less likely than men to be employed in supervisory positions (73%, versus 79% for men). The sex gap in supervision may have diminished slightly between the 1970s and 1980s, but it appears to be of comparable magnitude. These differences just fail to be statistically significant for each of the two time periods, 1972-1979 and 1980-1989.

I draw two conclusions from these results. First, because supervisory responsibility is such a fundamental indicator of managerial status, and because nearly three of four women managers supervise others, these data indicate that most women managers are managers in fact and not just in title. Although many women may be office managers with a small number of women subordinates, these data do not support the hypothesis that there has been a wholesale upgrading of women with no supervisory status into the ranks of management. A second inference that supports the same conclusion is the fact that the sex gap in supervisory status has not grown during this period. Had firms bestowed managerial titles on large numbers of women who had no supervisory authority, we would see the sex gap in authority grow over time. Yet no indication of such a divergence is evident in these data. Again, the data support the conclusion that women have held their own, if not advanced, as their numbers increased.

A second important finding in Table 6.3 is that men are much more likely to be located at higher levels of management. Over half of the male managers, versus only one in three female managers, reported that their subordinates in turn supervised others. This difference persisted into the 1980s. Women managers also have less autonomy than their male counterparts, as they are more likely to report having a boss. There were no differences in distance from the top of the organization, in that roughly three of four male and female managers reported that their boss had a boss. Table 6.3 leaves us with the slightly odd result that men are further from the bottom of their organizations than women, but at similar dis-

Table 6.3 Proportions Reporting Supervisory and Subordinate Status by Sex and Time Period Among Managers, GSS Data

Variable	Total		1972–1979		1980–1989	
	Men	Women	Men	Women	Men	Women
Do you supervise	78.98	73.15*	79.38	71.43	78.73	73.75
anyone? (% yes)	(1.42)	(1.96)	(2.27)	(3.93)	(1.83)	(2.26)
	(N = 823)	(N = 514)	(N = 320)	(N = 133)	(N = 503)	(N = 381)
Do your subordinates	54.53	34.14*	56.40	29.79*	53.18	35.61*
supervise anyone?	(1.97)	(2.46)	(3.14)	(4.74)	(2.52)	(2.88)
	(N = 643)	(N = 372)	(N = 250)	(N = 94)	(N = 393)	(N = 278)
Do you have a boss?	59.81	65.84**	58.94	58.65	60.38	68.29**
	(1.67)	(2.07)	(2.67)	(4.29)	(2.15)	(2.36)
	(N = 861)	(N = 341)	(N = 341)	(N = 133)	(N = 520)	(N = 391)
Does your boss have	71.09	73.61	73.47	72.00	69.58	74.06
a boss?	(2.02)	(2.39)	(3.16)	(5.22)	(2.62)	(2.69)
	(N = 505)	(N = 524)	(N = 196)	(N = 75)	(N = 309)	(N = 266)
Would not work if	23.76	25.61	23.62	25.29	23.83	23.35
had enough money	(1.54)	(2.06)	(2.67)	(5.21)	(1.88)	(2.22)
	(N = 766)	(N = 449)	(N = 254)	(N = 85)	(N = 512)	(N = 364)
Rank-ordered preference for:						
Meaningful work	1.90	1.63*	1.86	1.57*	1.91	1.65*
	(.04)	(.04)	(.07)	(.09)	(.05)	(.05)
Chances for	2.47	2.44	2.50	2.47	2.46	2.43
advancement	(.04)	(.04)	(.07)	(.10)	(.05)	(.05)
High income	2.58	2.77*	2.69	2.97*	2.51	2.71*
	(.03)	(.04)	(.06)	(.09)	(.04)	(.05)
Job security	3.91	3.93	3.92	3.89	3.90	3.94
	(.04)	(.04)	(.06)	(.09)	(.05)	(.05)
Short hours	4.15	4.22	4.02	4.10	4.21	4.26
	(.04)	(.04)	(.06)	(.10)	(.05)	(.05)
	(N = 899)	(N = 580)	(N = 325)	(N = 132)	(N = 574)	(N = 448)

NOTE: Standard errors are in parentheses.
$*p < .01$; $**p < .05$, differences in means between men and women.

tances from the top. This incongruity may be reconciled by the fact that men tend to be salaried managers in larger organizations. This would enable men to supervise more layers of subordinates while remaining the same distance from the top. Unfortunately, these data do not include a measure of firm size that would enable us to substantiate this inference.

Do these differences in supervisory status have an impact on income? To facilitate this analysis, I created an index of supervisory level: 0 indicating no subordinates, 1 representing the presence of subordinates, and 2 indicating that subordinates also supervise. A parallel index of subordinate status was constructed from the questions regarding bosses. I estimated a series of regression equations parallel to those presented in Table 6.2 to test the impact of supervisory status and other measures on the sex gap in income. The first notable result (data not shown) is that women managers' incomes have risen relative to men's over time, net of the overall trend toward higher wages (the Year*Female term is positive). The results obtained on the GSS data confirm the results of the CPS data that the sex gap in incomes among managers has declined over the last 20 years.

Another striking result of these GSS analyses is that the addition of training, work effort, and industry variables has little impact on the positive trend in women managers' incomes. The Year*Female coefficient remains close to constant across Models 1 through 4. Thus, the relative increase in women's incomes is not due to a change in women's attributes relative to men's on the variables included in these models. The principal caveat required for this generalization is that it may not apply to work experience, which neither these data nor the CPS data measure directly.

The results also indicate that the index of supervisory status has a positive effect on income. (A test of an interaction between female and supervisory status failed to indicate that women obtain any lower returns from supervisory status than their male counterparts.) Interestingly, more levels of management above the respondent also had a positive effect on income. I interpret this somewhat unexpected result as evidence that larger organizations with more levels of hierarchy tend to pay their managers more than smaller organizations. This interpretation is bolstered by the fact that the addition of industry controls attenuates this effect, a result one would expect, because the industry measures are a loose proxy for organizational size.

Overall, the impact of the two measures of supervisory status on the sex gap in income is modest. The introduction of these variables reduces the direct negative effect of sex on income by only a small amount. After adding these measures in Model 4, the female coefficient falls 3.1%, from −.813 to −.788.

The effects of education, hours worked, and potential experience are all positive, as expected. Experience squared is negative, again following well-established findings. Marital status has no direct impact on income, but once interaction terms are introduced in Model 5, being married has a negative impact on income for women and a positive impact on income for men. This result corresponds with the findings of other studies on the influence of marriage on wages (Korenman & Neumark, 1991). The sign on the two measures of the presence of children is negative for women managers, but only the measure of children under age 6 achieves statistical significance in these data. I tested whether women have lower returns to experience; in these data the sign for this interaction is in the expected (negative) direction but is not statistically significant.

The controls for education, hours, experience, marital status, children at home, supervisory status, and industry together contribute significantly to the explained variance (R^2 rises from .160 to .351 when these variables are included), yet only a modest fraction (14.5%) of the sex gap in income among managers is accounted for by these factors. The negative coefficient for females is −.942 in Model 1 and −.805 in Model 4, leaving 85.5% of the male-female differential unexplained. The addition of interaction terms in Model 5 makes a direct comparison of Model 1 and Model 5 inappropriate. Further, the positive time trend is only slightly diminished by the addition of these controls.

In additional analyses not shown, I repeated the interaction tests of gender and industry trends previously discussed for the CPS data. The results, again in concordance with the CPS findings, indicated no significant industry by gender by time trend interactions. I also conducted tests of interactions of earnings trend by gender by level of supervisory status. Again, the failure of these tests to reveal any statistically significant differences indicates that the economic gains made by women managers are not confined to the lowest or highest levels but have been distributed throughout the ranks of management.

Overall, the GSS results corroborate the findings on the narrowing of the sex gap in wages among managers obtained for the CPS data. In addition, they indicate that the role of supervisory status in explaining the sex gap in incomes among managers is small and that the changing attributes of men and women are not responsible for the positive time trend for women.

Gender Differences in Work-Related Values

Data on sex differences in work-related values can shed light on two questions: Whether women managers are paid less because their workplace goals differ from those of men and whether the positive trends over time in the relative position of women managers is due to their changing work orientation. Table 6.3 presents the means of each of six measures of work-related values. When asked whether they would continue to work even if they had all the money they needed to live comfortably, the great majority of both men and women reported that they would work even if they could afford not to, with no gender difference evident. These results on commitment to work are similar to Bielby and Bielby's (1988) findings on work effort.

The next five questions involved asking respondents to rank-order the importance of five aspects of a job. The rank-ordering of these five job attributes was the same for men and women. Both sexes ranked meaningful work first; chances for advancement second; high income third; no danger of being fired fourth; and working hours are short, lots of free time fifth. Thus, there are broad similarities in the attributes of jobs favored by men and women managers. Although the rank order was the same for men and women, there were nonetheless differences in the preferences expressed for two of the five measures. The mean ranking for meaningful work was higher for the women, whereas the importance attached to high income was higher for the men. Both of these differences were evident in both the 1970s and 1980s, with no discernible trend toward convergence. Thus, the trends over time in the relative position of women managers cannot be attributed to changes in these orientations.

Yet the presence of these modest differences does not necessarily explain the sex gap in wages. In analyses not shown here, I found that the stated preference for meaningful work does not predict wages. Both the zero-order and controlled regression analyses indicate no statistically significant effects. The preference for high income, in contrast, is positively associated with wage rates, yet the addition of this measure reduces the net sex gap in wages by only a small amount. Because the coefficient on the measure of the preference for high income is small, and because the sex difference in means is small, this variable reduces the sex gap in wages by only 0.7%. These results indicate that adding direct measures of work-related values to wage equations reduces the sex gap in earnings only slightly and does not affect the positive time trend for women managers documented above. Although it is always possible that other questions might have a larger effect, other work-related values are probably related to one or more of the measures included in this analysis and so would not have a very different effect on the wage equation or on the time trend. Moreover, we may be overstating the impact of values by ignoring the reciprocal causal impact of earnings and other work experiences on values.

Discussion and Conclusions

These results indicate that the substantial growth of women in management has coincided with a narrowing of the gender gap in wages and no widening of the gender gap in authority. The notion that the entry of women into management represents a wholesale subterfuge on the part of corporations trying to present themselves as supportive of opportunities for women is not consistent with the results in this chapter. Although there are undoubtedly many instances of women who have managerial titles without corresponding pay or authority, the predominant trend has been toward real, if slow, progress into management on the part of women. Consequently, the skeptical readings of the statistics on the entry of women into management—the glorified-secretary, resegregation, and title-inflation hypotheses—do not receive direct support, although there was some support for the title-inflation view, based on the declining ratio of managerial to nonmanagerial salaries.

The measures of segregation indicate modest declines in the extent of occupational and industrial segregation between male and female managers and a substantial increase in the chances of men and women managers sharing the same specialty. This finding is at odds with the resegregation thesis, as well as the resistance-to-threats hypothesis. Female managers rank work-related values in the same order as their male counterparts. The small difference in the preference for high income that was evident in the data was associated with only a tiny portion of the sex gap in wages and does not explain the observed changes over time. Women managers, however, continue to trail their male counterparts in both earnings and authority. Despite the positive trends documented here, both in wages and in attitudes, female managers have a long way to go before they reach parity with their male counterparts.

The present results also differ from several studies that have noted an escalation in job titles. Smith and Welch (1984) presented clear evidence for reassignment of women during the early 1970s, yet the gains for women managers have been steady over the last 20 years, extending well after this initial response to EEO regulations. Strang and Baron (1990) found that the greater the presence of both men and women, the greater the proliferation (but not necessarily inflation) of job titles. My results do not prove that no women were artificially reassigned to managerial titles; they merely show that this process has not been the predominant trend, or if reassignments did occur, they coincided with enough wage gains for women managers to enable them to close the gap with their male counterparts.

The narrowing sex gap in wages among managers, coinciding with a substantial rise in the number of women managers, is consistent with Kanter's strength-in-numbers view—that increasing representation of women tends to improve their position within organizations—whereas it is inconsistent with the contrasting Blalockian resistance-to-threats thesis. However, the analysis of variation across industries and occupations indicates that the extent of change for women did not vary (either positively or negatively) with the proportion employed.

These results are inconsistent with the findings of Pfeffer and Davis-Blake (1987), who found that increases in the proportion of women employed resulted in lower wages, both cross-sectionally and longitudinally, in a study of college administrators. Differences between these two studies may in part be accounted for by many differences in methodology. The present analysis is much broader in scope but less detailed in the available measures. The focus here has been on the earnings of individuals, with particular focus on the sex gap in wages; Pfeffer and Blake-Davis examined the salary of positions, with special attention to a depressing effect of the percentage of females in the position on earnings. Thus it may well be the case that women have been able to narrow the gap between themselves and men even though they are being paid less than men had previously been paid in the same position.

Yet I do not believe that all of these methodological differences will ultimately explain all of the disparity in results. I feel the differences in these studies ultimately reflect the fact that the present study taps broad-scale forces beyond the confines of a single setting. A complete analysis of the impact of growing numbers of women requires an analysis of dynamics internal to organizations, as well as an analysis of external cultural, social, and political forces. The Kanter and Blalock hypotheses specify organizational responses to demographic shifts, yet these responses are likely to depend on why the numbers of women are changing. When men leave an occupation in decline, leaving room for the entry of women, the likely result is lower pay for the position, as Reskin and Roos (1990) documented in a number of cases. When the entry of women is the result of federal legislation, the expanding number of women M.B.A.s, and the rise of women's aspirations and expectations, the process may well be different and have different outcomes. The remarkable uniformity of the rate of change for women across industries, managerial occupations, and supervisory levels suggests that broad political, cultural, and social changes may be responsible for these trends. Local organizational factors undoubtedly explain variation across firms, but this operates on a level more detailed than the measures available in this analysis.

The results obtained here do not offer an immediate explanation for the narrowing of the sex gap in wages among managers. The data indicate that this change is not due to changes in the attributes of women managers, nor to changes in the distribution of women managers across industries and occupations within management. The narrowing of the sex gap in earnings among managers parallels a similar trend in the labor force as a whole, a trend that has been proceeding slowly but surely throughout the 1980s. Economists have tended to attribute this trend to a growth in women's labor force experience (Goldin, 1990; Hayes, Hauser, & Santi, 1990; O'Neill and Polachek, 1991; Smith & Ward, 1984), although the evidence to date remains far from definitive. Despite their claims to the contrary, the results by O'Neill and Polachek (1991) indicate that more of the narrowing of the wage gap was due to the change in the coefficients than change in the characteristics. In other words, women are catching up to men more because they are getting a better return on their attributes than because they increased their human capital investments. We cannot directly test this possibility with these data, because no direct measure of experience is available, yet none of the available measures in either data set explained more than a fraction of the positive time trend for women.

More detailed research on the processes that perpetuate the glass ceiling in certain organizations while undermining it in others is needed. Systematic evidence regarding organizational cultures, as well as structural attributes of organizations that tend to promote greater opportunities for women, also needs to be collected. Finally, a number of large corporations have begun intensive programs to promote opportunities for women and minorities, in recognition of the fact that these groups represent the bulk of the labor force growth over the next decade (Johnston & Packer, 1987). A comparative analysis of the successes and failures of these efforts would be particularly informative.

Notes

1. This estimate is based on a reanalysis of results reported in Jacobs, 1989a and 1989b. Change in sex segregation is measured at the three-digit occupational level. Nearly 6 million women are listed as managers in 1989, compared with 175,000 lawyers, 100,000 doctors, 300,000 computer specialists, 100,000 natural scientists, 130,000 engineers, and 32,000 architects (U.S. Department of Labor, Employment and Earnings, January 1990).

2. The categories are: officials and managers, professionals, technicians, sales, office/clerical, craft (skilled), operatives (semi-skilled), laborers (unskilled), and service workers. The definition of management for the purposes of EEOC filing is "Occupations requiring administrative personnel who set broad policies, exercise overall responsibility for execution of these policies, and direct individual departments or special phases of a firm's operations. Includes: officials, executives, middle management, plant managers, department managers, superintendents, salaried supervisors who are members of management, purchasing agents and buyers, and kindred workers" (Office of Management and Budget, *EEO Standard Form 100, Rev. 2-83, Employer Information Report EEO-1*). This definition is similar to that employed in the 1980 Census, yet it does not specifically exclude clerical supervisors, which the Census specifically included within the rubric of clerical workers.

3. The CPS data indicate whether individuals were assigned the top code as a result of their own response to the earnings question or whether they were "top-coded" as a result of CPS procedures. In the latter case, individuals were assigned an annual earnings figure of $112,000, which takes into account the distribution of earners over $50,000 in 1987. In 1969, such a small fraction were top-coded that no adjustment was made.

References

Abowd, J. M. (1991). Does performance-based managerial compensation affect corporate performance? *Industrial and Labor Relations Review, 43,* S52-73.

Acker, J. (1990). Hierarchies, jobs, bodies: A theory of gendered organizations. *Gender and Society, 4,* 139-158.

Ball, K. (1991, August 26). Study finds few women hold top executive jobs. *Washington Post,* p. A-11.

Baron, J. N., Mittman, B. S., & Newman, A. E. (1991). Targets of opportunity: Organizational and environmental determinants of gender integration within the California civil service, 1979-1985. *American Journal of Sociology, 96,* 1362-1401.

Bielby, D., & Bielby, W. (1988). She works hard for the money: Household responsibilities and the allocation of work effort. *American Journal of Sociology, 91,* 759-799.

Bird, C. (1990). High finance, small change: Women's increased representation in bank management. In B. Reskin & P. Roos (Eds.), *Job queues, gender queues* (pp. 145-166). Philadelphia: Temple University Press.

Blalock, H. M., Jr. (1967). *Toward a theory of minority-group relations.* New York: John Wiley.

Boyd, M., & Mulvihill, M. A. (1990, August). *Patriarchy and post-industrialism in the service economy.* Paper presented at the meetings of the American Sociological Association, Washington, DC.

Bradley, H. (1989). *Men's work, women's work.* Minneapolis: University of Minnesota Press.

Bridges, W. P., & Nelson, R. L. (1989). Markets in hierarchies: Organizational and market influences on gender inequality in a state pay system. *American Journal of Sociology, 95,* 616-658.

Fierman, J. (1990, July 30). Why women still don't hit the top. *Fortune,* p. 42 passim.

Freeman, S.J.M. (1990). *Managing lives: Corporate women and social change.* Amherst: University of Massachusetts Press.

Garland, S. B. (1991, August 19). Throwing stones at the glass ceiling. *Business Week,* p. 29.

Goldin, C. (1990). *Understanding the gender gap: An economic history of American women.* New York: Oxford University Press.

Hayes, J. A., Hauser, R. M., & Santi, L. (1990). *Industrial changes and the gender gap in earnings, 1969-1984* (Working Paper 90-04). Madison: Center for Demography and Ecology, University of Wisconsin, Madison.

Jacobs, J. A. (1989a). Long-term trends in occupational segregation by sex. *American Journal of Sociology, 95,* 160-173.

Jacobs, J. A. (1989b). *Revolving doors: Sex segregation and women's careers.* Stanford, CA: Stanford University Press.

Jencks, C. S., Perman, L., & Rainwater, L. (1988). What is a good job? A new measure of labor market success. *American Journal of Sociology, 93,* 1322-1357.

Johnston, W. B., & Packer, A. E. (1987). *Workforce 2000: Work and workers for the twenty-first century.* Indianapolis, IN: Hudson Institute.

Kanter, R. M. (1977). *Men and women of the corporation.* New York: Basic Books.

Korenman, S., & Neumark, D. (1991). Does marriage really make men more productive? *Journal of Human Resources, 26,* 282-307.

Lieberson, S. (1980). *A piece of the pie: Blacks and white immigrants since 1880.* Berkeley: University of California Press.

Miller, A. R. (1980). Occupational statistics and labor force analysis. *Proceedings of the American Statistical Association, Social Statistics Section,* 108-115.

Olson, J. E., & Frieze, I. H. (1987). Income determinants for women in business. In A. H. Stromberg, L. Larwood, & B. A. Gutek (Eds.), *Women and work: An annual review* (Vol. 2, pp. 173-206). Beverly Hills, CA: Sage.

O'Neill, J., & Polachek, S. (1991). *An analysis of recent trends in the male-female wage gap.* Unpublished manuscript, Department of Economics, Baruch College, City University of New York.

Pfeffer, J., & Baron, J. N. (1988). Taking the workers back out: Recent trends in the structuring of employment. In B. M. Staw & L. L. Cummings (Eds.), *Research in organizational behavior* (Vol. 10, pp. 257-303). Greenwich, CT: JAI Press.

Pfeffer, J., & Davis-Blake, A. (1987). The effects of the proportion of women on salaries: The case of college administrators. *Administrative Science Quarterly, 32,* 1-24.

Powell, G. (1988). *Men and women in management.* Newbury Park, CA: Sage.

Priebe, J. A. (1985). *1970 census sample with industry and occupation descriptions.* Unpublished manuscript, U.S. Bureau of the Census, Washington, DC.

Reskin, B. F., & Roos, P. (1990). *Job queues, gender queues: Explaining women's inroads into male occupations.* Philadelphia: Temple University Press.

Reskin, B. F., & Ross, C. (1992). Job segregation, authority, and earnings and female and male managers. *Work and Occupations, 19*(4), 342-365.

Smith, J. P., & Ward, M. P. (1984). *Women's wages and work in the twentieth century.* Santa Monica, CA: Rand Corporation.

Smith, J. P., & Welch, F. (1984). Affirmative action and labor markets. *Journal of Labor Economics, 2,* 269-301.

Smith, V. (1990). *Gender and flexibility in the workplace: A review of some recent trends.* Unpublished manuscript, Department of Sociology, University of Pennsylvania.

Strang, D., & Baron, J. N. (1990). Categorical imperatives: The structure of job titles in California state agencies. *American Sociological Review, 55,* 479-495.

Treiman, D. H., Bielby, W. T., & Cheng, M. (1988). Evaluating a multiple-imputation method for recalibrating 1970 U.S. census detailed industry codes to the 1980 standard. *Sociological Methodology, 18,* 309-345.

U.S. Bureau of the Census. (1989). *Statistical abstract of the United States, 1989* (109th ed.). Washington, DC: U.S. Bureau of the Census.

U.S. Department of Labor, Bureau of Labor Statistics. (1990). *Employment and earnings.* Washington, DC: Author.

Wolf, W., & Fligstein, N. D. (1979). Sex and authority in the workplace. *American Sociological Review, 44,* 235-252.

7

Gender, Power, and Postindustrialism

MONICA BOYD
MARY ANN MULVIHILL
JOHN MYLES

Women and Men in Canada's Postindustrial Transition

Throughout this century, Canada led the way in the transition to a post-industrial labor market. The shift of employment into services began sooner in Canada than elsewhere (Singelmann, 1978), and services account for a larger share of total employment in Canada than in any other developed nation (Organization for Economic Cooperation and Development [OECD], 1988, Table 7). A postindustrial labor market is one where most labor is now employed in the provision of services and advanced technologies that release labor from direct production (Block, 1987, p. xx). This does not mean that manufacturing no longer matters. Manufacturing does matter, as a generator both of wealth and of employment (Cohen & Zysman, 1987). Manufacturing now generates more information and data-based occupations (engineers, lawyers, accountants, designers, clerks) or producer services, whereas the "direct producers"—craft workers and factory operatives—continue to decline. At the same time, productivity gains in goods production are releasing more labor for what could be called "people services," including the welfare state industries (health education and welfare) and retail and personal services (the

AUTHORS' NOTE: The analysis presented in this chapter was supported by a grant from the Social Sciences and Humanities Research Council of Canada. This chapter was previously published in *The Canadian Review of Sociology and Anthropology, 28*(4), 1991. Reprinted by permission.

178

"servant" industries such as food and accommodation). The concept of postindustrialism captures both dimensions.[1]

Postindustrialism, then, has a double meaning: a change in the mix of labor required to produce a fixed quantity of goods and a change in the amount or share of labor required for goods production. The first change has been manifested in the shift of employment into producer services (engineering, legal, financial, etc.) and the second in a shift of employment into consumer services, both personal and social.

Based on the classification of Singelmann and his associates (Browning & Singelmann, 1978; Singelmann, 1978; Wright & Singelmann, 1982), we document the parameters of this transition for Canada between 1941 and 1986 in Table 7.1. We divide the economy into seven broad sectors. The extractive sector includes agriculture, forestry, fishing, and mining. The transformative sector is composed of all manufacturing industries, construction, and utilities. Distributive services include transportation, communication, and wholesale trade. Although often counted as part of the service economy, distributive services (e.g., railways) grew as part of the Industrial Revolution and were often considered synonymous with it. Producer services are composed of firms that mainly provide services to other firms providing goods and services. They include banking and finance, insurance, real estate, lawyers' offices, labor unions, and miscellaneous business services. In contrast, the remaining service industries are primarily consumption oriented. These include social services (health education and welfare), public administration (federal, provincial, and local government), consumer services (accommodation, food, and personal services), and retail services.

The distributions in Table 7.1 (panel 1) show the marked decline in employment in extractive industries from 32% in 1941, to 14% in 1961, and then to the current 7%. Employment shares in the transformative sector began to decline after 1951. However, the raw numbers underlying these shares (not presented here) indicate that until the 1980s, this was not because employment in manufacturing, construction, and utilities was declining in any absolute sense, but because employment in this sector was not growing as quickly as in services. Only between 1981 and 1986 do we see "deindustrialization" in the sense of a real absolute decline in manufacturing employment. In distributive services, the share of employment grew at the beginning of the period and subsequently leveled off (Table 7.1, column 5).

During this same period, the share of employment in services (producer through retail services) rose from 31% in 1941 to 58% by 1986.

Table 7.1 Percentage Distribution of Industrial Sectors, Total, Female and Male Labor Force, Canada, 1941–1986

	Total N (1)	Percent Total (2)	Extractive (3)	Transformative (4)	Distributive (5)	Producer (6)	Social Services (7)	Public Administration (8)	Consumer Services (9)	Retail (10)
Panel 1, Total Labor Force										
1941	4,364,562	100.0	32	28	10	4	5	3	9	10
1951	5,218,596	100.0	21	33	12	4	7	5	7	11
1961	6,313,257	100.0	14	30	13	6	10	8	8	11
1971	7,944,985	100.0	9	29	12	9	14	8	7	12
1981	11,600,985	100.0	7	27	12	12	14	8	8	12
1986	12,371,675	100.0	7	24	11	13	15	8	10	12
Panel 2, Female Labor Force										
1941	828,719	100.0	2	22	5	6	18	3	32	12
1951	1,151,309	100.0	3	25	8	8	20	4	17	15
1961	1,724,318	100.0	5	19	7	9	24	5	16	14
1971	2,659,970	100.0	5	17	7	11	27	6	13	15
1981	4,676,740	100.0	3	15	8	15	24	7	13	15
1986	5,284,865	100.0	4	14	7	15	25	7	14	15
Panel 3, Male Labor Force										
1941	3,535,843	100.0	38	29	11	3	3	3	4	10
1951	4,067,287	100.0	26	35	13	3	3	6	4	10
1961	4,588,939	100.0	18	35	15	5	5	9	4	10
1971	5,285,015	100.0	11	36	14	7	8	9	5	10
1981	6,924,250	100.0	10	35	15	10	8	8	6	10
1986	7,086,810	100.0	9	32	14	11	8	8	7	11
Panel 4, Females as a Percent Within Industry Sectors										
1941	—	19	2	15	10	31	63	19	67	22
1951	—	22	4	17	15	40	64	18	56	31
1961	—	27	10	17	15	40	66	18	60	35
1971	—	33	17	19	20	44	64	26	58	42
1981	—	40	19	23	26	51	68	37	61	49
1986	—	43	23	24	27	51	69	40	61	50

SOURCE: Dominion Bureau of Statistics, *Eighth Census of Canada 1941* (Vol. 7, Table 17); *Ninth Census of Canada 1951* (Vol. 4, Table 16); *1961 Census of Canada* (Vol. 3, Part 2, catalogue 94-518, Table IA); and Statistics Canada, *Census 1986. Industrial Trends, 1951-1986* (catalogue 93-152) (Tables 1 and 2).

NOTE: The 1970 Standard Industrial Codes (SIC) were recoded as follows: Extractive (SIC 001-099); Transformative (SIC 101-421; 572-579); Producer Services (SIC 701-737; 851-869; 891-899); Social Services (SIC 801-831); Public Administration (SIC 902-991); Consumer (SIC 841-849; 871-879; 881-886); Retail (SIC 631-699). Data for 1941-1961 were grouped to conform to this classification. The data for 1941 include persons in active service. For 1951 and 1961, the data exclude a few persons seeking work who have never been employed; and for 1971 and 1981, the data exclude unemployed persons 15 years of age and over who had never worked or who had worked only prior to January 1970 or January 1980, as applicable. *N*s represent the sum of the numbers for the various sectors. Also excluded are persons for whom industry was not specified or defined.

180

Growth was most pronounced in producer and social services. The share of employment in consumer services initially declined between 1941 and 1951, mainly reflecting the decline in female domestic workers, and then remained relatively stable until 1981.[2] During the 1980s, however, the consumer service sector has been the single most important source of new jobs, accounting for 211,590 out of the 770,790 jobs added to the economy. Retail service has also been an important source of employment growth, adding nearly 130,000 new jobs to the economy between 1981 and 1986.

These general parameters of the postindustrial transition in Canada are documented elsewhere, and they hold few surprises (Magun, 1982; McInnis, 1971; Meltz, 1965, 1969; Picot, 1986; Smith, 1978). However, the sex-specific features of these changes have not been documented in a continuous series for the postwar period.[3] As we show in Table 7.1, postindustrial trends differ in important ways for men and women.

The stereotypical worker who appears in the pages of the history of industrial capitalism has been the male blue-collar worker employed in goods production (resource extraction, manufacturing, utilities, and construction) and in distribution (railways, trucking, and communications). The data in Table 7.1 show that this stereotype is far from dead. Despite the dramatic decline in the percentage of men in the extractive industries (a result of declining employment in agriculture), the majority of men (56%) were still employed in goods production (extractive and transformative industries) and distributive services in 1986. In contrast, only one quarter of women were employed in these traditional industrial sectors of the economy. By 1986, women represented about a quarter of total employment in goods and distribution, but between 40% and 70% of employment in the other service industries (Table 7.1, panel 4).

Over the whole period the percentage of men in the transformative sector changed only modestly, rising after the war and then declining slightly in the eighties. The main change in employment shares until the eighties took the form of declining employment in the extractive sector (especially in agriculture) and increasing employment in services. Conversely, for women, employment shares in the extractive sector were negligible from the beginning.[4] Instead, the female experience of the transition is one of declining employment in the transformative sector— from 25% in 1951 to 14% in 1986. The share of female employment increased substantially in producer services (largely finance and insurance industries) and in social service industries.[5]

The change in the industrial mix of employment for men and women tells only part of the story of postindustrialism, however. For women, the more dramatic shift in work patterns over this period was the movement from unpaid domestic labor to paid employment. Between 1941 and 1986, the percentage of all women in the paid labor force more than doubled, and women's share of total employment increased from 19% to 43% (Table 7.1, panel 4, column 2). Female shares of employment grew in all sectors. Over the 45-year period, women moved to a position of numerical dominance in producer, social, and consumer services, to parity with men in retail services, and to 40% of employment in public administration.

In sum, for men, postindustrial employment has largely meant a shift from agriculture to services and, until recently, relatively little change in goods production and distribution. For women, it has meant a shift from unpaid domestic labor into paid employment in services. And it is the latter change—the shift from unpaid domestic labor—that has contributed most to the growth in service employment. In other words, if unpaid domestic labor were counted as an industry in the usual classifications, we would describe postindustrialism in terms of the shift from unpaid to paid service work and put less emphasis on the "goods to services" metaphor.

Despite the fact that service employment has become an increasingly common destiny for both men and women, the structure of postindustrial labor markets is sex segregated. Relative to their share of total employment, women are underrepresented in goods and distribution but outnumber men in producer, social, and consumer services. Although sex segregation across the eight sectors declined over every period, the largest changes occurred from 1941 to 1951 and from 1961 to 1971, with relatively modest decennial change since then.[6]

Gender and Power in the Postindustrial Economy

A large research agenda emerges from the shift of employment to services and from increased rates of female labor force participation. Studies trace the persistence of occupational segregation over time (Armstrong & Armstrong, 1984; Connelly, 1978; Fox & Fox, 1987; Smith, 1978), compare the skill levels of occupations held by women and men (Boyd, 1990b; Myles & Fawcett, 1990), document the movement of women into the clerical occupations (Lowe, 1980, 1986), examine the role of women as a reserve army (Connelly, 1978; Marchak, 1987), and analyze women's occupational status and mobility (Boyd, 1982, 1985; Cuneo & Curtis, 1975; Goyder, 1985; Marsden, Harvey, & Charner, 1975).

As important as these dimensions of gender inequality are, they do not go to the heart of the matter of most concern to feminist scholarship— namely, the underlying relations of effective power that produce these unequal outcomes, the social as opposed to the material division of labor. Social relations of production are relations of "effective power over persons and productive forces" (Cohen, 1978, p. 63), including the in- struments and materials used in production and the capacities and skills of those who use them. Together, the social relations of production constitute what Marx called an economic structure, that is, "a framework of power in which producing occurs" (Cohen, 1978, p. 79). Relations of production are the building blocks of classes—the positions that are con- stituted by the intersection of these relations (Cohen, 1978, pp. 85-86).

Feminist theory sharply questions the gender neutrality of conven- tional class analysis. The historical gendering of class relations during the transition to industrial capitalism has been well-documented (e.g., Hartmann, 1976, 1981; Sokoloff, 1980, 1988; Ursel, 1986). With the decline of the household economy, hierarchically defined gender rela- tions were brought inside the factory gate to become part of a capital- ist and, theoretically, universalistic labor market. The subordination of women in the household was reproduced in the relations of power and authority of the capitalist firm. In short, the economic structure of indus- trial capitalism acquired a social form derived not merely from a logic based on the imperatives of capital accumulation—the logic of the mar- ket. It also incorporated social forms derived from the patriarchal house- hold. From this perspective, gender subordination in the market is inte- gral to analyses of the economic structure, producing outcomes that are gender asymmetrical, or "gendered" (Acker, 1988, 1989a).

There are at least four reasons to expect significant change in the way social relations are gendered in postindustrial economies. The first has to do with numbers. The growth in female employment can only be ab- sorbed in one of two ways: by a decline in the number of sex-segregated work environments or by an increase in the number of work environ- ments that are predominantly or exclusively female. If the former occurs, then Kanter's law of "relative proportions" should begin to operate. Drawing on Simmel, Kanter (1977, pp. 206ff.) points out that numbers are key elements shaping the corporate environment. Stereotyping, tokenism, and isolation characterize environments where women are a minority, producing performance pressure and differential patterns of evaluation. Accordingly, she concludes that as the ratio of women to men in organizations begins to rise, we should expect patterns of social relations between men and women to shift as well (p. 209).

Alternatively, if the increase in the number of women takes the form of an increase in the number of exclusively female work environments, then the number of work sites where women have access to positions of power and authority over other women should also increase. This distinction should also make clear that it is possible for the distribution of men and women within classes to become more alike without changing social relations between men and women. An economy completely segregated by sex, where men regulate men and women regulate women, can also produce class distributions undifferentiated by sex. A distinguishing feature of our empirical analysis is our ability to examine relations of authority between men and women, not just sex differences in the distribution of power and authority.

There are three additional reasons to think that gender differences in relations of power and authority might abate in postindustrial labor markets. The first is the very "modernity" of the service industries. The growth of personal, business, and social services is a contemporary phenomenon, and, as Stinchcombe (1965) has shown, the organization of labor within firms, industries, and occupations tends to bear the imprint of the historical period of their foundation and growth. Baron and Newman (1990), for example, show that wage differentials between men and women are greater in "old" than in "new" job categories.

As well, state employment is more prevalent in the service sector, and studies of earnings differentials between women and men have shown the gender gap in earnings has narrowed in the public sector (Boyd & Humphreys, 1979; Denton & Hunter, 1982). Finally, postindustrial labor markets—and especially social and business services—tend not only to be knowledge intensive but also credential intensive. High levels of formal education tend to be required for entry, and job-relevant skills are acquired through the educational system, rather than through on-the-job training and apprenticeship programs. In principle, this should benefit women, who are typically excluded from on-the-job training programs but who tend to have slightly higher levels of formal education than men (Myles & Fawcett, 1990).

Despite these reasons for anticipating some degendering of power relations in the service sector, the limited empirical work that directly addresses issues of gender differences in power and authority in the labor market offers less ground for optimism. Most notable is Cuneo's (1985) examination of census data, in which he concludes that "women have been increasingly excluded from gaining access to such positions as managers, officials, supervisors and forepeople in a ratio equal to their representation in the labor force" (p. 486). Cuneo does not examine gender differences by economic sector. But in view of the correlation among the underlying time trends, the implication is that the growth of the service sector and women's numerical dominance in the service industries have not appreciably altered their relative position in the power structure of the workplace. The empirical question we address in the remainder of this chapter is the extent to which the gendered organization of production relations persists within what are decidedly modern sectors of a postindustrial economy.

Research Design and Data

Our analysis is based on a family of measures related to decision making, hierarchical location, authority, and autonomy, which are described in Appendix A. These are the same measures that have been used in the construction of several class typologies used to describe the gendered distribution of classes (Clement, 1990; Wright, Costello, Hachen, & Sprague, 1982). Class typologies of the sort constructed by Wright (1978), Clement (1990), and others represent an effort to reduce the complexity of production relations—to identify positions in the economic structure—in ways that are theoretically and historically meaningful, on the one hand, and empirically feasible, on the other.

Such typologies are useful when they are intended to isolate particular production relations (or a combination of them) that are theoretically pertinent for the explanation of some other social process, such as class conflict, the formation and distribution of ideologies and beliefs, or even income inequality.[7] But they are decidedly less useful when the purpose is to study production relations themselves. Although typologies have the advantage of reducing complexity, they also obscure their underlying components. The reason is that all such typologies are based on theoretical choices to privilege some production relations over others or on the particular way in which a subset of production relations intersect.

Employees who supervise the labor of others but also have decision making powers over the allocation of capital are typically classified as managers or executives, and the fact that they also do supervisory work is lost in the process. Those responsible for the allocation of capital and labor to different uses may or may not be responsible for directing and disciplining labor. Similarly, some supervisors are closely regulated in their work, whereas others have significant autonomy. Some have powers to discipline their subordinates, whereas others only coordinate the work of others. The result is that any such typology can potentially conceal as much as it reveals about the gendered structure of production relations.

Our strategy is to study production relations directly, to "unpack" the conventional class typologies into their constituent elements.[8] We also extend the analysis to consider production relations not usually included in such typologies. Concrete positions in an economic structure are constructed out of production relations. However, individuals always exist in a matrix of production relations that are unlikely to be exhausted by any class typology or the subset of production relations used in its construction.

The data are from the Canadian Class Structure Survey (CCSS), collected by means of a multistage probability sample in Canada's 10 provinces during the winter of 1982-1983. Completed interviews were obtained in 76% of total eligible households. Results presented here are weighted to reflect both sample design and post facto adjustments for age and sex composition by region and employment status (Black & Myles, 1986, pp. 7-8). Our analysis focuses on a subsample consisting of respondents who were currently employed or unemployed for a year or less. This corresponds to the "experienced labor force" concept used in recent Canadian censuses. The CCSS was conducted in the depths of the greatest recession experienced by Canadian workers since the 1930s, when unemployment was especially high. The use of the experienced labor force as a universe helps us to correct for distortions introduced by this cyclical effect on the composition of our sample.

For both substantive and methodological reasons, we exclude employers and the self-employed from our analysis. Sex differences in ownership of capital have been documented elsewhere (Carroll, 1987; Cuneo, 1985), and the specific contribution of our analysis lies in the examination of the distribution and relations of control and authority among employees. Moreover, because it was presumed that employers and the self-employed held powers of decision making and authority by definition, many of the questions used in this analysis were not asked of this segment of the labor force. It should be kept in mind, however, that by focusing exclusively on employees, our analysis generates conservative estimates of sex differences in subordination-domination in the labor force.

The subsample is made up of 1,761 respondents (787 women and 974 men). Because of this sample size, we could not use the detailed eight-sector industrial classification employed in the analysis of census data in Table 7.1. Instead, we use a three-sector industry classification based on three important divisions for women:

1. the goods-producing and distributive sectors, which are predominantly male industries (this corresponds to a combined extractive-transformative-distributive sector)
2. commercial services, including producer, consumer, and retail services
3. public services, including the social services (health, education and welfare) and public administration

Previous research indicates that the commercial-public service division is important in that it is the public sector that provides the majority of high-wage, high-skill jobs for women (Boyd, 1990a; Boyd & Humphreys, 1979; Denton & Hunter, 1982; Myles & Fawcett, 1990).

The distributions by sex, within and between sectors, are shown in Table 7.2 and confirm the basic observations made previously concerning the sexual division of labor by industry. In the employed labor force, men (59%) are much more concentrated in the goods sector than women (22%). Women are a minority (24%) of all those employed in goods production but a majority of those employed in both commercial services (61%) and public services (60%).

In analyzing these data, we make use of conditional probabilities (percentages) and differences in conditional probabilities (percentage differences between men and women). A main concern is to test hypotheses about the difference of differences (interaction effects) between sectors.[9] We want to know whether gender differences are smaller or larger in the modern, postindustrial sectors of the labor market. We report a large number of such interactions in our tables, all of which lead to similar conclusions but which in general are not statistically significant.[10] This means the observed interactions may be an artifice of sampling error or of sample size (there are few women in goods and distributive services and fewer still with significant powers).

Table 7.2 Sample Distributions by Sex and Industrial Sectors, Employee Population, Canada, 1982

	Total (1)	Female (2)	Male (3)
Panel 1: Numbers, Unweighted			
Total	1,761	787	974
Goods and distribution	753	175	578
Commercial services	499	312	187
Public services	509	300	209
Panel 2: Percent Distribution by Sex[a]			
Total	100	100	100
Goods and distribution	42	22	59
Commercial services	30	41	21
Public services	28	37	20
Panel 3: Sex Distribution Within Sectors[a]			
Total	100	45	55
Goods and distribution	100	24	76
Commercial services	100	61	39
Public services	100	60	40

SOURCE: Canadian Class Structure Project, 1982.
a. Percentages based on data that are weighted to adjust for the sample design.

However, the pattern of interactions between gender and sector is consistent across a large number of measures, and in the concluding section we turn to census data to help us overcome the problems of sample size. Because the census includes all jobs in the economy, we are not faced with the problem that results may be due to sampling error. Moreover, the large number of cases allows us to do a more detailed industry analysis than is possible with the CCSS. With the census data we are also able to measure changes over two time periods—1971-1981 and 1981-1986. The weakness of the census is that we are compelled to measure production relations with conventional occupational categories. Our classification of census occupations is based on that of Pineo, Porter, and McRoberts (1977), but the fact that we are able to reproduce similar results with different databases and using alternative measures gives us considerable confidence that there is more than sampling or measurement error to support our conclusions.

Distributional Differences in Power

1. Autonomy

One form of power exercised by employees is the capacity to exercise control over their own work. Here we consider two broad aspects of such control—conceptual autonomy and task autonomy. Conceptual autonomy refers to the requirement in a job to conceptualize or design important aspects of a product or service. Task autonomy refers to the conditions under which the task is actually accomplished (control or the pace of work, how and when one does one's work, etc.).

In the CCSS, measuring conceptual autonomy was a matter of considerable importance because of the analytical significance of the category of semi-autonomous workers in Wright's (1978) original class schema. All respondents were asked:

> Is yours a job in which you are required to design important aspects of your own work and to put your ideas into practice? Or is yours a job in which you are not required to design important aspects of your own work or to put your ideas into practice, except perhaps in minor details?

Respondents who indicated they were required to design important aspects of their work were then asked in an open-ended question to provide an example of how they designed their own work and put their ideas into practice. The examples were then coded according to a rating scale of high, medium, low, and no autonomy according to a protocol initially designed for the American version of the survey and that the two principal investigators of the Canadian survey were able to replicate with an acceptably high level of reliability. The main purpose of this procedure was to eliminate exaggerated claims to autonomy. As Clement and Myles (1994) show, the resulting classification of autonomous employees is a valid measure of self-direction and job complexity (skill).

Task autonomy is measured with a simple yes or no response to five questions asking respondents whether they can regulate their own working hours, take time off without loss of pay, control the pace of their work, introduce new tasks on the job, and determine how they do their work.

The results (Table 7.3) show there are more jobs with significant conceptual and task autonomy in the service industries than in the goods

Table 7.3 Autonomy and Control Over Work by Industrial Sector, Canada, 1982

	Goods and Distribution			Commercial Services			Public Services		
	Female (1)	Male (2)	Difference (3)	Female (4)	Male (5)	Difference (6)	Female (7)	Male (8)	Difference (9)
Conceptual autonomy	100	100	0	100	100	0	100	100	0
High	7	13	-6	7	22	-15	31	52	-21
Medium	8	18	-10	14	26	-12	10	10	0
Low	10	14	-4	13	8	5	6	6	0
None	75	55	20	66	44	22	53	32	21
Task autonomy, percent yes[a] to:									
Can decide working hours	19	24	-5	24	37	-13	22	29	-7
Can take time off without accounting	29	26	3	29	35	6	20	31	-11
Can slow down pace of work	48	42	6	41	57	-16	36	52	-16
Can introduce own new task	36	41	-5	45	59	-14	51	59	-8
Can decide to do own job	66	70	-4	68	83	-15	71	79	-8

a. The percentage indicating *no* may be calculated by subtracting the figures for *yes* from 100. For example, of all female employees in the goods sector, 19% can decide working hours. Eighty-one percent of female employees in the goods sector cannot (100 − 19 = 81).

and distribution sector, but men have clearly appropriated such jobs disproportionately to their numbers. At high levels of conceptual autonomy, the gender gap is only 6 percentage points in goods and distribution but rises to 15 and 21 percentage points in commercial and public services, respectively.

The patterns for task autonomy are even more surprising. If anything, women tend to have a small advantage over men in goods and distribution. This pattern is reversed in the service sector, where men have a decided advantage in both commercial and public services on most items.

2. Decision Making

A distinguishing feature of the history of all industrial capitalist economies is the "decomposition of the functions of capital." With the rise of the large corporation, traditional powers associated with legal ownership—effective control over the allocation of capital, labor, and the means of production—are delegated to a new middle class of managers and professionals. To measure the distribution of decision making powers among employees, respondents were asked seven questions concerning their participation in policy decisions related to budget-setting, investment, and workplace organization, as well as the form of their participation in each decision. For presentational purposes, we use a summary measure indicating whether the respondent claims to be a decision maker on any of the seven items or takes part in the decision making process in an advisory capacity. The distribution of decision makers, advisers, and non-decision makers by sex for the total labor force and by sector is presented in Table 7.4. A second indicator of relative power position—the respondent's self-placement in the managerial hierarchy—is presented in Table 7.5.

Both measures tell a remarkably consistent story. As indicated by the pattern of percentage differences, rather than narrowing the gender gap, differences in the distribution of power are larger in both commercial and public services than in the industrial sector of the economy. In goods and distribution, there is a gender difference of 7%, which rises to 14% in public services and 15% in commercial services. There is a 2-point difference in the percentage of men and women who claim top or middle management positions in goods and distribution, a difference of 8% in commercial services and 11% in public services.

Table 7.4 Decision Making by Sex and Industrial Sector, Canada, 1982

	Goods and Distribution			Commercial Services			Public Services		
	Female (1)	Male (2)	Difference (3)	Female (4)	Male (5)	Difference (6)	Female (7)	Male (8)	Difference (9)
Decision role	100	100	0	100	100	0	100	100	0
Decision maker	8	15	-7	11	26	-15	19	33	-14
Adviser	4	6	-2	7	5	2	6	11	-5
Non-decision maker	88	79	9	82	69	13	75	56	19

Table 7.5 Managerial Self-Placement by Sex and Industrial Location, Canada, 1982

	Goods and Distribution			Commercial Services			Public Services		
	Female (1)	Male (2)	Difference (3)	Female (4)	Male (5)	Difference (6)	Female (7)	Male (8)	Difference (9)
Managerial self-placement	100	100	0	100	100	0	100	100	0
Top, upper	4	5	-1	2	10	-8	2	8	-6
Middle	3	4	-1	4	4	0	3	8	-5
Lower	1	3	-2	3	4	-1	1	0	1
Supervisor	12	14	-2	11	14	-3	13	24	-11
Nonmanagerial	80	76	4	80	68	12	81	60	21

Table 7.6 Authority Measures by Sex and Industrial Sector, Canada, 1982

	Goods and Distribution			Commercial Services			Public Services		
	Female (1)	Male (2)	Difference (3)	Female (4)	Male (5)	Difference (6)	Female (7)	Male (8)	Difference (9)
Percent of total who supervise others	24	37	-13	28	41	-13	19	35	-16
Type of authority	100	100	0	100	100	0	100	100	0
Sanctioning	17	27	-10	14	28	-14	16	25	-9
Task	4	5	-1	7	7	0	5	5	0
Nominal supervisor	4	5	-1	7	6	1	6	6	0
Nonsupervisory	75	63	12	72	59	13	73	64	9

3. Authority

It is within the supervisor-subordinate relation that the majority of people have their most immediate experience of the exercise of power. Experientially, senior executives and the powers they wield may be quite remote from the day-to-day life of most workers, whereas the exercise of authority by one's immediate superior is a recurring and ongoing reality at all levels of the firm.

In Table 7.6, we show the percentages of men and women by sector who supervise others (line 1) and the type of authority they exercise over subordinates. Among those with authority, we distinguish between those who have sanctioning authority (the capacity to impose positive or negative sanctions on others) and task authority (those whose power is limited to coordinating the labor of others). Finally, there is a small residual category of "nominal supervisors," those with neither sanctioning or task authority.

The magnitude of the gender gap in supervisory authority (the proportion of men and women with subordinates, line 1, Table 7.6) is the same in goods/distribution and in commercial services, and it is only slightly larger in state services. If we consider types of authority, however, the difference between the percentage of men and women who not only supervise but also can discipline their subordinates (sanctioning authority) is substantially larger in commercial services than in the goods sector. In contrast, sex differences in public services are somewhat smaller than in the goods sector.

Thus far, the pattern we have identified across a wide variety of measures of power, authority, and autonomy all lead to a similar conclusion. Rather than eroding the traditional sexual division of power, Canada's postindustrial labor market appears to be contributing to its consolidation and even its growth. Neither modernity nor the numerical dominance of women in the service industries has reduced the unequal access of women to positions of power and authority or even to jobs with high levels of self-direction. Cross-sectional differences, of course, tell us nothing about trends over time, a point to which we return shortly. They do point to a remarkable feature of postindustrial labor markets, however. In the traditional sectors of an industrial economy where most employees are male, the exercise of power takes the form of men ruling other men. Only in the modern, female service industries do men begin to rule over women in large numbers. In the following section we document the extent and consequences of this development.

4. Authority Relations Between Women and Men

There are many possible reasons to account for the unequal access of men and women to positions of power and authority in the contemporary workplace. For example, female employees typically tend to be younger and are more likely to have experienced labor force interruptions than male employees. The implications for relations between men and women, however, are startling. In goods and distribution, the majority of employees are men. As a result, men who rule tend to rule other men. In the service industries, in contrast, the majority of employees are women, and those subject to male authority are mainly women. This is shown in Table 7.7.

The CCSS asked all respondents who claimed to have subordinates for information on the sex composition of those they supervised. In Table 7.7 we summarize this information by classifying sex of subordinates into three categories—male only, female only, and mixed. In goods and distribution, 67% of men with subordinates supervise men only, and only 33% have female subordinates. In commercial services, the numbers are reversed: 69% of men with subordinates have female subordinates, and 31% supervise only other men. In public services the corresponding figures are 74% and 26%, respectively. In contrast, women with subordinates in all three sectors typically have authority only over other women—60% in the goods sector, 64% in commercial services, and 64% in public services. Between 36% and 40% of all women with authority have some or exclusively male subordinates in the three sectors.

Two broad conclusions follow from these results. First, the direct exercise of authority by men over women becomes widespread only in the service industries. The pattern observed in goods and distribution, where men supervise other men, is quite consistent with an internal promotions policy. However, the new pattern of men supervising women in female-dominated job ghettos appears to be inconsistent with this rule. It implies differential promotions of men or at least more male seniority.

Second, women are put in positions of authority mainly in female job ghettos, irrespective of sector. There are more women with authority in the service industries simply because there are more of these ghettos, not because women are more likely to be given authority over men.

The latter conclusion is confirmed dramatically in Table 7.8, where we show the distribution of responses to a question that asked respondents the sex of their immediate superior. The question structure allowed for the possibility that a respondent might be supervised or report to more

Table 7.7 Sex of Subordinates by Industrial Sector, Canada, 1982

	Goods and Distribution	Commercial Services	Public Services
Females with subordinates			
Sex of subordinates	100	100	100
Male only	15	11	5
Female only	60	64	64
Mixed	25	25	31
Males with subordinates			
Sex of subordinates	100	100	100
Male only	67	31	26
Female only	2	13	22
Mixed	31	56	52

than one person. Hence there is a small residual category (mixed) of respondents who report to or are supervised by both a man and a woman.[11] Only rarely do men have a female superior (Table 7.8, panel 2). In goods and distribution, 3% of all men have a female superior, in public services the figure is 10%, and in commercial services 15%. Most women in goods and distribution have male superiors, but these women represent a small fraction of all employed women. In commercial services 56% of women have male superiors, and in public services the figure is 47%.

Gathering these results together suggests the following. The majority of women with authority exercise that authority over other women. About one third of women with subordinates have at least one male subordinate, but these are unusual men, accounting for only 7% of the male labor force. The implication is that unequal access to positions of authority and power is mainly a result of "antimatriarchy." Men are not, or will not be, ruled by women. Under these conditions, women achieve positions of authority almost exclusively within female job ghettos.

In a curious way, then, numbers do matter: Women gain access to positions of authority, but only when it is unlikely that men will be subject to that authority. These results confirm England's (1979) observation that resistance to sex equality is greatest when it involves face-to-face relations of power in the workplace. Our data do not allow us to explain this apparent resistance of men to the exercise of power by

Table 7.8 Sex of Supervisor by Industrial Sector, Canada, 1982

	Goods and Distribution	*Commercial Services*	*Public Services*
Females	100	100	100
Female superior	31	42	52
Male superior	67	56	47
Mixed	2	1	1
Males	100	100	100
Female superior	2	12	10
Male superior	97	85	90
Mixed	1	3	0

women. We do, however, conclude, that this fact must be the starting point of any effort to explain the position of women in the economic structure of modern capitalism.

5. Evidence From the Census

Our survey results suggested that gender differences in workplace power and authority are more pronounced in services than in traditional industrial sectors of the economy. As we indicated, however, tests for interaction effects across the three industrial sectors generally fell below conventional standards of statistical significance, especially when we corrected for the design effect (1.5) of the CCSS sample. From this, we might conclude that there are no differences across industry sectors. Alternatively, it may be that our sample size is simply too small to detect these differences. Our analysis of census data supports the latter interpretation.

As another way of examining gender differences in power and authority, we turn to unpublished industry by occupation distributions from the Canadian censuses of 1971, 1981, and 1986. We examine the percentages of female and male labor in managerial and supervisory[12] occupations, following the Pineo et al. (1977) classification. Census occupations provide inferior measures of power and authority, because unlike the CCSS, the census provides no detailed probing of actual duties, responsibilities, and powers of managers and supervisors. The advantages of the census are the large number of observations and the ability to track changes over time. We are also able to return to the more detailed industry classification used in the introduction.

Percentage distributions and differences between men and women in managerial and supervisory occupations for 1986 are shown in Table 7.9. The results support our survey findings concerning sector differences in the gendering of class relations, but the pattern of differences varies for managerial versus supervisory categories and by detailed industry. In producer services, social services, and public administration, the gender gap in management positions is typically twice as large or more than that found in other industries. These are the high-wage, high-skill sectors of the service economy, and here the gender gap is most accentuated. In contrast, at the supervisory level the gender gap is largest in the low-wage, low-skill consumer and retail services.

Census data can also tell us about trends over time. In management occupations, gender differences declined after 1971 in the extractive industries, social services, public administration, and consumer services. They rose or were stable in other parts of the economy (Table 7.10). There was a more consistent downward trend in sex differences in supervisory occupations across all industries except for the extractive industries.

It is instructive, however, to further disaggregate the managerial occupations to see where in the hierarchy women have been making gains or losses. As Boyd (1990b, footnote 11) observes, women have tended to gain most in lower-level managerial and administrative support functions. This conclusion is confirmed when we divide managers into high- and middle-level managers, following the Pineo-Porter-McRoberts classification. As we show in Table 7.11, the gender gap in high-level management has increased since 1971 in all industries except social services. Conversely, the gender gap has fallen among middle managers in all industries except retail trade. In short, there have been two offsetting trends in the labor market: Women have been improving their position relative to men in lower-level management and supervisory jobs but losing ground relative to men in upper-level executive positions.

Conclusion

The shift of employment from goods to services and the massive incorporation of women into the paid labor force are defining and insepa-

Table 7.9 Percentage of Women and Men in Managerial and Supervisory Occupations by Industry, Canada, 1986

	Extractive (1)	Transformative (2)	Distributive (3)	Producer Services (4)	Social Services (5)	Public Administration (6)	Consumer Services (7)	Retail (8)
Females	100.0	100.0	100.0	100.0	100.0	100.0	100.0	100.0
Management	6.0	4.8	6.3	8.2	3.8	14.6	2.5	2.8
Supervisors	1.7	3.5	5.6	4.7	1.0	2.6	9.5	12.4
All others	92.3	91.7	88.2	87.1	95.2	82.8	87.9	84.8
Males								
Management	8.2	7.5	9.1	14.8	9.1	18.8	5.8	5.0
Supervisors	5.4	8.8	10.8	7.5	1.7	3.0	18.3	23.2
All others	86.3	82.4	80.1	77.7	89.2	78.2	75.9	74.8
Difference (Female – Male)								
Management	-2.3	-2.8	-2.9	-6.7	-5.3	-4.2	-3.2	-2.2
Supervisors	-3.7	-6.6	-5.2	-2.8	-0.7	-0.4	-8.8	-10.9

Table 7.10 Differences in Percentage of Women and Men in Managerial and Supervisory Occupations by Industry, Canada, 1971, 1981, 1986

	Extractive (1)	Transformative (2)	Distributive (3)	Producer Services (4)	Social Services (5)	Public Administration (6)	Consumer Services (7)	Retail (8)
1. Management occupations								
1971	-3.4	-2.3	-2.3	-6.5	-6.3	-6.5	-3.5	-1.3
1981	-2.1	-3.5	-3.4	-8.9	-5.8	-6.0	-3.4	-2.4
1986	-2.3	-2.8	-2.9	-6.7	-5.3	-4.2	-3.2	-2.2
2. Supervisory occupations								
1971	-3.5	-9.3	-9.3	-7.6	-0.1	-0.8	-11.1	-17.9
1981	-4.2	-7.3	-6.4	-2.7	-0.9	0.1	-10.9	-12.6
1986	-3.7	-6.6	-5.2	-2.8	-0.7	-0.4	-8.8	10.9

Table 7.11 Differences in Percentage of Women and Men in High- and Middle-Level Management Occupations by Industry, Canada, 1971, 1981, 1986

	Extractive (1)	Transformative (2)	Distributive (3)	Producer Services (4)	Social Services (5)	Public Administration (6)	Consumer Services (7)	Retail (8)
1. High level management								
1971	-0.3	-1.2	-1.5	-4.1	-5.3	-2.3	-0.5	-1.0
1981	-0.5	-1.5	-2.9	-6.6	-5.0	-3.3	-0.6	-1.8
1986	-0.7	-1.8	-2.9	-5.6	-4.8	-3.0	-0.7	-1.7
2. Middle management								
1971	-3.1	-1.1	-0.7	-2.4	-1.0	-4.2	-3.0	-0.3
1981	-1.6	-2.0	-0.5	-2.3	-0.8	-2.7	-2.8	-0.6
1986	-1.5	-1.0	0.1	-1.0	-0.5	-1.1	-2.5	-0.5

rable features of postindustrial labor markets. How we interpret the significance of this historical transformation depends critically on the precise nature of the question being asked. Significance for whom? And for what? The service economy is not cut from a single cloth. Relative to historical and emergent patterns in goods production, the service industries provide a complex mix of high-wage, high-skill employment (the information economy and welfare state industries) and low-wage, low-skill employment (the servant industries). The one constant of the service industries, however, is the numerical dominance of women. The service economy is where most women work.

However, women have not converted their numerical strength in the service industries into power. Our findings on the differential location of men and women in hierarchies of power and authority show that women are less likely than men to occupy positions of power. Our examination of the relations of authority between men and women indicate that women rarely are supervisors or managers of men, although men rule over both men and women. Census data indicate that the inroads of women into management are primarily at the lower rungs. Both census and survey results also show that gender differences in access to management and supervisory positions are largest in those service industries where women are in a majority. Together these results indicate that the service economy not only represents the continuation of female subordination, but also represents its consolidation.

Our results also underscore the observation of Bielby and Baron (1986), among others, who have pointed out the importance of firm-level analyses for understanding the dynamics of gender inequality. Even when there is convergence in the male and female distributions of power and authority, this tells us little about the relations of power and authority *between* men and women. It is quite possible to produce identical class or occupational distributions for men and women, even when perfect segregation exists at the level of the firm or work setting. Our analysis of the sex composition of supervisors versus supervisees indicates that despite an increase in female supervisors and lower-level managers, few men are subject to female authority, and women mainly get access to authority in female job ghettos.

Our results have some bearing for feminist theorizing about gender inequality in the workplace, as well. Recently Acker (1988, 1989a, 1989b) has argued that gender is so fundamental to hierarchical structure that alteration of the gender order tends to threaten the hierarchy itself (Acker, 1988, p. 482). Our research does not explore the processes that produce these gendered social relations. But our results on the relations of power and authority between men and women do indicate the embeddedness of gender in hierarchical relations. Our results, in fact, invert the traditional problematic of why men rule over women. Our findings on the near absence of men being supervised by women suggest a very powerful "iron law of anti-matriarchy"—men will not be governed by women. This suggests recasting the traditional question of why women are subordinate to men and asking why are men seldom, if ever, subordinate to women. This latter question creates different theoretical and empirical questions and sensitizes us to the gender hierarchies in analyses of class relations.

Appendix A

Construction of Variables on Decision Making, Authority, Managerial Self Placement, and Autonomy, Canadian Class Structure Project

A. The *decision-making variable* is constructed from responses to the following questions

　1. Are you personally involved even just to provide advice on:
　　a. Decisions to increase or decrease the total number of people employed in the place where you work?
　　b. Policy decisions to significantly change the products, programs, or services delivered by the organization for which you work?
　　c. Decisions to change the policy concerning the routine pace of work or the amount of work performed in your workplace as a whole or some major part of it?
　　d. Policy decisions to significantly change the basic methods or procedures of work used in a major part of your workplace?
　　e. Decisions concerning the budget at the place where you work?
　　f. Deciding the overall size of the budget?
　　g. General policy decisions about the distribution of funds within the overall budget of the place where you work?
　2. How do you usually participate in this decision? Do you make the decision yourself; make the decision as a voting member of a group; make the

decision subject to approval; or only provide advice? [Asked following each of 1a. through 1g.]

CONSTRUCTION: Respondents who indicated they make the decision themselves, make the decision as a voting member of a group, or, make the decision subject to approval for any *one* of 1a. through 1g. are coded as decision makers. Of the residual, those who indicated they provide advice for any *one* of questions 1a. through 1g. were coded as adviser managers.

B. The *authority variable* is constructed from responses to the following questions:

Sanctioning Authority:

1. Do you have any influence on:
   a. Granting a pay raise or a promotion to a person you supervise?
   b. Preventing a person you supervise from getting a pay raise or promotion because of poor work or misbehaviour?
   c. Firing or temporarily suspending a person you supervise?
   d. Issuing a formal warning to a person you supervise?

Respondents answering yes to any *one* of a. through d. were coded as having sanctioning authority.

Task Authority:

2. As part of your job, are you directly responsible for:
   a. Deciding the specific tasks or jobs to be done by the people you supervise?
   b. Deciding what procedures, tools, or materials they use in doing their work?
   c. Deciding how fast they work, how long they work, or, how much work they have to get done?

Respondents who answered yes to any *one* of a. through c. were coded as having task authority.

Nominal Authority

3. As an official part of your main job, do you supervise the work of other employees or tell other employees what work to do?

Respondents who answered yes to this question but no to questions 1a. through 1d. and 2a. through 2c. were coded as having nominal authority.

C. The *managerial self-placement variable* was constructed from responses to the following question:

Which of the following best describes the position which you hold within your business or organization?

Top Managerial

Upper Managerial

Middle Managerial

Lower Managerial

Supervisory

Non-Management Position

D. The *autonomy variable* was constructed from responses to the following questions:

1. First, is yours a job in which you are required to design important aspects of your own work and to put your ideas into practice? Or is yours a job in which you are not required to design important aspects of your own work or to put your ideas into practice, except perhaps in minor details?

   No, not required = no autonomy.

   Yes, answer next question.

2. Could you give an example of how you design your work and put your ideas into practice? The specific examples were coded according to the following criteria:

   High: indicates an ability to design broad aspects of the job, engage in nonroutine problem solving on a regular basis, and put one's ideas into practice in a regular and pervasive way.

   Moderate: ability to design limited aspects of the job, engage in relatively routine forms of problem solving, and within fairly well defined limits, put one's ideas into practice.

   Low: virtually no significant ability to plan aspects of the job, problem solving a marginal part of the job, and only in unusual circumstances can put one's ideas into practice.

Notes

1. In its original incarnation, the concept of postindustrialism was deployed by mainstream practitioners of what Giddens (1976) calls "industrialization" theory to make sense of emergent trends and patterns that were inconsistent with the conventional concepts and categories of this perspective (see Myles, 1990). If emergent patterns could not be adequately understood with a theory derived from "the logic of industrialism" (Kerr, Dunlop, Harbison, & Myers, 1964), then presumably a theory based on "the logic of postindustrialism" was necessary (Bell, 1973). Our use of the term is less ambitious. As Block (1987, p. 27) observes, the concept of postindustrialism (like post-Keynesian or post-Fordist) is a negative one. It does not designate the kind of economy or society we are moving toward but only the kind of economy and society we are leaving behind. It means simply that societies have moved beyond industrialism—an historical, not a logical, category. But we also use the term differently than Block, for whom postindustrialism represents "the development of new productive forces that come into conflict with capitalist social relations" (Block, 1987, p. 107). It is not capitalist social relations that are threatened by postindustrialism but a particular *historical* form of those relations. The Fordist labor process based on mass production technology, in which semiskilled labor is combined with product-specific machinery to produce a large volume of standardized goods for homogenous markets, is now breaking down (Piore & Sabel, 1984). However, the empirical terrain subsumed by the Fordism/post-Fordism metaphor is too narrow. As Mahon (1987) observes, analyses of postwar labor markets that derive from this perspective have been constructed largely around blue-collar work in manufacturing. However, the distinctive feature of advanced capitalist labor markets is that most employment is now in services.

2. Fluctuations from 8% in 1961 to 7% in 1971 (Table 7.1, panel I, column 9) should not be overinterpreted, given rounding procedures. Carried to the first decimal place, the percentages are actually 7.6 and 7.4 for 1961 and 1971, respectively.

3. Although Armstrong (1984) and Smith (1978) assemble industry data by sex, they use the major groups of the census industrial classification (SIC).

4. The slight increase in 1961 and 1971 in the percentages of females in extractive industries reflects an increase in the percentages of women in mining and quarrying, as well as in agriculture.

5. The decline in the percentage of women employed in the transformative sector was not because their share of jobs in this sector declined but because their share of employment in this sector grew less quickly than in services.

6. Indices of dissimilarity for the female and male labor force distributed across the eight categories in Table 7.1 are: 48.5, 40, 40, 35.5, 34 and 31.5 for 1941, 1951, 1961, 1971, 1981, and 1986, respectively.

7. But this also means that there is no single typology that can provide an all-purpose tool for class analysis.

8. A more extensive "unpacking" within a comparative framework is presented in Clement and Myles (1994).

9. For this reason we do not use log-linear models, which tend to be insensitive to interactions in the probabilities, for the good reason that such models are multiplicative in form and only additive in their logs.

10. Tests of significance for interactions (difference of differences) were made with Jim Davis's CHIP program designed for the analysis of contingency tables.

11. It should be emphasized that these results refer only to the respondent's immediate superior. Many respondents will be at the end of a longer chain of command with a different sex composition than indicated here.

12. The census distinguishes between "foremen" and "supervisors," which we aggregate into a single supervisory category.

References

Acker, J. (1988). Gender, class and the relations of distribution. *Signs, 13*(3), 473-497.

Acker, J. (1989a). The problem with patriarchy. *Sociology, 23*(May), 235-240.

Acker, J. (1989b). Making gender visible. In R. A. Wallace (Ed.), *Feminism and sociological theory* (pp. 65-81). Newbury Park, CA: Sage.

Armstrong, P. (1984). *Labour pains: Women's work in crisis.* Toronto: The Women's Press.

Armstrong, P., & Armstrong, H. (1984). *The double ghetto* (rev. ed.). Toronto: McClelland and Stewart.

Baron, J., & Newman, A. (1990). For what it's worth: Organizations, occupations and the value of work done by women and nonwhites. *American Sociological Review, 55,* 155-175.

Bell, D. (1973). *The coming of post-industrial society.* New York: Basic Books.

Bielby, W., & Baron, J. (1986). Men and women at work: Sex segregation and statistical discrimination. *American Journal of Sociology, 91*(4), 759-799.

Black, D., & Myles, J. (1986). Dependent industrialization and the Canadian class structure: A comparative analysis of Canada, the United States, and Sweden. *Canadian Review of Sociology and Anthropology, 23*(2), 157-181.

Block, F. (1987). *Revising state theory: Essays in politics and postindustrialism.* Philadelphia: Temple University Press.

Boyd, M. (1982). Sex differences in the Canadian occupational attainment process. *Canadian Review of Sociology and Anthropology, 19*(1), 1-28.

Boyd, M. (1985). Educational and occupational attainments of native-born Canadian men and women. In M. Boyd, J. Goyder, et al. (Eds.), *Ascription and achievement: Studies in mobility and status attainment in Canada* (pp. 229-295). Ottawa: Carleton University Press.

Boyd, M. (1990a). *Employment and skill: Men and women in Canada's service economy.* Paper presented at the annual meeting of the Canadian Sociology and Anthropology Association 1990 Learned Societies Conference, Victoria, British Columbia.

Boyd, M. (1990b). Sex differences in occupational skill: Canada, 1961-1986. *Canadian Review of Sociology and Anthropology, 27*(August), 285-315.

Boyd, M., & Humphreys, E. (1979). *Labour markets and sex differences in Canadian incomes* (Discussion Paper No. 143). Ottawa: Economic Council of Canada.

Browning, H., & Singelmann, J. (1978). The transformation of the U.S. labour force: The interaction of industry and occupation. *Politics and Society, 8*(3-4), 481-509.

Carroll, W. K. (1987). Which women are more proletarianized? Gender, class and occupation in Canada. *Canadian Review of Sociology and Anthropology, 24*(4), 571-585.

Clement, W. (1990). Comparative class analysis: Locating Canada in a North American and Nordic context. *Canadian Review of Sociology and Anthropology, 27*(November), 462-486.

Clement, W., & Myles, J. (1994). *Relations of ruling: Class and gender in postindustrial societies.* Montreal: McGill-Queens University Press.

Cohen, G. A. (1978). *Karl Marx's theory of history: A defence.* Princeton, NJ: Princeton University Press.

Cohen, S., & Zysman, J. (1987). *Manufacturing matters: The myth of the post-industrial economy.* New York: Basic Books.

Connelly, P. (1978). *Last hired, first fired: Women and the Canadian work force.* Toronto: The Women's Press.

Cuneo, C. J. (1985). Have women become more proletarianized than men? *Canadian Review of Sociology and Anthropology, 22*(4), 465-495.

Cuneo, C., & Curtis, J. E. (1975). Social ascription in the educational and occupational status attainment of urban Canadians. *Canadian Review of Sociology and Anthropology, 12,* 6-24.

Denton, M., & Hunter, A. A. (1982). *Equality in the workplace: Economic sectors and gender discrimination in Canada* (Discussion Paper Series A No. 6). Ottawa: Labour Canada, Women's Bureau.

England, P. (1979). Women and occupational prestige: A case of vacuous sex equality. *Signs, 5*(2), 252-265.

Fox, B., & Fox, J. (1987). Occupational gender segregation of the Canadian labour force, 1931-1981. *Canadian Review of Sociology and Anthropology, 24*(August), 374-397.

Giddens, A. (1976). Classical social theory and the origins of modern social theory. *American Journal of Sociology, 81*(January), 703-729.

Goyder, J. (1985). Occupational mobility among women. In M. Boyd, J. Goyder, et al. (Eds.), *Ascription and achievement: Studies in mobility and status attainment in Canada* (pp. 297-333). Ottawa: Carleton University Press.

Hartmann, H. (1976). Capitalism, patriarchy and job segregation by sex. *Signs, 3,* 137-168.

Hartmann, H. (1981). The unhappy marriage of Marxism and feminism: Towards a more progressive union. In L. Sargent (Ed.), *Women and revolution* (pp. 1-42). Boston, MA: South End Press.

Kanter, R. (1977). *Men and women of the corporation.* New York: Basic Books.

Kerr, C., Dunlop, J. T., Harbison, F., & Myers, C. (1964). *Industrialism and industrial man.* New York: Oxford University Press.

Lowe, G. (1980). Women, work and the office: The feminization of clerical occupations in Canada, 1901-1931. *Canadian Journal of Sociology, 5,* 354-365.

Lowe, G. (1986). Mechanization, feminization and managerial control in the early twentieth-century office. In C. Heron & R. Storey (Eds.), *On the job: Confronting the labour process in Canada* (pp. 177-209). Kingston/ Montreal: McGill-Queens University Press.

Magun, S. (1982). The rise of service employment in the Canadian economy. *Relations Industrielles, 37*(3), 528-555.

Mahon, R. (1987). From Fordism to ?: New technology, labour markets and unions. *Economic and Industrial Democracy, 8,* 5-60.

Marchak, P. (1987). Rational capitalism and women as labour. In H. J. Maroney & M. Luxton (Eds.), *Feminism and political economy* (pp. 197-212). Toronto: Methuen.

Marsden, L., Harvey, E., & Charner, I. (1975). Female graduates: Their occupational mobility and attainments. *Canadian Review of Sociology and Anthropology, 12*(November, Part I), 385-405.

McInnis, R. M. (1971). Long-run changes in the industrial structure of the Canadian work force. *Canadian Journal of Economics, 4*(3), 353-361.

Meltz, N. M. (1965). *Changes in the occupational composition of the Canadian labour force, 1931-1961* (Department of Manpower and Immigration). Ottawa: Queen's Printer.

Meltz, N. M. (1969). *Manpower In Canada 1931-1961: Historical statistics of the Canadian labour force* (Department of Manpower and Immigration). Ottawa: Queen's Printer.

Myles, J. (1990). States, labour markets and life cycles. In R. Friedland & S. Robertson (Eds.), *Beyond the marketplace: Rethinking economy and society* (pp. 271-299). New York: Aldine de Gruyter.

Myles, J., & Fawcett, G. (1990). *Job skills and the service economy* (Working Paper No. 4). Ottawa: Economic Council of Canada.

Organization for Economic Cooperation and Development. (1988). *Labour force statistics: 1966-86*. Paris: Author.

Picot, W. G. (1986). *Canada's industries: Growth in jobs over three decades* (Catalogue 89-507E). Ottawa: Statistics Canada.

Pineo, P., Porter, J., & McRoberts, H. A. (1977). The 1971 census and the socioeconomic classification of occupations. *Canadian Review of Sociology and Anthropology, 13,* 71-79.

Piore, M., & Sabel, C. (1984). *The second industrial divide*. New York: Basic Books.

Singelmann, J. (1978). *From agriculture to services* (Vol. 69, Sage Library of Social Research). Beverly Hills, CA: Sage.

Smith, N. (1978). *Distributive differentiation by sex in Canada*. M.A. thesis, Department of Sociology and Anthropology, Carleton University, Ottawa.

Sokoloff, N. (1980). *Between money and love*. New York: Praeger.

Sokoloff, N. (1988). Contributions of Marxism and feminism to the sociology of women and work. In A. H. Stromberg & S. Harkness (Eds.), *Women working* (2nd. ed., pp. 116-131). Mountain View, CA: Mayfield.

Stinchcombe, A. L. (1965). Social structure and organizations. In J. G. March (Ed.), *Handbook of organizations* (pp. 142-193). Chicago: McNally.

Ursel, J. (1986). The state and the maintenance of patriarchy: A case study of family, labour and welfare legislation in Canada. In J. Dickinson & B. Russell (Eds.), *Family, economy and the state* (pp. 150-191). Toronto: Garamond.

Wright, E. O. (1978). *Class, crisis and the state*. London: NLB.

Wright, E. O., Costello, C., Hachen, D., & Sprague, J. (1982). The American class structure. *American Sociological Review, 47,* 709-726.

Wright, E. O., & Singelmann, J. (1982). Proletarianization in the changing American class structure. *American Journal of Sociology, 88*(Supplement), 176-209.

PART III

Career Processes and Trends

8

Cumulative Versus Continuous Disadvantage in an Unstructured Labor Market

Gender Differences in the Careers of Television Writers

WILLIAM T. BIELBY
DENISE D. BIELBY

In the television industry in 1982, employed women writers earned 70 cents for each dollar earned by males. Among male television writers, median earnings doubled between 1982 and 1990 and grew each year throughout that period, with the exception of the 1988 strike year (see Figure 8.1 and Table 8.1). Over the same period, median earnings of women grew just as much, but the trend was much more erratic. By 1990, women writers were still earning, on average, 70 cents for each dollar earned by males. In this chapter, we explore the underlying labor market dynamics that produce this gender gap in earnings among writers in the television industry.

The primary goal of our empirical analysis is to compare two models of labor market dynamics. The first is a model of *cumulative disadvan-*

AUTHORS' NOTE: This research was completed with support from the National Science Foundation (SES 89-10039) and the Academic Senate of the University of California, Santa Barbara. We thank Jerry Jacobs and Barbara Reskin for their comments on an earlier draft.

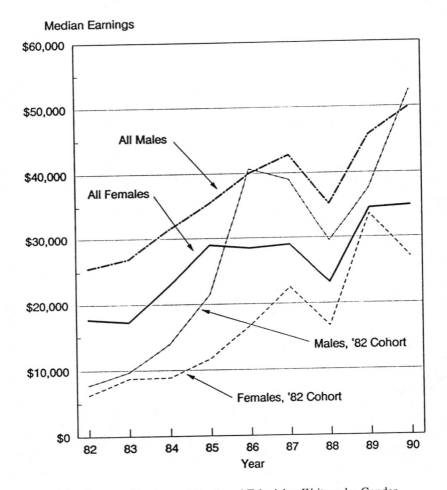

Figure 8.1. Median Earnings of Employed Television Writers, by Gender, 1982-1990

tage whereby differential access to opportunity is increasingly conse-quential over the course of writers' careers. According to this model, males benefit more than females from access to career opportunities, and as a result small gender differences at entry into the career generate increasingly divergent earnings trajectories over time. The second is a model of *continuous disadvantage* whereby the contributions of women writers are uniformly devalued across career stages. According to this

Table 8.1 Total Writers, Employed Writers, and Percentage Employed, Median Earnings of Employed Writers, Average Years in WGA of Employed Writers, and Average Age of Employed Writers, by Gender, 1982–1990

Year	Total Writers	Employed Writers	Percentage Employed	Median Earnings	Average Years in WGA	Average Age
Females						
1982	1,011	402	40	$17,761	5.7	39.1
1983	1,069	413	39	$17,303	5.9	39.0
1984	1,147	439	38	$22,903	6.3	39.3
1985	1,225	455	37	$29,000	6.9	39.8
1986	1,316	521	40	$28,495	7.1	40.0
1987	1,422	575	40	$29,000	7.2	40.6
1988	1,499	545	36	$23,221	7.7	40.7
1989	1,592	609	38	$34,625	7.9	40.9
1990	1,687	627	37	$35,000	8.1	41.2
Percent Change						
1982–1990	67	56		97	42	5
Males						
1982	3,583	1,624	45	$25,552	10.1	43.8
1983	3,724	1,585	43	$26,902	10.3	43.7
1984	3,888	1,625	42	$31,500	10.3	43.7
1985	4,091	1,719	42	$35,500	10.6	43.9
1986	4,324	1,837	42	$40,004	10.5	43.7
1987	4,595	1,937	42	$42,750	10.3	43.5
1988	4,759	1,828	38	$35,306	10.6	43.2
1989	4,974	1,953	39	$45,750	10.4	43.2
1990	5,198	2,024	39	$50,000	10.6	43.1
Percent Change						
1982–1990	45	25		96	5	−2

model, the barriers faced by women writers begin at entry into the industry and pose a constant source of disadvantage over the course of their careers.

A secondary goal of our empirical analysis is to examine whether there has been a measurable erosion during the 1980s in the career barriers faced by women writers in the television industry, regardless of whether the underlying dynamic is one of cumulative or continuous disadvantage. On one hand, over the period from 1982 through 1990, women have increased their representation in decision-making roles in production (e.g., as writer-producers of successful series) and, to a lesser extent, in programming, although barriers to career advancement for women have been documented and widely publicized (Bielby & Bielby, 1987b, 1989). On the other hand, as described below, the labor market for television writers is highly unstructured, making it difficult to identify the specific structures and practices that place women at a disadvantage and to design, implement, and enforce effective remedies. Accordingly, gender differences in labor market dynamics may or may not exhibit a trend of *declining disadvantage* over time, and we assess whether such a trend exists in our statistical models.

Below, we first describe the labor market for television writers and discuss implications for gender differences in career trajectories. We then describe our data and models for evaluating alternative conceptualizations of the labor market. After presenting the results of our analysis, we discuss implications for future research on the entertainment industry and for labor market issues more generally.

The Market for Television Writers

Technically, a television writer is a salaried employee in an industry dominated by about a dozen large corporations. Nearly half of all writers are employed by the television divisions of the seven major motion picture studios (Columbia/Sony, Time-Warner, Universal-MCA, Paramount, Fox, MGM, and Disney). Together, the major studios, the three networks, and the five or six largest independent production companies account for about two thirds of all employment.

However, the employment relation for television writers is closer to the kind of short-term contracting typical of craft administration of production (Stinchcombe, 1959) than to the bureaucratically organized internal labor market typical of large firms. Writers are employed for the duration of a project, which might be as short as a few weeks for work on a single telefilm, pilot, or episode of a prime-time series. Most secure (and potentially most lucrative) is employment as a writer-producer on an ongoing prime-time series. Those series last anywhere from a few weeks to a few years, but even on the most enduring series there is considerable turnover among the production staff from season to season. In short, television writers attempt to sustain careers by moving from project to project, perhaps working for dozens of employers over a period of a few years.

Although this project-oriented employment is similar in many ways to work in the construction trades, the labor market differs from that found in craft administration of production in one important respect: The quality of the work cannot be unambiguously evaluated based on technical and measurable features of the finished product. Instead, the quality of work and the competence of the writer is evaluated post hoc based on whether or not the product is seen by large numbers of viewers with the demographic traits most valued by advertisers. Moreover, the size of the audience for a writer's work is influenced by many factors that are beyond the control of the individual writer.

DiMaggio (1977) has described the organization of production surrounding this kind of work as a "brokerage" administration of production. In "culture industries" such as the television industry, the inherent conflict between creative and commercial interests creates unique problems of governance that cannot be effectively resolved with either a bureaucratic authority hierarchy or a craft system based on short-term contracting. Instead, in popular culture industries, brokers mediate between artists (e.g., writers) and managers (e.g., network programmers), performing the monitoring function that resides in authority relations in a bureaucracy and in professional standards and contract specifications in craft administration. According to DiMaggio,

> Like craft administrators, brokerage administrators lack professional competence to build a finished product and must defer to specialists beneath them on the organizational charts; but unlike craft administrators, they can never be certain exactly what professional competence is or who may be expected to possess it. Artists, and often brokers themselves, can only be evaluated post hoc on the basis of success, or on the basis of reputation or track record. (p. 442)

In television production, brokerage occurs among individual artists, projects (series), and networks purchasing those projects. The brokers in this system are established writer-producers. Among network executives, these individuals have reputations for successfully developing new projects, overseeing their production, and managing the inherent conflict between artistic and commercial interests. DiMaggio describes the specific arrangements in the television industry as a *centralized* brokerage system:

> In such a system, management exerts strong pressures upon creators, and innovation and diversity are, in most cases, successfully minimized. Brokers represent management's views to creators; they themselves are subject to

vertical communication through multiple hierarchies of control; decisions to fund products are made by committee; and management personnel are involved in the creative process itself. (p. 443)

Finally, the evaluation of professional competence in culture industries is unique in that it is driven by fashion (Hirsch, 1972). Thus, although reputations are built on past success, it is only success in arenas that remain fashionable that contributes to a writer's marketability. As a result, the "human capital" that is acquired through labor market experience atrophies rapidly, and only very recent experience yields a return in the market.

Implications for Gender Differences in Career Trajectories

Faulkner and Anderson (1987) argue that short-term contracting in a highly uncertain and unstable business environment supports a process of cumulative advantage in career trajectories (see also Allison, Long, & Krauz, 1982). Their data on the careers of film producers and directors strongly support their assertion, and we expect to see a similar pattern among writers in the television industry.

A cumulative advantage process per se need not imply that women experience a cumulative *disadvantage,* especially if men and women begin their careers with comparable resources. Moreover, because only recent experience is valued in the market, gender differences in the continuity of labor force participation—a factor emphasized in human capital accounts of the wage gap (Polachek, 1979)—should not place women writers at a significant disadvantage.

However, there are features of brokerage administration that might pose barriers that have a continuous impact on the careers of women writers. One is the highly skewed sex ratio within the industry. The network executives who make decisions about program procurement and scheduling and those at the production companies who make decisions about financing new projects are almost always white males. Women constitute less than 15% of the executive producers of prime-time programs and less than 25% of the writers working in television. With decisions being made in the context of high levels of ambiguity, risk, and uncertainty, social similarity is likely to have a significant impact on how writers' reputations are evaluated (Kanter, 1977). As a result, women writers are likely to remain peripheral to decision makers' social networks and thus have limited access to well-placed producers and programmers.

A second feature that might place women at a disadvantage is the typecasting of writers. In his study of musical directors working in feature film, Faulkner (1983) describes how artists must balance the trade-off between short-term employment security arising from stylistic specialization versus the long-term threat to artists' careers from being typecast. An artist who is labeled too narrowly risks falling out of fashion as tastes change. The careers of television writers are likely to be subject to similar processes. Moreover, the typecasting of television writers is also likely to be shaped by cultural stereotypes. Because of sex stereotyping, women writers may be subject to *role encapsulation* (Kanter, 1977). Employment of women who defy conventions is likely to be viewed as especially risky. Thus women writers are likely to encounter barriers to career advancement due to the limited range of writing opportunities open to them.

In sum, in the television industry, both the business environment and the labor market are characterized by high levels of risk and uncertainty. The matching of individual writers to employment opportunities is brokered by a small number of writer-producers whom network executives rely on to manage the inherent conflict between creative and commercial interests. In such a system, women writers are disadvantaged by limited access to informal networks and by typecasting of writers by gender. In terms of career trajectories, the dynamics of disadvantage might take on one of two forms: cumulative disadvantage, whereby differential access to opportunity is increasingly consequential over the course of the career, or continuous disadvantage, whereby gender barriers pose a constant source of disadvantage at every career stage. Regardless of whether the underlying dynamic is one of cumulative or continuous disadvantage, women's increased representation in broker roles may be contributing to a pattern of declining disadvantage over time.

Data, Measures, and Models

The data for our study describe the employment and earnings trajectories of 6,935 television writers, 5,167 of whom were employed at least once during the period from 1982 through 1990. These data are from the employment and membership records of the Writers Guild of America, West (WGA). They cover nearly all writing for episodic series and films for television produced in Hollywood. Not included are news, sports, and other nonfiction programming, game shows, and the daytime dramas produced in New York. Also not included in our analyses are data on a small number of writers for whom information on age is not available (see Bielby & Bielby, 1989, for details).

Our model is a pooled cross-sectional time-series specification of the form

$$Y_{ict} = a + b_1 X_i + b_2 W_{it} + Z_c + d_t + e_{ict,}$$ 8.1

where Y_{ict} is log earnings for the ith individual in cohort c in year t, and cohort is defined as year admitted to membership in the WGA. Attributes of individuals that do not vary over time (e.g., minority status) are included in X_i, and individual traits that vary over time (e.g., years of experience) are included in W_{it}. The term Z_c captures effects on earnings that are unique to a specific cohort over time, whereas d_t captures year-specific effects on earnings. The disturbance, e_{ict} is assumed to have zero mean and constant variance and to be uncorrelated with the other independent variables.

Minority status and gender are represented by binary (0-1) variables, coded 1 for minority and female, respectively. Work experience is measured in two ways. The first is years of membership in the WGA.[1] Because less than half of all writers are employed in any given year (see Table 8.1), years of membership does not equal years of employment experience. Consequently, in some models we also include binary variables for lagged employment status 1, 2, and 3 years prior to year t.

Age is measured as year t minus year of birth. Year effects are captured by eight binary variables, with 1982 as the reference category. We expect writers who began their careers prior to the mid-1970s to be disadvantaged in the labor market, and therefore cohort effects are captured by two binary variables, the first coded 1 for those admitted to the WGA prior to 1971 and the second coded 1 for those admitted between 1971 and 1975. Finally, our models include a binary variable coded 1 if the writer received earnings from work in feature films during year t.

Cumulative Versus Continuous Disadvantage: Hypotheses

Table 8.2 summarizes our hypotheses regarding the determinants of earnings under alternative conceptualizations of labor market dynamics.

Table 8.2 Hypothesized Effects of Independent Variables on Earnings for Different Models of Labor Market Dynamics

Variable	Cumulative Disadvantage	Continuous Disadvantage	Declining Disadvantage
Female	–	–	–
Experience (years in industry)	Inverted U	Inverted U	Inverted U
Lagged employment	+	+	+
Lagged earnings	+	+	+
Control variables			
Age	Inverted U	Inverted U	Inverted U
Pre-1971 cohort	–	–	–
1971–1975 cohort	–	–	–
Minority	–	–	–
Film earnings	–	–	–
Year (except strike year)	+	+	+
Gender interactions			
Female ×			
Experience	–	0	?
Lagged Employment	–	0	?
Lagged Earnings	–	0	?
Year	?	?	–

NOTE: + = variable is hypothesized to increase earnings; – = variable is hypothesized to decrease earnings; 0 = no relationship is hypothesized; ? = no prediction is made.

The main effects of gender, experience, and control variables are assumed to be the same across models. Each assumes a net negative effect of being female, effects of years of experience that increase at a decreasing rate, and positive effects of prior employment and earnings.

We assume that, net of experience, the contributions of older writers are disadvantaged in the labor market (D. Bielby & Bielby, 1991). The net age-earnings profile is expected to take the shape of an inverted U, peaking at a relatively young age. Similarly, we expect writers who began their careers prior to 1975 to be disadvantaged and hypothesize negative effects for the binary variables denoting year of entry prior to the mid-1970s. Opportunities for minority writers are constrained due to widespread typecasting by race and ethnicity (Bielby & Bielby, 1987b, 1989), and thus we hypothesize a negative net effect of minority status.

Some writers find occasional work in television, even though the focus of their careers is in the field of feature films. For many of these writers, employment in television is incidental to their work in the area of feature films (for example, they may receive compensation for a television spin-off from a successful film). Others might seek out work in television only when employment is unavailable in the film industry. Accordingly, we expect employment in feature film in year t to be negatively associated with television earnings in that year.

Because the collective bargaining agreement specifies annual increases in minimum compensation for virtually all types of writing assignments in television, we expect earnings to increase annually from 1982 through 1990, with one exception. A strike in 1988 halted production for several months, so we expect earnings in that year to fall substantially below earnings for the previous year.

The three models of labor market dynamics—cumulative disadvantage, continuous disadvantage, and declining disadvantage—are differentiated by their implications for interaction effects by gender. We choose between the cumulative disadvantage and continuous disadvantage models based on interaction effects between gender and experience, between gender and prior employment, and between gender and prior earnings. The cumulative disadvantage model assumes that access to opportunity early in the career pays off more for men than for women. As a result, the gender gap in wages is expected to increase with experience, as suggested in the trend for the cohort of writers who began their careers in 1982, as portrayed in Figure 8.1.[2] According to the cumulative disadvantage model, the net returns to experience, lagged employment, and lagged earnings are expected to be lower for women than for men.

According to the continuous disadvantage model, a pervasive bias against women affects them equally through all stages in their careers. The disadvantage at entry is neither greater nor worse than at later stages in the career. Thus the continuous disadvantage model implies no interaction between gender and measures of experience, prior employment, and prior earnings.

Neither the cumulative disadvantage nor the continuous disadvantage model provides an explicit prediction about the size and direction of the Gender × Year interaction. Over time and net of all other factors in these two models, the wage gap between men and women might be increasing, decreasing, or not changing at all. In contrast, according to the model of declining disadvantage, there is a trend toward an erosion of gender barriers and a resulting decline in the gender gap in wages over time. Whether the underlying dynamic is one of cumulative or continuous disadvantage, forces are at work that are slowly but surely dismantling the sources of that disadvantage.

In sum, if we find strong evidence of lower returns among women than among men in the effects of experience, prior employment, and prior earnings, then the cumulative disadvantage model will be favored over the continuous disadvantage model. In contrast, if there is a large net effect of gender but no interaction of gender with measures of experience, prior employment, or prior earnings, then the continuous disadvantage model will be favored. Regardless of the outcome of this comparison, a large negative interaction of female by year will provide evidence of declining disadvantage.[3] Absence of such an interaction will suggest that the barriers faced by women writers have persisted throughout the 1980s, despite women's increasing representation in positions of power and responsibility and despite increased attention to the problem of gender bias in the industry.

Findings

Tables 8.1 and 8.3 present a portrait of a career in television writing as a "revolving door" (Jacobs, 1989) for both men and women. Over the period from 1982 through 1990, the number of writers pursuing work in television has grown substantially more than the amount of available work, with the rate of employment declining accordingly from 40% to 37% among women and from 45% to 39% among men (Table 8.1). Over the same period, women have increased their representation among total writers (from 22% to 24.5%) and employed writers (from 19.8% to 23.7%).

Consistent with Faulkner and Anderson's (1987) notion of careers in Hollywood as a series of short-term contracts, Table 8.3 shows a high degree of discontinuity in the employment of both women and men writers (also see Bielby & Bielby, 1987a). For example, about a fourth of those employed in the industry in 1982 were not among those working in television the following year. It was also found that nearly half of those working in 1982 were not employed 8 years later. Similarly, over a fourth of those employed as television writers in 1990 were new to the industry, and fewer than half of those employed in that year were working as television writers 5 years earlier.

The employment patterns portrayed in Tables 8.1 and 8.3 suggest that the high level of risk and uncertainty in the business context facing programmers and producers also characterizes the careers of individual

Table 8.3 Stability of Employment, by Gender and Year

Subsequent Employment of Those Employed in Year 1982 – Percent Employed, by Year (n = 2,026)			Prior Employment of Those Employed in 1990 – Percent Employed, by Year (n = 2,651)		
Year	*Females*	*Males*	*Year*	*Females*	*Males*
1982	NA	NA	1982	34	41
1983	74	75	1983	36	43
1984	69	68	1984	40	46
1985	65	66	1985	43	50
1986	65	64	1986	49	57
1987	61	62	1987	58	62
1988	57	56	1988	59	63
1989	58	55	1989	71	74
1990	52	51	1990	NA	NA

writers. It is in precisely this kind of environment that the sources of gender bias are likely to be subtle and indirect, subject to the stereotypes and preconceptions of decision makers who place a premium on social similarity in order to establish trust and avoid risk (Ruble & Ruble, 1982; Salancik & Pfeffer, 1978). Tables 8.4 and 8.5 present the results of statistical analyses designed to determine how these sources of bias are embodied in labor market dynamics.

Our strategy was to estimate and contrast models with and without gender interactions under three alternative specifications. The first specification (Models 1 and 2) includes our measure of experience but not lagged employment and lagged earnings. This specification has the advantage of exploiting all 9 years of data from 1982 through 1990, reflecting the earnings trajectories of the 5,167 writers who worked at least once during that period. The second specification (Models 3 and 4) adds binary variables for whether a writer was employed in years $t-1$, $t-2$, and $t-3$. Because data on employment are not available for years prior to 1982, estimates for this specification are based on a shorter time span—from 1985 through 1990—and pertain to the 4,564 writers who worked at least once during this period. The final specification (Models 5 and 6) includes effects of earnings in years $t-1$ and $t-2$ and is limited to writers with at least one employment spell of 3 consecutive years between 1983 and 1990 (i.e., nonzero earnings in years t, $t-1$, and $t-2$). Accordingly, the results of this specification apply to a select subgroup of

Table 8.4 Earnings Regressions, Pooled Cross-Sectional Time-Series Models, OLS Estimates

Variable	Model 1	Model 2	Model 3	Model 4
Cohort				
Pre-1971	−0.185**	−0.175**	0.178**	0.169**
1971-1975	−0.098**	−0.092	0.169**	0.167**
Year				
1983	0.048	0.055	—	—
1984	0.152**	0.176**	—	—
1985	0.246**	0.267**	—	—
1986	0.302**	0.328**	0.084*	0.082
1987	0.403**	0.425**	0.203**	0.194**
1988	0.179**	0.188**	−0.053	−0.075
1989	0.440**	0.473**	0.256**	0.250**
1990	0.475**	0.480**	0.308**	0.276**
Experience	0.118**	0.116**	−0.011*	−0.010
Experience^2	−0.002**	−0.002**	0.001**	0.001**
Minority	−0.221**	−0.190**	−0.116	−0.045
Age × 10	0.053	0.053	−0.064	−0.008
Age^2 × 10	−0.004**	−0.004**	−0.002*	−0.000*
Film earnings	−0.202**	−0.196**	−0.091**	−0.090**
Employed—Lag 1	—	—	0.776**	0.765**
Employed—Lag 2	—	—	0.435**	0.467**
Employed—Lag 3	—	—	0.447**	0.448**
Female	−0.216**	−0.137	−0.249**	−0.228**
Gender Interactions				
Female ×				
Experience	—	0.012	—	0.002
Experience^2	—	−0.001*	—	−0.000
1983	—	−0.041	—	—
1984	—	−0.117	—	—
1985	—	−0.105	—	—
1986	—	−0.122	—	0.015
1987	—	−0.101	—	0.045
1988	—	−0.042	—	0.096
1989	—	−0.140	—	0.030
1990	—	−0.020	—	0.140
Film	—	−0.032	—	—
Minority	—	−0.109	—	−0.228
Employed—Lag 1			—	0.044
Employed—Lag 2			—	−0.134
Employed—Lag 3			—	−0.011
Constant	9.916	9.897	9.894	9.868
Root MSE	1.413	1.413	1.296	1.296
R^2	0.080	0.080	0.210	0.210
N (person-years)	20,717	20,717	14,629	14,629

(Continued)

Table 8.4 (Continued)

	Numerator df	F Ratio	Numerator df	F Ratio
Tests:				
All interactions	12	1.431	11	1.288
Experience interactions	2	6.339**	2	0.906
Lag employment interactions	—	—	3	1.509
Year interactions	8	0.512	5	0.74

*$p < .05$; **$p < .01$.

2,415 more successful writers with relatively continuous employment histories in the television industry.

Results for the first two specifications (Models 1 through 4) appear in Table 8.4, and those for the third specification (Models 5 and 6) are shown in Table 8.5. Overall, the results provide extremely strong support for a model of continuous disadvantage and fail to support a model of cumulative disadvantage. First, in each instance, a global test of the gender interactions failed to reject the null hypothesis of no interaction (see row labeled "all interactions" at the bottom of Tables 8.4 and 8.5). Models 2, 4, and 6 provide no significant improvement in fit over Models 1, 3, and 5, respectively. Second, specific tests of the Gender × Experience interactions failed to reject the null hypothesis in two of the three comparisons, and in the third (Model 1 vs. Model 2), the gender difference in the effect of experience is opposite in direction to that implied by the cumulative advantage model (see row labeled "experience interactions" at the bottom of Tables 8.4 and 8.5). Third, we failed to reject the hypothesis that the effects of prior employment on earnings are identical for men and women (see row labeled "lag employment interactions" at the bottom of Table 8.4 and the coefficient for lagged employment in Table 8.5). Finally, the small but significant interactions of gender and lagged earnings (see row labeled "lag earnings interactions" in Table 8.5) are opposite in direction to the hypothesis derived from the cumulative advantage model (.012 and −.001 for the linear and quadratic interaction terms, respectively). In short, there is no evidence that men receive higher returns than women with respect to the effects of years of experience, prior employment, and prior earnings on current earnings. That is, there is no evidence that the sizable overall gender difference in earnings is due to a small disadvantage faced by women at entry that accelerates through a process of cumulative disadvantage.

Nonetheless, the results for the models with no gender interactions show a remarkably large net disadvantage faced by women writers com-

Table 8.5 Earnings Regressions, Effects of Prior Earnings Among Those Employed in 3 Consecutive Years: Pooled Cross-Sectional Time-Series Models, OLS Estimates

Variable	Model 5	Model 6
Cohort		
Pre-1971	−0.036	−0.035
1971–1975	0.002	0.003
Year		
1986	−0.047	−0.029
1987	−0.034	−0.026
1988	−0.380**	−0.395**
1989	0.093*	0.111**
1990	0.010	0.037
Experience	0.013*	0.012
Experience^2	−0.000	−0.000
Minority	−0.038	0.003
Age × 10	−0.348**	−0.346**
Age^2 × 10	0.002*	0.002*
Film earnings	−0.144**	−0.144**
Log earnings—Lag 1	0.517**	0.506**
Log earnings—Lag 2	0.211**	0.209**
Employed—Lag 3	0.082**	0.115**
Female	−0.106**	−0.514*
Gender Interactions		
Female ×		
Experience	—	0.007
Experience^2	—	−0.000
1986	—	−0.087
1987	—	−0.039
1988	—	0.061
1989	—	−0.081
1990	—	−0.121
Minority	—	−0.116
Log earnings—Lag 1	—	0.048
Log earnings—Lag 2	—	0.004
Employed—Lag 3	—	−0.143
Constant	4.009	4.112
Root MSE	0.961	0.961
R^2	0.455	0.456
N (person-years)	8,579	8,579

	Numerator df	F Ratio
Tests:		
All interactions	11	1.554
Experience interactions	2	0.654
Lag earnings interactions	2	3.172*
Year interactions	5	1.188

$*p < .05$; $**p < .01$.

pared to men of similar age, experience, minority status, and recent employment history. Holding these factors constant, women face a net earnings disadvantage of approximately 22% (Model 1) to 25% (Model 3). Moreover, when we examine the relatively advantaged group of writers who have employment spells in television of 3 consecutive years (Model 5), women still earn 11% less than men with similar experience and comparable levels of earnings in the previous 2 years. In short, there is substantial evidence that in the 1980s women television writers faced formidable obstacles to career advancement regardless of age, years of experience, or pattern of employment.

Results in Tables 8.4 and 8.5 show no evidence of declining disadvantage. In each instance, we failed to reject the null hypothesis of no Gender × Year interactions (row labeled "year interactions" at the bottom of Tables 8.4 and 8.5), and there is no evidence of a declining effect of gender over time in the estimates of those interactions for Models 2, 4, and 6. In short, with respect to the impact of gender on earnings, the structure of disadvantage was essentially static during the 1980s. The net gender gap in wages was as large at the end of the decade as it was in the 1980s.

Our findings are surprisingly definitive. The pattern of coefficients is consistent with only one of the three models we posed: the model of continuous disadvantage. Our confidence in our results is reinforced by two other features of our analysis. First, by using a pooled cross-sectional design, we are exploiting both intra- and interindividual variation, and with such large sample sizes we certainly would have detected substantively significant interactions had they existed.[4] Second, the pattern of coefficients for the control variables is almost exactly as hypothesized. Year effects increase monotonically, with the exception of the strike year. Older writers and those from the earliest cohorts face a net disadvantage, as hypothesized.[5] Minority writers are disadvantaged according to Model 1, although Models 3 and 5 show this to be largely mediated by differences between minority and nonminority writers in prior employment and earnings. Model 1 shows an impact of years of experience that increases at a decreasing rate (peaking at about 28 years). However, Model 3 suggests that net of the pattern of very recent employment, additional years of experience in the industry actually place writers at a disadvantage in the labor market (although this pattern is not replicated in Model 5). Finally, as hypothesized, the effect of work in feature film is consistently negative in our models.

The estimates in Tables 8.4 and 8.5 provide no evidence of a declining gender gap in earnings. However, those specifications do not test for the possibility that some gender barriers are eroding; they apply only for the most recent cohorts. We subsequently modified Models 1 and 3 by adding two terms: a binary variable coded 1 for recent cohorts (writers who began their careers in 1988, 1989, or 1990) and an interaction— Female × Recent Cohort (results not reported in Table 8.4). The results provide our only evidence that, at least for some women writers, opportunities are improving. For the modified Model 3, the estimate for the interaction term is .24, almost exactly offsetting the main effect of gender, and it is statistically significant ($t = 2.638$, $p < .01$). For the modified Model 1, the estimated interaction term is .19, nearly offsetting the main effect of gender. However, in this model, the interaction term is not quite significant in a two-tailed test ($t = 1.886$, $p = .059$). Together these results suggest that women writers in more recent cohorts do not face the same disadvantages that limit the earnings of more experienced women writers. Moreover, when the results are disaggregated by including separate main and interaction effects for each of the three cohorts, the point estimates suggest improving earnings prospects for successive cohorts. Once again, however, the Gender × Cohort interactions are statistically significant for Model 3 ($p < .05$) but not for Model 1 ($p = .17$). Furthermore, it remains to be seen whether gains experienced by recent cohorts of women will be sustained over their careers.

In sum, our results suggest that women writers in the television industry face gender barriers that reduce their earnings substantially, compared to men of similar age and experience. These disadvantages persist throughout the career, reflecting a process of continuous disadvantage rather than one of cumulative disadvantage. Overall, there is little evidence that the barriers faced by women writers have eroded over the past decade, with the possible exception of a recent improvement in the earnings prospects faced by women writers just starting their careers.

Summary and Conclusions

The earnings gap between men and women writers with comparable years of experience in the television industry is approximately 25%. We have shown that women writers face disadvantages in the labor market throughout their careers. Although opportunities may have improved for women in very recent cohorts, we detected little evidence that the gender gap in earnings narrowed overall during the 1980s. In contrast, in most other sectors of the labor market, the gender gap in earnings among men and women in the same occupation and industry is much smaller than what we find for women television writers, and it is shrinking over time (Goldin, 1990). Thus it appears that the television industry has been insulated from social and economic changes that have improved earnings prospects for women more generally.

Research on other occupations and industries attributes extreme gender segregation to the sex labeling of jobs and sex-specific demand (Bielby & Baron, 1986; Reskin & Roos, 1990). In contrast, the career barriers that women face in the television industry arise from somewhat different mechanisms. Even though typecasting produces an unequal distribution of men and women across genres, segregation is far from complete. For example, women wrote for 90% of the prime-time series broadcast during the 1990-1991 season, and no series could be described as "women's work." Men account for at least 40% of the writers of every series, even those, such as *China Beach* and *Designing Women,* that have had large female audiences (Bielby & Bielby, 1992). In short, there is little evidence that men successfully exclude women from the most successful writing or that men are fleeing newly feminized areas of the profession. Instead, continuous disadvantage appears to be sustained by more subtle forms of discrimination. In the male-dominated world of studio and network executives, male writers are better known and are perceived as better risks than equally successful female writers. As a result, male writer-producers are more likely to get long-term development deals and multiple-series commitments from the networks. Our findings suggest that men gain this advantage early in their careers and are able to sustain it over the years, even as they work alongside women.

The features of the labor market for television writers underlying the dynamic of continuous disadvantage also make it resistant to change. Although most television writers are legally and technically employees of large organizations, the actual circumstances of their employment are similar to those of outside contractors hired for the duration of a short-term project. As a result, gender barriers to career advancement cannot be linked to formal organizational structures and policies, such as segregated internal labor markets or biased hiring and promotion criteria (Roos & Reskin, 1984). Therefore, dismantling gender barriers is not as simple as identifying and changing official organizational structures and practices.

Instead, the lines of authority and responsibility for making decisions regarding the hiring and compensation of television writers are often blurred. A typical television series is a joint venture between the executive producer's small production company and the major studio financing the production. The executive producer responsible for assembling a writing staff is likely to be reporting to one executive employed by the studio and another employed by the network. These executives represent the often differing commercial interests of two large organizations, and each is likely to demand input into decisions regarding the hiring and compensation of writers. Moreover, in decision making about creative personnel, criteria for a successful outcome are always ambiguous, and a large body of research demonstrates that social similarity in general and gender stereotypes in particular are likely to influence decisions under such conditions (Brewer & Kramer, 1985; Salancik & Pfeffer, 1978; Tetlock, 1985). Therefore, with no effective accountability regarding a policy of equal opportunity and blurred lines of authority, it is not clear who would establish such a policy and how accountability and enforcement might be implemented.

The same features of the labor market that sustain gender barriers may also explain why opportunities appear to be improving for recent cohorts of women. Although the typecasting of writers limits women's opportunities for employment outside of specific genres, it is precisely those genres in which women are overrepresented that have been the most successful with audiences in recent years. For example, data for prime-time network series during the 1986-1987 season reveal that women writers were twice as likely to find employment on situation comedies as on action-adventure dramas (Bielby & Bielby, 1989). Since then, situation comedies have proliferated on the network schedule, whereas the number of action dramas has declined substantially (W. Bielby & Bielby, 1991). As a result, the number of women in executive producer and supervising producer roles has increased, as well. In 1986-1987, women held such roles on 14 of the 88 series appearing on the three major networks. During the 1991-1992 season, women filled those roles on 30 network series, including highly rated shows such as *Roseanne, Designing Women, The Cosby Show, Murphy Brown, Golden Girls, Empty Nest, Home Improvement, Perfect Strangers, Doogie Howser, M.D., L.A. Law,* and *Northern Exposure.* If social similarity does indeed influence the decision making of those in broker roles, then an increased representation of women in such roles is likely to improve the employment prospects for women television writers in general.

Unfortunately, so long as typecasting of women by genre persists, these gains may be short-lived, for the popularity of specific genres is highly cyclical (Bielby & Bielby, 1990). Eventually, the situation comedy will again fade in popularity, as it did in the mid-1970s. Women's gains in writer-producer roles outside this genre have been more limited, restricting opportunities for them to occupy broker roles in other areas (Steenland, 1990). Moreover, creative interests in the television industry are subordinated to commercial interests, and until women significantly increase their representation in top executive positions at the major studios and networks, women's opportunities are likely to remain vulnerable to trends in the popularity of specific genres.

The research reported here demonstrates that gender difference in the labor market for television writers is characterized by a dynamic of continuous disadvantage. Our evidence linking that dynamic to the brokerage system of administration and the business context of the industry has been indirect. Our future research will examine these issues more directly. For example, we are currently collecting longitudinal data on women's representation in writer-producer roles and in executive positions at the major studios and networks. With that data, we will be able to explore the relative impact of typecasting by genre and the gender composition of decision-making roles on women's employment prospects. To assess how formal networks of interorganizational relations affect women's careers, we will examine gender differences in the relationship between agency representation and career success. Talent agents have the power to link writers to production companies, and we hypothesize that an agency's ties to those companies are more beneficial to men's careers than to women's. In completing this research program, we expect to develop a better understanding of gender bias in the labor market for television in particular and in the sources of bias in unstructured labor markets more generally.

Notes

1. We do not count years of experience prior to 1950 because there was very little original writing for television done before that year. Therefore, years of experience is $(t - $ admit year) if admit year was 1950 or later and $(t - 50)$ if year of admission to the WGA was 1949 or earlier.

2. In 1982, 55 women and 130 men from the 1982 cohort were employed. By 1990, only 33 women and 80 men from the 1982 cohort were employed.

3. Strictly speaking, if the cumulative disadvantage model is favored over the model of continuous disadvantage, then a process of declining disadvantage would imply a three-way interaction between time, gender, and the effects of experience, prior employment, and prior earnings.

4. Moreover, inspection of collinearity diagnostics indicates that our failure to detect interactions is not due to inflated levels of sampling variation and covariation.

5. In Models 1, 3, and 5, the curvilinear age effects are negative throughout the age range in our sample. In Model 1, point estimates imply an age effect ranging from $-.019$ at age 30 to $-.042$ at age 60. In Model 3, the effects range from $-.020$ at age 30 to $-.033$ at age 60. In Model 5, the corresponding effects range from $-.021$ at age 30 to $-.008$ at age 60.

References

Allison, P. D., Long, J. S., & Krauz, T. K. (1982). Cumulative advantage and inequality in science. *American Sociological Review, 47,* 615-625.

Bielby, D. D., & Bielby, W. T. (1991, November). *Older writers' participation in television production.* Paper presented at the annual meeting of the Gerontological Society of America, San Francisco.

Bielby, W. T., & Baron, J. N. (1986). Men and women at work: Sex segregation and statistical discrimination. *American Journal of Sociology, 91,* 759-799.

Bielby, W. T., & Bielby, D. D. (1987a). *Employment opportunities for television writers: Continuity and change from 1960 to the present.* Los Angeles: Writers Guild of America, West.

Bielby, W. T., & Bielby, D. D. (1987b). *The 1987 Hollywood writers report: A study of ethnic, gender and age employment practices.* Los Angeles: Writers Guild of America, West.

Bielby, W. T., & Bielby, D. D. (1989). *The 1989 Hollywood writers report: Unequal access, unequal pay.* Los Angeles: Writers Guild of America, West.

Bielby, W. T., & Bielby, D. D. (1990, August). *Organizational concentration and the diversity of network television programming.* Paper presented at the annual meeting of the American Sociological Association, Washington, DC.

Bielby, W. T., & Bielby, D. D. (1991, August). *"Tried and true is dead and buried": Genre, institutionalized decision-making, and claims to uniqueness in prime time television.* Paper presented at the annual meeting of the American Sociological Association, Cincinnati, OH.

Bielby, W. T., & Bielby, D. D. (1992). *The 1992 Hollywood writers report.* Los Angeles: Writers Guild of America, West.

Brewer, M. B., & Kramer, R. M. (1985). The psychology of intergroup attitudes and behavior. *Annual Review of Psychology, 36,* 219-243.

DiMaggio, P. (1977). Market structure, the creative process, and popular culture: Toward an organizational reinterpretation of mass culture theory. *Journal of Popular Culture, 11,* 433-451.

Faulkner, R. R. (1983). *Music on demand: Composers and careers in the Hollywood film industry.* New Brunswick, NJ: Transaction Books.

Faulkner, R. R., & Anderson, A. B. (1987). Short-term projects and emergent careers: Evidence from Hollywood. *American Journal of Sociology, 92,* 879-909.

Goldin, C. (1990). *Understanding the gender gap: An economic history of American women.* New York: Oxford University Press.

Hirsch, P. M. (1972). Processing fads and fashions: An organization-set analysis of cultural industry systems. *American Journal of Sociology, 77,* 639-659.

Jacobs, J. A. (1989). *Revolving doors: Sex segregation in women's careers.* Stanford, CA: Stanford University Press.

Kanter, R. M. (1977). *Men and women of the corporation*. New York: Harper & Row.

Polachek, S. W. (1979). Occupational segregation among women: Theory, evidence, and a prognosis. In C. B. Lloyd, E. S. Andrews, & C. L. Gilroy (Eds.), *Women in the labor market* (pp. 137-157). New York: Columbia University Press.

Reskin, B. F., & Roos, P. (1990). *Job queues, gender queues: Explaining women's inroads into male occupations*. Philadelphia: Temple University Press.

Roos, P. A., & Reskin, B. (1984). Institutional factors affecting job access and mobility for women: A review of institutional explanations for job segregation. In B. F. Reskin (Ed.), *Sex segregation in the workplace: Trends, explanations, remedies* (pp. 235-260). Washington, DC: National Academy Press.

Ruble, D. N., & Ruble, T. L. (1982). Sex stereotypes. In A. G. Miller (Ed.), *In the eye of the beholder: Contemporary issues in stereotyping* (pp. 188-252). New York: Praeger.

Salancik, G. R., & Pfeffer, J. (1978). Uncertainty, secrecy, and the choice of similar others. *Social Psychology, 41,* 246-255.

Stinchcombe, A. (1959). Bureaucratic and craft administration of production. *Administrative Science Quarterly, 4,* 168-187.

Steenland, S. (1990). *What's wrong with this picture?* Washington, DC: National Commission on Working Women.

Tetlock, P. E. (1985). Accountability: The neglected social context of judgment and choice. In L. L. Cummings & B. M. Staw (Eds.), *Research in organizational behavior* (Vol. 7, pp. 297-332). Greenwich, CT: JAI Press.

9

Occupational Sex Segregation and Women's Early Career Job Shifts

RACHEL A. ROSENFELD
KENNETH I. SPENNER

One of the most obvious characteristics of the labor market in the United States and elsewhere is the high degree of sex segregation (Blau & Ferber, 1986; Reskin & Hartmann, 1986). Occupational sex segregation in the United States has declined over recent decades and is somewhat lower for recent as compared with older workers. But in 1986 it was still true that almost 60% of women who were employed would have had to change occupational category for their occupational distribution to be the same as men's (Beller, 1984; Jacobs, 1989). Further, occupational sex segregation cuts across other segmentations of the labor market and the economy (Coverdill, 1988; Edwards, 1979; Zucker & Rosenstein, 1983). At the same time, a number of researchers (Corcoran, Duncan, & Ponza,

AUTHORS' NOTE: The Career Development Study data used here were collected by Luther B. Otto, Project Director, and Vaughn R. A. Call and Kenneth I. Spenner, Project Associates, with support provided by the U.S. Office of Education and Washington State University (Wave 1) and by the Boys Town Center and the National Institute of Education (NIE-G-79-0046) (Wave 2). The Carolina Population Center, the Institute for Research in Social Science (both at the University of North Carolina—Chapel Hill), and grants from the Duke University and University of North Carolina—Chapel Hill University Research Councils helped support the research reported in this chapter. We are grateful to Robert Jackson for his expert programming, Trond Petersen for access to his duration analysis program, Jenny Manlove for excellent research assistance, and Paula England, Jerry Jacobs, Richard Landerman, and anonymous reviewers for their constructive comments.

1984; England, 1982; Jacobs, 1989; Rosenfeld, 1983, 1984) have found that the boundaries between "male" and "female" occupations are permeable. Such mobility would appear to undermine arguments that the labor market is patterned by sex (Sørensen, 1983).

Jacobs (1989) proposes a theory of "revolving doors" to reconcile the seeming contradiction between a high degree of sex segregation and mobility between occupations that are predominantly male and predominantly female. Across their work lives, some women gain access to sex-atypical occupations, but a variety of institutional and less formal social controls put pressures on them to leave these occupations. Although there are some gains in occupational sex integration, gross mobility among occupations with different sex types is greater than net change: "Thus occupational segregation by sex persists, even though the same women do not stay in female-dominated occupations" (Jacobs, 1989, p. 48).

These studies of movement among *occupational* categories may overstate the extent to which people have access to sex-atypical *jobs* (Jacobs, 1989, pp. 145-146). Jobs are much more sex-segregated than occupations. Baron and Bielby (1985), for example, report an index of dissimilarity of 96 for organizational job titles. Almost 60% of their firms were perfectly sex-segregated in that no job contained workers of both sexes.[1] Given this segregation, some job shifts that look like moves to atypical positions when sex composition is measured at the occupation level may actually be sex-typical jobs. Further, such shifts may be part of sex-typical careers. For example, a university secretary who became a departmental office manager would be classified as moving from a women's to a man's job, even though this change was part of a "female" career (see also Baron, 1990; Baron, Davis-Blake, & Bielby, 1986).[2]

Ideally, to discover how sex-atypical jobs fit into people's work careers, one would need data on the sex composition of specific job titles across the work life. Such data are rare and usually limited in terms of population and occupations included. Most inferences about sex segregation and mobility among jobs with different gender types are based on occupational, not job, data. Our study does not have information on the sex composition of jobs either. Its contribution, though, is that it examines complete work histories for a cohort of young women. Previous work has generally only compared jobs' occupational sex composition at two times (see Corcoran et al., 1984, for a partial exception). The strategy here is to use job histories to follow women through their early work careers to see how jobs that are part of sex-atypical occupations contribute to these careers.

We first replicate and extend the description of job mobility across occupational gender-type boundaries using job shift data. We demonstrate again that there is considerable movement across these boundaries, as well as some directionality to the flows. In addition to looking at the patterns of movement, we examine job duration in sex-typical as compared with sex-atypical occupations to try to judge the importance for career trajectories of jobs in sex-atypical occupations. We also look at the reasons for and outcomes of different types of job moves to identify some of the pushes and pulls behind moves across occupational sex types.

We then examine predictors of different types of job shifts. There are at least four overlapping explanations for women's mobility between typically male and typically female occupations. One is that women who stay with or move to male occupations had less typically female socialization, higher career ambitions, and greater work commitment. Second, there are theories that typically female jobs better match many women's intermittent labor force participation (Wolf & Rosenfeld, 1978). Based on such discussions, we would expect that changes in family composition would predict leaving a job in a sex-atypical occupation more strongly than leaving a job in a sex-typical occupation. A third type of explanation focuses on the rewards from different types of jobs. For women, sex-atypical jobs may bring higher wages and opportunity (Rosenfeld & Spenner, 1988) even while involving pressures to leave (but see also Padavic & Reskin, 1990). To the extent that women take predominantly male jobs to gain higher wages, more challenging work, and greater advancement opportunity, we might expect to find that those in higher-level and better-paying female jobs are slower to leave for a predominantly male occupation. Fourth, different types of employers may be more or less open to giving women access to nontraditional jobs and job opportunity, whether because of labor needs or legal compulsion. Government employment, in particular, has been subject to greater control with respect to gender equity, such that one might find slower movement from male occupations there and perhaps faster movement to them.

Finally, we discuss some exploration of total job histories. If the process is really one of a revolving door, then it is necessary to examine all the pieces of a work career to see when and how women go between male and female jobs. Further, looking at a work career over a significant period of time might make it possible to see which women are not part of this process.

Data

The Washington State Career Development Study provided the data for our analyses. The original population included juniors and seniors in Washington State public high schools during the 1965-1966 academic year. An in-school questionnaire was administered in a stratified sample of schools ($N = 6,728$). In 1979, when the respondents were entering their 30s, telephone interviews of nearly 90%, or 5,849 of the original participants, obtained computer-assisted month-by-month education, family, and work histories for the years since leaving high school. Additionally, 84% of the 1979 interviewees completed a mail questionnaire, and most respondents gave signed release for access to their high school transcripts (for complete sample, design, and instrumentation information, see Otto, Call, & Spenner, 1981).

The characteristics of these respondents are similar to those for their cohort in the state of Washington and in the United States as a whole. The only major differences are that the 1979 respondents had slightly higher socioeconomic origins and achievements compared with national samples and that only 2% were nonwhite compared with 4% for the state of Washington and 12% nationally. There is evidence that occupational sex segregation and mobility differ by race/sex groups (Corcoran et al., 1984; Rosenfeld, 1984). Unfortunately, given the small proportion of nonwhites in our sample, we were not able to make race comparisons. Further, although the Career Development Study included both women and men, in this chapter we use only the women's data.[3]

The respondents finished high school just when the contemporary women's movement was beginning. If they went directly from high school to college, they received their bachelor's degrees at the time when affirmative action legislation was being put into effect. They were building their work careers in a period when occupational sex segregation was declining. At the same time, "youth" jobs were extremely sex-segregated (Greenberger & Steinberg, 1983), and job turnover was higher at younger as compared with later ages. Some of what might look like a move away from sex-typical occupations could be a move away from early temporary jobs. Although we cannot separate age from period effects here, we can comment on how mobility patterns vary by age.

Further, in the prediction of job-shift rates we include employment history among our independent variables to control for experience-related differences in turnover that could be confounded with changes in the rate of holding jobs in sex-segregated occupations.

The job histories begin with the first full-time job after high school and cover all full-time jobs thereafter to 1979, with a full-time job defined in the Career Development Study as one of at least 25 hours a week held for at least a month;[4] 2,532 women had at least one full-time job. To examine the origins, destinations, and duration of jobs in sex-typical and sex-atypical occupations, it was necessary to restructure the data set into records based on jobs. Each record in this reorganized data set contains information for a given job, which we refer to as the *reference job,* and for the jobs held before (*prior job,* if any) and after (*next job,* if any) the reference job. In addition, the record includes data on any periods of nonemployment before or after the reference job, on family status and educational level at the beginning of this job, on changes in these over the course of the job, and on high school characteristics (such as mother's work status and student's aspirations). Unlike most studies of mobility between occupations with different sex compositions, we did not require that women be employed on two specific dates or have continuous employment (Baron, 1990).

The measure of gender type is based on the percentage of males in the job's three-digit occupational code in the 1970 Census. Except in a very few cases where there was not a valid occupational code, this information is available for each job in each woman's history. Women held jobs across the period 1966-1979, and the percentage of males in an occupation might have changed. Rytina and Bianchi (1984), however, show that although the sex composition of some occupations changed over the 1970s, for the most part these changes were not so large as to change the gender type of an occupation (see Reskin & Roos, 1990, for case studies of occupations that had large changes in their sex composition between 1970 and 1980).

The image of boundaries and barriers between male and female jobs suggests that we need to go from a continuous measure of percentage of males in an occupation to a categorical measure of gender type. Researchers have done this in many different ways: considering a job atypical when a majority of the incumbents are of the other sex (e.g., Corcoran et al., 1984; Rosenfeld, 1984); starting with women's representation in the labor force and labeling occupations that have a given degree of female over- or underrepresentation as female or male (e.g.,

Beller, 1984; Rytina & Bianchi, 1984); looking for breaks in the distribution of percentage male to set cutoffs (e.g., Wolf & Rosenfeld, 1978); and analyzing patterns of mobility to identify blocks that are internally homogeneous (e.g., Jacobs, 1989).

In this chapter we use Jacobs's results from the latter approach for 1980-1981 Current Population Survey job changers. This is a compromise between using predetermined, often ad hoc boundaries and using our own sample's mobility patterns, which can vary with period changes in women's job opportunities, to set occupational gender types. Occupations 1%-29% male are considered "female," 30%-69% male are considered "unlabeled," and 70% or more male are considered "male."

Description of Job Histories and
Occupational Gender-Type Mobility

The Career Development Study women tend to have jobs in female-dominated occupations across their histories: Almost two thirds of their jobs are in occupations that are less than 30% male (see marginals in Table 9.1). This is a higher proportion than for the National Longitudinal Survey of Mature Women in either 1967 or 1977, perhaps because of some decline with age in extent of sex segregation (e.g., Jacobs, 1989; Rosenfeld, 1983) or because of the overrepresentation of movers, as we discuss below. For this cohort, there does seem to be movement out of female occupations over job shifts: The proportion of women in male occupations increases between the reference and next job, whereas the proportion in female occupations declines.

Underlying this pattern, we find considerable movement across gender barriers. As Table 9.1 shows, the correlation of percentage male between pairs of jobs is only .37, a figure very close to those reported by others using different samples and different conceptions of mobility (e.g., England, 1982; Jacobs, 1989; Rosenfeld, 1984). Jacobs (1989) and Rosenfeld (1984) found the flow away from sex-atypical occupations to be stronger than the flow to them, although neither Hachen (1988) nor Waite and Berryman (1986) found that occupational sex composition affected the probability or rate of a job change. The flow in these data does tend to be stronger toward female than male occupations: Of job shifts beginning in a female occupation, 12% result in a job in a male occupation; of those beginning in a male occupation, 35% have the next job in a female occupation.[5]

Table 9.1 Occupational Gender Type for Job Pairs[a]

| Reference Job | *Next Job Percent*[b] | | | | |
	Female	*Unlabeled*	*Male*	*(Reference Job Marginals)*[c]	*n*
Female (0%–29% male)	72.5	15.5	12.0	100.0 (63.1)	3,908
Unlabeled (30%–69% male)	43.9	36.6	19.5	100.0 (20.9)	1,267
Male (≥ 70% male)	34.8	19.7	45.5	100.0 (16.0)	822
(Next job marginals)	(61.3)	(20.5)	(18.2)	(100.0)	5,997

a. Sex composition measured at the level of three-digit 1970 Census occupation codes.
b. Pearson correlation: percentage male reference job with percentage male next job occupation = 0.37 ($p < .001$).
c. Includes those without a "next" job, $N = 8,615$.

Job histories offer the advantage of comparing more than two time points or career stages. At the same time, such comparisons may over-represent the movers, whereas those who do not change jobs or who leave the labor force are those who maintain sex segregation (e.g., Baron, 1990; Cain, 1984). Our multivariate analysis of job-changing rates uses information on stayers and those who exit the labor force as well as movers, although it is still true that those who change jobs frequently contribute more jobs to a given analysis. We control for this by including total number of jobs held by an individual as one independent variable. Most women, though, did have at least one job change (which could have included a period of nonemployment between jobs): Fewer than 15% had only one job, contributing only 4% to all jobs in these histories. Those who held only one job were more likely than other women to be in female occupations (68%) and less likely to be in male occupations (11.1%). However, those holding only two jobs (only one job shift) had gender-type distributions and mobility outflows almost identical to those for the sample as a whole (results not shown).

Further, over their complete job histories, a sizable proportion of women moved between male and female occupations: 17% of the sample members went from a female to a male occupation at least once and 11% moved at some time in their early work lives from a male to a female

Table 9.2 Work History Prevalence of Moves, by Occupational Gender Type (*N* = 2,532)

Women With at Least One Move	Percentage
Female to male	17.4
Female to unlabeled	21.7
Male to female	10.7
Male to unlabeled	6.0
Unlabeled to female	20.4
Unlabeled to male	9.8

occupation, as indicated in Table 9.2, which has women rather than jobs as the unit of analysis (see also Corcoran et al., 1984, for comparable results).

Our results, then, add to the preexisting body of evidence that many people do not spend their entire work lives in sex-typical occupations. The question we seek to help answer in this chapter is what this movement means in terms of the importance of sex-atypical jobs in a work career and the correlates and determinates of moves between typical and atypical occupations.

One hypothesis is that sex-atypical jobs are relatively minor parts of careers; such jobs are held for only a short time or are part of early job shopping. This would be consistent with the stronger flow toward as compared with the flow away from jobs in sex-typical occupations. There is no indication in Table 9.3 that jobs in predominantly female occupations are longer than those in other types of occupations, consistent with the findings of Hachen (1988) and Waite and Berryman (1986).

An additional way of describing job shifts, and of getting a sense of factors attracting or compelling a move, is in terms of why the shift was initiated. Women were asked why they left each job they held. We focus on male and female occupations (as defined above) here and in the rest of the chapter, given that the extremes of the sex composition distribution are of the most interest (see Table 9.4). There is evidence that women gain from moving to jobs in male as compared with female occupations: A greater proportion of these moves, from both male and female occupations, is made to obtain "better jobs, promotions."

Table 9.3 Average Duration of Jobs in Months, by Occupational Gender Type: Reference Jobs

	Observed Duration[a]	Estimate Duration[b]
Female	20.49 (23.54)	16.03
Unlabeled	18.92 (21.38)	15.50
Male	19.76 (22.51)	17.61

NOTE: Numbers in parentheses are standard deviations.
a. Includes censored cases.
b. Constant hazard rate model.

Table 9.4 Reason for Leaving Reference Job, by Occupational Gender Types in Percentages

	Next Occupation	
Reference Occupation	Female	Male
Female		
Involuntary termination, temporary layoff	7.84	6.20
Better job, promotion	24.14	35.47
Other work reason	10.80	8.97
Marriage, children, family	26.34	18.37
Returned to school	5.29	5.34
Illness, health	1.52	2.56
Other	24.08	23.08
Total[a]	100.01	99.99
(N)	(2,833)	(468)
Male		
Involuntary termination, temporary layoff	12.24	16.31
Better job, promotion	16.43	32.09
Other work reason	15.73	14.97
Marriage, children, family	18.18	10.43
Returned to school	7.69	1.87
Illness, health	3.15	2.41
Other	26.58	21.92
Total	100.00	100.00
(N)	(286)	(374)

a. Totals differ from 100 because of rounding.

Analysis (not shown) of average levels of wages, status, substantive complexity, and skill requirements across pairs of jobs provides additional evidence for this characterization: Going from a female to male occupation results in increases in these job characteristics, on average, whereas going from male to female occupations leads to average loss on all dimensions except for substantive complexity (see for similar conclusions, Rosenfeld, 1984; Wolf & Rosenfeld, 1978). These averages, however, are the result of changes, often-large, in both directions for any particular kind of shift; the variation in outcomes is great within a given category.

None of the mean changes is significantly different from 0 at conventional levels of significance. Women do not inevitably gain from going to a predominantly male occupation nor lose from moving to a predominantly female one, despite descriptions of predominantly male occupations as providing higher job rewards. Further, there is a suggestion that women are indeed pushed out of male occupations: Relatively more of the moves from these occupations, especially to other male occupations, are involuntary.

Those moving from a given occupational type to a female occupation are more likely than those moving to a male occupation to say they left their job because of family reasons, which is consonant with the idea of female occupations as those that accommodate women's family responsibilities.[6]

Many of these results fit stereotypic characterizations of male as compared with female jobs and careers. Jobs in male as compared with female occupations are better on a number of dimensions. Women are more likely to leave the male jobs involuntarily, perhaps in part because they were "last hired, first fired" but perhaps because of other problems with being the "wrong" sex for a job. Jobs in predominantly female occupations appear to fit family circumstances somewhat better than do jobs in predominantly male occupations. At the same time, there is a large amount of variation in outcomes and job-leaving reasons across types of job shifts.

In looking at pieces of careers so far, to a large extent we have not taken into account timing or censoring of job shifts, nor have we looked systematically at other dimensions of women's lives. We do this in the next section by predicting rates of jobs shifts of various kinds.

Rates of Leaving Jobs

Models

To see what predicts how fast women move to different destinations from jobs in sex-typical as compared with sex-atypical occupations, we use event history models (Allison, 1984; Kalbfleisch & Prentice, 1980; Petersen, 1986; Tuma & Hannan, 1984). Models are of the form

$$ln\ (r_{jk}) = a + X\mathbf{b} + X(t)\mathbf{b(t)} + ct,$$

where r_{jk} is the rate of movement from state j to state k, a is a constant, X is a matrix of variables that are fixed at the beginning of a job (e.g., high school job attitudes, employment experience before this job), $\mathbf{b}$ is a vector of coefficients, $X(t)$ is a matrix of variables that can change over a job (e.g., marital status, number of children), $\mathbf{b(t)}$ is the vector of coefficients associated with these variables, and c indicates the degree and direction of duration dependence (Gompertz functional form).

Data Structure

As we described above, we rearranged the women's work histories into sets of jobs. For the analysis here, we focus on movement from the reference job. The rates are based on time in this job. When the next activity in a women's work history was nonemployment or part-time employment (fewer than 25 hours a week), we skipped over this period to the next full-time job, if any.

For some women, a particular reference job was the current one at the time of the interview. For other women, this was the last job in their histories, followed by nonemployment. Further, not all shifts from a given type of job are of interest in a particular model. If we focused on job shifts from female to male occupations, for example, we would actually observe such shifts only for those making this kind of move. But all women beginning a particular set of jobs in a female occupation would be at risk of this kind of move, even if the reference job were the last in the job history or led to a female or sex-neutral occupation. We do not throw out the latter cases. They contribute information to the estimation of coefficients but are treated as censored at the time of the interview or end of a job that leads to nonemployment (with no further jobs) or to a job with a gender type other than that of particular interest.

Within a given job, when a woman upgraded her educational credentials, had a child, had a child reach the age of 6 years, or changed marital status, the data set contains a new record reflecting the new configuration of independent variables. At the same time, it retains how far into the job such changes occurred, which permits estimation of duration dependence (i.e., the effect, if any, of time spent in that particular job; Petersen, 1986). Most research reports negative duration dependence for jobs, at least for job shifts across employers (Felmlee, 1982): The longer a person has been in a job, the less likely she is to leave, interpreted as inertia, accumulation of benefits, job security, and so on.

Independent Variables

Differences among individuals can give the appearance of negative duration dependence: Those predisposed to leave a given situation tend to leave earlier, whereas those predisposed to remain stay longer. Unmeasured differences among individuals can also cause correlation between records when a given individual contributes more than one record to a data set, as is true here.

Statistical solutions to the problems that arise from unobserved individual differences—unobserved heterogeneity—are neither robust nor easy to implement in practice. An alternative is to try to measure explicitly the characteristics of individuals that best represent their propensity to move. Hutchison (1988) points out that "individual heterogeneity at any given time, and the individual's history so far, are to some extent different sides of the same coin. . . . Thus one would expect that including a number of items of past history . . . would have an effect virtually the same as formally allowing for unobserved heterogeneity" (p. 269). Here we include among the independent variables the number of jobs a particular woman reported in her work history, as well as other aspects of her employment history discussed below.

Substantively, we include four sets of independent variables: high school work attitudes and expectations; educational credentials; family status; and job and employment characteristics. These tap various dimensions of early expectations and work orientation, family constraints, jobs' relative "goodness," and properties of the employer. Table 9.5 provides descriptions of the variables. The most striking feature of the descriptive statistics is similarity of individual characteristics by type of job shift, despite some differences in the nature of the reference job. Of course, it should be kept in mind that some respondents contribute spell segments to both sets of means, given movement between typically female and typically male occupations.

High School Work Attitudes and Expectations

As can be seen in Table 9.5, typically male occupations do not necessarily have higher status than typically female occupations, which are concentrated in lower white-collar occupations (England, 1979; Jacobs & Powell, 1987). To the extent that moves to typically male occupations bring status increases for those with a given level of education and other characteristics, however, women with expectations for higher-status jobs would be predicted to move more quickly from a typically female occupation and perhaps more slowly from a typically male occupation. A woman with a 2-year college degree, for example, who in high school aspired to a higher-level job, might be more likely at a given time to leave a secretarial job for an administrative one than would someone with lower expectations. Those who thought they would be relatively more committed to employment would be expected to move more slowly from predominantly male occupations and more quickly away from predominantly female occupations if it is true that male jobs require such commitment (Polachek, 1981).

Even if the assumptions about the net relationships between attitudes and expectations and occupational gender types are correct, however, we might fail to find the effects we hypothesize with measures of high school attitudes. People's work attitudes and aspirations are not fixed before they enter the labor market full-time but change with both their job experiences and also other individual and political changes. Jacobs (1989) argues that "the pressure for women to pursue female-dominated positions does not end in childhood. It is continually reinforced and recreated throughout young adulthood. . . . Many women internalize these values, whereas others successfully challenge the constraints imposed on them. These two groups of women are not as distinct as many assume" (p. 48). He finds so much change in sex-type of aspirations

Table 9.5 Variable Descriptions (Means and Standard Deviations), by Occupational Gender Type of Reference Jobs

			Referent Occupation			
			Female		Male	
Concept/Indicator	Time Referent	Description	Mean[a]	(SD)	Mean[a]	(SD)
Background						
High school occupational expectations	High school	Duncan socioeconomic status score	54.07	(18.26)	57.62	(18.12)
High school work orientation[b]	High school	"Which of the following statements best describes what you think your *interests* and *desires* will be for most of your adult life?" 1. Homemaking will be my major interest. I will not want to work after I am married. 2. Homemaking will be my major interest, but I will want to work occasionally or work part-time. 3. Homemaking will be my major interest, but I will also want to work most of the time. 4. Work will be my major interest, but I will also want to have a family and be a homemaker. 5. Work will be my major interest. I will not want to spend much effort in homemaking. 6. Work will be my only interest. I will not want to spend much effort in homemaking.	2.67	(1.09)	2.74	(1.12)
Educational status						
Highest credential	t_s^c	0 = high school dropout 1 = high school graduate 2 = Associate of Arts 3 = B.S., B.A.	1.38	(0.79)	1.61	(0.96)

			\multicolumn{2}{}{}	\multicolumn{2}{}{}
		4 = M.S., M.A.		
		5 = Ph.D., M.D., J.D., other professional degree		
Added schooling	t	0 = no; 1 = yes (includes part-time schooling)	0.15 (0.35)	0.13 (0.33)
Family status				
Single	t_s	0 = no; 1 = yes (never married)	0.27 (0.45)	0.23 (0.42)
Divorced	t_s	0 = no; 1 = yes (married prior to t_s)	0.11 (0.31)	0.14 (0.35)
Children under 6 years of age	t_s	Number of children under age 6	0.34 (0.62)	0.38 (0.64)
Job and labor market position				
Wages	t_e	In dollars (adjusted to April 1979 value)	5.00 (2.12)	5.84 (2.95)
Reference job status	t_s	Duncan socioeconomic status score × 10	454.12 (176.47)	509.49 (234.68)
Occupation category:				
Professional/managerial	t_s	Collapsed from three-digit occupational codes	0.10 (0.31)	0.53 (0.50)
Lower white-collar			0.64 (0.48)	0.17 (0.38)
Blue-collar (including farm)			0.01 (0.12)	0.22 (0.42)
Service			0.24 (0.43)	0.07 (0.25)
Hours employed	t_s	Average hours per week (up to 70)	40.35 (5.68)	42.48 (8.52)
Employer sector	t_s	0 = other; 1 = government employee	0.25 (0.43)	0.20 (0.40)
Prior spells—firm shifts	Prior job spells	0 = all prior jobs (if any) with same employer; 1 = one or more prior firm shifts	0.54 (0.50)	0.70 (0.46)
Prior spells—full-time job experience	Prior job spells	In months	32.00 (31.45)	48.11 (37.68)
Duration/heterogeneity				
Duration	t	In months	20.74 (22.90)	20.38 (22.68)
Number of jobs	All spells	Total number of full-time jobs per respondent	5.12 (2.85)	5.80 (3.38)
n			3,743	894

a. Mean calculated across all job segments (i.e., includes spell segments censored by time-varying covariates). Only cases with no missing data.

b. Scores here were based on a scale of 1 to 6, following responses to the question listed under description.

c. t_s = measured at the start of the spell segment; t_e = measured at the end of the spell segment; t = measured over entire spell segment.

per se for young adults that he says such attitudes are not predictive of later occupational mobility (see also review in Marini & Brinton, 1984). Rexroat and Shehan (1984) report that young women who in the late 1960s expected to be employed at age 35 tended actually to be employed, but so were many of those who had expected to be housewives, in part in response to changes in their family status.

Education Credentials

Educational level is a major predictor of occupational attainment. If, for a particular woman, a job in a predominantly male occupation is a "better" one (in terms of pay, working conditions, and opportunity potential) than a job in a predominantly female occupation, we would expect to see those with more education and with increases in education leaving the job in the female occupation more quickly or the job in the male occupation more slowly. Not all "better" atypical jobs, however, require more education: For example, women in typically female white-collar clerical jobs have been able to improve their income by moving to blue-collar predominantly male jobs (Walshok, 1981).

Previous work (Jusenius, 1975) suggests possible curvilinear effects of education on moving to an atypical job. Given that sample members were selected toward the end of high school, it is not surprising that only a very few failed to complete high school. We therefore use a linear measure of credentials. As mentioned above, educational credentials is a time-varying covariate. Additional education during a job that did not lead to a new credential is simply indicated as a dummy variable.

Family Status

Much of the discussion of women's work lives has focused on the constraining effect of their family responsibilities (Becker, 1981), although empirical research has not consistently found such effects on work outcomes net of women's employment histories (Duncan & Corcoran, 1984). Further, research has not necessarily shown that jobs with a greater proportion of females do have characteristics, such as flexibility, that would make them easier to combine at a given time with family work (Glass, 1990). To the extent that women tend to be in predominantly female occupations because these are—or are perceived to be—easier to combine with family responsibilities, we should find that women who are married and have more young children move faster to jobs in typically female occupations and more slowly to jobs in predominantly male occupations. Again, measures of marital status and number of children under age 6 are allowed to vary over time in a particular job.

Job and Employment Characteristics

The literature on job shifting has found that although higher credentials increase the rate at which a person leaves a job, especially across employers, higher job rewards slow the rate (Felmlee, 1982; Rosenfeld, 1992; Sørensen & Tuma, 1981). We include reference job wages and status as measures of job rewards. To see whether a particular type of occupation has an effect, we also ran our models two other ways (not shown), replacing socioeconomic status with occupational categories (with the contrast professional/managerial versus other occupations and with a set of dummies for lower-white-collar, blue-collar, and service, with professional/managerial as the reference category). Given that professional and managerial occupations of a given gender type are often the ones characterized as offering not only high rewards but also requiring career commitment and training, we might expect to see those in these occupations leaving them more slowly. We will report these results where they differ from those shown.

We also measure whether the employer is a government agency to see if perhaps better benefits and promotion opportunities for women in such jobs exert some holding power or even allow faster movement to a male occupation (DiPrete, 1989). Whether the person changed firms before the reference job is a measure of whether the person had the potential to be in a firm-internal labor market, with the potential for upward mobility even within a gender type (Althauser, 1989).

All of the jobs in our sample's histories were held at least 25 hours a week, which is still less than the official cutoff for full-time work. We include hours employed to see whether more hours worked indicates a commitment to a particular job and therefore a slower rate of movement out of it, net of other characteristics. As discussed before, months of full-time employment before beginning the reference job controls for where this job falls in a woman's work history, although it can also indicate behavioral commitment to the labor market and job-acquired human capital.

Race

The equations also include race (white/nonwhite) as an additional control variable, although the proportion nonwhite is very low. We do not include this variable in estimating moves from jobs in predominantly male occupations that ended in a typically male occupation because of collinearity between race and hours employed.

Results

Table 9.6 shows the results of the event history analysis. The last line gives the rates per month estimated from the histories. The fastest movement is within a given gender type, especially between jobs in predominantly female occupations. The slowest rates are between gender types. Consistent with what we saw in the mobility tables, movement out of a male occupation is faster than moving to a sex-atypical occupation.

What predicts how fast a woman's job shifting takes her across gender-type boundaries? Contrary to other research, we find some effects of high school attitudes.[7] Those who planned to put relatively more emphasis on employment leave a job in a typically male occupation for one in a typically female occupation more slowly. This effect is fairly large: A one-unit increase on the work orientation scale results in a 24% decrease in the rate of moving from a predominantly male to a predominantly female occupation (i.e., $100 \cdot (\exp[-.274] - 1) = 100 \cdot (.76 - 1)$). Based on the estimated rate, the inverse of which gives the duration in a given state, this would translate into about 1.75 years longer spent in a job in a predominantly male occupation before going to a predominantly female occupation.

Those who expected to be in higher status occupations moved more quickly from a job in a predominantly female occupation to one in a predominantly male occupation, a 7% increase for each 10 status points. This does not necessarily mean that these women went to jobs in predominantly male occupations simply to move up in status, although on average there was a small, nonsignificant increase. Alternative explanations would be that those who expected to hold higher status occupations were those for whom predominantly female jobs were temporary jobs before entering more typically male careers (e.g., being a clerical worker before getting a job in wholesale sales) or were part of typically female career ladders (the secretary who became office manager). When we entered the set of three occupational categories rather than reference job socioeconomic status, however, this effect was no longer significant, which could be consistent with any of these explanations.[8]

Table 9.6 Prediction of Job Shift Rate Classified by Occupational Gender Type of Origin and Destination Jobs

	Type of Shift			
	FF	*FM*	*MF*	*MM*
Race	−.044	.314	−1.121	—
	(.136)	(.452)	(.522)	
High school work orientation	−.029	.052	−.274*	−.132
	(.020)	(.051)	(.072)	(.068)
High school occupational	.0004	.007*	−.006	.007
expectations (SEI)	(.001)	(.003)	(.004)	(.005)
Educational credentials	−.083*	−.072	−.274*	.241*
	(.033)	(.081)	(.099)	(.077)
Added formal education during job	−.155*	−.070	.106	−.201
(1 = yes; 0 = no)	(.063)	(.159)	(.207)	(.218)
Divorced	−.058	.091	−.304	−.199
(1 = yes; 0 = no)	(.082)	(.191)	(.270)	(.240)
Single, never married	−.217*	−.133	.162	−.138
(1 = yes; 0 = no)	(.056)	(.145)	(.191)	(.169)
Number of children < 6 years of age	−.040	.301*	−.219	.084
	(.044)	(.091)	(.143)	(.132)
Employer = government	−.024	−.326*	.099	.024
(1 = yes; 0 = no)	(.059)	(.153)	(.199)	(.179)
Hours employed (up to 70)	−.006	−.005	.008	.007
	(.004)	(.012)	(.009)	(.008)
Reference job SEI	−.00001	.0003	−.0009*	−.0009*
	(.0002)	(.0004)	(.0003)	(.0003)
Wages	−.078*	−.020	−.101*	−.027
	(.011)	(.033)	(.040)	(.032)
Previous firm shift(s)	−.216*	.085	.359	−.165
(1 = yes; 0 = no)	(.061)	(.158)	(.198)	(.196)
Months of full-time work previously	−.013*	−.009*	−.025*	−.005
	(.001)	(.003)	(.004)	(.003)
Total number of jobs	.153*	.170*	.129*	.141*
	(.006)	(.018)	(.023)	(.018)
Duration	−.003*	.004	−.003	.001
	(.001)	(.003)	(.005)	(.004)
Constant	−2.588	−6.391	−.848	−4.540
Spells	3,743	3,743	894	894
Completed transitions	1,976	308	192	224
Estimated constant rate	.037	.006	.015	.018

NOTE: FF = female to female; FM = female to male; MF = male to female; MM = male to male. Standard deviation shown in parentheses.
*$p < .05$, two-tailed.

We argued that the intensity of past and contemporary employment could also tap workforce commitment, which is hypothesized to increase mobility across gender-type boundaries in the direction of sex-atypical occupations and slow return to sex-typical ones. Hours employed has no effect here. Past employment slows all job shifting, but especially that from a male occupation to a female one, which would be consistent with the argument that workforce commitment as displayed in work behavior affects gender-type mobility.

The effects of the family variables are not those expected based on many descriptions of typically female occupations as those that accommodate family life. Women with more small children are those who move most quickly out of a job in a predominantly female occupation to one in a predominantly male occupation, each additional child increasing the rate by about 35%. An after-the-fact explanation would be that women with more children need more money and better benefits, as well as more flexibility, all of which are more likely to be found in occupations with a greater percentage male (Glass, 1990), net of other job and incumbent characteristics.

Some discussions about moving across gender-type boundaries emphasize the search for better jobs. Education gives potential access to such jobs. It does not appear to stimulate faster mobility from jobs in sex-typical to jobs in sex-atypical occupations, although those with higher educational credentials stay longer in a job in a typically male occupation before moving to one in a predominantly female occupation.

Contrary to what we had expected, higher wages and status do not slow a woman's move to a sex-atypical occupation, although those who are in male occupations go more slowly to female occupations when they have higher wages and status. When, however, we substitute whether the job is in the professional/managerial category for socioeconomic status, we find this is significant also for moving from a predominantly female to predominantly male occupation: Those who are professionals or managers at a given time have a rate of leaving a typically female for a typically male occupation that is 67% slower than for those in other categories (coefficient = −1.094, standard error = .289).

Being employed by the government does not give women an advantage in moving quickly to a sex-atypical occupation but might provide benefits and work conditions making such a move less attractive. Most of the effect of government employment, however, appears to be that of occupational category: When we include a dummy for professional/

managerial occupation rather than socioeconomic status, the variable for government employment is no longer significant.

Thus some explanations for women's boundary shifting hold up in this analysis. There are hints that higher expectations, commitment to employment, and credentials speed movement across gender types to a male occupation. Higher job rewards do retain women in male, and to some extent, female occupation jobs, although government employment does not appear to have an independent effect. Family constraints, however, have no predicted effects.

We can compare predictors of rates at which women move across occupational gender types with predictors of job shift rates within occupational types. Overall, the two types of processes differ, as indicated by comparing the log-likelihood ratios for models that collapse shifts to sex-typical and sex-atypical destinations with those that estimate such shifting separately (with a difference of 878.3, 17 degrees of freedom, for moves from female occupations and of 253.1, 16 degrees of freedom, for moves from male occupations). For moves from predominantly female occupations, individual effects of high school expectations and of children are significantly different, but so are the patterns of significant predictors. Those with higher educational credentials and additional education are somewhat more likely to stay longer on a job in a predominantly female occupation when this is part of a set of jobs in predominantly female occupations. Getting additional education, for example, decreases the rate of leaving one job in a predominantly female occupation for another one by about 14%, increasing duration in the job by about 4.5 months. This could be because at least some of these jobs are in the female professions, which might account as well for the nonsignificant effect of job socioeconomic status in this model. Including occupational category or categories rather than socioeconomic status did reduce the effect of educational credentials so that it was no longer significant, although the effect of educational change continued to be significant.

Single women, who supposedly have fewer family constraints on their employment, shift jobs more slowly in the context of a female occupational career. Those women with higher wages and perhaps employed in internal labor markets (with advancement opportunity) also leave one female job for another more slowly.

One could take these results as evidence that moves set in sex-typical occupations are part of "real" rather than random careers (for example, the effect of being a professional in retaining a woman in a predominantly female occupation or of staying within a firm on moving to another predominantly female job), perhaps because we have a group of relatively young and relatively well-educated white women. Those who had stayed with the same firm moved more quickly from a job when it was part of a set of jobs in sex-typical occupations. (Those in sex-atypical jobs who were not part of firm-internal labor markets went more quickly to sex-typical occupations, an effect significant by a one-tailed test.)

Perhaps because we controlled for relevant aspects of these women's life histories, there is significant negative duration dependence only for female jobs that lead to other female jobs. This is consistent with the idea that typically female jobs do not offer advancement opportunity (Felmlee, 1982; Glass, 1990) but could also indicate that we do not characterize the forces behind this kind of shift as well as we do for other kinds of shifts.

Moves between jobs in male occupations offer the pattern expected in vacancy mobility, where movement upward in a job system depends on higher jobs opening up, with eligibility for these openings depending on time in the system and human capital resources (Rosenfeld, 1992). Only for moves between jobs in predominantly male occupations do we see the positive effect of education found in the general research on job shifting, with each higher educational level increasing the rate of mobility by a bit over 27% (decreasing the duration by about a year). This effect differs significantly from that for moves from male to female occupations. Having achieved higher status, on the other hand, slows mobility, with one explanation being that there are fewer higher positions to attain. Months of previous employment has a statistically different and nonsignificant effect here, which is in line with the explanation that the difference between resources and rewards captures effects of time exposed to job opportunities when mobility is driven by job vacancies.

Overall, there do seem to be differences in the process of women's job shifting by whether it occurs within sex-typical occupations, within sex-atypical occupations, or across occupational gender-type boundaries. Many hypotheses about how variables should work in generating these shifts, for example, about family effects, are not supported. In terms of the metaphor of revolving doors, the results suggest that the door spins at different speeds and sends women in different directions depending on the type of move.

Conclusions and Discussion

Many women move back and forth between male and female jobs. The flow is somewhat stronger toward than away from sex-typical occupations. Looking at reasons for and outcomes from job shifts, we found that moves to jobs in male occupations sometimes bring increased job rewards and that moves to jobs in female occupations are sometimes prompted by family considerations. But we also found considerable variation in why women moved to an occupation of a different gender type. In predicting rates of individuals' movement across gender boundaries, we found evidence supporting explanations for such movement that focus on aspirations and work commitment, the search for better jobs, and perhaps employers' gender equity. We found almost no support for family-based explanations. Job-shifting within female occupations suggests that at least some women are pursuing real careers within this context, whereas predictors of job movement within typically male occupations fit what would be expected for careers in vacancy chains, sometimes equated with internal labor markets.

One problem with the analysis is that we have only measures of labor supply, none of labor demand. Job changes depend on not only the characteristics of the job changer but also the distribution of accessible job openings. At the same time, another problem could be that the sex-type categories are not "clean" ones, because they combine sex-typical and sex-atypical careers within each occupational gender type. Even linking pairs of jobs, we do not get a sense of the total career line (Rosenfeld, 1992). As an initial exploration of differences in complete career histories, we randomly selected 10 job histories that included at least one shift from a predominantly male to a predominantly female occupation and 10 histories that included at least one shift from a predominantly female to a predominantly male occupation. Looking across the occupations and industries of the jobs in these histories, we found three types of career patterns. One is a "disorderly" or perhaps youth career, with a set of rather short, generally unrelated jobs. One woman, for example, was a secretary (female occupation), bowling alley attendant (male), waitress (female), construction laborer (male), and cook (unlabeled), among other jobs.

A second type of career is one that appears more "typically female," especially after the first few jobs, even if it includes jobs in occupations that are disproportionately male. One woman, for example, was a cashier for most of her working life, with one 3-year stint as a sales manager in a department store or for a mail-order business. The third type of career one sees among these examples of women who move across gender-type boundaries is that of a real move to a male career line. A woman who spent 10 years in typically female occupations for the telephone company then became a telephone installer and repairer. This may have been as a result of the discrimination suit against AT&T.

At the same time, looking across the job histories of a sample of young women, we saw considerable variation in how such shifts fit into their work—and family—careers. For at least some women, going to a sex-atypical occupation appeared to be part of going through the revolving door: These jobs were not ones they held for long and were not related to other parts of their job histories. For other women, moves to sex-atypical occupations were either a continuation of their prior jobs or appeared to represent a real switch to a typically male career line. It is not surprising, then, that the patterns of correlates and predictors of job shifts were no stronger than they were. The general picture is consistent with the one Jacobs (1989) presents in that, rather than rational, life-long plans for careers, there is "short-term decision making that is responsive to social pressure and the extent of available opportunities" (p. 169).

Our results point to the need to identify career lines as sex-typical, sex-atypical, or mixed (for an example of how such career lines might be identified, see Abbott & Hrycak, 1990). A given piece of a career line (a succession of jobs) can, of course, be of a given type, then change as a person moves through later jobs. Further, we need more studies that look at how hiring, transfer, promotion, and firing occur (e.g., Levinson, 1975; Padavic & Reskin, 1990) to see how the demand side also works in shaping a sex-segregated occupational structure.

Notes

1. See also Blau (1977) who found that firms tended to be more sex-segregated than their occupational composition would indicate, Reskin and Roos (1990) who document resegregation of jobs within occupations as the overall sex composition of the occupation changes, and Hachen (1988) who shows that there are sex differences in authority moves within occupations.

2. Indeed, the category of "executive, administrative, managerial" is one that has become increasingly female (Rytina & Bianchi, 1984). Some of the change in sex composition may reflect real advances of women into management, but some may hide continued sex segregation of careers.

3. Considering only women's careers is consistent with much of the concern about sex segregation that has focused on the consequences for women as a group excluded from relatively better jobs and pay. In further work, we would like to compare the experiences of women and men. Men are in occupations that are more sex-segregated than those of women (e.g., Rosenfeld, 1984), yet much of the occupational sex integration between 1960 and 1970 was the result of men entering the predominantly female professions. Men's chances of sharing an occupation with women have increased, although they are still somewhat lower than women's chances of sharing an occupation with men (Jacobs, 1989). Across their work lives, some men also move between typical and atypical occupations (Jacobs, 1989), with the outcomes and predictors depending on their race (Rosenfeld, 1984). And men may also face pressures on the job from being the "wrong" gender (e.g., Schreiber, 1979).

4. Although we know when a woman held a job of fewer than 25 hours a week, we have no details on the characteristics of such a job.

5. Although these patterns are stronger for younger job shifting, they are still apparent in shifts at somewhat older ages. Of the job shifts undertaken before age 26, 68% were from female occupations. Eleven percent of these shifts were to a male occupation, whereas 42% of the shifts from male occupations were to jobs in female occupations. After women turned 26, 54% of the reference jobs were predominantly female. Seventeen percent of the shifts from female occupations were to male occupations, and 24% of those from male occupations were to sex-typical occupations. As women sort out their lives, some may be more likely to pursue or fall into atypical job paths. Further, this cohort may have been especially affected by Equal Employment Opportunity (EEO) and Affirmative Action legislation. It is not possible to differentiate among age, period, and cohort effects here, but the multivariate analysis will control for other characteristics that can change with age, such as education and family status, as well as incorporating information from those who did not change jobs at older ages, as we discuss later.

6. The time between ending a job and beginning the next is slightly longer, on average, for those leaving a job in a female as compared to a male occupation, although the variance is large and the difference not statistically significant: 7.61 months for completed jobs in a female occupation (SD = 16.71), 6.04 months for completed jobs in a male occupation (SD = 14.33). The average difference is consistent with Wenk and Rosenfeld's (1992) finding that women were nonemployed longer when they left their jobs for family rather than other reasons. There was almost no difference by occupational gender type in whether a particular job led to a period of nonemployment as compared with leading directly to another job.

7. We have directional hypotheses about many effects we estimate, for which we should therefore use one-tailed tests. In Table 9.6, we indicate, however, the results of two-tailed tests with p values less than .05. These tests are the equivalent of one-tailed tests with p values less than .025—if the results are in the hypothesized direction. Some of our results are in the direction the opposite of what we expected, so we sacrifice statistical power to find these effects. A theoretical justification for this is that our hypotheses are based on stereotypes about jobs with different gender types, and we do not have confidence that these stereotypes are accurate. We mention the few estimates that are in the predicted direction and would be statistically significant at the .05, but not .025, level by a one-tailed test.

8. In other analyses, we also included whether the mother worked when the respondent was in high school as an indicator of role modeling. This variable had no effect on the rate at which women left a typically female job for one in a typically male occupation. Because of the large amount of missing data on this variable, we did not include it for the rest of the analysis.

References

Abbott, A., & Hrycak, A. (1990). Measuring resemblance in sequence data. *American Journal of Sociology, 96,* 144-185.

Allison, P. (1984). *Event history analysis: Regression for longitudinal event data.* Newbury Park, CA: Sage.

Althauser, R. (1989). Internal labor markets. *Annual Review of Sociology, 15,* 143-161.

Baron, J. (1990). Are the doors revolving or still locked shut? *Contemporary Sociology, 19,* 347-349.

Baron, J., & Bielby, W. (1985). Occupational barriers to gender equality. In A. Rossi (Ed.), *Gender and the life course* (pp. 233-251). New York: Aldine.

Baron, J., Davis-Blake, A., & Bielby, W. (1986). The structure of opportunity: How promotion ladders vary within and among organizations. *Administrative Science Quarterly, 31,* 248-273.

Becker, G. (1981). *A treatise on the family.* Cambridge, MA: Harvard University Press.

Beller, A. (1984). Trends in occupational segregation by sex and race, 1960-1981. In B. Reskin (Ed.), *Sex segregation in the workplace* (pp. 11-26). Washington, DC: National Academy Press.

Blau, F. (1977). *Equal pay in the office.* Lexington, MA: D. C. Heath.

Blau, F., & Ferber, M. (1986). *The economics of women, men and work.* Englewood Cliffs, NJ: Prentice-Hall.

Cain, P. S. (1984). Commentary. In B. Reskin (Ed.), *Sex segregation in the workplace* (pp. 87-90). Washington, DC: National Academy Press.

Corcoran, M., Duncan, G. J., & Ponza, M. (1984). Work experience, job segregation, and wages. In B. Reskin (Ed.), *Sex segregation in the workplace* (pp. 171-191). Washington, DC: National Academy Press.

Coverdill, J. (1988). The dual economy and sex differences in earnings. *Social Forces, 60,* 970-993.

DiPrete, T. (1989). *The bureaucratic labor market.* New York: Plenum.

Duncan, G., & Corcoran, M. (1984). Do women "deserve" to earn less then men? In G. Duncan (Ed.), *Years of poverty, years of plenty* (pp. 153-172). Ann Arbor: University of Michigan, Institute for Social Research.

Edwards, R. (1979). *Contested terrain.* New York: Basic Books.

England, P. (1979). Women and occupational prestige: A case of vacuous sex equality. *Signs, 5,* 252-265.

England, P. (1982). The failure of human capital theory to explain occupational sex segregation. *Journal of Human Resources, 17,* 358-370.

Felmlee, D. (1982). Women's job mobility processes within and between employers. *American Sociological Review, 47,* 142-151.

Glass, J. (1990). The impact of occupational segregation on working conditions. *Social Forces, 68,* 779-796.

Greenberger, E., & Steinberg, L. (1983). Sex differences in early labor force experience. *Social Forces, 62,* 467-486.

Hachen, D. (1988). Gender differences in job mobility rates in the United States. *Social Science Research, 17,* 93-116.

Hutchison, D. (1988). Event history and survival analysis in the social sciences, II: Advanced applications and recent developments. *Quality and Quantity, 22,* 255-278.

Jacobs, J. (1989). *Revolving doors: Sex segregation and women's careers.* Stanford, CA: Stanford University Press.

Jacobs, J., & Powell, B. (1987). *Women's occupational status: A revised metric for comparing men and women.* Unpublished manuscript, University of Pennsylvania, Department of Sociology.

Jusenius, C. (1975). Occupational change, 1967-71. In *Dual Careers* (Vol. 3, pp. 21-35). Columbus: Ohio State University Center for Human Resource Research.

Kalbfleisch, J., & Prentice, R. (1980). *The statistical analysis of failure time data.* New York: John Wiley.

Levinson, R. (1975). Sex discrimination and employment practices. *Social Problems, 22,* 533-543.

Marini, M., & Brinton, M. (1984). Sex typing in occupational socialization. In B. Reskin (Ed.), *Sex segregation in the workplace* (pp. 192-232). Washington, DC: National Academy Press.

Otto, L., Call, V.R.A., & Spenner, K. (1981). *Design for a study of entry into careers.* Lexington, MA: D. C. Heath.

Padavic, I., & Reskin, B. (1990). Men's behavior and women's interest in blue-collar jobs. *Social Problems, 37,* 613-628.

Petersen, T. (1986). Estimating fully parametric hazard rate models with time-dependent covariates. *Sociological Methods & Research, 14,* 219-246.

Polachek, S. (1981). Occupational self-selection: A human capital approach to sex differences in occupational structure. *Review of Economics and Statistics, 58,* 60-69.

Reskin, B., & Hartmann, H. (Eds.). (1986). *Women's work, men's work.* Washington, DC: National Academy Press.

Reskin, B., & Roos, P. (1990). *Job queues, gender queues.* Philadelphia: Temple University Press.

Rexroat, C., & Shehan, C. (1984). Expected versus actual work roles of women. *American Sociological Review, 49,* 349-358.

Rosenfeld, R. A. (1983). Sex segregation and sectors. *American Sociological Review, 48,* 637-655.

Rosenfeld, R. A. (1984). Job changing and occupational sex segregation: Sex and race comparisons. In B. Reskin (Ed.), *Sex segregation in the workplace* (pp. 56-86). Washington, DC: National Academy Press.

Rosenfeld, R. A. (1992). Job shifting and career processes. *Annual Review of Sociology, 18,* 39-61.

Rosenfeld, R. A., & Spenner, K. (1988). Women's work and women's careers. In M. Riley (Ed.), *Social structure and human lives* (pp. 285-305). Newbury Park, CA: Sage.

Rytina, N., & Bianchi, S. (1984). Occupational reclassification and changes in distribution by gender. *Monthly Labor Review, 107,* 11-17.

Schreiber, C. T. (1979). *Changing places: men and women in transitional occupations.* Cambridge, MA: MIT Press.

Sørensen, A. (1983). Sociological research on labor markets. *Work and Occupations, 10,* 261-287.

Sørensen, A., & Tuma, N. (1981). Labor market structures and job mobility. In D. Treiman & R. Robinson (Eds.), *Research in social stratification and mobility* (Vol. 1, pp. 67-94). Greenwich, CT: JAI.

Tuma, N., & Hannan, M. (1984). *Social dynamics.* New York: Academic Press.

Waite, L., & Berryman, S. (1986). Job stability among young women: A comparison of traditional and nontraditional occupations. *American Journal of Sociology, 92,* 568-595.

Walshok, M. (1981). *Blue collar women.* Garden City, NJ: Doubleday.

Wenk, D., & Rosenfeld, R. A. (1992). Women's employment exit and reentry. *Research in Social Stratification & Mobility, 11,* 127-150.

Wolf, W., & Rosenfeld, R. A. (1978). Sex structure of occupations and job mobility. *Social Forces, 56,* 823-844.

Zucker, L., & Rosenstein, C. (1983). Taxonomies of institutional structure: Dual economy reconsidered. *American Sociological Review, 46,* 869-884.

10

Trends in Occupational and Industrial Sex Segregation in 56 Countries, 1960–1980

JERRY A. JACOBS
SUET T. LIM

Although occupational sex segregation in the United States has attracted the interest of scholars from diverse fields, less attention has been directed to international comparisons. In particular, little research has examined trends in sex segregation in a variety of countries. This chapter attempts to begin to fill this gap.

Occupational sex segregation, although remaining stable in the United States over most of the century (England, 1981; Jacobs, 1989a), has been slowly but steadily declining since 1970. The proportion of women who would have to change occupations to be distributed in the same manner as men declined from 67.6% in 1970 to 57.3% in 1986 (Jacobs, 1989a). Is this development part of an international trend? Is this pattern evident throughout highly industrialized countries? Are developing countries moving in the same direction? Do men and women experience workplace trends in the same way? What factors are associated with declines in sex segregation? These are the questions addressed in this chapter.

AUTHORS' NOTE: An earlier version of this chapter was presented at the annual meeting of the Population Association of America held in New Orleans, April 1988. We wish to thank Andrea Beller, Ester Boserup, Robin Leidner, Patricia Gwartney-Gibbs, Patricia Roos, and Vicki Smith for their comments.

Sex Segregation and Income Inequality

Sex segregation is of interest largely because of its connection with the gender gap in wages. Women earn less than men in part because they work in female-dominated occupations. In 1986, women working full-time in the United States brought home 64% of men's earnings. Although the sex gap in wages has narrowed in recent years, the annual earnings of women in 1986 constituted the same fraction of men's earnings as in 1955.[1] Earnings are lower in female-dominated occupations than in male-dominated occupations with similar educational requirements. Analyzing occupational data, Treiman and Hartmann (1981) estimated that 35% to 39% of the gender gap in wages is due to the sex segregation of occupations. Individual-level analyses show smaller but still substantial effects of sex segregation on women's wages. Sorensen (1989) found that 20% of the earnings gap is attributable to occupational sex segregation and another 16% due to sex segregation across industries. A recent U.S. Bureau of the Census report (1987) indicated that 17% to 30% of the wage gap between men and women is due to women's concentration in female-dominated occupations.[2]

Studies such as these attempt to measure the direct effect of sex segregation on wages. But there are indirect effects as well. For example, sex differences in education and experience are usually seen as voluntary, the result of the free choices of women. Yet if women's educational choices partly reflect their views of the limited occupational choices available to them, then an estimate of the total wage consequences of sex segregation should include a portion of the education effect. Similarly, if women leave the labor force because their jobs are not sufficiently rewarding, then the experience gap reflects an additional indirect effect of sex segregation. Adding these indirect effects of discrimination to the unexplained residual typically attributed to discrimination pushes the portion of the wage gap due to discrimination well above the conventional 50% estimate (Madden, 1985).

Kalleberg and Rosenfeld (1990), on the basis of an analysis of four countries, suggested that there may be no connection across countries between the level of occupational sex segregation and the gender gap in wages. Blau and Ferber (1986) are equally skeptical. Indeed, for the 10 countries for which they present both sex segregation and wage data, there is only a weak negative relationship between sex segregation and the male-female income gap ($r = -.02$). However, this relationship may be weak in part because Blau and Ferber's sex-ratio data are for manufacturing only, whereas the degree of segregation is computed across the labor force as a whole. As we will discuss, comparing occupations across countries is treacherous. Our analysis primarily focuses on changes over time in individual countries, rather than cross-sectional comparisons. We posit that a decline in sex segregation contributes to a decline in male-female earnings inequality, although the available data do not permit us to test this assumption.

To our knowledge, no one has documented the contribution of sex segregation to the sex gap in wages in developing countries. Yet the sex segregation of work is often cited as a principal cause of women's economic disadvantage. Whereas numerous cases of women being paid less than men for identical work are cited (Bisilliat & Fieloux, 1987; Joekes, 1985), more typical is the case in which women are excluded from better-paying jobs. The sectors in which women are concentrated vary from place to place, whether it be the concentration of women in low-skilled jobs in the semiconductor industry in Korea (Horton & Lee, 1988), the relegation of women to back-breaking work in subsistence agriculture in Africa or Latin America (Deere & Leon, 1987), or the concentration of women in handicraft production in northern India (Weston, 1987). In each case, the evidence indicates that the differentiation of women's work from men's work is responsible for women's economic plight. Thus we expect that sex segregation at work is associated with women's economic disadvantage and is correlated with temporal changes in the economic position of women relative to men.

Comparative Data on the Division of Labor by Sex

Although occupational sex segregation in the United States has been the focus of a great deal of scholarly attention, efforts to place the United States in the context of international trends have been limited. The research to date has been almost exclusively cross-sectional (Blau & Ferber, 1986; Gaskin, 1979; Roos, 1985) and has left the question of change over time—the focal point of this chapter—essentially unexplored (for notable exceptions, see Gwartney-Gibbs, 1988; Hakim, 1992; Jin & Stevens, 1987; Lyson, 1986).

Comparative anthropological research on the sex-typing of work reveals that tasks allocated to men in one society are often allocated to women in others (Friedl, 1975; Murdock & Provost, 1973; Rogers, 1978; Sanday, 1981; Whyte, 1978). On the basis of this evidence, it is difficult to conclude that the specific economic roles women perform are determined by their reproductive role or by their household obligations (Jacobs, 1989b).

Several studies have attempted to quantify sex segregation in work in different countries. Boserup (1970) demonstrated that the sexual division of labor remains highly varied as the countries of the developing world move toward more urban and industrial economies. She documented wide variations across Africa, Asia, and Latin America in the representation of women in agriculture, trading, clerical work, and administration. Boulding (1976) presented data on the division of labor in 86 countries and reported indices of segregation that varied from less than 5 to nearly 80 across eight broad occupational groups. Ferber and Lowry (1977) described the variation in labor force participation and occupational representation for 157 countries for which International Labor Organization (ILO) data were available. Miller (1972) documented variation in industrial sex segregation across 85 countries and suggested there was no relationship between the level of economic development and the degree of segregation observed. Similarly, Roos (1985) reported variation in the representation of women across 14 broad occupational categories for 12 industrial societies and indicated that there were significant differences in the level of occupational segregation by sex among these countries. More detailed occupational measures would presumably show even greater variation, although comparable detailed occupational data are difficult to obtain.

Ward (1984) examined the determinants of women's labor force participation and women's share of industrial, agricultural, and service-sector employment across 105 countries in 1975. She was particularly interested in the effect on women's economic activity of the position of countries in the world system, as measured by the structure of foreign trade and the level of multinational investment. Most recently, Charles (1992) attempted to explain variations in the level of segregation in 25 mostly developed countries.

In this chapter, we focus on change over time in sex segregation, rather than on variations in the division of labor by sex across societies. Whereas comparisons across countries can be misleading due to variations in the nature of work in different societies, in the way occupational data are reported, and in the cultural acknowledgement of women's labor force activity (Dixon, 1982), focusing on change over time for particular countries avoids most of these difficulties. We ask whether sex segregation has increased or declined in a wide range of countries between 1960 and 1980. We also examine whether the changes were experienced in the same way by men and women. Finally, we ask whether basic indicators of socioeconomic modernization, such as per capita Gross National Product (GNP), urbanization, women's labor force participation rate, total fertility rate, and women's educational levels can explain changes in the level of sex segregation over time.

Trends in Sex Segregation

We test three competing hypotheses regarding trends in sex segregation in the labor force:

1. Sex segregation is increasing in developing societies and persisting in industrial societies.
2. Sex segregation is declining in both developing and industrial societies.
3. Sex segregation increases during the initial stages of economic development but declines with greater economic advancement.

A great deal of recent research has sought to document the plight of women in the Third World. This research has highlighted the invisibility of much of the work women do (Deere & Leon, 1987; Dixon, 1982; Rogers, 1979; United Nations, 1980), the substantial (and sometimes preponderant) economic contributions made by women (Lele, 1986; New Internationalist, 1985; UNESCO, 1981), the sometimes blatant wage discrimination against women (Afshar, 1985; Bisilliat & Fieloux, 1987), the arbitrary distinctions among work activities constructed to maintain women's economic disadvantages (Afshar, 1987; Humphrey, 1987), the terrible conditions under which women often work (Nash & Fernandez-Kelly, 1983; Smith, Collins, Hopkins, & Muhammad, 1988), and the burden of hours of extensive household work that begins after an exhausting day of wage labor (Bisilliat & Fieloux, 1987; Lele, 1986; UNESCO, 1981). (Useful reviews of this literature are found in Ward, 1988, and Mukhopadhyay & Higgins, 1988; see also Joekes, 1987; Tinker, 1990; Ward, 1990.)

Many women in developing countries no doubt work under harsh conditions for little pay. For example, Tamil women often work 10 or 12 hours picking tea leaves on plantations in Sri Lanka, only to return home to begin their second shift, preparing meals and caring for their families without the labor-saving technology that women in industrialized countries can depend on (Bisilliat & Fieloux, 1987).

Much of the recent research on women and work in the Third World is pessimistic about the effects of economic development on the status of women. According to Nash (1988), for example, "Ethnographic evidence points to a sharpening of the cleavages along racial and gender lines during the expansive decades of capitalist penetration throughout the world" (p. 12). Similarly, Ward (1988) concludes that "a growing body of macro and micro research has documented that, during development, women's economic status relative to men's has stagnated, particularly in currently developing countries or countries in the periphery of the capitalist world system. Over time, the women's position has continued to decline" (pp. 17-18). Finally, Greenhalgh (1985) maintains that "since publication of Ester Boserup's pioneering book, *Woman's Role in Economic Development,* in 1970, a growing body of literature has documented the decline in women's status that has accompanied the development of capitalism in many parts of the world" (p. 265).

Feminist observers have attributed this condition to the intersection of international forces with local gender-based arrangements. Some writers have stressed the role of Western influence in undermining women's economic position in non-Western societies. Boserup and others have argued that the European presence in colonial societies elevated men's status over that of women, as men obtained control over new agricultural technology for the production of cash crops (Boserup, 1970; Etienne & Leacock, 1980; Lele, 1986). This pattern continued as development projects continued to favor men. A 1980 United Nations development report acknowledged that "women's lack of access to modern technology [was] closely linked to the pervasive bias against women in technical education and training" (p. 11).

Feminists writing from Marxist and world-systems perspectives have emphasized the role of the internationalization of industrial capitalism in the deterioration of women's status (Mies, 1988; Nash & Fernandez-Kelly, 1983; Smith et al., 1988; Ward, 1984). Nash and Fernandez-Kelly, for example, point to the spread of highly exploitative conditions in textile, electronics, and garment industries in developing countries as evidence of the intensifying differences between men and women. In each case, external pressures have interacted with patriarchal institutions internal to each society to erode the economic position of women.

Although these authors do not develop specific predictions regarding trends in sex segregation, we may nonetheless derive from their perspective the expectation that sex segregation increased. The operative mechanism in this approach is that women are economically disadvantaged because they are excluded from the types of work men do. Thus Afshar (1985) cites the "feminization of agriculture" (p. xii), particularly in Africa and Latin America, and Ward (1988) points to the "feminization of the informal sector" (p. 25) in many countries, concluding that "most women around the world are located in the agricultural, service or informal sectors" (p. 25). When women are found in manufacturing, often young single women take transitory jobs in low-wage, female-dominated industries such as textiles and electronics in countries including the Philippines, Taiwan, South Korea, and Singapore (Nash & Fernandez-Kelly, 1983). If the sex segregation of work is crucial to the disadvantaged position of women, the decline in women's status should coincide with a decline in the degree of occupational and industrial overlap between men and women—in other words, an increase in sex segregation at work.

Few have argued that sex segregation is increasing in industrial societies. Rather, pessimists have held that declines in sex segregation will be slow or nonexistent for many reasons, including rigidities in the structure of labor markets (Roos & Reskin, 1984), the persistence of women's domestic obligations (Fuchs, 1988), patriarchal institutions and ideologies (Hartmann, 1976), and the persistence of labor market discrimination (Bergmann, 1986). Thus our first hypothesis is that sex segregation is increasing in developing economies while remaining stable in industrial economies.

Both neoclassical economic theory and one strand of sociological theory predict the demise of arbitrary sex-linked differences in labor market behavior. In sociology, the industrial society thesis holds that industrialism tends to eradicate ascriptive criteria. The implication of this view is that sex segregation declines as the institutional requisites of industrial society come to the fore (Bernard, 1968; Smelser, 1968). This expectation has been the foil for studies that find a stable pattern of sex segregation in the United States over much of the century (England, 1981; Gross, 1968; Jacobs, 1989a). Different versions of this approach emphasize different causes for this decline. Some stress educational changes that reduce productivity differentials between men and women (Schultz, 1981). Other authors (Davis & van den Oever, 1982; Ridley, 1968) emphasize the demographic dimension of modernization. They reason that declines in fertility associated with economic advances result in the increased participation of women in a broad spectrum of economic activities. Specifically, as fertility declines and longevity increases, women spend a greater proportion of their lives in the labor force, which results in a convergence between men and women in investments in skills and career pursuits and eventually in a rise in feminist movements that further challenge sex-role differentiation. The implication is that the status of women will improve due to a decline in sex segregation at work.

In discussing the modernization perspective, several caveats should be made. First, as we noted above, the status of women varies considerably among preindustrial societies (Bradley, 1989; Sanday, 1981; Whyte, 1978). We should not assume that the condition of women before industrialization was uniformly low. Second, it is now recognized that there is no single route to industrialization. Different countries draw on preexisting cultural and institutional arrangements and do not conform to a single optimum approach, as divergent success stories in Japan, Germany, and Sweden attest. Third, the resurgence of religious fundamentalism in Islamic countries and elsewhere should give pause to sweeping generalizations concerning changes in women's status. Nonetheless, this view offers a clear prediction that can be tested empirically.

A second perspective that predicts a decline in sex segregation is that of neoclassical labor economics. The rise of competitive market forces is predicted to erode discriminatory barriers in the economy because discrimination costs those who discriminate. Although this perspective might not account for the wide variations in the level of sex segregation found among different countries, it may nonetheless be useful in predicting the direction of change.

Both modernization and neoclassical economic theory predict that sex segregation will decline in the same fashion for developed and developing societies. Industrial society (or economic efficiency) is expected to erode the importance of ascriptive (discriminatory or nonefficient) characteristics in the labor market. This view has generally been interpreted as predicting decline in the sexual division of labor. A leading neoclassical labor historian has been quite explicit about this prediction: "There is no a priori reason why men and women should or ought to be distributed identically across occupations. But there is a presumption that movements over time in the index [of dissimilarity] should reflect changes in the attributes of the two groups that make them more alike" (Goldin, 1990, p. 75).

One final note about the prediction of a decline in sex segregation: Scholars who study trends in sex segregation rarely discuss politics explicitly (Beller, 1982). Although this study does not include direct measures of political change, we should note its potential effects. The women's movement has become an international force during the period considered (Iglitzin & Ross, 1986). To the extent that we observe a decline in sex segregation, we may attribute a portion of such changes to the rising political influence of women. Our second hypothesis, then, is that sex segregation is declining in both developing and industrialized economies.

Our last hypothesis derives from Sinha's (1968) work on women's labor force participation (see also Durand, 1975). Sinha argued that women's economic contributions decline during the early stages of modernization but increase in later stages. As the agricultural and traditional sectors contract, women's traditional economic contributions may be undercut. Women may also be at a disadvantage in competing with men in the face of high unemployment that often characterizes rapidly growing cities at the onset of industrialization. This pattern is reversed in later stages of development, as the growth in jobs in the modern sector draws in women. This reasoning may be extended to predict increasing sex segregation at the onset of industrialization and declining sex segregation thereafter. Although Durand (1975) found little longitudinal support for this thesis with respect to women's labor force participation, this hypothesis continues to be explored by those interested in the labor force participation of women in developing countries (Park, 1990). Thus our third hypothesis is that sex segregation is increasing in the least developed countries while declining in the most developed countries.[3]

Little comparative evidence on changes in women's status over time exists for the contemporary period. The few longitudinal studies to date focus on determinants of women's labor force participation (Singelmann & Tienda, 1979; Ward & Pampel, 1985) rather than on trends in sex segregation. Miller (1972) examined whether an inverse correlation exists between economic development and industrial sex segregation. She found little evidence of such a pattern in a cross-sectional examination of 61 countries, but she did not have enough longitudinal data to examine changes for particular countries.

In a review of ILO data, Sivard (1985) indicated that sex segregation remains high. She suggests that there have been some slow declines in recent years, but she does not present data supporting this conclusion. She does show that sex differences in manufacturing wages in 24 of the 26 countries examined have narrowed between 1960 and 1980, surely an optimistic sign. However, we do not have comparative data on wages in other sectors and so do not know whether the overall sex gap in wages is declining. The picture is complicated by the fact that the proportion of women in manufacturing has increased in some countries but has declined in others. The available literature does not settle the issue of recent trends in income or occupational and industrial sex segregation.

Data and Methods

Longitudinal data on occupation and industry trends for as many countries as were available were culled from published tables in ILO yearbooks. We included only those countries for which data employing standard categories were available for three time points, corresponding as closely as possible to 1960, 1970, and 1980. Because data on a given country are not reproduced in every ILO yearbook, we searched volumes from 1955 to 1986 to compile the most complete set of data possible. The ILO data are derived from population censuses and labor force surveys from each country. We drew data from the ILO yearbook Tables 4A and 4B from 1955 to 1963 and Tables 2A and 2B after 1964. The data were tabulated by sex and employment status, with Tables 4A and 2A covering the economically active population by industry and Tables 4B and 2B showing the distribution of labor force by occupation. Appendices available from the authors list, for occupation and industry, respectively, the countries we considered, the years to which the data pertain, and the ILO volumes from which the data were obtained.

Whereas some countries used their own system of classification or modified versions of the ILO standard, by 1980 most countries reported the data in the standard classification system recommended by the ILO. However, the ILO standard itself changed over time, so we had to create a uniform set of categories for our analysis. The original classification system, published in 1958, was revised in a 1968 ILO publication.

The revised occupational standard has two fewer categories than the older version. The categories of miners, transportation workers, and production-process workers (Categories 5, 6, 7/8) were collapsed into one category in the later version (Category 7-9). In order to have comparable data over time, we used the broader classification system, the 1968 revised standard, with a loss of detail for the sake of comparability. In our calculations, the figures for Categories 5, 6, 7/8 in the earlier years were grouped to match the one category for the later years. All other categories remained essentially the same. The main loss of cases came from countries that collapsed categories together; most commonly administrative and managerial fields were combined with those doing clerical work. The category "inadequately described" was omitted in our calculations. Consequently, the occupational indexes are based on seven categories: professional, administrative, clerical, sales, service, agricultural, and production-related work.

The revised standard classification system for industry status has nine categories, compared with eight in the older classification. The principal change is that services are divided into business and personal services. In our calculation of indexes, we used the 1958 standard classification system to obtain comparable data over time. The industrial indexes are based on eight categories: agriculture, mining, manufacturing, construction, electricity, transportation, service, and commerce.[4]

Countries were excluded if they employed their own classification system or if they reported data for fewer than three consecutive time points. We made one exception to this rule for Israel, which reported data on seven industrial categories for all time points. We excluded countries with very small populations and those with large changes in the population that are not accounted for by normal population growth (i.e., countries that have experienced boundary changes). Unfortunately, we were forced to exclude all formerly Soviet bloc countries, as well as most African countries, due to insufficient data.

We obtained data for 56 countries: 50 countries are included in our industry analysis and 39 in our occupation analysis. For 33 countries we have both industry and occupation data, for 17 countries industry data only, and for 6 countries occupation data only.

Data Validity and Reliability:
The Parallel Lines Hypothesis

The principal difficulty with these data is that they are highly aggregated. With only eight industry and seven occupational categories available for longitudinal analysis, a fundamental question is whether we can derive meaningful results from these data. We maintain that even though these data understate the level of segregation they may nonetheless serve as a useful indicator of the trend in segregation.

We considered two potential problems with the aggregated ILO data. The first is the validity of these data as an indicator of the degree of sex segregation in the workplace, which may be severely underestimated as a result of the high level of aggregation. Women and men are not evenly distributed within broad occupational and industrial groups. Indeed, Bielby and Baron (1984) have shown remarkably high levels of sex segregation within a sample of firms. Consequently, the higher the level of aggregation, the smaller the proportion of actual segregation captured by one's measure. The second problem concerns the reliability of the data on trends. The gross units of analysis may misrepresent trends over time because they may capture an increasingly small proportion of overall segregation, as specializations proliferate. England (1981) emphasized this point in her study of trends in occupational segregation by sex. The reliance on standardized categories may be deceptive, in that the underlying phenomenon may become increasingly remote from the measures employed.

Given these potential difficulties, it is important to examine whether major fields constitute an appropriate unit of analysis. Our analysis of international trends in sex segregation rests on this premise, which we refer to as the "parallel lines" assumption. We assume that trends in sex segregation tracked by more detailed data would parallel the trends we present. The more detailed the measure, the higher the segregation we expect to observe. But we maintain that the relatively coarse ILO data are reliable barometers of the direction and perhaps even the rate of change in segregation.

Four types of data suggest that aggregated measures of segregation show the same patterns of change as more detailed data. First, data on trends in occupational segregation in the United States indicate that whether one measures sex segregation with detailed occupational data or with aggregated occupational data, the direction of change is the same (Jacobs, 1986). Moreover, these data indicate that the rate of change is roughly similar at the detailed and aggregated levels.

A study of the sex segregation of college majors in the United States obtained a similar finding. An aggregated measure of field of study was constructed to facilitate an analysis of trends between 1948 and 1980. Indexes of segregation (D) and isolation (P*) were calculated for the major categories and for the most detailed available categories, for 1952, 1960, 1970, and 1980 for bachelor's, master's, and doctoral degrees. An analysis based on 24 majors yielded trends parallel to those obtained from the most detailed data available (by 1980, the detailed data consisted of several hundred fields). Not only did both measures move together over a period of 30 years, but the rate of change over time was similar at both levels of measurement (Jacobs, 1985).

Analyses of residential segregation also indicate that detailed data produce results that mirror those for more aggregated measures. For residential segregation, block-level data are more detailed than census tract data. Careful analysis has revealed that measures of segregation calculated at the census tract level parallel those at the block level (Taeuber & Taeuber, 1965). In short, the coarser measure is lower but varies across space and over time in accord with the more detailed measure.

We tested this parallel lines thesis with data from eight countries for which both detailed and aggregated data were available: Canada, Guyana, Ireland, New Zealand, Panama, Singapore, the United States, and Venezuela. The results are presented in Table 10.1. The aggregated categories correspond to the seven standard ILO categories; the number of detailed categories varies by country. We find in seven of the eight cases that the trends obtained with the broad ILO occupations match those obtained with more detailed occupational data from each country's census. Moreover, the rate of change is roughly similar for these different units of measurement. The sole exception is Venezuela, where the aggregated data suggest a slight increase in segregation, whereas the detailed data indicate a slight decline. However, the difference between these two measures is not large: The detailed measure shows a decline of less than 1%, whereas the aggregate measure shows an increase of 6.6%. These results suggest that the parallel lines assumption, although not mathematically a necessity, nonetheless obtains with regularity. These data speak directly to both the issue of validity and that of reliability: Aggregated data understate the degree of sex segregation, but they do so in a consistent fashion; these data also provide us with a reliable measure of time trends.[5]

The only argument we are aware of that runs counter to the parallel lines assumption is that of Reskin and Roos (1990), who examined the "resegregation" of occupations in the United States between 1970 and 1980. They questioned whether the apparent decline in occupational segregation during this period is real. They examined a number of occupations that are flipping from predominantly male to predominantly female and concluded that the resegregation of such occupations has vitiated much of the apparent gains women have made. The evidence that Reskin and Roos compiled will make a significant contribution to our understanding of the maintenance of sex segregation.

One might conclude from this work that declines in sex segregation measured at the aggregate level do not correspond with changes occur-

Table 10.1 Comparison of Detailed Aggregated Measures of Sex
            Segregation

	Time Span	N Occupations Aggregated (Detail)	Initial Segregation Aggregated (Detail)	Final Segregation Aggregated (Detail)	Change Aggregated (Detail)
Canada	1951–1961	7	52.8	49.8	−5.7%
		(19)	(62.6)	(58.8)	(−6.1%)
Guyana	1946–1960	7	29.7	37.4	+25.9%
		(19)	(41.3)	(48.7)	(+17.9%)
Ireland	1951–1961	7	41.3	42.2	+2.2%
		(19)	(52.2)	(55.3)	(+5.9%)
New Zealand[a]	1971–1981	7	42.8	41.9	−2.1%
		(80)	(62.5)	(57.6)	(−7.8%)
Panama	1950–1960	7	53.5	65.5	+16.1%
		(19)	(65.2)	(74.0)	(+13.5%)
Singapore	1957–1966	7	35.8	28.8	−19.6%
		(19)	(50.2)	(42.9)	(−14.5%)
United States[b]	1970–1980	7	41.4	34.9	−15.7%
		(483)	(67.6)	(59.8)	(−11.5%)
Venezuela	1950–1961	7	51.3	54.7	+6.6%
		(19)	(67.7)	(67.3)	(−0.6%)

NOTE: Unless otherwise specified, the data reported here were compiled by Ann Miller from the censuses of these countries. She collapsed these data into a consistent set of occupational classifications. These data are located in the files of the Population Studies Center at the University of Pennsylvania.
a. Detailed data obtained from Gwartney-Gibbs (1988).
b. Detailed data obtained from Jacobs (1989a). These figures employ 1980 Census detailed occupational categories for both years.

ring at a more detailed, intraoccupational level. Yet Reskin and Roos do not demonstrate that the decline in sex segregation during the 1980s is a temporary by-product of resegregation. Resegregation might temporarily reduce the observed level of segregation, but in the long run, resegregation would lead to a resurgence of segregation. Consider the effects of resegregation at three points in time. If the only change between Time 1 and Time 2 is that several occupations began to change their sex composition from male dominated to female dominated, then segregation measured at Time 2 would indeed be lower than at Time 1, as the occupations in question would be temporarily less skewed by sex. However, at Time 3, when this transition was complete, we would see sex segregation return to its Time 1 level. But because sex segregation is continuing to decline in the United States, albeit slowly (Jacobs, 1989a), we conclude that the process of resegregation has not stemmed the overall trend toward declining segregation. Despite Reskin and Roos's (1990) valuable analysis, we maintain that trends in sex segregation measured at different levels of analysis generally move together.

A secondary difficulty has to do with the underreporting of women's labor force participation in many parts of the world, particularly in agriculture (Dixon, 1982; Lyson, 1986; Miller, 1972), although it also is endemic in the informal sector as well. Consequently, we measure segregation for the entire labor force and for the nonagricultural labor force. This procedure also helps to adjust for the widely varying proportion of individuals working in agriculture from country to country.

Finally, our analysis is less vulnerable to underreporting of women's labor force participation than it is to changes in reporting procedures. If the underreporting of women's economic activity remained constant over time, our measures would still capture the trends in behavior. However, if reporting changes had occurred in the interim, we would need to distinguish real changes in behavior from changes in documentation.

Dimensions of Segregation

Most research on occupational segregation by sex has employed one measure of segregation: D, the index of dissimilarity. This index measures the main dimension of segregation: the degree to which two groups are unevenly distributed over a set of categories. The index of dissimilarity has a convenient interpretation: It represents the proportion of women who would have to change occupations for women to be distributed in the same manner as men. D is symmetrical: The same proportion of men would have to change occupations for men to be distributed in the same manner as women. We also present results for a size-standardized measure of segregation, which allows us to determine what trends in segregation would have been if the relative size of occupations (or industries) had remained constant over time.[6]

Although uniform reliance on this measure has been helpful in comparing the results of different studies, we examine other dimensions of segregation as well. Massey and Denton (1988) surveyed a wide range of measures of segregation and suggested that isolation is a nonspatial dimension of segregation that complements the dimension of unevenness represented by the index of dissimilarity.

The isolating effect of segregation depends on the relative size of groups in which men and women find themselves working, as well as the level of segregation. Lieberson (1980) fruitfully employed an index of the probability of intergroup contact, P*, in recent studies of residential segregation (Lieberson & Carter, 1982; Massey & Denton, 1988). In the nonspatial context we are considering, this measure represents the chances of sharing an industry or occupation with a member of the opposite sex, not the chances of personal contact per se. This index has been used in studies of sex segregation only to a limited extent (Jacobs, 1985, 1986, 1989b). This index supplements the standard index of dissimilarity by indicating the way in which each group experiences segregation. Two different settings with equal levels of segregation but different proportions of women will give women different probabilities of sharing an occupation or industry with each other, a feature of segregation revealed by P*. Another important property of this measure is that the probability of sharing an occupation or industry differs from the perspective of each group. When experiencing a given level of segregation, the majority group will always have a lower chance of encountering the minority: The minority is less isolated from the majority.[7] We add a discussion of the P* index to the standard discussion of segregation in examining trends in occupational sex segregation. We refer to segregation as the degree of unevenness measured by the familiar index of dissimilarity, D, and of isolation as the probability of sharing an industry or occupation with a member of the opposite sex as measured by P*.

Results

Occupational Segregation

Table 10.2 presents findings for trends in the index of dissimilarity for 1960, 1970, and 1980 and whether there was an increase or a decrease in sex segregation between 1960 and 1980. Results are presented by continent. We present North and South American countries together, and we append Australia and New Zealand to the Asian countries. For the Americas, we note that most countries (10 of 13) experienced a decline in occupational sex segregation between 1960 and 1980. The exceptions were Ecuador, Peru, and Paraguay. For Asia, a bare majority of countries (7 of 12) experienced declines in sex segregation. In Europe, trends in segregation are mixed. Eight of 14 countries experienced increases, and only 6 experienced declines during this period.

Table 10.2 also presents size-standardized indexes of dissimilarity. These results enable us to distinguish compositional changes from the effect of the changing mix of occupations. A clearer pattern emerges for this measure than for the unstandardized index. Sex segregation would have declined in every American country and all Asian countries except India if the relative size of occupational groups had remained the same. For Europe, the size-standardized measure shows declines in the majority of cases (10 of 14), with Austria, Denmark, France, and Switzerland the exceptions. This suggests that growing occupations are more segregated by sex than average, and so the declining sex segregation of occupations is sometimes reversed by the countervailing trend in the occupational mix.

We analyzed the compositional changes responsible for the increases in overall occupational sex segregation in countries where D increased but the size-standardized D declined. Unfortunately, no simple pattern emerged. The decline in farm employment in most countries tended to contribute to an increase in the extent of sex segregation, as agriculture tends to be more integrated by sex than other occupational groups (especially when women's contributions are adequately reported). However, there were exceptions to this pattern. In Greece, for example, farming was more skewed by sex than other occupations in 1961, and in the ensuing 20 years it became less skewed while declining in size. Thus farming contributed less to sex segregation in Greece in 1981 than in 1961. Greek women were overrepresented in agriculture in 1961, with more than two thirds of the women in the labor force engaged in agriculture, compared with less than half of the men. By 1981, the agricultural labor force had contracted, with less than one third of the women and a little more than one quarter of the men working on farms. The ratio of women's representation in agriculture to men's declined from 1.39 to 1.18. (Men were a numerical majority in agriculture at both points in time: This ratio refers to the proportion of women in agriculture versus the proportion of men in agriculture.) The same pattern obtained in Sweden, where men were disproportionately represented in agriculture in 1960. Agricultural employment declined but became less skewed toward men, contributing to a decline in occupational sex segregation.

In most cases, the growth of professional, administrative, and clerical occupations contributed to an increase in sex segregation, as men's rep-

Table 10.2 Trends in Occupational Segregation, 1960–1980

	Index of Dissimilarity (D)				Size-Standardized D			
	1960	*1970*	*1980*	*1960–1980*	*1960*	*1970*	*1980*	*1960–1980*
Americas								
Canada	.492	.434	.424	–	.437	.385	.373	–
Chile	.512	.500	.427	–	.407	.404	.407	–
Costa Rica	.589	.568	.498	–	.488	.460	.422	–
Dominican Republic	.631	.214	.485	–	.490	.315	.413	–
Ecuador	.486	.473	.573	+	.406	.399	.402	–
El Salvador	.623	.621	.408	–	.431	.464	.381	–
Mexico	.389	.397	.335	–	.362	.302	.303	–
Panama	.645	.599	.587	–	.485	.485	.451	–
Paraguay	.436	.488	.480	+	.375	.369	.391	–
Peru	.309	.399	.345	+	.327	.377	.352	+
United States	.419	.407	.384	–	.406	.398	.368	–
Uruguay	.428	.414	.349	–	.465	.409	.427	–
Venezuela	.551	.551	.504	–	.514	.510	.480	–
Asia								
Brunei	.419	.349	.417	–	.408	.297	.355	–
India	.135	.138	.156	+	.355	.335	.298	–
Japan	.239	.253	.251	+	.272	.290	.272	–
Korea	.136	.197	.183	+	.323	.325	.259	–
Kuwait	.562	.539	.529	–	.547	.599	.575	+
Malaysia	.256	.201	.168	–	.376	.263	.231	–
Philippines	.257	.302	.251	–	.288	.303	.256	–
Singapore	.356	.241	.212	–	.400	.298	.259	–
Syria	.427	.248	.412	–	.501	.341	.371	–
Thailand	.087	.096	.108	+	.317	.270	.217	–
Australia	.468	.476	.471	+	.419	.429	.407	–
New Zealand	.482	.428	.419	–	.452	.432	.396	–
Europe								
Austria	.364	.337	.392	+	.305	.301	.315	+
Denmark	.487	.454	.497	+	.459	.415	.509	+
France	.344	.389	.383	+	.343	.374	.372	+
Germany	.375	.352	.364	–	.332	.316	.309	–
Greece	.207	.238	.228	+	.280	.268	.230	–
Ireland	.461	.460	.476	+	.459	.451	.442	–
Italy	.176	.234	.246	+	.146	.253	.302	+
Luxembourg	.511	.544	.489	–	.430	.441	.418	–
Netherlands	.481	.449	.399	–	.447	.425	.424	–
Norway	.552	.487	.479	–	.504	.449	.439	–
Portugal	.372	.226	.270	–	.487	.337	.284	–
Sweden	.490	.393	.432	–	.493	.391	.438	–
Switzerland	.379	.374	.392	+	.355	.414	.401	+
United Kingdom	.440	.422	.444	+	.455	.434	.441	–

resentation disproportionately grew in administrative and professional occupations and women's representation grew in clerical occupations. But again, exceptions to these generalizations are evident. In Ireland, Thailand, and Paraguay, clerical occupations grew while becoming less segregated by sex.

The growth of manufacturing and service employment had highly varied effects on sex segregation. In Australia, Italy, Korea, Ecuador, and Paraguay, the growth of manufacturing reduced sex segregation, whereas in Peru, Switzerland, Ireland, Greece, and Thailand, manufacturing increased its contribution to sex segregation during this period. For services, a similarly mixed pattern was evident: In Australia, Korea, Ecuador, and Paraguay, growing employment in service occupations increased sex segregation, whereas in Switzerland, Peru, and Ireland, the reverse pattern appeared.

We expected the nonagricultural occupations to show greater declines in sex segregation. Because agriculture is generally a relatively integrated occupation, as it shrinks, sex segregation should increase. We expected that this might cancel out declines in other sectors of the economy. But the occupational results do not support this expectation. The number of cases in which sex segregation declines remains about the same when agriculture is removed from the analysis. Removing agriculture deletes one decline from the American scorecard, adds one decline to the Asian scorecard, and adds two cases of decline to the European scorecard.[8] Size-standardized analyses removing agriculture show three fewer cases of declines for the Americas (10 of 13) and for Asia (8 of 12) than when all sectors are included. In Europe, the size-standardized measure removing agriculture produces the same direction of change as that which includes agriculture.[9]

Three objections may be raised to this summary of results: First, many of the changes involve very small declines in segregation; second, for a number of countries, segregation increased during the 1960s and then declined during the 1970s; and third, for some countries, like the Dominican Republic, the decennial figures are so volatile as to be implausible. The first point weakens but does not undermine our conclusions. If we treat as unchanged countries where there is, say, less than a 5% change, then the generalization of a decline in the size-standardized measure of segregation applies to 24 of 39 countries, with no change in 10 others and only five cases of clear increases. In other words, ignoring small changes reduces the exceptions as much as those cases that fit the rule. On the second point, most of the countries where direction of change differed did so only to a limited extent. Of course, it may well be the case that countries did experience declines in one period and increases in another. Finally, the Dominican Republic is the only case where very large changes point in opposite directions in different decades. It is consequently excluded in the multivariate analysis. In other cases, changes tend to be smaller and the two decades tend to move in consistent directions.

Industry

Thirteen of 15 American countries saw declines in industrial sex segregation, as indicated in Table 10.3. For Europe and Asia, the trends were mixed. In 10 of the 17 Asian countries examined, declines in industrial sex segregation were evident, with 6 countries increasing and 1—Thailand—remaining unchanged. In Europe, segregation in 9 countries declined, whereas 6 countries (Austria, Belgium, Finland, Greece, Hungary, and the United Kingdom) showed increases.

A more consistent pattern emerges when the size-standardized measure is examined: Sex segregation then declines in 13 of 15 American countries, with Ecuador and Paraguay as exceptions. Every European country shows a decline in industrial sex segregation. For Europe, there were consistent compositional declines; however, in 6 of 15 countries, these compositional changes were offset by countervailing structural changes. For Asia, the size-standardized measure showed declines in all but two countries—India and Nepal.

To summarize, the composition of industries and occupations is rarely moving toward a greater segregation of men and women. In most countries, declines or approximate stability were evident. However, in 11 of the 15 cases where industrial sex segregation increased, especially in Asia and Europe, the changing mix of industries (structural change) offset the compositional changes and was responsible for the net increase in segregation.

Removing agriculture does not change the overall scorecard for trends in industrial segregation, although the trends in a number of individual countries change between slightly negative and slightly positive.[10] Removing agriculture from the size-standardized industrial analyses has no effect on the direction of change. For industry, as for occupation, the removal of agriculture does not produce a pattern of greater declines.

Table 10.3 Trends in Industrial Segregation

	Index of Dissimilarity (D)				Size-Standardized D			
	1960	1970	1980	1960–1980	1960	1970	1980	1960–1980
Africa								
Egypt	.258	.326	.450	+	.476	.380	.300	−
Morocco	.339	.365	.311	−	.502	.471	.503	+
South Africa	.539	.334	.379	−	.538	.511	.444	−
Tunisia	.221	.500	.306	+	.461	.550	.494	+
Americas								
Argentina	.405	.382	.398	−	.533	.494	.485	−
Barbados	.326	.327	.163	−	.510	.487	.321	−
Canada	.384	.349	.296	−	.463	.411	.307	−
Chile	.506	.450	.353	−	.583	.563	.540	−
Costa Rica	.641	.571	.493	−	.591	.578	.516	−
Dominican Republic	.692	.210	.405	−	.627	.200	.424	−
Ecuador	.480	.515	.410	−	.536	.505	.452	−
Guatemala	.659	.664	.624	−	.589	.639	.555	−
Guyana	.384	.432	.430	+	.524	.524	.469	−
Mexico	.357	.377	.307	−	.416	.352	.267	−
Panama	.623	.554	.491	−	.449	.473	.418	−
Paraguay	.494	.568	.551	+	.582	.632	.549	−
Peru	.343	.424	.312	−	.505	.529	.422	−
United States	.329	.293	.274	−	.433	.378	.400	−
Venezuela	.525	.468	.380	−	.496	.432	.396	−
Asia								
Brunei	.381	.336	.291	−	.462	.408	.297	−
Hong Kong	.237	.239	.219	−	.320	.331	.397	+
India	.139	.127	.156	+	.266	.282	.290	+
Indonesia	.081	.109	.125	+	.422	.520	.408	−
Iran	.542	.497	.305	−	.649	.631	.544	−
Israel	.367	.324	.330	−	.470	.333	.355	−
Japan	.209	.207	.196	−	.403	.411	.384	−
Korea	.072	.151	.163	+	.513	.446	.388	−
Kuwait	.487	.503	.499	+	.642	.634	.496	−
Malaysia	.240	.170	.163	−	.331	.360	.402	+
Nepal	.049	.054	.064	+	.219	.351	.312	+
Philippines	.266	.415	.321	+	.640	.616	.533	−
Singapore	.307	.268	.193	−	.398	.354	.333	−
Sri Lanka	.176	.207	.168	−	.438	.480	.359	−
Thailand	.085	.088	.085	+	.401	.364	.404	+
Australia	.355	.308	.321	−	.490	.395	.371	−
New Zealand	.360	.308	.271	−	.484	.422	.355	−

(Continued)

Table 10.3 (Continued)

	Index of Dissimilarity (D)				Size-Standardized D			
	1960	*1970*	*1980*	*1960–1980*	*1960*	*1970*	*1980*	*1960–1980*
Europe								
Austria	.303	.280	.320	+	.490	.446	.422	–
Belgium	.325	.295	.342	+	.489	.453	.439	–
Denmark	.346	.297	.343	–	.433	.391	.309	–
Finland	.269	.319	.325	+	.431	.396	.388	–
Germany	.292	.243	.282	–	.470	.423	.424	–
Greece	.201	.220	.209	+	.481	.393	.374	–
Hungary	.171	.214	.247	+	.370	.359	.380	+
Ireland	.423	.395	.376	–	.520	.487	.457	–
Luxembourg	.497	.493	.399	–	.575	.513	.437	–
Netherlands	.394	.362	.371	–	.491	.412	.390	–
Portugal	.579	.294	.224	–	.603	.407	.477	–
Sweden	.439	.396	.386	–	.484	.405	.373	–
Switzerland	.355	.305	.204	–	.552	.424	.387	–
United Kingdom	.302	.310	.341	+	.446	.412	.394	–

**Trends in the Chances of
Sharing Occupations and Industries**

Table 10.4 presents the results for men's probability of sharing an occupation with women and women's probability of sharing an occupation with men. The corresponding industry figures are presented in Table 10.5. Men increased their chances of working in the same occupation as women in 11 of 13 American countries (all except Ecuador and Paraguay), in 8 of 12 Asian countries (India, Japan, Syria, and Thailand are exceptions), and in 12 of 14 European countries (Austria and Greece are exceptions). In most of the countries examined, then, men may perceive significant changes in women's roles. However, women have lower chances of sharing an occupation with men in 10 of 13 American countries (all except Chile, Costa Rica, and Peru), in 8 of 12 Asian countries (the same exceptions as mentioned above), and in 13 of 14 European countries (all except Greece).

What is remarkable, then, is that the changes that occurred during this period were experienced differently by men and women. The differences in trends for men and women reflect the growth in women's labor force participation. When more women enter the labor force, men's contact with women increases but working women's contact with men declines.

Table 10.4 Trends in the Probability of Sharing an Occupation

	Men's Chances of Sharing With Women (P*MW)				Women's Chances of Sharing With Men (P*WM)			
	1960	*1970*	*1980*	*1960–1980*	*1960*	*1970*	*1980*	*1960–1980*
Americas								
Canada	.217	.266	.313	+	.565	.529	.460	−
Chile	.163	.175	.244	+	.548	.566	.551	+
Costa Rica	.109	.138	.172	+	.541	.566	.604	+
Dominican Republic	.071	.212	.204	+	.560	.709	.532	−
Ecuador	.128	.133	.101	−	.643	.642	.620	−
El Salvador	.123	.125	.274	+	.565	.460	.528	−
Mexico	.151	.165	.227	+	.689	.700	.679	−
Panama	.128	.166	.186	+	.515	.511	.508	−
Paraguay	.179	.170	.155	−	.666	.612	.616	−
Peru	.195	.169	.208	+	.688	.689	.692	+
United States	.261	.294	.347	+	.542	.502	.466	−
Uruguay	.195	.231	.345	+	.582	.568	.497	−
Venezuela	.134	.167	.208	+	.588	.575	.555	−
Asia								
Brunei	.151	.160	.192	+	.746	.755	.657	−
India	.307	.170	.198	−	.665	.812	.779	+
Japan	.363	.361	.350	−	.566	.562	.573	+
Korea	.278	.337	.351	+	.684	.613	.609	−
Kuwait	.042	.062	.111	+	.839	.815	.751	−
Malaysia	.236	.290	.310	+	.705	.670	.660	−
Philippines	.323	.276	.350	+	.594	.605	.573	−
Singapore	.163	.231	.345	+	.735	.717	.586	−
Syria	.225	.104	.141	−	.621	.866	.760	+
Thailand	.476	.461	.460	−	.502	.514	.513	+
Australia	.234	.249	.281	+	.564	.533	.487	−
New Zealand	.202	.244	.276	+	.596	.569	.533	−
Europe								
Austria	.343	.334	.334	−	.509	.530	.489	−
Denmark	.233	.292	.350	+	.501	.491	.381	−
France	.298	.290	.326	+	.552	.533	.492	−
Germany	.309	.314	.320	+	.546	.559	.536	−
Greece	.308	.266	.251	−	.645	.684	.695	+
Ireland	.205	.208	.225	+	.581	.595	.568	−
Italy	.241	.257	.302	+	.724	.690	.615	−
Luxembourg	.189	.180	.240	+	.512	.506	.479	−
Netherlands	.184	.209	.276	+	.616	.605	.531	−
Norway	.165	.218	.305	+	.550	.553	.433	−
Portugal	.145	.242	.366	+	.647	.681	.548	−
Sweden	.223	.295	.350	+	.523	.535	.413	−
Switzerland	.247	.285	.298	+	.572	.557	.529	−
United Kingdom	.281	.292	.303	+	.503	.513	.458	−

Table 10.5 Trends in the Probabilty of Sharing an Industry

	Men's Chances of Sharing With Women (P*MW)				Women's Chances of Sharing With Men (P*WM)			
	1960	*1970*	*1980*	*1960–1980*	*1960*	*1970*	*1980*	*1960–1980*
Africa								
Egypt	.074	.060	.058	–	.892	.891	.866	–
Morocco	.107	.154	.171	+	.818	.707	.746	–
South Africa	.156	.245	.257	+	.570	.568	.579	+
Tunisia	.298	.054	.194	–	.638	.859	.693	+
Americas								
Argentina	.177	.208	.222	+	.636	.614	.589	–
Barbados	.340	.331	.402	+	.488	.511	.465	–
Canada	.230	.286	.372	+	.621	.586	.527	–
Chile	.166	.190	.261	+	.568	.624	.601	+
Costa Rica	.106	.144	.177	+	.544	.586	.626	+
Dominican Republic	.074	.199	.229	+	.582	.743	.587	+
Ecuador	.147	.141	.180	+	.675	.693	.701	+
Guatemala	.092	.095	.107	+	.616	.606	.658	+
Guyana	.190	.203	.215	+	.646	.614	.623	–
Mexico	.156	.102	.224	+	.713	.827	.674	–
Panama	.139	.178	.208	+	.546	.540	.560	+
Paraguay	.185	.166	.157	–	.628	.600	.635	+
Peru	.193	.170	.211	+	.693	.697	.703	+
United States	.284	.341	.388	+	.584	.556	.516	–
Venezuela	.148	.177	.232	+	.646	.622	.608	–
Asia								
Brunei	.152	.149	.210	+	.754	.776	.720	–
Hong Kong	.269	.310	.330	+	.670	.622	.599	–
India	.306	.171	.197	–	.666	.814	.780	+
Indonesia	.264	.312	.311	+	.717	.652	.647	–
Iran	.085	.111	.175	+	.765	.723	.729	–
Israel	.260	.285	.319	+	.590	.605	.561	–
Japan	.364	.364	.356	–	.567	.567	.583	+
Korea	.281	.336	.364	+	.701	.618	.582	–
Kuwait	.046	.066	.114	+	.910	.867	.772	–
Malaysia	.234	.285	.313	+	.714	.672	.646	–
Nepal	.400	.289	.343	–	.587	.700	.643	+
Philippines	.346	.255	.317	–	.553	.574	.565	+
Singapore	.166	.221	.323	+	.764	.714	.615	–
Sri Lanka	.202	.221	.249	+	.762	.731	.712	–
Thailand	.474	.463	.460	–	.501	.513	.512	+
Australia	.217	.284	.325	+	.655	.616	.554	–
New Zealand	.216	.267	.313	+	.645	.630	.607	–

Table 10.5 (Continued)

	Men's Chances of Sharing With Women (P*MW)				Women's Chances of Sharing With Men (P*WM)			
	1960	1970	1980	1960–1980	1960	1970	1980	1960–1980
Europe								
Austria	.352	.346	.341	–	.522	.551	.545	+
Belgium	.239	.267	.308	+	.647	.636	.564	–
Denmark	.278	.306	.373	+	.576	.592	.485	–
Finland	.343	.367	.402	+	.528	.500	.464	–
Germany	.325	.329	.351	+	.565	.590	.556	–
Greece	.299	.251	.246	–	.635	.683	.685	+
Hungary	.334	.381	.409	+	.602	.543	.493	–
Ireland	.214	.218	.237	+	.611	.629	.607	–
Luxembourg	.215	.208	.281	+	.576	.592	.567	–
Netherlands	.194	.220	.255	+	.675	.657	.618	–
Portugal	.148	.236	.363	+	.569	.670	.539	–
Sweden	.236	.295	.370	+	.555	.538	.452	–
Switzerland	.251	.303	.255	+	.584	.585	.447	–
United Kingdom	.315	.325	.350	+	.571	.565	.523	–

(When women are 40% of the labor force, a woman is more likely to share an occupation with another woman than when women constitute 20% of the labor force.) Declines in occupational sex segregation produce the opposite effect: They tend to increase both men's chances of sharing an occupation with women and women's chance of sharing an occupation with men. The increase in women's labor force participation overwhelmed the effect of changes in sex segregation in most places: Despite a majority of cases in which sex segregation declined, women's chances of sharing an occupation with men declined in a clear majority of cases.

This pattern emerges even more clearly in the industrial analysis. Men's probability of sharing an industry with women increased in every American country except Paraguay, in every European country except Greece and Austria, and in every Asian country except India, Thailand, and the Philippines. In the Americas, there were 8 cases (out of 15) of women having an increased chance of sharing an industry with men. (In American countries, the greater declines in industrial sex segregation outweighed the effect of the increase in women's labor force participation.) Women's probability of sharing the same industry with men declined in every European country except Austria and Belgium. In Asia, women's probability of sharing an industry with men declined in most (12 of 17) countries. Whether measured in terms of industrial or occupational trends, the experiences of men and women differ markedly.

Explaining Changes in Segregation

Table 10.6 presents two regression equations that attempt to explain industrial sex segregation. The independent variables are gross national product, women's labor force participation, the total fertility rate, the ratio of women's to men's literacy, and the ratio of women's to men's enrollment in higher education. We also examined the proportion of the population in urban areas, but because this variable was not significant in any of our models we omitted it from the models discussed below. Data were obtained from Sivard (1985).

The first equation is a cross-sectional equation that predicts sex segregation in 1980 from the independent variables in 1980. The second equation is a change-score equation that predicts changes in sex segregation from changes in the independent variables. In each case, we took the logistic transformation of the index of sex segregation because the index is a proportion bounded by zero and 1.

In the cross-sectional equation, all the coefficients are statistically significant, but only two of the five are consistent with the modernization hypothesis. Per capita GNP and women's education and literacy are all positively related to segregation, whereas the modernization perspective would predict the opposite in each case. In contrast, women's labor force participation and the total fertility rate both behave in the predicted direction (labor force participation for women is inversely related to segregation, whereas total fertility is directly related to segregation).

However, the cross-sectional model is not the preferred model in this case. As we noted above, comparisons of segregation between countries can be problematic because of the difficulties in comparing occupations and industries across countries. A change-score equation is likely to be more useful in this case.

The second equation in Table 10.6 presents the results of a regression analysis in which both the dependent and independent variables represent changes between 1960 and 1980. We find that a change in per capita GNP is positively related to change in sex segregation, again counter to the prediction of modernization theory. In the change-score equation, no

Table 10.6 Regression Equations Predicting Industrial Sex Segregation

Variable	Parameter Estimate	SE
(dependent variable: log of index of industrial segregation, 1980)		
Model 1		
Intercept	.967***	.150
GNP	.008***	.001
Women's relative education	.007**	.003
Women's relative literacy	.014***	.003
Women's labor force participation	−.022***	.004
Total fertility rate	.032***	.004
(dependent variable: change in log of index of industrial segregation, 1960–1980)		
Model 2		
Intercept	−.132	.104
Change, GNP	.009**	.004
Change, women's relative education	−.006*	.003
Change, women's relative literacy	.002	.005
Change, women's labor force participation	.003	.013
Change, total fertility rate	.015	.012
R^2	.100	

*$p < .10$; **$p < .05$; ***$p < .01$.

other variable is statistically significant. The signs of the coefficients for women's relative education and total fertility rate are consistent with the modernization hypothesis (rises in education and declines in fertility contribute to declines in segregation), whereas those for relative literacy and women's labor force participation are inconsistent with this perspective. (We also estimated a change-score equation that controlled for the initial level of sex segregation. The results parallel those obtained when no such control is introduced. Consequently, we do not have to take sides in the controversy over the appropriateness of controls for initial levels in change-score models; see Allison, 1990.)

We tested for the presence of a curvilinear relationship between per capita GNP and changes in segregation, as implied by the Sinha U-shaped curve hypothesis. We detected no evidence for this pattern: The coefficient for the interaction term was insignificant and opposite in direction to that predicted by the U-shaped curve thesis.

We also estimated these models for changes in occupational segregation, again with similar results. Each variable has the same effect in both the industrial and occupational cross-sectional models, and per capita GNP is the only variable that is close to being significant in the occupation change-score model. We present the industrial model because more cases of industrial data are available for the analysis.

Discussion

The overall picture appears mixed, as there is no consistent trend toward an increase or a decrease in sex segregation in developed or developing countries. Nor is it the case that one trend prevails in developed countries and another in developing countries. Mixed trends appear for industrial and occupational data in both Europe and Asia, whereas in the Americas, declines in segregation are generally evident. These data do not decisively support any of our three competing hypotheses.

However, compositional (size-standardized) changes generally have been moving in the direction of greater integration. This remarkably consistent pattern does constitute evidence for an optimistic view. Market forces, perhaps with some additional impetus from political pressures, have resulted in a more even distribution of women across occupational and industrial sectors. Thus we may expect continued declines in sex segregation if unimpeded by countervailing structural changes in the distribution of industries and occupations. Unfortunately, we should not view structural changes as temporary impediments to greater integration. The relative size of occupations and industries has been changing continually and will continue to do so. Any firm predictions about the direction of change are premature.

Another notable finding is that men's and women's experiences of change have differed markedly. In most countries, men have experienced a notable increase in the chances of being employed in the same occupational or industrial group as women, whereas women in the majority of countries experienced a decline in the chances of sharing an occupation or industry with men. This result offers a possible explanation for the observations of many researchers that opportunities for women are deteriorating: From women's point of view, the occupational and industrial structure appears more segregated than previously. Yet men may perceive that women are making substantial progress.

Finally, the extent of change between 1960 and 1980 is negatively related to economic growth and is not significantly related to changes in other measures, such as fertility, women's labor force participation, women's education and literacy, and urbanization. Thus the explanation for the changes we observe are generally inconsistent with those of the modernization perspective. Nor does the U-shaped curve hypothesis receive notable support: The least-developed countries do not show a consistent increase in sex segregation, nor does initial GNP level appear significant as an interaction term in the multivariate analysis.

The results presented here appear inconsistent with the bulk of recent writings, which have stressed the deterioration of women's economic position in developing countries. In the majority of cases, both occupational and industrial sex segregation are declining. However, these declines have been modest and do not foreshadow an imminent end to women's economic disadvantages. We trust our conclusion is not misinterpreted. We do not believe women and men benefit equally from industrialization nor that men and women are evenly distributed within the broad occupational and industrial classifications described in our data. We are convinced that women remain disadvantaged compared with men, and the growth of new industries and occupations hardly erases women's economic disadvantage. However, unless there is increasing segregation within the broad industrial and occupational categories available to us, our results suggest modest progress for women in gaining broader occupational and industrial opportunities in many countries.

The 1980s brought stagnation and decline to many developing countries. Perhaps the modest relative gains for women we document in some countries for the 1960s and 1970s did not continue into the 1980s, and some of these gains may have been replaced by setbacks. On the other hand, more attention has begun to be paid to women in the development process, and new initiatives may be able to avoid the most egregious institutional sexism of the past. Consequently, we will forgo the impulse to extrapolate from our findings to current and future trends.

We conclude by noting the highly aggregated nature of the data we examined. More detailed data would undoubtedly reveal higher levels of segregation. We have shown that trends obtained with aggregated data generally move in the same direction as those obtained with more detailed data. Nonetheless, additional detailed research, using census data from different countries over time, will be needed to more definitively delineate longitudinal trends in sex segregation. As noted above, our analysis is vulnerable to changes in reporting that may have occurred during the interim. We offer trends in sex segregation as one indicator of trends in the status of women. Additional research is needed to track other indicators of trends in the status of women in order to provide a fuller picture of recent changes and a basis for a more developed comparative analysis of the political economy of women's status.

Notes

1. A figure of 70% recently obtained a great deal of attention, but this statistic is not comparable to the familiar time-series data (see National Committee on Pay Equity, 1987, for a discussion of recent data on the sex gap in wages).

2. The 30% figure was reported for high school graduates and those without high school degrees. The 17% figure was for college graduates, but if one adds 12% for the sex segregation of college majors, the total effect of sex segregation for this group is 29%.

3. The conflicting perspectives regarding contemporary trends in women's status parallel historical debates regarding the effects of early industrialization on the status of women, as ably summarized by Bradley (1989).

4. In all, six industry categories are unchanged, although the order in which they appear has been changed. These include agriculture, mining, manufacturing, construction, transportation, storage, and communications, as well as inadequately described work. The category covering the utilities (electricity, etc.) was changed slightly by the deletion of sanitary services. Although sanitary services did not reappear under either of the revised service categories, we assume that workers who were previously classified under this status remained in the utilities category. The all-inclusive category of commerce was clarified in the revised version. The service category was also clarified, and workers can now be classified in either the business service sector or the personal service sector. The reasons for a country's exclusion may be obtained from the authors.

5. When an earlier version of this chapter was delivered at the 1988 Population Association of America annual meeting, Boyd and Myles (1988) presented apparently contradictory trend data on Canada. However, closer examination revealed that the discrepancy was due to the inclusion of agriculture in our analysis and its exclusion from Boyd and Myles's analysis. When one restricts the analysis to the same occupations, more detailed measures consistently move in the same direction as broader measures.

6. The formula for D is:

$$D = \tfrac{1}{2}\sum_{i=1}^{n} |(Wi/W) - (Mi/M)| \times 100$$

where Wi is the number of women in occupation i, W is the total number of women, Mi is the number of men in occupation i, M is the total number of men, and n is the number of occupations. D varies from 0 to 100, with 0 representing a perfectly even distribution and 100 representing perfect segregation.

The formula for the size-standardized index of dissimilarity is:

$$SD = \tfrac{1}{2}\sum_{i=1}^{n} |(Wi/Ti)/ - \Sigma(Wi/Ti)) - ((Mi/Ti)/ - \Sigma(MiTi))| \times 100$$

where Ti is the total number of men and women in occupation i, and other terms are defined as above.

7. The formula for $P* \cdot WM$, women's probability of contact with men, is:

$$P* \cdot WM = \sum_{i=1}^{n}((Wi/W) - (Mi/T))$$

where T is the total number of individuals in the labor force, and each of the other terms is defined as above.

8. Removing agriculture reversed the direction of change in occupational segregation for three American countries—El Salvador, Peru, and Uruguay—five Asian countries—India, Korea, the Philippines, Syria, and Thailand—and six European countries—France, Germany, Ireland, Italy, Switzerland, and Sweden.

9. Removing agriculture reverses the size-standardized occupational change from positive to negative in six countries: El Salvador, Peru, and Paraguay in the Americas and the Philippines, Australia, and New Zealand in Asia.

10. Removing agriculture reverses the direction of change in industrial segregation in four Asian countries: Iran, Japan, Nepal, and the Philippines. In Europe, Finland, Germany, Greece, Hungary, and Ireland change signs; in the Americas, only Guyana changes sign.

References

Afshar, H. (Ed.). (1985). *Women, work and ideology in the Third World.* London: Tavistock.

Afshar, H. (Ed.). (1987). *Women, state and ideology: Studies from Africa and Asia.* Albany: State University of New York Press.

Allison, P. (1990). Change scores as dependent variables in regression analysis. In C. Clogg (Ed.), *Sociological methodology* (Vol. 20, pp. 93-114). Oxford: Blackwell.

Beller, A. H. (1982). The impact of equal opportunity policy on sex differentials in earnings and occupations. *American Economic Review: Papers and Proceedings, 2,* 171-175.

Bergmann, B. (1986). *The economic emergence of women.* New York: Basic Books.

Bernard, J. (1968). The status of women in modern patterns of culture. *Annals of the American Academy of Political and Social Science, 375,* 3-14.

Bielby, W. T., & Baron, J. N. (1984). A woman's place is with other women: Sex segregation in the workplace. In B. Reskin (Ed.), *Sex segregation in the workplace: Trends, explanations, remedies* (pp. 27-55). Washington, DC: National Academy of Sciences Press.

Bisilliat, J., & Fieloux, M. (1987). *Women of the Third World.* Rutherford, NJ: Fairleigh Dickinson University Press.

Blau, F. D., & Ferber, M. A. (1986). *The economics of women, men and work.* Englewood Cliffs, NJ: Prentice-Hall.

Boserup, E. (1970). *Woman's role in economic development.* New York: St. Martin.

Boulding, E. (1976). *Handbook of international data on women.* Beverly Hills, CA: Sage.

Boyd, M., & Myles, J. (1988, April). *Skill upgrading or skill degrading: The impact of sex compositional changes in the Canadian occupational structure.* Paper presented at the annual meeting of the Population Association of America, New Orleans.

Bradley, H. (1989). *Men's work, women's work.* Minneapolis: University of Minnesota Press.

Charles, M. (1992). Accounting for cross-national variation in occupational sex segregation. *American Sociological Review, 57*(4).

Davis, K., & van den Oever, P. (1982). Demographic foundations of new sex roles. *Population and Development Review, 8*(3), 495-511.

Deere, C. D., & Leon, M. (1987). *Rural women and state policy.* New York: Westview.

Dixon, R. B. (1982). Women in agriculture: Counting the labor force in developing countries. *Population and Development Review, 3,* 534-566.

Durand, J. D. (1975). *The labor force in economic development: A comparison of international census data.* Princeton, NJ: Princeton University Press.

England, P. (1981). Assessing trends in occupational sex segregation, 1900-1976. In I. Berg (Ed.), *Sociological perspectives on labor markets* (pp. 273-294). New York: Academic Press.

Etienne, M., & Leacock, E. (Eds.). (1980). *Women and colonization: Anthropological perspectives.* New York: Praeger.

Ferber, M. A., & Lowry, H. M. (1977). Woman's place: National differences in the occupational mosaic. *Journal of Marketing, 41,* 23-30.

Friedl, E. (1975). *Men and women: An anthropologists' view.* New York: Holt, Rinehart & Winston.

Fuchs, V. R. (1988). *Women's quest for economic equality.* Cambridge, MA: Harvard University Press.

Gaskin, K. A. (1979). *Occupational differentiation by sex: An international perspective.* Unpublished doctoral dissertation, Department of Sociology, University of Michigan.

Goldin, C. (1990). *Explaining the gender gap.* Oxford: Oxford University Press.

Greenhalgh, S. (1985). Sexual stratification: The other side of "Growth with Equity" in East Asia. *Population and Development Review, 11*(2), 265-314.

Gross, E. (1968). Plus ça change. . . ? The sexual structure of occupations over time. *Social Problems, 16,* 198-208.

Gwartney-Gibbs, P. A. (1988). Sex segregation in the paid workforce: The New Zealand case. *Australian and New Zealand Journal of Sociology, 24*(2), 264-278.

Hakim, C. (1992). Explaining trends in occupational segregation: The measurement, causes and consequences of the sexual division of labour. *European Sociological Review, 8*(2), 127-152.

Hartmann, H. (1976). Capitalism, patriarchy, and job segregation by sex. In M. Blaxall & B. Reagan (Eds.), *Women and the workplace: The implications of occupational segregation* (pp. 137- 169). Chicago: University of Chicago Press.

Horton, J., & Lee, E.-J. (1988). Degraded work and devalued labor: The proletarianization of women in the semiconductor industry. In J. Smith et al. (Eds.), *Racism, sexism, and the world-system* (pp. 137-152). New York: Greenwood.

Humphrey, J. (1987). *Gender and work in the Third World: Sexual divisions in Brazilian industry.* London: Tavistock.

Iglitzin, L. B., & Ross, R. (Eds.). (1986). *Women in the world: 1975-1985. The women's decade* (2nd ed.). Santa Barbara, CA: ABC-Clio.

Jacobs, J. A. (1985). Sex segregation in American higher education. In L. Larwood, A. Stromberg, & B. Gutek (Eds.), *Women and work: An annual review* (Vol. 1, pp. 191-214). Beverly Hills, CA: Sage.

Jacobs, J. A. (1986). Trends in contact between men and women at work, 1971-1981. *Sociology and Social Research, 70*(3), 202-206.

Jacobs, J. A. (1989a). Long-term trends in occupational segregation by sex. *American Journal of Sociology, 95*(1), 160-173.

Jacobs, J. A. (1989b). *Revolving doors: Sex segregation and women's careers.* Stanford, CA: Stanford University Press.

Jin, K., & Stevens, G. (1987). Occupational sex segregation in Korea, 1960-1980. *Sociology and Social Research, 71,* 99-102.

Joekes, S. (1985). Working for lipstick? Male and female labour in the clothing industry in Morocco. In H. Afshar (Ed.), *Women, work and ideology in the Third World* (pp. 183-213), London: Tavistock.

Joekes, S. (1987). *Women in the world economy: An INSTRAW study.* New York: Oxford University Press.

Kalleberg, A., & Rosenfeld, R. (1990). A cross-national comparison of the gender gap in income. *American Journal of Sociology, 96*(1), 69-106.

Lele, U. (1986). Women and structural transformation. *Economic Development and Cultural Change, 34*(2), 195-221.

Lieberson, S. (1980). *A piece of the pie.* Berkeley: University of California Press.

Lieberson, S., & Carter, D. K. (1982). Temporal changes and urban differences in residential segregation: A reconsideration. *American Journal of Sociology, 88,* 296-310.

Lyson, T. A. (1986). Industrial transformation and occupational sex differentiation: Evidence from New Zealand and the United States. *International Journal of Comparative Sociology, 27,* 53-68.

Madden, J. F. (1985). The persistence of pay differentials: The economics of sex discrimination. In L. Larwood, A. Stromberg, & B. Gutek (Eds.), *Women and work: An annual review* (Vol. 1, pp. 76-115). Beverly Hills, CA: Sage.

Massey, D. S., & Denton, N. A. (1988). The dimensions of residential segregation. *Social Forces, 67,* 281-315.

Mies, M. (1988). *Women: The last colony.* London: Zed Books.

Miller, A. (1972). *The industrial distribution of women's employment: An international comparison.* Unpublished manuscript, University of Pennsylvania, Population Studies Center.

Mukhopadhyay, C. C., & Higgins, P. J. (1988). Anthropological studies of women's status revisited: 1977-1987. *Annual Review of Anthropology, 17,* 461-495.

Murdock, G. P., & Provost, C. (1973). Factors in the division of labor by sex: A cross-cultural analysis. *Ethnology, 12,* 203-225.

Nash, J. (1988). Cultural parameters of sexism and racism in the international division of labor. In J. Collins, T. K. Hopkins, & A. Muhammad (Eds.), *Racism, sexism, and the world system* (pp. 11-38). New York: Greenwood.

Nash, J., & Fernandez-Kelly, M. P. (Eds.). (1983). *Women, men and the international division of labor.* Albany: State University of New York Press.

National Committee on Pay Equity. (1987). *Briefing paper on the wage gap* (Mimeo). Washington, DC: Author.

New Internationalist. (1985). *Women: A world report.* New York: Oxford University Press.

Park, Y. J. (1990). *Women's labor force participation in Korea: Trends, levels, patterns and differentials during 1960-1980.* Unpublished doctoral dissertation, Graduate Group in Demography, University of Pennsylvania.

Reskin, B. F., & Roos, P. (1990). *Job queues, gender queues: Explaining women's inroads into male occupations.* Philadelphia: Temple University Press.

Ridley, J. C. (1968). Demographic change and the roles and status of women. *Annals of the American Academy of Political and Social Science, 375,* 15-25.

Rogers, B. (1979). *The domestication of women: Discrimination in developing societies.* New York: St. Martin.

Rogers, S. C. (1978). Woman's place: A critical review of anthropological theory. *Comparative Studies in Society and History, 20*(1), 123-162.

Roos, P. (1985). *Gender and work: A comparative analysis of industrial societies.* Albany: State University of New York Press.

Roos, P., & Reskin, B. (1984). Institutional factors contributing to sex segregation in the workplace. In B. Reskin (Ed.), *Sex segregation in the workplace: Trends, explanations, remedies* (pp. 235-260). Washington, DC; National Academy of Sciences.

Sanday, P. R. (1981). *Female power and male dominance: On the origins of sexual inequality.* London: Cambridge University Press.

Schultz, T. W. (1981). *Investing in people: The economics of population quality.* Berkeley: University of California Press.

Singelmann, J., & Tienda, M. (1979). Changes in industry structure and female employment in Latin America: 1950-1970. *Sociology and Social Research, 63,* 745-769.

Sinha, J. N. (1968). Dynamics of female participation in economic activity in a developing economy. *Proceedings of the World Population Conference, Vol. 4.* New York: United Nations.

Sivard, R. L. (1985). *Women . . . A world survey.* Washington, DC: World Priorities.

Smelser, N. J. (1968). Toward a theory of modernization. In N. J. Smelser (Ed.), *Essays in sociological explanation* (pp. 125-146). Englewood Cliffs, NJ: Prentice-Hall.

Smith, J., Collins, J., Hopkins, T. K., & Muhammad, A. (Eds.). (1988). *Racism, sexism and the world system.* New York: Greenwood.

Sorensen, E. (1989). Measuring the effect of occupational sex and race composition on earnings. In R. T. Michael, H. I. Hartmann, & B. O'Farrell (Eds.), *Pay equity: Empirical inquiries* (pp. 49-69). Washington, DC: National Academy Press.

Taeuber, K. E., & Taeuber, A. F. (1965). *Negroes in cities: Residential segregation and neighborhood change.* Chicago: Aldine.

Tinker, I. (1990). *Persistent inequalities: Women and world development.* New York: Oxford University Press.

Treiman, D., & Hartmann, H. (Eds.). (1981). *Women, work and wages: Equal pay for jobs of equal value* (Report of the Committee on Occupational Classification and Analysis, Assembly of Behavioral and Social Sciences). Washington, DC: National Academy Press.

UNESCO. (1981). *Women and development: Indicators of their changing role.* Paris: Author.

United Nations. (1980). *Rural women's participation in development.* New York: United Nations Development Programme.

U.S. Bureau of the Census. (1987). Male-female differences in work experience, occupation, and earnings: 1984. *Current Population Reports* (P-70, No. 10). Washington, DC: U.S. Government Printing Office.

Ward, K. B. (1984). *Women in the world-system: Its impact on status and fertility.* New York: Praeger.

Ward, K. B. (1988). Women in the global economy. In B. A. Gutek, A. H. Stromberg, & L. Larwood (Eds.), *Women and work: An annual review* (Vol. 3, pp. 17-48). Newbury Park, CA: Sage.

Ward, K. B. (1990). *Women workers and global restructuring.* Ithaca, NY: Industrial and Labor Relations (ILR) Press.

Ward, K. B., & Pampel, F. C. (1985). Structural determinants of female labor force participation in developed nations, 1955-1975. *Social Science Quarterly, 66,* 654-667.

Weston, A. (1987). Women and handicraft production in North India. In H. Afshar (Ed.), *Women, state and ideology: Studies from Africa and Asia* (pp. 173-185). Albany: State University of New York Press.

Whyte, M. K. (1978). *The status of women in preindustrial societies.* Princeton, NJ: Princeton University Press.

PART IV

Perspectives on Occupational Resegregation

11

Shifting Gender Boundaries

Women's Inroads Into Academic Sociology

PATRICIA A. ROOS
KATHARINE W. JONES

In recent years, social scientists have devoted considerable attention to occupational feminization. This research area grew since 1970, largely because there was little change in occupational sex composition prior to that time: Such segregation persisted at approximately the same level from 1900 to 1970 (Jacobs, 1989). Beginning in 1970 the aggregate level of occupational sex segregation began to decline (Beller, 1984; Jacobs, 1989). One reason for this was that women moved into a select number of occupations traditionally held by men. Although media pundits proclaimed that women were now gaining access to a greater variety of better-paying male jobs, a closer look at women's occupational inroads suggested need for caution in interpreting these gains (Reskin & Roos, 1990).

In this chapter, we investigate the reasons for women's greater access to academic sociology, one of the fields that began to feminize during the

AUTHORS' NOTE: A previous version of this chapter was published in *Work and Occupations*, 20(4), November 1993, 395-498. We thank Andrew Abbott for first suggesting this topic to us and Carla Howery for providing us with unpublished data. We also thank Denise Bielby, Lee Clarke, Judith Gerson, Lowell Hargens, Bettina Huber, Nicole Isaacson, Jacqueline Litt, Karen Miller-Loessi, Barbara Reskin, Susan Rovi, Kim Wittenstrom, and the Sociology Gender Group for comments on a previous draft. The research was supported in part by a Rutgers University Research Council Grant (2-02079).

1970s. We use the term *feminize* to indicate a growing representation of women, and not to suggest that women have become the predominant, or even the majority, sex. In the case of sociology, two parallel but distinct processes of feminization have occurred. First, women's representation rose most dramatically among sociology doctorates (about half of all doctorates now go to women). Second, women have also begun to join sociology faculties, albeit much more slowly. Although it is premature to determine definitively whether sociology faculties will further feminize, we are able to explore women's recent movement into academic positions. We focus, however, on the feminization of sociology's recruitment pool. Our analysis rests on a systematic review of research on women's accomplishments in sociology (and academia more generally), publications produced by sociology's professional society (the American Sociological Association), and other statistics on women and men in sociology.

Queuing and Changing Occupational Sex Composition

Reskin and Roos (1990, chap. 2; see also Reskin, 1991) theorized changing occupational sex composition as the operation of two queues: gendered labor queues (whereby employers rank workers) and job queues (whereby workers rank jobs). According to this perspective, changes in sex composition occur because employers change their ordering of workers in the labor queue or workers reorder their estimations of jobs. In addition, the number of elements (workers in the labor queues or jobs in the job queues) can change, leading to a greater (or lesser) probability of selection. Thus, for example, if men (theoretically at the top of the labor queue) disproportionately exit or fail to enter the queue, employers reach women (theoretically lower in the labor queue) more quickly.

The queuing perspective provides a powerful framework for understanding the social processes promoting occupational feminization. Reskin and Roos (1990) delineated several important explanations for changing sex composition in the occupations they examined. First, employers turned to women when faced with a shortage of male workers, occasioned either by occupational growth (where demand outstripped the number of available male workers) or by occupational decline (where men shunned deteriorating occupations). Second, employers sometimes turned to women because of a specific demand for women (e.g., because of antidiscrimination legislation, the desire to reduce labor costs, technological change, or the growth of a female clientele). Third, the percentage of women in the labor queue grew because more of them completed lengthy training, as in the professions. The extent to which each of these factors operated in sociology is the focus of this chapter.

The queuing perspective encompasses both demand and supply factors and thus represents a distinct improvement over explanations that focus solely on the characteristics and choices of individuals (Reskin, 1991). On the supply side, the queuing perspective allows for self-conscious choices of men and women. For example, men have often expressed their job preferences by voting with their feet to leave or avoid deteriorating occupations, represented in the queuing perspective as a shift in men's job queues. Similarly, women sometimes choose formerly male occupations because they provide higher earnings than traditionally female occupations, representing a rise of the occupations in their job queues. On the demand side, the queuing perspective reminds us that the choices of another labor market actor—employers—and an extra-labor market actor—the state—are important, as well. For instance, employers often raise women in their labor queues when they have a specific reason for preferring women (for example, when they introduce technologies that substitute traditionally female tasks for traditionally male ones; Roos, 1993). Similarly, government regulatory agencies can stimulate demand for women workers by enforcing affirmative action regulations aggressively.

Job queues and labor queues operate within a gendered social structure that shapes both individual workers' and employers' preferences. This social structure—the sex-segregated American occupational structure—comprises a set of boundaries that differentiate women and men in the workplace (Gerson & Peiss, 1985). Occupational feminization indicates that these gender boundaries are permeable (to use Gerson and Peiss's [1985] terminology). Because studies of occupational feminization target those work arenas where social norms regarding gender are in transition, they can show us how boundaries between men's and women's jobs emerge and change at specific historical moments. Gender boundaries shift as a consequence of interactions among particular labor market actors (e.g., employers, women, and men; Gerson & Peiss, 1985; Roos, 1993). As Connell (1987) argued, structure—in this case, a gendered occupational structure—is neither preexisting nor natural, but rather historically and socially constructed. Rather than being rigid, reified categories that leave individuals powerless, gender boundaries emerge from the interactions of individuals in the workplace. In turn, they constrain or enable the actions of individuals, and hence can limit or enhance individual opportunity. Structures, then, are always being renegotiated by individuals with different amounts of power to affect outcomes.

We illustrate this approach by examining, to the extent possible given our data, the shifting gender boundaries in academic sociology at two points in time. Our main purpose is to examine women's growing presence among sociology Ph.D.s since 1970, because that is where the most dramatic change has already occurred. We begin, however, by considering briefly the emergence of sociology as a discipline at the turn of the century, a time when women first entered sociology graduate departments in large numbers. Using insights from the queuing perspective, we investigate the choices of social actors, but also the ways in which their actions were shaped by processes outside their control (e.g., by the contraction of the academic labor market, discriminatory practices). Although it is too early to tell whether women will have full access to faculty ranks in sociology, our results provide some insight into this question, as well.

From the Past to the Present

Large numbers of (especially white, upper-class) women enrolled in sociology graduate programs between 1890 and 1920, the "golden era of women in sociology" (Deegan, 1991, p. 15). Unlike the 1970s, however, these women made virtually no headway into the professoriate, turning instead to other, related professions. In this section we examine why gender boundaries remained relatively stable in sociology's professoriate during this early period.

Sociology acquired legitimacy in the academy at the same time that women were gaining access to higher education as a whole. Between 1636 (when Harvard was founded) and 1837 (when Oberlin opened its doors to women), women were excluded from higher education in the United States. Even Oberlin's acceptance of women was "ostensibly to provide ministers with intelligent, cultivated, and thoroughly schooled wives" (Graham, 1978, p. 764). The major push for increasing women's opportunities in higher education emerged in the context of declining male enrollments (Graham, 1970, p. 1284); the Civil War, economic depression, and dissatisfaction with curricula led many men to avoid college education entirely. To bolster sagging tuition revenues, college trustees and presidents turned to women to replenish their undergraduate populations. As Graham (1970, p. 1284) reported, women's breakthrough into academe was thus attributable in part to economic exigencies rather than ideological pressure, although a context supportive of women's educational rights certainly existed at the time.

In this climate, women became an established presence in graduate sociology programs during the discipline's formative years (Deegan, 1978, 1991). Their numbers grew notably throughout the last decades of the 19th century: Morgan (1980, p. 3) found that the number of women graduate students majoring in sociology increased from 1 (of 13) in 1892–1893 to 34 (of 132) by 1900–1901. Women constituted 28% of graduate students majoring in sociology between 1888 and 1901 (p. 4). Not surprisingly, given their role as the major producers of sociology Ph.D.s, the University of Chicago and Columbia University enrolled the largest number of women sociology graduate students in the last decades of the 19th century. By 1901 Chicago had 35 and Columbia 31 women matriculating as sociology graduate students (p. 5). As was true for most graduate students at the time, not all of those enrolled actually graduated. By 1901, of the 117 women who had enrolled in graduate study in sociology, 24 had earned master's degrees and 9 had earned doctorates (p. 9).[1]

The More Things Change, the More They Stay the Same

Despite their increased presence in graduate programs, women made little headway into sociology faculties at the turn of the century. Indeed, an ideology promoting the separation of the sexes emerged in response to women's increasing numbers. Albion Small, the first chair of the Department of Sociology at the University of Chicago and a central figure in the early years of the American Sociological Society, believed in separating the sexes in educational institutions (Deegan, 1978, 1981). When it came to recruiting faculty at the University of Chicago, Small and his colleagues hired women only as adjuncts: Edith Abbott as an instructor and lecturer, Mary McDowell as an instructor, and Annie Marion McLean as an extension assistant professor of sociology. The Department of Household Administration, originally organized under the auspices of Chicago's Sociology Department, hired additional women (Deegan, 1978, p. 19). Thus the commitment of some male sociologists to a sex-segregated workplace helped to ensure that gender boundaries remained relatively immutable.

In 1905 a small group of influential male sociologists, including Albion Small and Lester Ward, organized what would eventually be called the American Sociological Association (ASA) (Deegan, 1981; Rhoades, 1981).[2] Women were virtually excluded from the early meetings of the association, participating (if at all) as discussants at professional meetings. Their participation sometimes elicited resistance (Deegan, 1981, pp. 16-17).[3] In response, women sociologists established their own network, centered around Jane Addams, to work on issues of interest to them.

Another development within the field also helped to foster lines of demarcation between the sexes. In the late 19th century, sociology as a discipline was very much concerned with social problems, and especially with the condition of disadvantaged members of society. As Morgan (1980) described it:

> Many students of the new science were directed to the [social] settlements as "sociological laboratories" in which they could observe segments of society in operation. It was thus assumed that there would emerge from this observation and involvement greater scientific understanding of society through its pathological manifestations. (pp. 9-11)

This orientation of the field was seen as particularly "fit" for women. In 1898 an instructor at Virginia's Randolph-Macon Women's College wrote of his sociology course as being:

> specifically adapted to meet the requirements of the ever-increasing demand for intelligent women in the management of the various charitable and philanthropic organizations of modern society. The object is to train the student to an intelligent grasp of the great social problems that confront us at this stage of our civilization, and to the solution of which the women of the future will be called upon in even larger measure to contribute. (In Morgan, 1980, pp. 15-16)[4]

At the same time that women were being drawn to sociology, however, the field itself was retreating from a focus on reform to "disinterested scientific objectivity and political neutrality" (Morgan, 1980, p. 11; for additional details, see Turner & Turner, 1990, chap. 1).[5] Facing limited options in academic sociology, women sociologists found their niche in the more practical side of the discipline (which male sociologists were abandoning) or migrated to other developing professions that were seen as more compatible with female sensibilities: social work, child/adult education and human development, and clinical psychology (Deegan, 1978, p. 12; Morgan, 1980, p. 11). Thus, despite women's increased entry into sociology graduate programs, the responses of male incumbents helped to ensure that very few women became sociology faculty.

Women's Entry Into Academic Sociology Since 1970

Women made few additional gains in academic sociology until the 1970s ushered in a whole new era of possibilities for women (Deegan, 1991, p. 18). Table 11.1 provides data on the number of doctorates in sociology from 1920 to 1991; Appendix A furnishes comparable data for doctorates from all fields and from all social sciences. As Table 11.1 documents, women held fewer than one in five sociology doctorates between 1920 and 1971, a situation that changed dramatically during the decade of the 1970s. In this section, we describe the feminization of sociology's recruitment pool; in the next, we explore at greater length the reasons for these changes.

Like men, women made their earliest moves into sociology's recruitment pools during the late 1960s and early 1970s (see Table 11.1). Although women made similarly dramatic inroads into the social sciences as a whole, and indeed into all doctorate fields (see Appendix A), for each comparison the percentage increase was largest for sociologists. During the latter half of the 1970s, women's increased representation among doctoral recipients occurred in the context of a notable decline in the total number of sociology doctorates: After hitting an all-time high of 734 in 1976, the number of doctorates dropped to 422 in 1987, only to inch up slowly since that time. In 1970 18% of new Ph.D.s were women; by 1980, 38% were. Women's representation among doctorates peaked in 1988 at 53% and has since hovered at 50%, approximately the same as the figure for all social scientists (49%) and notably higher than that for all disciplines (37%).

Data on graduate student enrollments (see Table 11.2) support the contention that sociology is once again increasing in popularity. Appendix B suggests a similar resurgence of social sciences in general during the late 1980s. After dropping to a low of 5,901 in 1986, the number of sociology graduate students in doctorate-granting institutions rose to 6,658 by 1989, an increase of 13%. This increase in the number of sociology graduate students is occurring among both women and men. The representation of women among sociology graduate students has

Table 11.1 Doctorates in Sociology, by Sex, 1920-1991

Panel A: Number of Doctorates Decade	Men	Women	Total	Percent Female
1920–29	176	32	208	15.4
1930–39	359	89	448	19.9
1940–49	478	99	577	17.2
1950–59	1,334	221	1,555	14.2
1960–69	2,090	442	2,532	17.5
Year				
1970	412	93	505	18.4
1971	471	115	586	19.6
1972	500	138	638	21.6
1973	445	154	599	25.7
1974	460	185	645	28.7
1975	470	210	680	30.9
1976	511	223	734	30.4
1977	488	237	725	32.7
1978	386	224	610	36.7
1979	400	232	632	36.7
1980	369	231	600	38.5
1981	363	242	605	40.0
1982	354	214	568	37.7
1983	309	216	525	41.1
1984	289	226	515	43.9
1985	227	234	461	50.8
1986	276	215	491	43.8
1987	254	168	422	39.8
1988	211	238	449	53.0
1989	214	222	436	50.9
1990	221	207	428	48.4
1991	235	231	466	49.6

Panel B: Percentage Change in Number of Doctorates	Men	Women	Total
1960–65	52.2	25.0	47.5
1965–70	102	166	111
1970–75	14.1	126	34.7
1975–80	−21.5	10.0	−11.8
1980–85	−38.5	1.3	−23.2
1985–91	3.5	−1.3	1.2

SOURCE: Unpublished data of the National Research Council (1973, 1980, 1992). Raw data used to calculate percentage change for 1960–1965 and 1965–1970 in Panel B are from National Research Council (1980).

Table 11.2 Sociology Graduate Students in Doctorate-Granting Institutions, 1981–1989

Year	Men	Women	Total	Percent Female
1981	3,481	3,569	7,050	50.6
1982	3,145	3,525	6,670	52.8
1983	3,046	3,330	6,376	52.2
1984	2,856	3,266	6,122	53.3
1985	2,836	3,166	6,002	52.7
1986	2,709	3,192	5,901	54.1
1987	2,888	3,442	6,330	54.4
1988	2,971	3,481	6,452	54.0
1989	3,072	3,586	6,658	53.9
Percentage change in numbers enrolled				
1981–85	−18.5	−11.3	−14.9	
1985–89	8.3	13.3	10.9	

SOURCE: National Science Foundation (1990, Tables, C-8, C-9).

remained fairly constant (approximately 54%) in the last half of the 1980s (see Table 11.2), slightly higher than the 49% figure for all social science graduate students in 1989 and markedly higher than the 37% figure for all graduate students (see Appendix B). The fact that the percentage of women among graduate students has remained stable since 1985 suggests that sociology faculties will not feminize further in the near future.

The data in Table 11.1 (Panel B) reveal two quite different recruitment patterns for women and men. Appendix A (Panel B) provides comparable data for all doctorates and all social science doctorates. The late 1960s was the big growth period for sociology Ph.D.s for both sexes, with men's numbers increasing by 102% and women's by 166%. Striking sex differences in sociology doctorate production first began to emerge in the early to mid 1970s, when men's growth slowed to 14% and women's remained at a high of 126%. From 1975 to 1985, a percentage decline in the number of men receiving doctorates was partially offset by a continued growth among women (although substantially slowed from previous years). Only in the 1985 to 1991 period did the number of men earning Ph.D.s begin to increase once again, while the number of women dropped slightly. For the most part, this overall sex difference is replicated for all doctorates and social science doctorates, although the decline in the number of male doctorates was more pronounced in sociology than in the other two groups (see Appendix A). This indicates that although the trend in sociology replicated what occurred in academia as a whole, and in the social sciences, the decline was greatest in sociology.

These striking increases in the number of women in sociology's recruitment pool have yet to make much of an impact on the overall representation of women in sociology faculties (see Table 11.3). In 1974, 24% of full-time sociologists employed at universities and colleges were women, a figure that increased by only three percentage points in 11 years.[6] Estimates are not substantially different for those working full time in 1985 at doctorate-granting and nondoctorate-granting institutions: 26% and 27%, respectively (see Table 11.3). As noted elsewhere (Huber, 1985; Kulis, 1988; Kulis, Miller, Axelrod, & Gordon, 1986), women's representation is somewhat higher in part-time positions. In 1985, women were 38%, 44%, and 36% of part-time sociologists at all universities and colleges, doctorate-granting institutions, and nondoctorate-granting institutions, respectively (National Science Foundation [NSF], 1985, Tables B-21 to B-26).

Employing different and more recent data, Beeghley and Van Ausdale (1990, p. 4) found the percentage female "at all ranks in [sociology] graduate programs" increased from 14% to 22% between 1979 and 1989. The comparable percentage increase for full and associate professors was from 10% to 18%. Given lengthy training requirements, women's greatest inroads are where one would expect them to be, in the nontenured ranks. Kulis (1988, Table 2) found that in 1984, women represented 40% of assistant professors in U.S. sociology departments (38% in "top-ranked" U.S. departments).[7] Recent data collected by the ASA (C. Howery, personal communication, 1993) suggest that by 1991–1992, women represented 29% of tenured and tenure-track sociology faculty. Disaggregating by rank shows that 46% of the assistant professors were women; the comparable figures for the associate and full professors were 30% and 20%, respectively.[8] There is also some evidence that women, like men, have bettered their tenure rates. For a sample of 4-year colleges and universities in 13 Western states, Kulis et al. (1986, p. 153) found that between 1979 and 1984 the percentage of tenured female sociologists rose from 44% to 56% (the comparable increase for men was 72% to 81%). In sum, women are apparently moving into academic sociology, although by 1991–1992 they still represented only about 3 of every 10 faculty members.

Taken as a whole these data reveal quite different patterns of behavior for men and women. Men were the first to lower sociology (and indeed

Table 11.3 Sociologists Employed Full-Time at Universities and Colleges, 1974–1985

Panel A: Numbers Employed Full-Time and Percent Female

Year	Men	Women	Total	Percent Female
All universities and colleges				
1974	7,672	2,376	10,048	23.6
1975	8,104	2,640	10,744	24.6
1976	8,501	2,927	11,428	25.6
1977	8,629	3,042	11,671	26.1
1978	8,475	3,027	11,502	26.3
1979	n.a.	n.a.	n.a.	—
1980	7,920	2,940	10,860	27.1
1981	7,790	2,957	10,747	27.5
1982	7,738	3,028	10,766	28.1
1983	7,613	2,872	10,485	27.4
1984	7,524	2,756	10,280	26.8
1985	7,463	2,703	10,166	26.6
Doctorate-granting universities and colleges				
1980	3,839	1,381	5,220	26.5
1984	3,538	1,212	4,750	25.5
1985	3,561	1,233	4,794	25.7
Nondoctorate-granting universities and colleges				
1980	4,081	1,559	5,640	27.6
1984	3,986	1,544	5,530	27.9
1985	3,902	1,470	5,372	27.4

Panel B: Percentage Change in Numbers Employed Full-Time

Year	Men	Women	Total
All universities and colleges			
1974–80	3.2	23.7	8.1
1980–85	−5.8	−8.1	−6.4
Doctorate-granting universities and colleges			
1980–85	−7.2	−10.7	−8.2
Nondoctorate-granting universities and colleges			
1980–85	−4.4	−5.7	−4.8

SOURCE: National Science Foundation (1981, Table B-21; 1985, Tables B-19, B-20, B-23 to B-26).

all academic fields) in their job queues: As represented by their Ph.D. production rates, men began to eschew training in sociology in the 1970s and early 1980s, substantially earlier than women (see Table 11.1 and Appendix A). Comparing Table 11.1 with Appendix A shows that this pattern of sex differences, although generally true of all fields and all social scientists, is more pronounced in sociology. Between 1965 and 1975 the percentage increase for women sociologists was greater than comparable figures for all doctorates or for only social science doctorates, and between 1975 and 1985 the percentage decrease for male sociologists was similarly greater. With fewer men in training programs, women's presence grew.[9] The numbers of women receiving sociology doctorates did not begin to slow dramatically until the late 1970s and early 1980s and, contrary to men's experiences, did not actually decline until the late 1980s.

Clearly the social processes fostering change operated differently for men and women, and especially so for male and female sociologists. In addition, women's inroads into sociology faculty positions have been slow, suggesting that gender barriers remain in the sociological marketplace. However, women's limited movement into full-time sociology faculties is attributable in part to the lengthy training required for academic careers. In addition, when the bottom fell out of the academic labor market in the 1970s, men as well as women had difficulty finding academic positions. As Table 11.3 shows, the total number of sociologists employed full time at universities and colleges peaked in 1977, and declined consistently through 1985.

More Women, Fewer Men

The queuing perspective helps to disentangle the various factors leading to the feminization of sociology's recruitment pool. In particular, we focus on what it was about the 1970s and 1980s that led more women but fewer men to choose advanced training in sociology. We explore three major explanations. First, the boom of academic sociology in the early postwar period, followed by its bust in the 1970s, increased and then reduced men's interest in the field. Research and development (R&D) funding for the social sciences, and for sociology in particular, dropped notably in the 1970s, and trends in several economic indicators suggested that the discipline was deteriorating (see below). In queuing language, men's ranking of sociology in their job queues has dropped since 1970, with important consequences for their choice of graduate training. Second, beginning in the 1970s university sociology departments developed a specific interest in hiring women, because of the salience of antidiscrimination legislation and because women sociologists generated pressure for change. There was an increased demand for women per se—women rose in academic employers' labor queues—in part because of the actions of extra-labor market actors (e.g., the federal government) and also because women sociologists themselves acted to enhance their standing in the field. Third, women themselves increasingly chose graduate training in sociology because the nature of sociology's subject matter lent itself to the inclusion of issues central to their lives. They thus increasingly supplied themselves to sociology's recruitment pools by choosing graduate training in the field.

Boom Versus Bust

The most likely explanation for men's declining interest in sociology was the deterioration of the field that began in the 1970s. As documented in Table 11.1 and Appendix A, prior to the 1970s academic sociology, like academia as a whole, was a booming enterprise. During the early postwar period, the growth in the field was attributable in part to increased federal funding for research in universities (Carter & Carter, 1981; see also Turner & Turner, 1990, chap. 4). Reflecting this expansion, total membership in the ASA increased fivefold between 1950 and 1972 (ASA, 1972c), and the number of sociology degrees awarded grew significantly: As Table 11.1 documents, the number of Ph.D.s increased by 48% and 111%, respectively, in the early and late 1960s. Notably both women's and men's participation grew during this period: The number of men increased by 52% and 102% in the early and late 1960s, respectively, whereas the comparable figures for women were 25% and 166%.

As we discussed above, during the 1970s sociology began to contract, and the effects of this became visible first in the actions of men. We examine several factors contributing to this contraction, including declines in governmental funding and the occupation's attractiveness to men in particular.

Declines in Governmental Funding and Support. One indicator of the field's decline was the drop in federal funding. Sociology, and the social sciences more generally, were particularly hard hit by the contraction of research funding and were the targets of bitter executive and legislative attacks (Prewitt & Sills, 1981). One of the early indications that academic social science was hitting rough waters was the resignation of the National Science Foundation's (NSF) highest-ranking social scientist, Lloyd G. Humphreys, in September 1971 to protest cuts in the science budget (ASA, 1971c). As the ASA newsletter *Socio-Log* (ASA, 1971c) noted at the time, these cuts were particularly significant for the social sciences:[10]

> It suggests once again that NSF is suspending some crucial programs now that the natural sciences have reaped their benefit and despite the apparent need for the social sciences to have their turn. It also underlines the determination of both NSF and OMB [Office of Management and Budget] to move Federal support programs off the campus and in applied directions. (p. 2)

The financial attack on universities continued apace, as federal agencies reduced or eliminated graduate student fellowships and training grants (ASA, 1971a, 1973a). Although the 1973 budget contained some assurances that academia would benefit from federal funds, the federal government placed increasing emphasis on applied rather than basic research, solving specific national problems, and nonacademic research. The latter emphasis was perhaps the most telling sign of declining support for the academy. Yet the *American Sociologist* (ASA, 1972b) remained relatively hopeful: "While sociology is not yet the queen of the social sciences in terms of its federal resources, there is ample provision for a princely life style as long as it is pursued on the king's own terms" (p. 1).

Federal funding for social science research continued to decrease in real dollars throughout the 1970s (Prewitt & Sills, 1981). Inflation, declining student enrollments, government demands for greater financial accountability, and the rising costs of procuring grants further weakened universities' financial status (Smith & Karlesky, reported in Rhoades, 1979). Figures 11.1a and 11.1b (see also Rhoades, 1980) illustrate these trends. Total R&D funds for sociology (in 1987 constant dollars) reached a peak of $312.3 million in 1972, only to drop notably after that date (see Figure 11.1a). The pattern for R&D funding of basic research in sociology was flatter, but also peaked at $54.1 million in 1972.[11] This pattern of improvement and then decline in funding recurs when we view sociology's total R&D funding as a percentage of total funding for social sciences and as a percentage of total funding for all fields. Figure 11.1b shows that sociology's relative position reached a peak in 1972, when the discipline received 38.9% of all the R&D funds targeted to the social sciences and 2.2% of the R&D funds for all fields.

a. In millions of dollars (in constant 1987$)

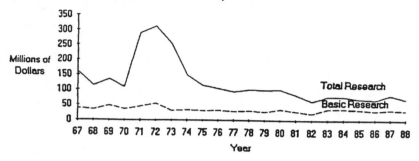

b. Total research (in percentages)

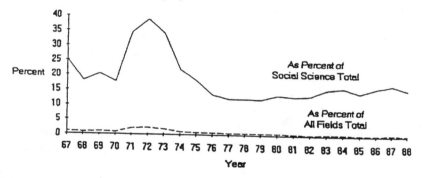

Figure 11.1. Federal Funding for Sociology, 1967-1988

SOURCE: From National Science Foundation (1987, Tables C-159A, C-159B, C-160A, C-160B).
NOTE: Total Research = federal obligations for total research (basic and applied). Basic Research = federal obligations for basic research. 1987 and 1988 data are estimates. Funding figures were standardized to 1987 constant dollars using Gross Domestic Product (GDP) deflators (Jankowski, 1992). In Figure 1b, sociology funding is presented as a percentage of total social science funding and as a percentage of total funding for all fields.

The deterioration in federal support reached crisis proportions in 1981 after the election of Ronald Reagan. The Carter administration had allocated an increase of 23.5% for fiscal year (FY) 1981 to NSF's social and economic science budget. Reagan's OMB proposed cutting the FY 1981 budget by 75%, or $30 million, as well as eliminating the entire budget of $98 million for instrumentation programs and programs to help women and racial/ethnic minorities (ASA, 1981c). The rationale was that "the support of these sciences is considered of relatively lesser importance to the economy than the support of the natural sciences" (OMB, 1981, as cited in Prewitt & Sills, 1981, p. 4).[12] Although the proposal to reduce the social science budget was defeated, and the debate showed broad bipartisan support, social scientists argued that the situation remained precarious because the administration's basic assumption had been that such disciplines were a "needless luxury" (Prewitt & Sills, 1981, p. 7).

The attacks on the social sciences did not come solely from the executive branch nor from Republicans. Democratic Senator William Proxmire also attacked academics through the mass media, and his notorious Golden Fleece awards further highlighted the vulnerability of academia (particularly social scientists) to political attacks. Responding to an attack on sociology professor Elaine Walster, Sewell (1975) argued that Proxmire obviously mistrusted the peer review system for NSF funding and favored research projects with short-term payoffs, without recognizing that applied and developmental projects may take years to come to fruition. Academic social science was thus in an unstable position during the 1970s. Federal funding was declining precipitously and the legitimacy of the social sciences was under attack. The federal government, through its granting agencies, placed increased emphasis on the significance and utility of social science research, especially in the short term.

The Decline of Sociology? Some have proclaimed that sociology is declining (e.g., Horowitz, 1992; see also Coughlin, 1992; Lynch, 1992).[13] To our minds, reports of sociology's decline have been vastly exaggerated. Indeed, Hargens (1990) found no empirical support for the assertion that sociologists have become increasingly discouraged with their field. Using data from the Carnegie Commission on Higher Education for 1969 and 1975 and the Carnegie Foundation for the Advancement of Teaching for 1984, he found no change over time in sociologists' perceptions about agreement on standards of scholarship nor on their assessments of the vitality of their field. Pointing out that sociology's changing age and sex composition has produced new specialties, Hargens (1990, pp. 205-206) attributed the view that sociology is declining to an overreliance on the perceptions of journalists and more established sociologists who work in traditional sociological fields. Tables 11.1 and 11.2 also suggest that the field is seeing an increasing number of recruits and that both women and men are contributing to that increase. Nonetheless, we did find evidence that sociology's overall position deteriorated in the 1970s on several important economic indicators. Sociology dropped in male job queues in the 1970s, and men began to avoid graduate training because it no longer provided the same opportunity for advancement.

One indicator of sociology's deterioration in the 1970s is that, like the overall national trend, real earnings in sociology dropped in the 1970s (ASA, 1972a): B. J. Huber (1985, p. 20) found that sociology faculty salaries declined 29% between 1975 and 1981.[14] NSF data for a sample of doctoral scientists (see Table 11.4) support the conclusion that sociology's real earnings declined in the late 1970s, although they did rebound during the 1980s (perhaps accounting in part for men's renewed interest in the field in the late 1980s). In constant 1987 dollars, the median earnings of sociology/anthropology doctorates employed full time in universities and 4-year colleges decreased by 21.1% from 1973 to 1981 and increased 16.4% from 1981 to 1989.[15] Equivalent figures for all scientists (and social scientists, excluding psychologists) showed a percentage decline of 15% (and 19%) between 1973 and 1981 and a percentage increase of 19% (and 18%) between 1981 and 1989 (data not shown in tabular form, but calculated from NSF, 1991, Table 9). Overall the patterns of decline, then increase for sociologists, social scientists, and all scientists were remarkably similar. Notably, sociology's drop in median earnings in the 1970s was greater than that experienced by either social scientists or all scientists, and their revival in the 1980s was less strong.

Salaries were not the only aspect of academia to deteriorate during the 1970s. Freeman (as cited in Carter & Carter, 1981, p. 483) characterized the 1970s as "the worst job market for Ph.D.s in American academic history." Universities responded by lowering promotion rates, increasing the number of nontenure-track positions (Huber 1985, p. 28), and raising student-faculty ratios (Tuckman, Caldwell, & Vogler, 1978). In addition, Perrucci, O'Flaherty, and Marshall (1983) found evidence at one large state university that those gaining tenure in the buyer's market of the 1970s needed to be more productive than those reaching the same status in the seller's market of the 1960s.

Prior to 1970, sociologists had few problems finding faculty jobs. However, in 1972 the bubble burst as supply caught up with demand (Finsterbusch, 1972). Some made dire predictions that only 44% of sociologists would be employed in graduate academic programs by 1980 (McGinnis & Solomon, 1973, p. 61). Others were more sanguine, noting that the number of students entering graduate schools had already begun to decline (Finsterbusch, 1972). However, the net number of new positions in sociology declined between 1971 and 1974, so that Finsterbusch (1974, p. 7) estimated that in 1974 about 400 sociology Ph.D.s did not

Table 11.4 Median Annual Salaries, Underemployment Rate, and
Underutilization Rate of Sociology/Anthropology Doctorates,
1973-1989

| | *Median Annual Salaries*[a] | | *Underemployment Rate*[b] | | *Underutilization Rate*[c] | |
| | | *1987* | *Social* | *Sociology/* | *Social* | *Sociology/* |
Year	*Actual $*	*Constant $*[d]	*Sciences*	*Anthropology*	*Sciences*	*Anthropology*
1973	19,100	46,281	1.5%	1.4%	2.5%	2.8%
1975	20,600	41,878	1.2	1.2	2.2	3.0
1977	22,200	39,735	2.4	2.0	3.7	4.5
1979	24,000	36,613	2.1	3.5	3.2	5.5
1981	28,800	36,520	1.7	2.7	2.5	4.3
1983	32,800	37,632	2.8	4.1	3.9	6.5
1985	37,300	39,525	3.3	6.5	4.3	8.4
1987	41,900	41,900	3.2	7.5	4.5	10.0
1989	46,100	42,520	2.8	5.4	4.0	8.2

SOURCE: National Science Foundation (1991, Tables 9, 14, 15).

a. Median annual salaries are for sociology/anthropology doctorates employed full time in universities and 4-year colleges.

b. Underemployment rate = ratio of those working part-time but seeking full-time jobs or who are working in a nonscientific job when a scientific job is preferred to total employment. Data are for a sample of doctorates. Changes in wording of questionnaires makes pre-1985 data not exactly comparable to later years (National Science Foundation, 1991, p. 58).

c. Underutilization rate = proportion of those in the total labor force who are either unemployed but seeking employment, working part-time but seeking full-time jobs, or working involuntarily in a nonscientific job. Data are for a sample of doctorates. Changes in wording of questionnaires makes pre-1985 data not exactly comparable to later years (National Science Foundation, 1991, p. 58).

d. Salary figures were standardized to 1987 constant dollars using Gross Domestic Product (GDP) deflators (Jankowski, 1992).

find jobs in academic sociology. The bottom seemed to have fallen out of the academic labor market, and this prompted sociologists to look elsewhere for jobs, in particular to the applied sector.[16]

As the academic labor market contracted, the number of unemployed sociologists rose 56% between 1975 and 1981, and women and racial/ethnic minorities were overrepresented among the unemployed (Huber, 1985, p. 41).[17] In the late 1970s unemployment for minority sociologists grew by 1,000% (Huber, 1985, p. 42).

Changes in the labor market also prompted the appearance of a two-tiered labor market: The number of nontenure-track and part-time positions rose throughout the 1970s (Huber, 1985; Tuckman et al., 1978; Van Arsdale, 1978; Whitt & Derber, 1979; for a broader view, see American Association of University Professors, 1992).

The growth of part-time and nontenure-track employment was a serious issue for sociology because it reflected and contributed to the occupation's deterioration. Part-time positions are often low paid: Tuckman et al. (1978, p. 187) found that part-timers were paid 25% to 35% less than full-timers, assuming equivalent rank structures. In addition, there were few benefits or chances for promotion for part-timers or so-called academic gypsies, who moved from one temporary position to another (for additional details, see ASA, Committee on the Freedom of Research and Teaching, 1986). Once again, women and racial/ethnic minorities were disproportionately represented in the part-time labor market (Whitt & Derber, 1979, p. 2).

To illustrate these trends more systematically, Table 11.4 presents underemployment and underutilization rates for a sample of doctoral social scientists and sociologists/anthropologists for 1973 through 1989. These data indicate that the general trend for sociology/anthropology doctorates in both the 1970s and the 1980s has been one of increasing underemployment and underutilization. Both underemployment and underutilization appeared to have peaked in 1987, with 7.5% of sociology/anthropology doctorates reporting themselves as underemployed and 10% as underutilized. Significantly, in all but 3 of the 18 comparisons, the underemployment and underutilization rates for sociology/anthropology doctorates were higher than those for the social sciences as a whole.[18]

Increased Demand for Women

At the same time that sociology was deteriorating in the 1970s, several factors helped to create a climate that increased the demand for women per se in academic sociology. First, partly in response to external pressure, the ASA strongly supported affirmative action in the early 1970s as a means to improve women's low status in the field. Second, women sociologists themselves became an important pressure group for change, organizing to enhance their status within the field.

Affirmative Action. In the post-Reagan/Bush 1990s, it is hard to remember that a climate supportive of affirmative action goals existed at the federal government level in the early 1970s. During these years, the Department of Health, Education, and Welfare (HEW) required universities with large government contracts to develop an affirmative action strategy outlining their plans to increase the number of women and racial/ethnic minorities they employed. Penalties were assessed for universities not complying with the HEW directives. Ample evidence of federal government support for affirmative action exists in both the national higher education media of the time and in ASA's *Footnotes*. As an article in a contemporary *ASA Footnotes* noted, by 1973 HEW had charged 350 educational institutions with discriminatory practices against women and was threatening to sever federal funding for those institutions failing to comply with the guidelines (Barnes, 1973). During the early 1970s, the *Chronicle of Higher Education* published a series of articles on the HEW guidelines and their aftermath, including descriptions of universities where federal grants were delayed because of inadequate affirmative action plans (e.g., Boffey, 1974; "Federal Laws," 1972; Fields, 1975; Logan, 1970; Semas, 1971; "U.S. Announces," 1972). As sociology's professional association, the ASA responded by urging sociology departments to "support and promote" affirmative action programs (Hill, 1973, p. 9). At least some sociology departments responded to such initiatives by increasing their efforts to recruit women and racial/ethnic minorities (e.g., Hill, 1983).

That some believed these affirmative action goals were successful can be documented in white men's subsequent claims of reverse discrimination. In 1973 *ASA Footnotes* reprinted a *Washington Post* article, "Reverse Bias Alleged in College Hiring" (Barnes, 1973, p. 4), which generated much comment in later issues (e.g., Borgatta, 1973, 1974; Huber, 1974). Two contemporary surveys suggested that some sociology department chairs interpreted affirmative action guidelines as preferential treatment for racial/ethnic minority and female job candidates (Borgatta, 1973; Lorch, 1973).[19] In response to the subsequent uproar over the directives, in 1973 HEW's Office of Civil Rights established an ombudsman to investigate complaints of preferential treatment and in 1974 issued a clarifying memorandum assuring colleges and universities that matters of assessing applicants' quality were best left to them (Fields, 1974b; Van Dyne, 1973).

Although sociologists continue to argue about the theory and effects of affirmative action, contemporary studies revealed that it produced limited results in practice, especially for racial/ethnic minorities (for such statistics for the 1970s, see Harris, 1975; Jackson, 1973; Williams, 1982; for information on the effects of affirmative action on women and racial/ethnic minorities' access to academe as a whole, see Exum, Menges, Watkins, & Berglund, 1984; Fields, 1974a; Menges & Exum, 1983; Weidlein, 1973). Jackson (1973, p. 3) noted that by 1973 only one third of sociology departments had set goals and timetables for hiring women and racial/ethnic minorities. Women's representation among faculty had increased somewhat (from 9% to 15% between 1970 and 1973), but hiring procedures had produced few advantages for people of color— African Americans were consistently 3% of total faculty during this same period, Asian Americans were 2%, Chicanos, .6%, Puerto Ricans, .2%, and Native Americans, .1%. Jackson also examined subtle indicators of departments' openness to women and racial/ethnic minorities, such as graduate courses in gender and race or ethnic studies, recognition of special contributions made by women and racial/ethnic minority faculty, and the number of leadership positions racial/ethnic minorities and women held. He found that most departments fared poorly on all these counts.

Kulis et al. (1986, p. 158) found equally discouraging results for racial/ethnic minorities in the western region of the United States in the early 1980s: In 1984, African Americans accounted for only 2.5% of full professors (and 3.0% and 6.2% of associate and assistant professors, respectively). The comparable percentages for Hispanics were 1.9%, 3.0%, and 5.2%, respectively. Kulis and Miller (1988, p. 337) argued that minority women, in particular, suffered from "double jeopardy" in academia, as indicated in their underrepresentation relative to both white women and men of their own race/ethnicity and their concentration in the South, in lower academic ranks, in undergraduate institutions, and at public colleges and universities. Segura and Jewell (1990, p. 3) concurred, arguing that faculty women of color encounter barriers to academic success not faced by their white colleagues: lack of sensitivity of colleagues and university administrators regarding extra demands on their time; the failure to recruit at less prestigious universities where most women of color train; their token status, which often includes the assumption of lower quality; and their marginality within departments and universities.

Pressure for Change. Some women did, however, move into faculty positions during the 1970s, although their status within departments remained lower than men's. As was true at the turn of the century, women themselves were a major force in this change. In 1969, the Caucus of Women Sociologists called on the ASA Council to produce listings of faculty and students by sex and to remove barriers to equality (Rhoades, 1981, p. 61).[20] Similar groups continued to lobby throughout the 1970s for fellowship programs, awards, staff positions, and greater representation in ASA activities (p. 67). In 1970 the Women's Caucus of the ASA met to examine women's position within sociology, and in 1971 the caucus reconstituted itself as Sociologists for Women in Society (SWS) (Banister, 1991, pp. 1, 190-192). This association was instrumental in lobbying to improve women's status within the discipline and in providing a supportive network for women.[21]

Unlike the turn of the century, the ASA responded to women's increasing demands by setting up a Committee on the Status of Women in Sociology (CSWS) (ASA, 1971b, 1973b) and appointing an Executive Specialist for Minorities and Women (Rhoades, 1981, p. 63). CSWS lobbied the ASA to enhance women's status in the profession, addressing issues as diverse as nepotism rules, recruitment procedures, maternity and paternity leave, and the rights of part-timers (ASA, 1971b; see also ASA, Committee on Freedom of Research and Teaching, 1986). *ASA Footnotes* also initiated a column on women and racial/ethnic minorities (ASA, 1973b, 1974b), which alerted readers that the ASA was committed to improving their position. Finally, the ASA was instrumental in encouraging the participation of racial/ethnic minorities and women in ASA committees and as elected officials.[22]

One final reason for the ASA's more favorable response to women's pressure for access during the 1970s, as compared with the turn of the century, was the large and growing number of women graduate students. Although it is difficult to know the direction of causality, anecdotal evidence abounds that women graduate students played an important role in individual departments in generating pressure to hire women faculty. In addition, as men's numbers in the recruitment pools dropped, these women eventually served as a larger proportion of the pool for academic employers looking to hire more women faculty.

Sociology's Changing Subject Matter

Several of the changes we have discussed thus far (e.g., declines in real earnings and federal R&D funding) also occurred in other social sciences. Although we focus on sociology, we are well aware that other social science fields have feminized as well. In 1950, for example, women earned 15% of all psychology doctorates, but by 1984 they earned over half (Howard et al., 1986, p. 1319) and by 1991, 61% (National Research Council [NRC], 1993b, p. 69). Women made fewer inroads into several other social science fields: In 1991 women constituted

20% and 27%, respectively, of doctorates in economics and political science/government (NRC, 1993b, p. 69). What led sociology (and presumably psychology) to be more receptive to women? Although we do not have the space to address this question fully here, we do offer one explanation for why women increasingly supplied themselves to sociology training programs: Sociology's subject matter lends itself to the inclusion of issues central to women's lives. As Stacey and Thorne (1985, pp. 301-302) noted, feminist perspectives have offered new insights into traditional sociological fields (e.g., organizations, occupations, deviance, stratification), led to reconceptualizations in other fields (e.g., in the study of mothering, rape, marriage), and allowed for the emergence of new research topics (e.g., sexual harassment, feminization of poverty, childbirth).[23]

Signs that interest in gender issues has increased are readily apparent. In the 1970s gender roles and women's issues gradually developed as legitimate fields of sociological inquiry. DeWolf, Skipper, Steed, & Alpaugh (1986, p. 151) found that the percentage of women listing gender or women's issues as an area of interest in the *ASA Guide to Graduate Departments* increased from 14% to 25% between 1975 and 1985 (the comparable percentages for men were .3% to 1.1%). Ward and Grant (1985, p. 146) found a steady increase in the proportion of gender articles published in prominent journals between 1974 and 1983—up from 14% to 21%.[24] Another important indicator of the popularity of gender issues is that by 1992 the sex and gender section topped the remaining ASA specialty sections in the total number of members (1,154, 40% of whom were graduate students; Lorber, 1992).

Women are likely drawn to sociology because the increasing attention paid to gender encourages scholars to address women's experiences in general and to relate these to their own experiences in particular. Since 1970, feminist theorists, and gender scholars in a variety of sociological fields, have pointed to the lack of serious investigation of gender issues. A dramatic influx of articles by women and about women, by both male and female researchers, has helped change the balance. Even if women did not explicitly wish to study gender, they may have felt that increased awareness within sociology about women's issues would translate into a more receptive work environment.

Despite notable achievements in introducing gender analyses into a plethora of sociological fields, women have yet to integrate fully. For example, whether by inclination, channeling, or mentoring relationships, women tend to be overrepresented in specialties such as family, medical, and gender sociology (Ward & Grant, 1985, p. 143; 1991). Ward and Grant (1991, pp. 121-124) found, for example, that women less often identified themselves as theorists (a high-status field within sociology), seldom wrote theory texts, and were infrequently mentioned in theory books. In addition, women's knowledge tends to remain separate from the main conceptual frameworks of sociology (Gould & Kern-Davies, 1977, p. 186; Stacey & Thorne, 1985). Studies of gender articles corroborate this intellectual segregation. Although Ward and Grant (1985) noted a steady increase in the number of articles published about women in prominent journals, they found that many of these simply examined sex differences. Articles that attempted to redefine concepts or methods or provide insight into previously neglected areas of women's lives were seldom cited. Articles that centered the analysis on women and offered new ways of thinking about the discipline were virtually absent from the most prominent journals.

Additional evidence that sociology is structured by sex emerges from studies of overlapping scholarly interests. Using joint memberships in ASA sections, Cappell and Guterbock (1992, p. 270) found that shared memberships in sociology's "visible colleges" are determined in part by common ascriptive characteristics (e.g., sex, race/ethnicity). Thus women are proportionately overrepresented in the family, sex and gender, medical, population, aging, and racial and ethnic minorities sections; similarly, people of color are disproportionately represented in the ASA Racial and Ethnic Minorities Section. Notably, its percentage of females and percentage of minorities are negatively correlated with a section's professional power.

Discussion

In this chapter we investigated the processes leading to the feminization of sociology's recruitment pool since 1970. Building on Reskin and Roos's (1990) queuing perspective, we use an instance of occupational feminization—academic sociology since 1970—to illustrate how and why occupations' gender boundaries shift. In particular, we look to the interactions of academic employers, women, and men to determine how gendered occupational structures emerge and change. In addition, we explore the role of extra-labor market actors (e.g., the federal government) in this process.

Our argument begins at the turn of the century. In line with expectations from the queuing perspective, women first gained access to higher education because economic exigencies led college administrators to search them out. As fewer men chose to enroll, women began to fill the educational slots. It was in this supportive climate that women first gained access to sociology graduate programs. But although they gained entry, they found little access to academic teaching positions. Women organized to defend their interests by establishing a separate women's network, centered around Jane Addams, but gender boundaries remained intractable. Their own professional association and most academic positions remained closed to them. Like their female counterparts in the 1970s, many opted for positions in the applied sector or closely related academic fields (e.g., social work, child and adult education).

Women remained a minority presence within sociology until the 1960s and 1970s, when they swelled the ranks of sociology graduate programs once again. In the late 1960s they were joining men in choosing sociology—a burgeoning field at the time—but by the early 1970s fewer of their peers in entering cohorts were male. Although men began to avoid graduate training in sociology, women continued to choose the field well into the 1970s. Thus understanding why sociology graduate programs feminized requires understanding both why fewer men—but more women—chose sociology in the 1970s and what structural conditions affected men's and women's decision making.

We focused on three explanations for men's exit and women's entry in the 1970s. First, academic sociology dropped in men's labor queues during the 1970s because, relative to other alternatives, the field was deteriorating. Federal funding for sociology declined notably throughout the 1970s, thereby reducing or eliminating graduate student fellowships and traineeships. Real earnings declined, as well, during the decade, and the buyer's market of the 1970s meant that fewer Ph.D.s could be guaranteed jobs at the end of their lengthy training. Unemployment rose, and those who were employed were often underemployed and underutilized. As the bottom fell out of the academic labor market, many new Ph.D.s looked elsewhere for jobs, most notably in the applied sector. A large number of those Ph.D.s moving into applied jobs were women; like their counterparts at the turn of the century, these women had a more difficult time finding jobs in the academic sector.

Second, women rose in academic employers' labor queues in part because of the increased salience of affirmative action goals and because they organized to pursue their self-interests. Although there is some debate as to the ultimate success of affirmative action programs, there is no doubt that such pressure existed. The number of articles on this issue in the ASA's newsletter and related publications increased dramatically during the 1970s, and allegations of reverse bias ensued. Women themselves reinforced that outside pressure by negotiating forcefully for their own interests. This took the form of establishing a separate professional association and setting up a committee to oversee their interests within the ASA. Thus, within the academic labor market, women successfully negotiated with academic employers to better their position within the field. Through its emphasis on affirmative action, the federal government—an extra-labor market actor—also succeeded in putting pressure on institutions of higher education to attend to women's concerns.

Finally, women raised sociology in their job queues because as a field of scholarly inquiry it permitted the inclusion of issues central to their lives. Sociological theory and methods could be put to good use in studying issues long of interest to women and, in return, be strengthened by the incorporation of women's experiences.

During the 1970s, gender boundaries thus shifted in sociology's graduate programs: Women are now as likely as men to enroll for Ph.D. training in sociology. We have already outlined several explanations for the greater permeability of sociology's gender boundaries in enrollments in recent decades. We close by speculating about whether such boundaries will shift as notably in sociology faculties. In the 1970s more women moved into sociology faculties. This in itself is a dramatic change from the relatively fixed boundaries facing women sociology graduates at the turn of the century. The most recent data we have on women's entry into faculty positions suggest that women represent approximately 46% of assistant professors in U.S. sociology departments, and 30% and 20%, respectively, of associate and full professors.

It is still too early to tell whether women will continue to move into faculty positions in the coming decades. Data suggest that the numbers choosing sociology are on the increase (see also Wright, 1990). Since hitting its nadir in 1987—when sociology graduated 422 Ph.D.s—the number of doctorates has steadily increased. Notably, the number of men entering the field began to increase in the late 1980s, after 10 years of decline. After peaking in 1988—when 238 women represented 53% of those earning Ph.D.s—the number of women has dropped somewhat. Also during the 1980s, real earnings began to increase slowly, and underemployment and underutilization rates for sociologists/anthropologists began to drop, as well. Prospects for a further shifting of sociology's gender boundaries, however, seem bleak without a rosier economic prognosis for higher education.

Although women's successes in sociology are clear, troubling traces of gender boundaries remain. Importantly, women have not been as successful at breaking into tenured associate and full professor positions as their overall numbers in the field would suggest. Only 3 in 10 full-time sociologists employed at universities are women. Women's progress into faculty positions has been slow, in part because of the lengthy training time required and because they entered the labor market in large numbers in a declining academic labor market. But women's (and racial and ethnic minorities') lack of access to the most prestigious ranks, their concentration in part-time work, and their intellectual segregation strongly suggest that discriminatory barriers remain in place in the sociological labor market.

Appendix A

Total Doctorates and Total Social Science Doctorates, by Sex, 1920–1991

Panel A: Number of Doctorates

	Total: All Fields				Social Sciences Total[a]			
Decade	Men	Women	Total	Percent Female	Men	Women	Total	Percent Female
1920–29	10,093	1,826	11,919	15.3	1,573	325	1,898	17.1
1930–39	21,870	3,784	25,654	14.8	2,994	562	3,556	15.8
1940–49	26,460	4,115	30,575	13.5	3,421	580	4,001	14.5
1950–59	72,254	7,972	80,226	9.9	12,182	1,510	13,692	11.0
1960–69	143,055	18,964	162,019	11.7	21,516	3,604	25,120	14.3

(Continued)

Appendix A *(Continued)*

Panel A: Number of Doctorates

	Total: All Fields				Social Sciences Total[a]			
Decade	Men	Women	Total	Percent Female	Men	Women	Total	Percent Female
Year								
1970	25,527	3,971	29,498	13.5	3,829	737	4,566	16.1
1971	27,271	4,596	31,867	14.4	4,265	924	5,189	17.8
1972	27,754	5,287	33,041	16.0	4,442	1,026	5,468	18.8
1973	27,670	6,085	33,755	18.0	4,547	1,211	5,758	21.0
1974	26,594	6,453	33,047	19.5	4,503	1,381	5,884	23.5
1975	25,751	7,201	32,952	21.9	4,544	1,522	6,066	25.1
1976	25,262	7,684	32,946	23.3	4,580	1,634	6,214	26.3
1977	23,858	7,858	31,716	24.8	4,348	1,725	6,073	28.4
1978	22,553	8,322	30,875	27.0	4,178	1,861	6,039	30.8
1979	22,302	8,937	31,239	28.6	3,969	1,992	5,961	33.4
1980	21,612	9,408	31,020	30.3	3,810	2,045	5,855	34.9
1981	21,465	9,892	31,357	31.5	3,945	2,197	6,142	35.8
1982	21,018	10,093	31,111	32.4	3,679	2,158	5,837	37.0
1983	20,749	10,533	31,282	33.7	3,690	2,406	6,096	39.5
1984	20,638	10,699	31,337	34.1	3,504	2,426	5,930	40.9
1985	20,553	10,744	31,297	34.3	3,388	2,377	5,765	41.2
1986	20,591	11,304	31,895	35.4	3,381	2,511	5,892	42.6
1987	20,938	11,425	32,363	35.3	3,297	2,492	5,789	43.0
1988	21,677	11,812	33,489	35.3	3,175	2,597	5,772	45.0
1989	21,811	12,507	34,318	36.4	3,263	2,693	5,956	45.2
1990	22,955	13,102	36,057	36.3	3,261	2,821	6,082	46.4
1991	23,686	13,765	37,451	36.8	3,101	3,026	6,127	49.4

Panel B: Percentage Change in Number of Doctorates[b]

	Men	Women	Total		Men	Women	Total
1960–65	67.8	68.9	67.9		40.1	35.8	39.5
1965–70	75.1	126.0	80.5		88.1	152.0	96.1
1970–75	.9	81.3	11.7		18.7	107.0	32.9
1975–80	−16.1	30.6	−5.9		−16.2	34.4	−3.5
1980–85	−4.9	14.2	.9		−11.1	16.2	−1.5
1985–91	15.2	28.1	19.7		−8.5	27.3	6.3

SOURCE: Unpublished data of the National Research Council (1973, 1993a).

a. Includes psychology.

b. Raw data used to calculate percentage change for 1960–1965 and 1965–1970 are from National Research Council (1980).

Appendix B

Total Graduate Students and Total Social Science Graduate Students in Doctorate-Granting Institutions, 1981–1989

	Total: All Fields				Social Sciences Total[a]			
Year	Men	Women	Total	Percent Female	Men	Women	Total	Percent Female
1981	218,854	110,848	329,702	33.6	55,708	42,383	98,091	43.2
1982	221,118	115,103	336,221	34.2	54,014	42,483	96,497	44.0
1983	225,878	117,193	343,071	34.2	50,568	41,491	92,059	45.1
1984	227,506	118,925	346,431	34.3	48,485	40,579	89,064	45.6
1985	233,003	123,019	356,022	34.6	48,313	41,977	90,290	46.5
1986	239,539	127,624	367,163	34.8	47,910	42,771	90,681	47.2
1987	242,299	130,162	372,461	34.9	48,495	44,464	92,959	47.8
1988	241,927	135,747	377,674	35.9	48,477	46,196	94,673	48.8
1989	243,525	141,500	385,025	36.8	49,549	48,188	97,737	49.3
Percentage change in numbers enrolled								
1981–85	6.5	11.0	8.0		−13.3	−1.0	−8.0	
1985–89	4.5	15.0	8.1		2.6	14.8	8.2	

SOURCE: National Science Foundation (1990, Tables C-8, C-9).
a. Includes psychology.

Notes

1. The increasing representation of women in graduate studies in sociology paralleled, and indeed contributed to, the educational inroads women were making in academia as a whole. In 1890, 18% of the 2,383 graduate students enrolled in all fields of graduate work were women. The comparable percentages for 1900 and 1930 were 30% and 39%, respectively (John, 1935, p. 13, Table 2, as cited in Morgan, 1980, p. 7).

2. When first established in 1905 the organization was called the American Sociological Society. In 1959 it became the American Sociological Association (Rhoades, 1981). The ASA remained small until the post-World War II period: Even as recently as 1960, the entire set of records for the association fit in four drawers (Turner & Turner, 1990, p. 151).

3. The lack of women's participation changed only slowly. As Jessie Bernard described her debut at the 1924 annual meetings of the American Sociological Society, "I was the only girl on the program, and I received applause both before and after my talk" (Bannister, 1991, p. 78).

4. Interestingly, at the time sociology was not yet taught at Randolph-Macon *Men's* College (Morgan, 1980, p. 15).

5. This debate would play out again later in sociology's development. In the 1930s, for example, sociologists debated whether sociology should be the scientific study of society or the study of social problems (Turner & Turner, 1990, p. 150).

6. Our estimates of those working full time in sociology faculties come from NSF's surveys of scientists and engineers employed at universities and colleges (NSF, 1981, 1985). These numbers include those in teaching and research positions at colleges and universities and thus are not equivalent to figures based on teaching faculty. In addition, NSF's sample is not equivalent to a survey of doctorates because the former includes those without doctorates. Any sample differences attributable to this are likely to be minimized in doctorate-granting universities, where full-time scientists and engineers likely have doctorates. Unfortunately, NSF discontinued this series, and there are no comparable data since 1985.

7. Kulis's (1988) sample consisted of "all four-year colleges or universities that had either a sociology department or a 'social science' department offering sociology courses." The sample was identified from the 1984 *ASA Directory of Sociology Departments.* Given women's overrepresentation in undergraduate departments, these percentages are likely higher than Beeghley and Van Ausdale's (1990) sample of "graduate departments of sociology." For other reviews of women's inroads into sociology, see Fava (1960), Hughes (1973), Miller, Kulis, Gordon, and Axelrod (1988a, 1988b), Nigg and Axelrod (1981), Patterson (1971), and Rossi (1970).

8. The ASA's survey was administered to 1,827 sociology departments or divisions in the spring of 1992. The response rate was 53%. The data we present represent only those 5,276 faculty who were either tenured or in tenure-track positions. The ASA data suggest that the representation of women is greatest at 2-year and liberal arts institutions: 36% of the tenured or tenure-track faculty at 2-year institutions were women compared with 34%, 30%, 25%, and 28% at liberal arts, comprehensive, doctorate, and research institutions, respectively (C. Howery, personal communication, 1993).

9. The pool of women trained to move into the graduate sociology slots was already large: Women have made up more than 60% of bachelor degree recipients in sociology since 1930 (Douglas Adkins, as cited in ASA, 1972c, p. 8). In 1987–1988, 69% of bachelors degrees in sociology went to women (U.S. Department of Education, 1991, p. 243).

10. The major newsletter of the ASA has undergone several name changes. From August 1971 to December 1971, it was called ASA *Socio-Log.* From January 1972 to December 1972, this newsletter merged with the *American Sociologist* and was published under the latter's name. In January 1973, the ASA moved once again to a separate newsletter format, with the initiation of *ASA Footnotes.*

11. Comparing the patterns in Figure 11.1a for total and basic research illustrates that the substantial increase in federal funding in the early 1970s was for applied rather than basic research.

12. The social science community fought back, rejuvenating its lobbying arm, the Consortium of Social Science Associations (COSSA). COSSA was instrumental in developing strategies to make its presence felt in Washington, including establishing its own office and preparing committee testimony (ASA, 1981a; Prewitt & Sills, 1981).

13. Horowitz (1992), for example, attributes the "decomposition of sociology" to "ideological thinking . . . [as] American sociology opted for a remedial vision of social welfare . . . while giving scant attention to the sources of social strife" (p. 33) and to its splintering into "a conglomerate of specialties" (p. 32). Recent or threatened closures or downsizings of sociology departments (e.g., Washington University, San Diego State) have intensified such concerns.

14. Whereas real salaries had grown by more than 2% per year between 1960 and 1970 (Dresch & Waldenberg, 1981, as cited by Huber, 1985, p. 18), real academic salaries for all disciplines decreased 21% in the 1970s (Huber 1985, p. 18; see also Carter & Carter, 1981).

15. Unfortunately, the available NSF data do not include separate figures for sociology, nor do they include salary figures separately by sex.

16. During the same years that academic jobs in sociology were disappearing, the applied sector (or sociological practice, as it is now called) expanded to offset these losses. Between 1975 and 1981, the size of the applied sector increased by a dramatic 189%, while the size of the academic sector diminished by 10% (Huber 1985, p. 35). Sociologists looked for employment outside academia in businesses, nonprofit organizations, or government agencies. The heightened awareness of the need to educate sociologists about alternative job opportunities was exemplified by the extraordinary proliferation of articles about nonacademic sociology in the field's major newsletter (ASA, 1974a, 1978a, 1978b, 1978c, 1978d, 1981b; Boros, 1980; Huber, 1983; Jackson, 1972; Motz, 1974; Wilkinson, 1980a, 1980b). Notably, B. J. Huber (1985, p. 38) found that between 1975 and 1981 women were more likely to move into government and nonprofit organizations in the applied sector, men into business/industry.

17. The Office of Scientific Personnel of the National Academy of Sciences found evidence on a national level that female academics were hit harder by job shortages than were their male counterparts ("Women Ph.D.s," 1971).

18. Sociology's underemployment and underutilization rates were always notably higher than those for all scientists. In 1987, 1.5% of all scientists reported that they were underemployed, and 2.6% reported that they were underutilized (NSF, 1991, Tables 14, 15). It is too early to determine if the decrease in both rates in 1989 constitutes a fluctuation or the beginning of a sustained decline in these rates. But the fact that this drop occurred in both rates in all three groups (sociologists/anthropologists, social scientists, and all scientists) strongly suggests that it is not simply a statistical artifact.

19. Echoes of these concerns continue into the present (e.g., Lynch, 1992).

20. Racial and ethnic minorities exerted similar pressure, establishing (for example) the Caucus of Black Sociologists and the Chicano Caucus (Rhoades, 1981, p. 67).

21. Similarly, activist women's groups within academe were sometimes successful in raising the issue of discrimination to a national level by pushing HEW to investigate their universities ("HEW Probing," 1970).

22. Although only 31% of nonstudent ASA members were female in 1987, women were 47% of elected officers and council members, 40% of council/presidential appointments, 30% of editorial boards, 43% of elected section officers and councils, and fully 63% of all elected ASA committee members. Similarly, although 10% of nonstudent ASA members, racial and ethnic minorities were 5% of elected officers and council members, 18% of council/presidential appointments, 3% of editorial boards, 13% of elected section officers and councils, and 14% of all elected ASA committee members (Huber, 1988, p. 4).

23. In comparison with sociology, the subject matter of economics and the profession itself have been less hospitable to women. According to a recent *New York Times* article (Uchitelle, 1993), the glass ceiling is thick for women in economics. Although 22% of all Ph.D.s in economics went to women over the past decade, they represent 20% of all assistant professors, and 8% and less than 4%, respectively, of associate and full professors. Women typically concentrate in the traditionally less prestigious people-oriented specialties (e.g., labor, trade, industrial organization). Perhaps symptomatic of the profession's lack of receptivity toward women is the negative response of the American Economic Association to repeated requests for child care for those attending their annual meetings (Uchitelle, 1993).

24. Although DeWolf et al. (1986) found that the proportion of male sociologists interested in gender studies was very low, it gradually increased between 1975 and 1985.

References

American Association of University Professors. (1992). *The status of non-tenure-track faculty.* Unpublished report, Washington, DC.

American Sociological Association. (1971a, November). Council reacts to reduced funding for graduate students. *Socio-Log, 1,* 1.

American Sociological Association. (1971b, October). Recommendations to improve status of women. *Socio-Log, 1,* 3.

American Sociological Association. (1971c, October). Top NSF social scientist resigns in protest. *Socio-Log, 1,* 2.

American Sociological Association. (1972a, May). Academic salaries losing to the cost of living. *American Sociologist, 7,* 1.

American Sociological Association. (1972b, February). 1973 federal budget revealing for social sciences. *American Sociologist, 7,* 1.

American Sociological Association. (1972c, October). How many are we? *American Sociologist, 7,* 8.

American Sociological Association. (1973a, March). Facts confirm rumors . . . training grants to terminate. *ASA Footnotes, 1.*

American Sociological Association. (1973b, August). Report of the committee on the status of women in sociology. *ASA Footnotes, 1,* 17, 21.

American Sociological Association. (1974a, April). Facts compiled from the directory . . . Non-academic employment of ASA members. *ASA Footnotes, 2,* 1.

American Sociological Association. (1974b, March). Minorities and women. *ASA Footnotes, 2,* 4-5.

American Sociological Association. (1978a, April). Alternative career opportunities outlined by sociologists. *ASA Footnotes, 6,* 1, 6.

American Sociological Association. (1978b, January). Is sociology relevant to the "real" world? Yes, but . . . . *ASA Footnotes, 6,* 1, 7.

American Sociological Association. (1978c, March). Non-academic settings: Breadth and depth needed in graduate training. *ASA Footnotes, 6,* 1, 5.

American Sociological Association. (1978d, February). Non-academic settings: Supportive of research. *ASA Footnotes, 6,* 1, 6.

American Sociological Association. (1981a, October). COSSA to continue budget monitoring. *ASA Footnotes, 9,* 1, 4.

American Sociological Association. (1981b, November). Non-academic employers surveyed. *ASA Footnotes, 9,* 1.

American Sociological Association. (1981c, March). OMB guts NSF social science budget. *ASA Footnotes, 9,* 1, 8-9.

American Sociological Association, Committee on the Freedom of Research and Teaching. (1986). *Guidelines for employment of part-time faculty in departments of sociology* (rev. ed.). Washington, DC: American Sociological Association.

Bannister, R. C. (1991). *Jessie Bernard: The making of a feminist.* New Brunswick, NJ: Rutgers University Press.

Barnes, B. (1973, May). Backlash mounts for women and minorities . . . Reverse bias alleged in college hiring. *ASA Footnotes, 9,* 4.

Beeghley, L., & Van Ausdale, D. (1990, December). Status of women faculty in graduate departments: 1973 and 1988. *ASA Footnotes, 18,* 3, 4.

Beller, A. (1984). Trends in occupational segregation by sex, 1960–1981. In B. F. Reskin (Ed.), *Sex segregation in the workplace: Trends, explanations, remedies* (pp. 11-26). Washington, DC: National Academy of Sciences.

Boffey, P. M. (1974, April 8). U. of Washington threatened with loss of federal contracts. *Chronicle of Higher Education, 8,* 7.

Borgatta, E. F. (1973, December). Affirmative action in action. *ASA Footnotes, 1,* 2, 6.

Borgatta, E. F. (1974, April). Rejoinder to Joan Huber. *ASA Footnotes, 2,* 4.

Boros, A. (1980, May). Applied sociology suggested as best generic term. *ASA Footnotes, 8,* 2.

Cappell, C., & Guterbock, T. (1992). Visible colleges: The social and conceptual structure of sociology specialities. *American Sociological Review, 57,* 266-273.

Carter, M. J., & Carter, S. B. (1981). Women's recent progress in the professions or, women get a ticket to ride after the gravy train has left the station. *Feminist Studies, 7,* 477-504.

Connell, R. W. (1987). *Gender and power: Society, the person and sexual politics.* North Sydney, Australia: Allen & Unwin.

Coughlin, E. K. (1992, August 12). Sociologists confront questions about field's vitality and direction. *Chronicle of Higher Education,* pp. A6-8.

Deegan, M. J. (1978). Women and sociology: 1890–1930. *Journal of the History of Sociology, 1,* 11-32.

Deegan, M. J. (1981, February). Early women sociologists and the American Sociological Society: The patterns of exclusion and participation. *American Sociologist, 16,* 14-24.

Deegan, M. J. (Ed.). (1991). *Women in sociology: A bio-bibliographical sourcebook.* New York: Greenwood.

DeWolf, P. L., Skipper, J. K., Jr., Steed, J., & Alpaugh, C. V. (1986). Gender roles and women's issues as an area of interest among sociologists: 1875–1985. *Sociological Inquiry, 56,* 149-155.

Exum, W. H., Menges, R. J., Watkins, B., & Berglund, P. (1984). Making it at the top: Women and minority faculty in the academic labor market. *American Behavioral Scientist, 27,* 301-324.

Fava, S. F. (1960). The status of women in professional sociology. *American Sociological Review, 25,* 271-276.

Federal laws and regulations concerning sex discrimination in educational institutions. (1972, October 24). *Chronicle of Higher Education,* p. 4.

Fields, C. M. (1974a, September 3). Affirmative action, 4 years after. *Chronicle of Higher Education,* pp. 1, 8-9.

Fields, C. M. (1974b, December 23). Colleges told: Hire the best-qualified. *Chronicle of Higher Education,* pp. 1, 8-9.

Fields, C. M. (1975, June 23). 29 universities warned U.S. may withhold contracts. *Chronicle of Higher Education,* pp. 1, 6.

Finsterbusch, K. (1972, December). The fall and rise of the academic job market for sociologists. *American Sociologist, 7,* 2, 8.

Finsterbusch, K. (1974, December). Academic job market report: Some good news and some bad news. *ASA Footnotes, 2,* 7.

Gerson, J. M., & Peiss, K. (1985). Boundaries, negotiation, consciousness: Reconceptualizing gender relations. *Social Problems, 32,* 317-331.

Gould, M., & Kern-Davies, R. (1977, November). Toward a sociological theory of gender and sex. *American Sociologist, 12,* 182-189.

Graham, P. A. (1970). Women in academe. *Science, 169,* 1284–1290.

Graham, P. A. (1978). Expansion and exclusion: A history of women in American higher education. *Signs, 3,* 759-773.

Hargens, L. L. (1990). Sociologists' assessments of the state of sociology, 1969–1984. *American Sociologist, 22,* 200-208.

Harris, J. R. (1975, January). Women and minorities in sociology: Findings from annual ASA audit. *ASA Footnotes, 3,* 4, 5.

HEW probing alleged employment bias against women on at least 18 campuses. (1970, November 9). *Chronicle of Higher Education,* p. 2.

Hill, R. J. (1973, August). Support and promote affirmative action programs. *ASA Footnotes, 1,* 9.

Hill, R. J. (1983). Minorities, women, and institutional change: Some administrative concerns. *Sociological Perspectives, 26,* 17-28.

Horowitz, I. L. (1992). The decomposition of sociology. *Academic Questions, 5,* 32-40.

Howard, A., Pion, G. M., Gottfredson, G. D., Flattau, P. E., Oskamp, S., Pfafflin, S. M., Bray, D. W., & Burstein, A. G. (1986). The changing face of American psychology: A report from the committee on employment and human resources. *American Psychologist, 41,* 1311–1327.

Huber, B. J. (1983, May). Sociological practitioners: Their characteristics and role in the profession. *ASA Footnotes, 11,* 6-8.

Huber, B. J. (1985). *Employment patterns in sociology: Recent trends and future prospects.* Washington, DC: American Sociological Association.

Huber, B. J. (1988, May). The status of minorities and women within ASA. *ASA Footnotes, 16,* 4, 8.

Huber, J. (1974, April). Comment on Edgar Borgatta, Affirmative action in action. *ASA Footnotes, 2,* 4.

Hughes, H. M. (Ed.). (1973). *The status of women in sociology, 1968–1972.* Washington, DC: American Sociological Association.

Jackson, M. (1972, October). Minorities and women in sociology: Are opportunities changing? *American Sociologist, 7,* 3-5.

Jackson, M. (1973, December). Affirmative action—Affirmative results? *ASA Footnotes, 1,* 3-4.

Jacobs, J. (1989). Long-term trends in occupational sex segregation. *American Journal of Sociology, 95,* 160-173.

Jankowski, J. (1992). *Memorandum regarding deflating R&D expenditures.* Unpublished memorandum dated March 16, 1992, National Science Foundation.

Kulis, S. (1988). The representation of women in top ranked sociology departments. *American Sociologist, 19,* 203-217.

Kulis, S., & Miller, K. A. (1988). Are minority women sociologists in double jeopardy? *American Sociologist, 19,* 323-339.

Kulis, S., Miller, K. A., Axelrod, M., & Gordon, L. (1986). Minorities and women in the Pacific Sociological Association region: A five-year progress report. *Sociological Perspectives, 29,* 147-170.

Logan, A. A. (1970, July 6). Universities told they must grant equal opportunity to women. *Chronicle of Higher Education,* p. 5.

Lorber, J. (1992, Fall). *From the chair* (ASA section on sex and gender newsletter). Washington, DC: American Sociological Association.

Lorch, B. R. (1973, August). Reverse discrimination in hiring in sociology departments: A preliminary report. *American Sociologist, 8,* 116-120.

Lynch, F. R. (1992, August). *Affirmative action's amazing grace: Challenging sociology's church of PC.* Paper presented at the Annual Meetings of the American Sociological Association, Pittsburgh.

McGinnis, R., & Solomon, L. (1973, May). Employment prospects for Ph.D. sociologists during the seventies. *American Sociologist, 8,* 57-63.

Menges, R. J., & Exum, W. H. (1983). Barriers to the progress of women and minority faculty. *Journal of Higher Education, 54,* 123-144.

Miller, K. A., Kulis, S., Gordon, L., & Axelrod, M. (1988a, April). Representation of women in U.S. sociology departments. *ASA Footnotes, 16,* 3.

Miller, K. A., Kulis, S., Gordon, L., & Axelrod, M. (1988b, November). Women's representation among graduate students in sociology. *ASA Footnotes, 16,* 8.

Morgan, J. G. (1980). Women in American sociology in the 19th century. *Journal of the History of Sociology, 2,* 1-34.

Motz, A. B. (1974, April). The challenge of new roles for sociologists in academic and non-academic settings. *ASA Footnotes, 2,* 2-3.

National Research Council. (1992). [Number of doctorates awarded in the United States, by fine field and sex, 1970–79 (Survey of Earned Doctorates)]. Unpublished data.

National Research Council. (1993a). [Number of doctorates awarded in the United States, by fine field and sex, 1970–79 (Survey of Earned Doctorates)]. Unpublished data.

National Research Council. (1993b). *Summary report 1991: Doctorate recipients from United States universities.* Washington, DC: National Academy Press.

National Research Council, Commission on Human Resources. (1980). [Doctorate recipients from United States universities by fine field of doctorate, sex and year of doctorate, 1958–1979]. Unpublished tables.

National Research Council, Office of Scientific Personnel. (1973). [Doctorates awarded from 1920 to 1971 by subfield of doctorate, sex, and decade]. Unpublished tables.

National Science Foundation. (1981). *Academic science, 1972–81: R&D funds, scientists and engineers, graduate enrollment and support.* Washington, DC: U.S. Government Printing Office.

National Science Foundation. (1985). *Academic science/engineering: Scientists and engineers.* Washington, DC: U.S. Government Printing Office.

National Science Foundation. (1987). *Federal funds for research and development: Fiscal years 1986, 1987, 1988,* Vol. 36. Washington, DC: U.S. Government Printing Office.

National Science Foundation. (1990). *Academic science and engineering: Graduate enrollment and support, Fall 1989.* Washington, DC: U.S. Government Printing Office.

National Science Foundation. (1991). *Characteristics of doctoral scientists and engineers in the United States: 1989, detailed statistical tables* (NSF 91-317). Washington, DC: U.S. Government Printing Office.

Nigg, J., & Axelrod, M. (1981). Women and minorities in the PSA region: Results of the 1979 survey. *Pacific Sociological Review, 24,* 107-128.

Patterson, M. (1971, August). Alice in wonderland: A study of women faculty in graduate departments of sociology. *American Sociologist, 6,* 226-234.

Perrucci, R., O'Flaherty, K., & Marshall, H. (1983). Market conditions, productivity, and promotion among university faculty. *Research in Higher Education, 19,* 431-449.

Prewitt, K., & Sills, D. L. (1981, December). Federal funding for the social sciences: Threats and responses. *ASA Footnotes, 9,* 4-8.

Reskin, B. F. (1991). Labor markets as queues: A structural approach to changing occupational sex composition. In J. Huber (Ed.), *Macro-micro linkages in sociology* (pp. 170-191). Newbury Park, CA: Sage.

Reskin, B. F., & Roos, P. A. (1990). *Job queues, gender queues: Explaining women's inroads into male occupations.* Philadelphia: Temple University Press.

Rhoades, L. J. (1979, November). Study reports trouble ahead for university research. *ASA Footnotes, 7,* 1, 4.

Rhoades, L. J. (1980, March). Federal funding level for social/behavioral sciences indicates low national priority. *ASA Footnotes, 8,* 4, 5.

Rhoades, L. J. (1981). *A history of the American Sociological Association, 1905-1980.* Washington, DC: American Sociological Association.

Roos, P. A. (1993). *Gender switch in the printing industry.* Unpublished manuscript, Rutgers University.

Rossi, A. S. (1970, February). Status of women in graduate departments of sociology, 1968-1969. *American Sociologist, 5,* 1-11.

Segura, D., & Jewell, K. S. (1990, December). Unique barriers women of color faculty encounter. *ASA Footnotes, 18,* 3, 9.

Semas, P. W. (1971, November 15). File an acceptable equal-employment plan or lose U.S. contracts, Columbia told. *Chronicle of Higher Education,* p. 5.

Sewell, W. H. (1975, May). Sewell responds to Proxmire on NSF funding of basic research. *ASA Footnotes, 3,* 2.

Stacey, J., & Thorne, B. (1985). The missing feminist revolution in sociology. *Social Problems, 32,* 301-316.

Tuckman, H. P., Caldwell, J., & Vogler, W. (1978, November). Part-timers and the academic labor market of the eighties. *American Sociologist, 13,* 184-195.

Turner, S. P., & Turner, J. H. (1990). *The impossible science: An institutional analysis of American sociology.* Newbury Park, CA: Sage.

Uchitelle, L. (1993, January 11). In economics, a subtle exclusion. *New York Times,* p. D1.

U.S. announces job-bias rules for colleges. (1972, October 10). *Chronicle of Higher Education,* pp. 1-2.

U.S. Department of Education. (1991). *Digest of education statistics: 1990.* Washington, DC: U.S. Department of Education, Office of Educational Research and Improvement, National Center for Education Statistics.

Van Arsdale, G. (1978, November). De-professionalizing a part-time teaching faculty: How many, feeling small, seeming few, getting less, dream of more. *American Sociologist, 13,* 195-201.

Van Dyne, L. (1973, February 5). Colleges' white men assail "preference" for minorities. *Chronicle of Higher Education,* p. 4.

Ward, K. B., & Grant, L. (1985). The feminist critique and a decade of published research in sociology journals. *Sociological Quarterly, 26,* 139-157.

Ward, K. B., & Grant, L. (1991). On a wavelength of their own? Women and sociological theory. In *Current Perspectives in Social Theory* (Vol. 11, pp. 117-140). Greenwich, CT: JAI Press.

Weidlein, E. R. (1973, August 27). Affirmative action has little impact on faculty hiring, study shows. *Chronicle of Higher Education,* pp. 1, 4.

Whitt, J. A., & Derber, C. (1979, November). Problem of professional nomads needs attention. *ASA Footnotes, 7,* 2.

Wilkinson, D. (1980a, March). Federal employment for sociologists? *ASA Footnotes, 8,* 4.

Wilkinson, D. (1980b, October). Skills assessment: Marketing our assets. *ASA Footnotes, 8,* 3.

Williams, P. R. (1982, December). Minorities and women in sociology: An update. *ASA Footnotes, 10,* 6-8.

Women Ph.D.s hurt more than men by job shortage, survey shows. (1971, January 11). *Chronicle of Higher Education,* p. 4.

Wright, R. A. (1990, November). Openings in sociology departments, 1984 to 1989. *ASA Footnotes, 18,* 15.

12

Male Flight From Computer Work

A New Look at Occupational Resegregation and Ghettoization

ROSEMARY WRIGHT
JERRY A. JACOBS

Does the sustained entry of significant numbers of women into an occupation precipitate a decline in status of that occupation? Does feminization inevitably result in occupational resegregation? Once the process of feminization has commenced, is ghettoization—the emergence of a highly internally stratified occupation—the only alternative to resegregation? We address these questions by examining one feminizing occupation—computer work.

Social scientists have vigorously debated the significance of recent changes in the economic status of women, and their observations point to both continuity and change. For example, although the sex gap in earnings has narrowed in the last decade, women working full-time, full-year

AUTHORS' NOTE: Authorship is shared equally. Address correspondence to Rosemary Wright, 10 Woods Lane, Chatham, NJ 07928. An earlier draft of this chapter was presented at the annual meeting of the Society for the Advancement of Socio-Economics, New York, March 1993, and the same material was published in *American Sociological Review,* August, 1994. This research was funded in part by a fellowship to Jerry A. Jacobs from the Russell Sage Foundation. We thank Paul Allison, Elaine Hall, Robin Leidner, Brian Powell, Vicki Smith, Ronnie J. Steinberg, Pamela Stone, Harrison White, and anonymous *ASR* reviewers for their helpful comments and suggestions.

still earn, on average, only 75% as much as their male counterparts. Moreover, about half of the narrowing of the gap has resulted from a decline in men's real earnings rather than from an increase in women's real earnings (Institute for Women's Policy Research, 1993).

Analysts have also drawn differing conclusions from the decline in the sex segregation of occupations in the last two decades: After remaining steady for most of the century, the proportion of employed women who would have had to change their occupations in order for women to be distributed in the same manner as men declined by roughly 18% during the 1970s and 1980s. Specifically, the index of dissimilarity by sex across detailed census occupational categories declined from 67 in 1970 to 55 in 1990. Women's entry into prominent male-dominated fields such as law and medicine has been especially widely heralded. Yet, for every woman who works as a lawyer, there are 170 women clerical workers, 50 women sales clerks, 20 waitresses, and 15 female nurse's aides (Jacobs, 1989a; Jacobsen, 1994; U.S. Bureau of Labor Statistics, 1989).[1] Women are still a long way from achieving integration with men at the workplace.

The resegregation thesis is one of the most intriguing interpretations of recent changes in women's occupational standing. It holds that women's entry into previously male-dominated occupations is not a stable outcome, but rather represents one phase in a process that generally ends in the reestablishment of sex-segregated work roles. Reskin and Roos (1990, hereafter, Reskin & Roos) present the most developed analysis of the resegregation process. They examine 14 cases in which, during the 1970s, women made significant inroads into previously male-dominated occupations; 11 cases are presented in their book, *Job Queues, Gender Queues.*[2] These case studies draw on a variety of historical, institutional, and documentary materials, as well as analyses of aggregated data on earnings trends for these occupations.

Reskin and Roos find a common pattern—that a shortage of male employees prompts employers to recruit women. The shortage of men is typically due to a decline in the status of the occupation, but it is sometimes compounded by a rapid increase in demand. In some cases, the impetus for the initial departure of men from an occupation is a technological shift that lowers skill levels and earnings in the field. Reskin and Roos also find that women are often concentrated in the least desirable niches in these occupations—niches with lower pay, fewer required skills, less autonomy, and limited promotion opportunities. Thus their analysis suggests that women's entry into previously male-dominated occupations frequently does not yield the degree of economic progress for women that we might expect.

Reskin and Roos's work, along with studies by a number of other scholars in this area (Cohn, 1985; Davies, 1982; Strober, 1984), raises the question of whether it is possible for women to successfully integrate a single occupation, let alone the labor force as a whole. These studies outline two processes—resegregation, where an occupation reverses from male-dominated to female-dominated, and ghettoization, where women become concentrated in low-status specialties within the occupation. In this chapter we examine these two processes in the context of computer work, an occupation that is becoming feminized. We use individual-level panel data that allow us to see who stayed, who left, and why. This study represents the first test of the resegregation/ghettoization hypotheses with microlevel data. We repeat our analysis for two computer specialties—systems analysis, a specialty studied by Reskin and Roos, and computer programming, historically the computer specialty with the greatest female representation.

We begin by outlining the logic underlying the processes of resegregation and ghettoization. We then develop six hypotheses regarding these processes. In some cases, these hypotheses flow rather directly from previous research in this area. In others, we had to draw out previously unarticulated implications of the literature in order to develop empirical tests. Using data from a variety of sources, we test these hypotheses by analyzing the career moves of computer workers during the 1980s.

Feminization and Resegregation

We define a *feminizing occupation* as one in which the representation of women is increasing. At first, feminization in a previously male-dominated field results in the occupation moving closer to parity with women's representation in the labor force as a whole—moving toward greater integration. If the representation of women continues to increase, surpassing the labor force average, we refer to the occupation as "resegregating"—becoming significantly more skewed in favor of women. Thus far, our usage follows Reskin and Roos, who refer to an occupation as resegregated "when an entire occupation or a major occupational specialty switches from a predominantly male to a predominantly female labor force" (p. 71).

The term "resegregating," however, has implications not only for women's representation, but also for the relative economic standing of men and women. As we define the term, resegregation implies that a newly feminized occupation is not as economically attractive as it had previously been. This devaluation can occur before or during the process of feminization. In contrast, movement toward real economic integration implies that an occupation maintains or even increases its economic attractiveness.

Combining these ideas produces a profile of a *resegregating occupation* that is characterized by two trends that run counter to gender equality:

1. Women, initially an underrepresented minority, continue to gain in number until the occupation becomes significantly skewed in favor of women rather than men.
2. The economic standing of the occupation relative to the labor force declines.

The decline in status sometimes precedes women's entry, as Reskin and Roos find, or it may coincide with and follow women's entry, as others have suggested (Strober, 1984).

What forces cause resegregation? One hypothesis is that men flee an occupation when they see the status of the occupation declining. This argument is central to Reskin and Roos's discussion of the queuing process that facilitates the feminization of previously male-dominated occupations:

> Most of the occupations or specialties we studied experienced a shortage of male workers during the 1970s not because they grew dramatically but because their rewards or working conditions deteriorated relative to other occupations for which male workers qualified, making them less attractive to male workers. (p. 42)

The status of the occupation might decline for many reasons, including technological change, organizational change, the rise of competition, the decline of union power, and other factors.

This perspective maintains that an occupation is frequently already in decline before women enter it in large numbers. The decline in its status prompts some men working in the occupation to leave and discourages other men from entering the occupation. The departure of large numbers of male incumbents from an occupation—which we refer to as "male flight"—plays a significant role in the resegregation process by magnifying the need for a new pool of workers. Employers, seeking to fill empty employment slots, recruit women. Although many factors are related to the decline in the desirability of an occupation to men, a leading cause is the decline in earnings. Reskin and Roos (1990) maintain that "a primary reason the occupations we studied failed to draw or retain enough men was that their earnings declined during the 1970s, relative to those of the male labor force as a whole" (p. 44).

A second hypothesis is that feminization itself can contribute to male flight from an occupation: Men may flee in response to women's entry because of deteriorating earnings, the stigma associated with doing "women's work," or both. First, feminization results in decreased earnings, which produces the economic motivation for male flight, as described above. A number of students of gender stratification have argued that feminization per se tempts employers to reduce wages. Strober (1984), for example, maintains that "once an occupation becomes a female occupation, employers will often lower its wage rate" (p. 149). Studies of comparable worth have demonstrated a tendency for female-dominated jobs and occupations to be paid less than male-dominated positions with similar educational requirements, job demands, and working conditions (England, 1992; Jacobs & Steinberg, 1990). Men may flee in response to women's entry because they anticipate that earnings will decline as feminization proceeds. Second, feminization may result in male flight because of the social stigma associated with working with women. Strober (1984) is unambiguous about this: "But men are reluctant to enter female occupations, primarily because of their low wages but also because they fear ridicule by other men and aspersions on their masculinity if they do" (p. 150).

Male flight is only one part—albeit an important part—of the resegregation process. It is logically possible for an occupation to become resegregated through a process of cohort replacement. Men already in an occupation might stay, whereas prospective entrants might choose other pursuits. Such a process would require several decades. However, none of the literature to date describes occupational resegregation as relying solely, or even principally, on cohort change. Moreover, the factors that deter young men from entering an occupation are presumably the same factors that prompt older men to leave it, although the two groups might not be equally susceptible to these factors.

The process of occupational resegregation is analogous to the process of invasion and succession that underlies residential segregation (Massey & Denton 1993; Reskin & Roos, 1990, p. 314). In both cases, the dominant group fears the loss of social status and economic position they believe will result from the growing presence of a socially devalued group. For white home owners, the fear is that the arrival of African Americans will lower property values and result in a decline in the standing of a neighborhood. The question addressed here is whether the same process contributes to the flight of men from feminizing occupations.

Ghettoization Versus Integration

Reskin and Roos's research is often associated with the notion of occupational resegregation, but in fact, the outcome in 9 of the 11 cases they discuss in their book was ghettoization rather than resegregation. Reskin and Roos define ghettoization as occurring "when women and men in the same occupational title typically perform different jobs" (p. 71). The disparate placement of men and women within an occupation results in women not achieving parity with men. For example, in the case of bakers, women mostly work in supermarkets baking prepackaged dough, while men continue to monopolize the more skilled positions in bakeries.

In some ways, the ghettoization of an occupation is the specialty-specific counterpart of occupational resegregation. In other words, in this case, it is a specialty, rather than the occupation as a whole, that undergoes resegregation. Although in principle the growth of an already feminized subspecialty can account for the ghettoization of an occupation, typically some specialties will become increasingly feminized, whereas others will see women enter in large numbers for the first time. We expect that the same processes that operate in explaining the feminization of an occupation account for the feminization of a specialty within an occupation.

Reskin and Roos note that ghettoization draws on differentiation in rewards between occupational specialties—differentiation that predated women's entry. However, they do not specify whether the inequality in rewards between specialties within an occupation grows or declines following women's entry. We maintain that this difference is theoretically important. If internal stratification increases as an occupation feminizes, then women's opportunities are undercut just when they are poised to seize them. On the other hand, if internal stratification declines as women enter, then the entry of women coincides with a reduction in existing sex stratification within an occupation. In the latter case, women not only grow in numbers, but at the same time receive rewards closer to those received by their male counterparts.

Our view stresses the trend in the status of women in the occupation during the period of feminization. In contrast, Reskin and Roos define ghettoization by contrasting it with a standard of genuine integration, which characterizes an occupation as truly integrated only if women "integrated all specialties within a desegregating occupation and if they found work in all industries in which the occupation is located and all establishments that employ occupational incumbents" (p. 71).

Although we agree with Reskin and Roos on the objective of complete equality, we believe ghettoization should be assessed in terms of trends, rather than in terms of this absolute standard. It is useful to distinguish cases where ghettoization is becoming more severe as a result of the entrance of large numbers of women from cases in which ghettoization is becoming more attenuated over time. We are not aware of any occupation in which women have achieved complete integration or complete economic equality. Nevertheless, we can differentiate occupations that are moving toward equality from those that are becoming more unequal. Thus, we focus on trends rather than on static measures because we want to assess the direction of change. This approach enables us to use the level of inequality in an occupation prior to the significant entry of women as a baseline for assessing change. In this way we can assess both the causes and consequences of increasing numbers of women in an occupation.

In our view, the following characteristics identify a *ghettoizing occupation:*

1. Women's representation in an occupation is not becoming so skewed that the entire occupation is becoming significantly female-dominated.

2. Women are increasingly concentrated in a limited number of specialties within the occupation, and these specialties may be becoming dominated by women. (An indicator of this trend is that the level of sex segregation within the occupation is increasing.)

3. The female-dominated specialties are lower in status than other specialties in the occupation, and their status is not increasing relative to the status of

other specialties. (One important indicator of relative status is relative salary, but other indicators, such as authority, prestige, skills, and promotion opportunities are also relevant.)

4. The sex gap in earnings within the occupation is constant or growing.

An *integrating occupation* implies several egalitarian trends, contrasting sharply with the trends described by resegregation and ghettoization:

1. Women's representation is moving toward parity.
2. Women are increasingly evenly distributed across industries and specialties within an occupation. In other words, the index of segregation is constant or decreasing. (This trend is just the opposite of ghettoization.)
3. The sex gap in earnings within the occupation is narrowing.
4. The economic standing of the occupation relative to the labor force as a whole is holding steady or improving.

In an integrating occupation, women are moving in the direction of economic parity within the occupation, which has the net effect of improving women's earnings relative to men in the labor force as a whole. The movement may be too slow for many reformers and may never be completely realized, but these criteria can distinguish trends in occupations.

Hypotheses

Resegregation

The first premise of the resegregation thesis is that a decline in the status of an occupation results in an exodus of men. We focus here on earnings—one prominent indicator of occupational status. We use the term *favorability ratio* to mean the ratio of earnings in an occupation to alternative earnings in other occupations in the labor force. Our first hypothesis is:

H_1: When men's earnings decline relative to alternative occupations in the labor force, men's exit rates from an occupation increase. Conversely, an increase in this favorability ratio reduces men's occupational exit rates.

A more general interpretation of queuing theory suggests a related hypothesis for both male and female exits. The exit rates for both men and women should depend on the changes in the favorability ratios for each—their earnings in a given occupation compared to their relevant alternatives in the labor force. For example, if the attractiveness of an occupation improves greatly in comparison to women's alternatives, while its attractiveness relative to men's alternatives remains unchanged, we would expect women's exit rates to decline relative to men's. If men's prospects in an occupation decline while women's remain unchanged, men's exit rates would be expected to increase. Note that for male flight to contribute significantly to resegregation, men's exits must exceed women's exits. Thus, our second hypothesis states:

> H_2: The male-female differential in exits parallels the difference in an occupation's attractiveness to men and women, relative to men's and women's occupational alternatives. (Men's exits exceed women's when their favorability ratio declines faster than women's favorability ratio.)

Our third hypothesis draws on the notion that women's entry per se prompts male flight.

> H_3: The more women enter an occupation, the more men leave. (The greater the proportion of women entering, the greater the proportion of men leaving.)

These hypotheses on resegregation are not sufficient to completely characterize career transitions because occupational exits take many forms: career switches out of computer work, moves into management, job losses (exits to unemployment), and exits from the labor force. The male flight prediction refers to overall attrition, yet there may be substantial sex differences in each specific exit process. These may reinforce one another, or they may cancel each other out. Consequently, we test the male flight thesis on aggregate exits, as well as on each separate type of exit.

Ghettoization

As noted above, the causal mechanisms responsible for ghettoization at the specialty level parallel those that produce resegregation at the occupational level. In other words, the process of male flight and female entry also pertains to those low-status specialties within an occupation that women are more likely to enter. Thus, our first three hypotheses regarding ghettoization are the same as resegregation Hypotheses 1, 2, and 3, except that we apply them to specialties within an occupation.

We propose three additional hypotheses for ghettoization. They involve the relative statuses of male-dominated and female-dominated specialties and how these statuses change with the feminization of an occupation. Ghettoization implies that women are increasingly represented in those segments of an occupation that have low and declining status. We rely principally on income to define status, although we examine data on specific work activities, as well. Sex segregation may also take a number of different forms, including segregation by specialty, industry, or work activity. Our fourth and fifth hypotheses are thus:

H4: As an occupation feminizes, women's representation increases in the low-status specialties, industries, and work activities within that occupation.

H5: Sustained entry of women into an occupation increases sex segregation within that occupation.

If, as Hypothesis 4 proposes, women generally enter low-status specialties in an occupation, then the gender gap in earnings within an occupation would increase as men increasingly monopolize the high-status specialties and leave the low-status ones for women. The growing segregation posited by Hypothesis 5 would also lead to increased earnings inequality between men and women. Our sixth hypothesis thus states:

H6: Ghettoization results in an increase in gender inequality in earnings and/or other rewards within an occupation.

The Feminization of Computer Work

We test our hypotheses using computer work as a case study. Currently, 32% of men and 43% of women in the labor force use a computer at work (U.S. Bureau of the Census, 1991a), but by our definition, not all of these are "computer workers." Following Hughes's (1971) dictum that function defines occupation, we use the Association for Computing Machinery's definition of computer professional: A computer worker is someone whose main function is to support *other* people's use of computer systems (Denning, 1991). On this basis, we include computer programmers, systems analysts, and computer scientists. We also include computer and systems engineers, for reasons given below.

Computer work represents a good test case of the hypotheses listed above for two principal reasons. First, it is a rapidly feminizing occupation. Women have become increasingly represented in computer work since at least 1971 (as we will see below in Figure 12.1)—women composed 36% of computer workers in 1991, up from 15% in 1971. Thus, computer work is a recently feminizing occupation that allows us to investigate its feminization processes. Second, leading analysts (Donato, 1990; Strober & Arnold, 1987) have claimed that computer work is a case conforming to the model. A reanalysis of such a case is an appropriate test of the perspective that resegregation and ghettoization are the outcomes of feminization.

The case study of systems analysts in the Reskin and Roos book attributes women's increasing representation in computer work to a number of factors, including the expansion of employer demand for computer workers (Donato, 1990). Nonetheless, Donato argues that declining earnings relative to the labor force as a whole during the 1970s dampened men's interest in this area and helped pave the way for women's entry:

> Women's greater representation in systems analysis . . . also resulted from a shortage of men able to meet the growing demand for computer specialists. Women's entry was spurred by sex stereotypes about male and female workers and by changes in the nature of the occupation and its technology that appear related to declining occupational rewards. Men responded to the last of these by leaving the computer field, thus helping to accelerate the demand for women workers. (Donato, 1990, p. 181)

Thus, Donato posits that declining earnings contributed to male flight for this particular specialty. She concludes that in the 1970s, systems analysis did not become a resegregated, female-dominated occupation, but rather that women became ghettoized in low-status industries with fewer economic and prestige rewards. "As women increasingly entered the field, they tended to be segregated into lower-paid specialties, while men monopolized the higher-paid jobs" (Donato, 1990, p. 182).

Strober and Arnold (1987), other leading analysts of gender and occupational resegregation, also consider the case of computer work and include a much wider array of computer specialties than did Donato. They show that men predominate in high-status specialties, such as electrical engineering, whereas women are concentrated in low-status occupations, such as data entry. They find a significant sex gap in wages, with women earning about 70% of their male counterparts. They also show that men and women are unequally distributed across industries— women are more likely to be employed in end-user industries than in computer manufacturing. Strober and Arnold's results are clearly consistent with a finding of ghettoization, as Reskin and Roos use this term. They conclude: "High tech may produce integrated circuits, but it does not necessarily produce an integrated work force or eliminate the female/male earnings differential" (Strober & Arnold, 1987, p. 172). However, their analyses are not specifically set up to test hypotheses regarding the resegregation and ghettoization processes. For example, they do not explore whether earnings declines precipitated the entry of women into such fields as computer programming and systems analysis. Further, their data do not allow them to test whether male flight is associated with women's entry.

Three other studies provide additional documentation of gender inequality across computer specialties (Donato & Roos, 1987; Glenn & Tolbert, 1987; Kraft & Dubnoff, 1983), although Arnold (1988) was unable to detect substantial gender inequality among recent computer science graduates of a California community college. Thus there is substantial evidence for the existence of gender inequality in computer work. The question addressed here is not whether gender inequality exists, but whether the changes occurring conform to the resegregation and ghettoization processes.

Several other considerations make computer work an especially interesting case. First, computer work is a relatively new field, having come into existence during World War II (Kraft, 1977). That computer work is a new field makes it appealing for the study of gender stereotyping, because it does not have a long history of being labeled "men's work" or "women's work." Although the newness of computer work may limit the generalizability of this case study, gender stereotyping in computer work borrows heavily from its occupational progenitor, electrical engineering. The experiences of women in computer work may thus be directly relevant for understanding women's progress in a variety of technically oriented, male-dominated professions, such as engineering, biotechnology, architecture, and finance.

Second, computer work's large size and rapid growth suggest that it is an important case in its own right. Employing one out of every four scientists (National Science Foundation, 1988), two of its specialties— computer programming and systems analysis—make computer work the third-fastest-growing occupation in the United States in the 1990s (Silvestri & Lukasiewicz, 1992).

Finally, computer work is simultaneously characterized by growth in demand and obsolescence of skills. Technology has changed constantly throughout the 50 years of computer work's existence. Computer workers have been required to thoroughly reskill through at least three major paradigm shifts, as well as partially reskill because of frequent changes in software, hardware, and programming philosophies (Abbott, 1988). Employers and employees are both faced with continually changing sets of required skills—skills that are different, not necessarily lesser: Studies conducted in the 1980s (Kuhn, 1989; Orlikowski, 1988; Tarallo, 1987) refute earlier claims of deskilling in computer work (Greenbaum, 1979; Kraft, 1977). In this fast-changing occupation, therefore, the number of jobs requiring new skills is rapidly growing, at the same time that the number of jobs requiring old skills is shrinking.

Under Reskin and Roos's queueing approach, employers rank men ahead of women for jobs in traditionally male occupations. In rapidly growing occupations, employers cannot find enough men to fill open positions and turn to women; in occupations with declining economic rewards, men leave jobs for alternatives in the labor force, opening the way for women. We argue that computer work meets both of these criteria: As computer jobs open up that require new skills, there should be an insufficient number of men to fill them. As the number of computer jobs that require old skills decrease, the earnings of men in those jobs should drop relative to their alternatives in the labor force. If the queueing model advanced by Reskin and Roos applies, we should see male flight from the old-skill computer jobs at the same time that we should see too few men available for the new-skill computer jobs.

Data and Methods

We marshal data from a variety of sources. Data on trends in the sex composition of computer specialties are drawn from the U.S. Bureau of Labor Statistics (1976-1992), which also provided data on the earnings of computer workers and the civilian labor force. Data on degrees received in computer science and engineering are from Vetter (1991, 1992) and the U. S. Department of Education (1992).

The bulk of our analysis examines microlevel data from the National Science Foundation's Survey of Natural and Social Scientists and Engineers (SSE). The SSE data set contains career histories of 46,049 scientists and engineers who were sampled as part of the 1980 Census and surveyed again in 1982, 1984, 1986, and 1989 (U.S. Bureau of the Census, 1991b). NSF stratified the sample to ensure sufficient numbers of women, computer specialists, and engineers. They defined scientists and engineers as individuals having a scientific, engineering, or related occupation, having 4 or more years of college (2, if engineering), and being in the experienced civilian labor force or "labor reserve" (National Science Foundation, 1984).[3]

We view computer work as a single occupation, because it is one occupation from a functional standpoint (Hughes, 1971) and from the standpoint of computer workers themselves (Denning, 1991). One indicator of this internal coherence of computer work is that it is especially difficult to demarcate specialties (Orlikowski, 1988). Debons, King, Mansfield, and Shirey (1981) illustrate this difficulty when they discover more than 300 job titles for computer professionals in a national survey of employers in the late 1970s. They report great difficulty in categorizing those job titles. Many computer workers' job and occupational titles are assigned to the residual category "not elsewhere classified" or its equivalent. A joint report of the Computer Science and Telecommunications Board and the Office of Scientific and Engineering Personnel of the National Research Council discusses this problem at length (Steering Committee on Human Resources in Computer Science and Technology, 1993, pp. 12-19).

Combining computer workers into a single field assures that we will capture the respondent as a computer worker, even if we can't be sure which specialty he or she would have chosen. Although management analysts sometimes exclude engineers (Orlikowski, 1988), the many close ties between computer science and engineering lead us to include engineers who provide computer support to others (Steering Committee on Human Resources in Computer Science and Technology, 1993). In fact, the field of computer science is an outgrowth of electrical engineering, and most computer science programs are in engineering schools (Abbott, 1988; Kraft, 1977).[4]

We include seven computer specialties or suboccupations in our analysis: computer programmer, computer systems analyst, other systems analyst, systems engineer, computer scientist, computer engineer, and other computer specialist.[5] This definition yields 6,162 respondents who declared a computer specialty in at least one of the four waves: Between 3,500 and 3,900 (of whom roughly 25% were women) were employed in computer work in each of the 4 survey years.[6] The numbers of respondents in our tables depend on the specific data and employment statuses required for each analysis. For certain key analyses, we test our results on each of these seven computer specialties; we report results for two particularly interesting cases, computer systems analysts and computer programmers. We also test whether engineering specialists and computer workers with engineering degrees differ in the patterns we report here.

As is the case with all panel data, the SSE is subject to attrition from wave to wave. The successive SSE response rates in 1982, 1984, 1986, and 1989 were 71%, 73%, 87%, and 83%, respectively (U.S. Bureau of the Census, 1991b). The cumulative attrition, consequently, is quite substantial. We do not think the sample attrition affects our results because we obtained virtually identical results when our analysis was restricted to the 1982 to 1984 period.

We examine four types of exits from computer work (exits overall, exits due to a career switch, exits into management, and exits from the labor force) for men and women for each of the four survey periods. As discussed above, separating each type of exit enables us to analyze the pattern of male departures in detail.

Our multivariate analysis considers whether gender differences in exits from computer work are due to factors other than gender itself. Each transition is treated as a separate case. Exits from each of the three transition periods are pooled into a single analysis. We test whether the exit rate is constant across the three periods of analysis. We also estimate the determinants of each of the four exit types separately. The effects of independent variables are estimated in logistic regression analyses.

Control variables in the analysis include several productivity-related measures and some indicators of the social composition of computer workers. We include the respondent's age, years of experience,[7] highest degree completed (none, associate degree, bachelor's degree, master's degree, M.B.A. degree, or professional/Ph.D. degree), and major field of study (computer science, business, engineering, math sciences, other technical field, nontechnical field). Other variables we include are the respondent's race (white, African American, Asian, other),[8] marital status (married, not married), and the presence of children in the home (two measures: children under age 6 and children between ages 6 and 17). We also include measures of the seven computer specialties (noted above) and seven broad industry categories (manufacturing, professional services, finance/insurance, utilities, education, government, and other). Appendix A gives 1984 values for these variables.[9]

Results

Resegregation

Earnings Comparisons. We begin our analysis by comparing the earnings of computer workers to earnings in the labor force as a whole, following the procedure employed by Reskin and Roos (1990). In Table 12.1, we compare earnings for full-time SSE computer specialists by sex to their counterparts across the labor force.[10] We also present ratios for earnings per year of education (the ratio of two ratios, as the name suggests), again following Reskin and Roos. For all survey years, male computer specialists earned well above the average male in the labor force (1.74 times as much in 1982, 1.84 times as much in 1989). Thus, women's entry into computer work did not coincide with a decline in men's earnings. The earnings advantage has remained; but the advantage is lower when earnings per year of education is the measure employed.

These data do not support the notion of declining attractiveness, which Donato (1990) claims has contributed to the feminization of systems analysis. Men may not have had an economic impetus to flee computer work, either prior to or in response to women's entry. Nevertheless, yearly fluctuations in the economic advantage of men in computer work enable us to test whether changes in men's *relative economic status* are related to their flight from computer work. The earnings ratio for men during the period studied ranged from a high of 1.84 to a low of 1.66. Female computer specialists boasted an even higher earnings ratio compared to the female labor force (2.46 in 1982, 2.49 in 1989). The education-adjusted ratios also remained higher for women than for men. On strictly economic grounds, then, one would expect computer work to be quite attractive to women workers.[11]

Although the economic status of computer work did not change dramatically during the 1980s, the proportion of women continually increased. Women's representation among computer workers grew 3.8 percentage points between 1982 and 1984, 2.1 percentage points between 1984 and 1986, and .4 percentage points between 1986 and 1989.[12] Women's representation increased for each of the three time periods examined. Hypotheses 1 and 2 predict that changes in relative earnings drive exits from computer work; Hypothesis 3 predicts that feminization also drives male exits. Although the earnings stimulus is limited to year-to-year variability rather than a sustained decline, the feminization impetus is clearly present throughout this period.

Table 12.1 Labor Force Earnings Ratios: Computer Workers From the SSE, 1982 to 1989

Earnings Ratio	Computer Men to Male Labor Force[a]				Computer Women to Female Labor Force[b]			
	1982	1984	1986	1989	1982	1984	1986	1989
Labor force earnings[c]	1.74	1.80	1.66	1.84	2.46	2.54	2.39	2.49
Labor force earnings to education[d]	1.30	1.35	1.25	1.39	1.95	2.02	1.80	1.99
Reference earnings[e]	20,336	22,643	25,296	28,291	12,013	13,666	15,425	18,253
Reference years of education[f]	12.7	12.8	12.8	12.8	12.7	12.7	12.8	12.8
Number of cases	2,671	2,689	2,631	2,532	822	792	748	688

a. Ratios directly correspond to those in Table 2.2, page 45, of Reskin and Roos.
b. Ratios directly correspond to those in Table 2.4, page 62, of Reskin and Roos.
c. Ratio of mean earnings of full-time respondents on the SSE to reference earnings in table.
d. Numerators are mean earnings divided by median years of education of full-time respondents on the SSE; denominators are reference earnings divided by reference years of education.
e. Mean earnings of male or female full-time wage and salary workers 16 and older (U.S. Bureau of Labor Statistics, unpublished data).
f. Median years of education for male or female members of civilian labor force 16 and older (U.S. Bureau of Labor Statistics, unpublished data). 1988 values used for 1989 due to change of bureau's method.

Exit Rates. Table 12.2 compares data on exit rates for men and women. Overall, in each of the three periods examined, men were more likely to leave computer work than were women. This finding is consistent with the notion of resegregation: Disproportionate male attrition reinforces the tendency of an occupation to become female-dominated, whereas disproportionate female attrition inhibits the feminization of an occupation.

Table 12.2 also shows year-to-year fluctuations in exit rates and earnings ratios for men and women. This analysis focuses on Hypotheses 1 and 2, which posit a connection between earnings and exits for men and women. The results for men's exits oppose the predictions of Hypothesis 1, which holds that a decline in men's relative earnings should stimulate men's flight. Men's exit rates declined, while their relative earnings

Table 12.2 Comparison of Exit Rates and Earnings Ratios: Computer Workers From the SSE, 1982 to 1989

Variable	1982–1984		1984–1986		1986–1989	
	Men	Women	Men	Women	Men	Women
Change in earnings ratio	.06	.08	–.14	–.15	.18*	.10*
Predicted change in exit rates (Hypothesis 1)	—	—	[+]	—	[–]	—
Predicted change in exit rates (Hypothesis 2)	—	—	[+]	[+]	[–]	[–]
Overall exit rate (percent)	27.6*	21.4*	27.2*	23.0*	32.4*	25.9*
Change in exit rate (percent)	—	—	–.4	1.6	5.2@	2.9@
Number of cases	2,358	772	2,449	799	2,432	750

* = Male-female difference significant at $p < .05$.
@ = Time-trend difference significant at $p < .10$.
[+] = Exit rate increases.
[–] = Exit rate decreases.

declined as well (1984 to 1986); men's exit rates increased while their relative earnings increased (1986 to 1989). If we apply the same reasoning to women, we find that the 1984 to 1986 period saw a decline in relative earnings and an increase in exits. However, the final period saw both relative earnings and exits rise, the reverse of the logic that changes in the former produce opposite changes in the latter. Thus the year-to-year changes in exits for women respond to earnings in closer accord with Hypothesis 2 than do those for men, but the fit is not particularly close for either group. Thus Hypotheses 1 and 2, which connect earnings decline and occupational attrition, do not hold up well.

Table 12.3 presents the exit rates and entry rates for men and women for each period by type of exit: exits from the labor force, career switches (moves to noncomputer, nonmanagement jobs), moves into management, and moves to unemployment. The salient results from Table 12.3 regarding exits are:

1. In all three periods, exits from computer work were substantial, with between one fourth and one third of computer workers leaving the field.
2. In all three periods, men left computer work more often than did women.

Table 12.3 Percentages of Men and Women Entering and Exiting Computer Work: Computer Workers From the SSE, 1982 to 1989

Computer Work Exits/Entrances	1982–1984			1984–1986			1986–1989		
	Men	Women	Difference	Men	Women	Difference	Men	Women	Difference
Exits (percentage)									
From the labor force	1.0	5.3	-4.3**	1.8	3.5	-1.7*	3.9	4.3	-.4
To a career switch	16.2	7.5	8.7**	14.9	8.3	6.6**	17.1	8.7	8.4**
To management	9.6	8.2	1.5	9.6	8.9	.7	9.8	10.7	-.8
To unemployment	.8	.4	.4	.9	2.4	-1.5**	1.6	2.3	-.7
Total percent exiting computer work	27.6	21.4	6.2**	27.2	23.0	4.2*	32.4	25.9	6.5**
Number of cases	2,358	772	—	2,449	799	—	2,432	750	—
Entrances (percentage)									
To the labor force	.3	1.8	-1.5**	.3	2.3	-2.0**	.3	2.7	-2.4**
From a career switch	20.2	13.1	7.0**	17.9	9.7	8.2**	18.6	9.7	8.9**
From management	6.5	2.9	3.7**	6.5	6.0	.5	8.7	7.0	1.8
From unemployment	.9	1.0	-.1	.6	.3	.4	.9	.9	.0
Total percent entering computer work	27.9	18.8	9.1**	25.3	18.3	7.0**	28.5	20.2	8.3**
Number of cases	2,449	799	—	2,432	750	—	2,362	703	—

NOTE: Numbers may not add due to rounding errors.
*p < .05; **p < .01 (two-tailed tests).

3. In all three periods, women left the labor force more often than did men (two of these differences are statistically significant).

4. Men made more career switches (moves to noncomputer, nonmanagement positions) than did women.

5. Moves to management did not differ by sex.

6. In all three periods, few computer specialists were unemployed, and, with one small exception, no gender gap in unemployment was evident.

Our findings regarding the low unemployment levels for computer workers are consistent with other studies of the computer field. With the tremendous demand for computer personel, there was little unemployment during this period for either men or women (National Science Foundation, 1988). There are several possible explanations for the lack of a gender gap in moves into management. First, some evidence suggests that, in general, women are catching up to men in management (Jacobs, 1992). Other analysis of the SSE data (Wright, 1992) indicates that there is significant mobility between management and computer work in both directions. A computer worker's move to management does not necessarily mean a promotion, nor are promotions in computer work solely the province of people who accept management occupational titles (Eskow, 1990). Finally, although both men and women may have managerial titles, women may well be moving into management positions with less status and authority than those held by men (Kraft & Dubnoff 1983; Reskin & Ross 1992).

Gender differences are evident in two types of exits: Women leave the labor force more often than do men, whereas men switch to fields outside computer work more often than do women. Women's disproportionate exit from the labor force is consistent with the age composition of women in the SSE pool: 85% of the female SSE sample in 1986 was between ages 21 and 45—the childbearing and early childrearing years during which women are more likely to leave the labor force than are men. Men, in contrast, tend not to leave the labor force until retirement; 70% of the male SSE sample in the same year were in the same age group.

For career switches (moves to nonmanagement, noncomputer occupations), men's exit rates were higher than women's. These moves may have significant implications for gender inequality: Previous research (Wright, 1990) suggests that lateral career switches out of computer work may well lead to subsequent promotional advantages.

The substantial turnover of computer workers facilitates the relatively rapid feminization of the field, because it generates new employment opportunities for women. However, many of those who leave computer work do return; thus, a more complete analysis requires understanding of both exits and entries. One estimate suggests that in 1986, 39% of entering computer scientists and systems analysts had previous computer experience (Carey, 1989). Net exit rates take both entrances and exits into account. The SSE data are not ideally suited for a complete analysis of new entrants, because the population is restricted to individuals who were already scientific and technical specialists in 1980. An analysis of entrances from this population is, however, useful for comparison to exits into the same population.

We analyzed the entry into computer work by scientific and technical workers from the SSE panel. The second panel of Table 12.3 shows the rates of entry from each of four employment statuses for the three time intervals considered. The entrants shown were from the larger SSE panel: Any 1980 scientist or engineer entering computer work was included, whether or not he or she had previously worked as a computer profes-sional. In each period, men entered computer work from other fields at a higher rate than women. Men were more likely to switch careers into computer work and to enter from managerial positions, whereas women were more likely to enter if they had previously left the labor force. Combining exits and entries in Table 12.3, the net outflow for men was smaller than for women in each survey period, despite the lower attrition of women in computer work. (In one period, 1982 to 1984, the exits and entrances for men were about the same.) The feminization of computer work, thus, appears to have been aided by the relatively high turnover of computer workers, but it proceeded despite the greater net turnover of women. The large and growing number of women did not deter male scientists, engineers, and other technical workers from entering computer specialties.

Exits and Earnings. To further examine the exit differences presented in Table 12.3, we used logistic regression to explore the variability in each type of move: We estimated the odds of exiting computer work between survey waves (2-year or 3-year intervals).[13] We estimated models that combined all exits into a single analysis and others that treated each exit type separately.

A series of logistic regression models were estimated for all exits from computer work, in which controls for background, education, period, occupation, and industry were gradually added (see Table 12.4). In the initial model, the variable "male" was entered into the equation by itself and had a positive coefficient. This indicates that, before other factors are taken into account, the odds of men's exiting computer work exceeds those of women. This is consistent with the results in Table 12.3 and appears to support the resegregation perspective, in that men leave more than women.

The most striking result in Table 12.4, however, is that as additional variables were added to the model, the male coefficient quickly changed sign and became statistically significant in the opposite direction. In other words, once relevant controls are introduced, men are *less* likely than women to leave computer work. Background variables (age and experience), education, and computer specialty all contributed to the reversal. The principal finding supporting the resegregation perspective was the excess male attrition from computer work. Yet this finding does not hold after the introduction of simple, relevant controls in our multivariate analysis.

The earnings variable in the analysis in Table 12.4 was individual earnings in a given year divided by the average male labor force earnings in the same year. This variable consistently failed to predict exits. In other words, there appears to be no support for the notion that either men or women were more likely to leave computer work when their earnings declined relative to the rest of the labor force.

We were so surprised and puzzled by this result that we examined a total of 43 alternative measures of the relative economic status of computer specialists. We followed the same pattern of individual earnings compared to yearly aggregates, varying the aggregates. We considered four alternative reference groups: all technical workers, all computer workers, all those sharing one's specialty, and all technical workers in one's industry. We adjusted for education, following the procedure we used in Table 12.1. We changed the five reference groups to be sex-specific and adjusted for education again.

We then constructed four additional earnings measures: the female-to-male earnings ratio at the specialty level, the female-to-male earnings ratio at the industry level, the individual's earnings (with no specified reference group), and the individual's earnings trajectory in the preceding interval. Finally, we reanalyzed each of the male and sex-specific earnings ratios with lagged earnings data, using the earnings ratios from the previous interval, on the grounds that it may take men some time to react to the trend in earnings. Values for the subset of these measures that reflect male reference groups in the same interval are shown in Appendix A. Results (not shown) indicate that none of these measures reliably

Table 12.4 Logistic Regression Coefficients for All Exits From Computer Work on Selected Variables: Computer Workers From the SSE, 1982 to 1989

Variable	Model 1	Model 2	Model 3	Model 4	Model 5	Model 6	Model 7
Male	.16*	.02	-.13	-.16*	-.21**	-.21**	-.21**
BACKGROUND							
Race							
White		—	—	—	—	—	—
Black		-.23	-.18	-.18	-.20	-.20	-.20
Asian		-.26*	-.34**	-.34**	-.28*	-.28*	-.28*
Other		.34*	.29	.28	.23	.23	.23
Married		.26**	.23**	.23**	.21**	.20**	.20**
Children under age 6 at home		-.07	-.06	-.04	-.03	-.03	-.03
Children ages 6-17 at home		-.09	-.07	-.08	-.06	-.06	-.06
Age		.01	.01	.01	.01*	.01*	.01*
Years of experience		.02*	.01	.01	.00	.00	.00
EDUCATION							
Degree							
None			.23	.21	.10	.10	.10
Associate			.61***	.58**	.45*	.44*	.44*
Bachelor's			—	—	—	—	—
Master's			.08	.07	-.06	-.05	-.05
M.B.A.			.34*	.33*	.24	.24	.24
Professional/Ph.D.			.25*	.24*	.11	.11	.11
Major							
Computer science				—	—	—	—
Business				.39**	.33*	.33*	.33*
Engineering				1.05***	.68***	.67***	.67***
Math sciences				.24*	.16	.16	.16

Other technical	—	—	.45***	.43***	.32**	.33**	.33**
Nontechnical	—	—	.53***	.50***	.45***	.46***	.46***
PERIOD							
1982–1984	—	—	—	.29***	.19*	.18*	.18*
1984–1986	—	—	—	-.21**	-.25**	-.26**	-.26**
1986–1989	—	—	—	—	—	—	—
SPECIALTY							
Computer programmer	—	—	—	—	-.90***	-.90***	-.90***
Computer systems analyst	—	—	—	—	-.66***	-.66***	-.66***
Other systems analyst	—	—	—	—	.77***	.77***	.77***
Systems engineer	—	—	—	—	.23	.23	.23
Computer scientist	—	—	—	—	.53***	.52***	.52***
Computer engineer	—	—	—	—	-.41**	-.41**	-.41**
Other computer specialist	—	—	—	—	—	—	—
INDUSTRY							
Manufacturing	—	—	—	—	—	-.05	-.05
Professional Services	—	—	—	—	—	-.03	-.03
Finance/insurance	—	—	—	—	—	-.08	-.08
Utilities	—	—	—	—	—	.05	.05
Education	—	—	—	—	—	-.08	-.08
Government	—	—	—	—	—	-.08	-.08
Other industry	—	—	—	—	—	-.14	-.14
	—					—	—
Labor force earnings ratio	—	—	—	—	—	—	-.00
−2 Log Likelihood	7,946.45	7,848.69	7,667.46	7,612.24	7,342.33	7,340.20	7,340.18
Chi-square[a]	6.23*	103.98***	285.22***	340.44***	610.35***	612.48***	612.49***
Degrees of freedom	1	9	19	21	27	33	34
Percent concordant pairs	20.3	56.1	62.9	64.0	68.4	68.5	68.5

NOTE: $N = 7,558$.

a. Chi-square significance given with degrees of freedom.

$*p < .05$; $**p < .01$; $***p < .001$ (two-tailed tests).

357

predicts male exits from computer work. In other words, when other relevant influences on exit rates are accounted for, exits are not predicted by year-to-year fluctuations in the earnings of computer specialists, using earnings measures relative to any of a wide range of reference groups.

These results run counter to Hypotheses 1 and 2. They contradict Hypothesis 1 because they indicate male attrition is not determined by earnings changes. They contradict Hypothesis 2 because they indicate male attrition is less likely than female attrition when individual attributes are controlled (Hypothesis 2 holds that the difference between male and female departures should reflect earnings differences alone).

Our focus here is not on the effects of the control variables themselves, but rather, controlling for other factors, whether there is an excess or deficit in male exit rates relative to women. Nevertheless, the coefficients for the control variables in Table 12.4 shed interesting light on the process of attrition from computer work. Persistence in computer work declines with experience, a result consistent with the high turnover rate discussed above. Attrition varies little across industry, but varies substantially across specialty: Programmers are more likely to persist, and systems engineers are more likely to leave. Those with computer science degrees are more likely to persist in computer work than those with degrees in other fields, such as business or engineering. Differences in persistence across educational levels diminish markedly once specialties are controlled. Asians are more likely to persist in computer work than their white counterparts, perhaps dueto the greater difficulties Asians experience in obtaining promotions (Tang, 1991).

Because women's representation in computer work leveled off after 1986, we wanted to examine whether the determinants of attrition changed during this period. The analyses presented in Table 12.4 indicate that there are indeed period effects. Computer workers were most likely to exit in 1982 to 1984 and least likely to exit in 1984 to 1986. However, there were no significant period interaction effects. In other words, we could not reject the null hypothesis that the effects of earnings and other key variables on attrition were constant during the periods considered.

Economic factors are likely to account for the period effects in Table 12.4. The 1982 to 1984 period included the recession that peaked at the end of 1982; overall it was a time of decreasing layoffs and increasing consumer confidence, as measured by initial claims for unemployment insurance and the Conference Board's index, respectively. These trends reversed in the 1984 to 1986 period: It was a time of increasing layoffs and decreasing consumer confidence, as measured by the same indicators. Both periods had high rates of unemployment, compared to the 1986 to 1989 period (Haver Analytics, 1992). These factors are all likely to affect individuals' assessments of the risks of leaving computer work—in different ways to different destinations.

Table 12.5 repeats the analysis presented in Table 12.4 for career switches (exits to nonmanagement, noncomputer work), exits from the labor force, and moves into management. This table reveals the reasons for the reversal of the male exit advantage: In each case, the male coefficient is smaller in the controlled analysis (Model 7) than is observed in the zero-order relationship (Model 1). The addition of control variables to the analysis reduces men's advantage in the case of career switches, reinforces women's advantage in the case of exits from the labor force, or turns men's advantage (which was not statistically significant) into a disadvantage for moves into management.

Most of men's advantage in career switches out of computer work is due to differences in specialty and background characteristics, such as major field of study. Once these differences are controlled, only a small male advantage persists. We see that women's advantage in exits from the labor force increases when controls are imposed. No significant gender difference in moves into management is evident until the earnings ratio measure is introduced; this analysis indicates that high earners, who are disproportionately men, are more likely to become managers, but are less likely to switch careers or leave the labor force.

These results illuminate the processes that underlie the combined exit results in Table 12.4. Specifically, for men the higher rate of exits from computer work reverses when controls are imposed, because education, experience, and specialty account for most of the male excess in career switches, and at the same time enhance women's advantage in exits from the labor force.[14]

Sex Composition Effects. Table 12.6 presents a summary of the effects of sex composition on male exits. This analysis is designed to test Hypothesis 3—whether the growing presence of women in computer work prompts men to leave the occupation. The regressions included men only and controlled for all variables in Model 7 (except the variable "male") presented in Tables 12.4 and 12.5. Two measures of percentage female were considered separately: specialty percentage female and industry percentage female. The mean values for these variables are given at the bottom of Appendix A. None of the percentage

Table 12.5 Logistic Regression Coefficients for Three Types of Exits From Computer Work on Selected Variables: Computer Workers From the SSE, 1982 to 1989

Variable	Career Switches		Labor Force Exits		Moves to Management	
	Model 1	Model 7	Model 1	Model 7	Model 1	Model 7
Male	.71***	.27*	-.80***	-1.85***	.02	-.24*
BACKGROUND						
Race						
White	—	—	—	—	—	—
Black	—	.07	—	.17	—	-.75**
Asian	—	-.18	—	-.09	—	-.34*
Other	—	.25	—	-1.49	—	.21
Married	—	.11	—	1.21***	—	.22
Children under age 6 at home	—	-.13	—	.10	—	-.03
Children ages 6-17 at home	—	-.02	—	-1.45***	—	.28**
Age	—	.02*	—	.11***	—	-.03**
Years of experience	—	-.01	—	.02	—	-.00
EDUCATION						
Degree						
None	—	-.02	—	-.29	—	.29
Associate	—	.46*	—	.40	—	.27
Bachelor's	—	—	—	—	—	—
Master's	—	-.07	—	-.33	—	.05
M.B.A.	—	-.08	—	-.14	—	.45*
Professional/Ph.D.	—	.23	—	-.43	—	.03
Major						
Computer science	—	—	—	—	—	—
Business	—	.38	—	.01	—	.39*
Engineering	—	1.06***	—	.01	—	.28
Math sciences	—	.21	—	.31	—	.11

	(1)	(2)	(3)	(4)	(5)	(6)
Other technical	—	.52**	—	.12	—	.27
Nontechnical	—	.67***	—	−.13	—	.38*
PERIOD						
1982–1984	—	.64***	—	−.22	—	−.05
1984–1986	—	−.07	—	−.67**	—	−.29*
1986–1989	—	—	—	—	—	—
SPECIALTY						
Computer programmer	—	−.79***	—	.11	—	−1.28***
Computer systems analyst	—	−.99***	—	.09	—	−.62***
Other systems analyst	—	1.14***	—	.79	—	.53
Systems engineer	—	.70***	—	.05	—	−.38
Computer scientist	—	1.11***	—	.44	—	−.22
Computer engineer	—	−.10	—	−1.37*	—	−.71***
Other computer specialist	—	—	—	—	—	—
INDUSTRY						
Manufacturing	—	−.08	—	.17	—	−.05
Services	—	−.05	—	−.00	—	−.03
Finance/insurance	—	−1.05***	—	.53	—	.09
Utilities	—	−.06	—	.20	—	.29
Education	—	−.03	—	−.80	—	−.03
Government	—	−.23	—	.11	—	.03
Other industry	—	—	—	—	—	—
Labor force earnings ratio	—	−.01***	—	−.00**	—	.01***
Number of cases	6,637	6,637	6,080	6,080	6,553	6,553
−2 Log Likelihood	4,578.64	3,773.11	1,595.79	1,226.25	4,250.36	3,969.71
Chi-square[a]	49.91***	855.44***	25.96***	395.50***	.06	280.71***
Degrees of freedom	1	34	1	34	1	34
Percent concordant pairs	22.5	79.2	32.7	86.9	19.6	68.7

a. Chi-square significance given with degrees of freedom.
*$p < .05$; **$p < .01$; ***$p < .001$ (two-tailed tests).

Table 12.6 Logistic Regression Coefficients for the Effect of Percentage Female on Men's Exits From Computer Work: Computer Workers From the SSE, 1982–1989

Percentage Female	Exits From Computer Work	Exits From the Labor Force[a]	Exits to a Career Switch	Exits to Management
Specialty	.01 (.03)	—	.00 (.04)	.06 (.04)
Industry	−.03 (.03)	—	−.05 (.05)	−.07 (.05)
Number of cases	5,607	4,438	4,964	4,821

NOTE: Numbers in parentheses are standard errors. None of the coefficients was significant at $p < .05$ in two-tailed tests.
a. Men's exits were so few that the regressions did not converge.

female coefficients presented in Table 12.6 are significant, which indicates that the variation in exit rates in the observed data is not a function of the variation in the rates of entry by women into computer work. Because the tests of the effect of percentage female are conducted at the specialty and industry levels, there may not have been enough variation to detect sex composition effects. On the other hand, we did not find large coefficients with large standard errors. Rather, the estimated effects were small. Hypothesis 3, which holds that feminization prompts men to leave, is not confirmed.

Ghettoization

Systems Analysis and Computer Programming. Recall that our first three hypotheses for ghettoization at the specialty level parallel the three hypotheses for resegregation at the occupational level. We repeat our analysis for two computer specialties, computer systems analysts and computer programmers. We chose systems analysis to match Donato's (1990) case study, and computer programming because it is the lowest in status and has been historically the most female-dominated computer specialty. Table 12.7 presents exit rates by sex for these two specialties to each of five destinations. (Note that moves to other types of computer work are now added as a destination.) Men are less likely than women

Table 12.7 Percentages of Men and Women Exiting From Computer Systems Analysis and Computer Programming: Computer Workers From the SSE, 1982 to 1986

Type of Exit	1982–1984			1984–1986		
	Men	Women	Difference	Men	Women	Difference
Percentage from computer systems analysis						
To other computer work	22.3	20.9	1.3	23.1	22.3	.8
From the labor force	1.2	5.2	−4.0**	1.1	3.4	−2.3*
To a career switch	4.6	3.8	.8	4.5	4.0	.5
To management	7.5	8.1	−.7	8.7	8.3	.4
To unemployment	1.0	.3	.7	.7	2.8	−2.0*
Total from computer systems analysis	36.5	38.4	−1.9	38.1	40.7	−2.6
Number of cases	831	344	—	843	327	—
Percent from computer programming						
To other computer work	34.6	40.6	−6.0	33.7	36.2	−2.5
From the labor force	.8	5.3	−4.5*	2.4	4.7	−2.3
To a career switch	7.6	3.0	4.6*	8.3	7.1	1.2
To management	4.2	4.5	−.3	3.6	2.4	1.2
To unemployment	0	0	0	1.2	1.6	−.4
Total from computer programming	47.3	53.4	−6.1	49.2	52.0	−2.8
Number of cases	237	133	—	252	127	—

NOTE: Numbers may not add due to rounding errors.
*$p < .05$; **$p < .01$ (two-tailed tests).

to leave these two specialties, a result that contradicts the premise of the resegregation perspective. The sex-specific differences for each destination conform to the patterns documented in Table 12.3. The differences in moves to other computer work are small and not statistically significant.

Regression analyses of overall exits from these two specialties were conducted for the 1982 to 1984 and 1984 to 1986 periods (a change in SSE coding categories made it imposible to continue the analysis through 1989). The results (not shown) generally match the results in Table 12.4: The male coefficient declines as additional control variables are added, yet neither case starts with a positive male coefficient, and the male coefficient is not statistically negative in the final model. Thus, ghettoization hypotheses 1, 2, and 3 are not supported in this analysis. In other words, when the analysis is restricted to these two specialties, men's exits are not related to earnings decline, men do not leave more than women once other factors are controlled, and men do not leave in response to women's entry.

Analyses comparable to those presented in Table 12.7 for the other five specialties yielded quite comparable results. Specialties vary in the *level* of turnover, with exits from other systems analysis, a declining field, being especially high. However, the specialties did not vary in terms of the gender pattern of exits described in Table 12.7. We also estimated regression equations predicting exits from all seven specialties. Although the analyses provided some interesting details beyond what we report here, the key results regarding the effect of earnings on attrition are consistent with those found for computer systems analysis and computer programming.

Ghettoization by Specialties. Figure 12.1 presents trends in the representation of women in computer work for six computer specialties.[15] The percentage of women in computer work (excluding engineers) rose from 15% to 35% between 1971 and 1986. When electrical and electronic engineers are included, women's representation is somewhat lower, but the time trend remains the same. The rate of increase has varied by specialty. Whereas women's share of computer programming jobs increased from 23% in 1971 to 34% in 1991, women's representation among operations systems researchers and analysts increased even faster during the same period, jumping from 9% to 43%.

The three additional hypotheses specific to ghettoization also receive little support in this analysis. First, the greatest number of women in computer work have not entered the lowest-status computer specialties (Hypothesis 4). Of the four computer specialties shown in Figure 12.1, computer programming is the lowest-paid specialty. Yet women's representation among computer systems analysts and operations systems analysts, the second- and third-highest-paid specialties, respectively, grew much faster during the 1970s and 1980s than women's representation among programmers. On the other hand, women have made only modest inroads into electrical engineering, the highest-paid specialty of the four fields included in the U.S. Bureau of Labor Statistics (1976-1992) data.

Another test of Hypothesis 4 analyzes data on work activities from the SSE survey. For the 15 work activities listed in the SSE, women were

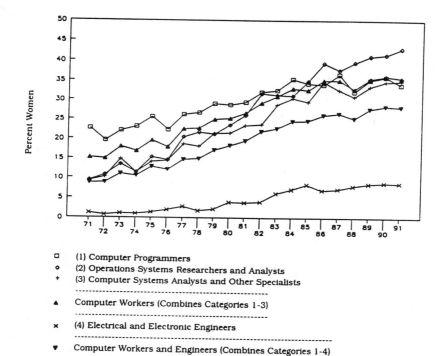

Figure 12.1. Women's Representation Among Computer Workers, 1971-1991
SOURCE: U.S. Bureau of Labor Statistics (1976-1992), supplemented by the bureau's unpublished data for 1971-1974. Data for computer systems analysts and other specialists were estimated because of 1983 changes in the bureau's occupational groups. Details are in note 15.

indeed most represented in the lowest-paid areas.[16] For example, women were underrepresented in management and consulting (the highest paid) and were overrepresented in teaching and training (the lowest paid). The Spearman rank-order correlation of activity earning level and women's representation in 1982 was −.46. However, women's representation in the lowest-paid work activities did not increase over the years studied. The change in women's representation between 1982 and 1989 was unrelated to the earnings in the activity ($r = .02$). Thus, the ghettoization of women across work activities neither grew nor shrank as women's representation in the field increased. Thus, Hypothesis 4, which holds that the growth in women's representation will be concentrated in the lowest-paid fields within an occupation, is not confirmed in either the specialty or the work activity analyses.

Hypothesis 5 posits that the process of ghettoization generates an increase in sex segregation across specialties when large numbers of women enter a field. Jacobs (1989b) showed that this was not the case for law or medicine, and we find that it is no more true for computer work. The degree of sex segregation across computer specialties, as measured by the index of dissimilarity, declined somewhat during the 1970s and 1980s: Using data from the U.S. Bureau of Labor Statistics, as measured across the four specialties in Figure 12.1 (computer programmers, operations systems researchers and analysts, computer systems analysts and other specialists, and electrical and electronic engineers), the index of dissimilarity declined from 61.5 in 1971 to 47.7 in 1981 to 41.8 in 1991. As measured across three computer specialties (excluding engineers), the index declined from 25.5 in 1971 to 6.1 in 1981 to 4.3 in 1991. We conducted the same analysis for Strober and Arnold's (1987) wider set of computer specialties and found much the same result: Between 1970 and 1980 the degree of sex segregation across occupations declined from 59.1 in 1970 to 47.2 in 1980 (calculated from Strober & Arnold, 1987, p. 145).

We expected similar results, although with less of a trend, in our analysis of the SSE data, because the population in the SSE is restricted to experienced computer workers, and our analysis was limited to just a 4-year period (because of a change in categories). The level of sex segregation as measured across seven SSE specialties increased less than 1%, rising from 18.0% in 1982 to 18.6% in 1986, although this increase was not statistically significant. Using the U.S. Census Bureau's (1991b) grouping of computer specialties (excluding engineers and other systems analysts), the index declined from 7.2 in 1982 to 4.6 in 1986. Occupational sex segregation across industries and work activities also declined slightly for the SSE panel.[17] In all three sets of data we analyzed, the entry of women did not result in an increase in ghettoization, but rather there was either no change or a modest decline in sex segregation across specialties. Thus, Hypothesis 5—feminization is associated with increased segregation across fields—receives little support from our analysis.

Finally, Hypothesis 6 predicts that ghettoization within an occupation results in an increased gap in earnings between men and women. In 1989 women computer workers earned 88% of the salaries of their male counterparts, and the gap between men and women narrowed slightly during the 1980s for all computer workers and also for each of the seven specialties examined between 1982 and 1986. In 1982 women computer specialists working full-time earned 84% as much as their male counterparts. This fraction rose to 85% in 1984 and 88% in 1986, where it remained through 1989 (cf. Donato & Roos, 1987; Glenn & Tolbert, 1987). The sex gap in earnings also narrowed in all seven SSE industry groups between 1982 and 1986—the years with comparable occupational and industry data. Results of regression analyses of the SSE data (not shown) indicate that more than half of the sex gap in earnings is due to identifiable human capital differences, and the unexplained sex gap in wages has declined over time. Thus Hypothesis 6—feminization results in an increased gender gap in earnings—is also not supported in this case study.

Discussion

We have examined in detail several hypotheses culled from the literature on the processes of occupational resegregation and ghettoization. Our results are not consistent with the predictions of these hypotheses. The data indicate that during a period of rapid feminization of computer work, the earnings of computer specialists did not decline relative to the labor force as a whole. Men left computer work more often than did women, but they were also more likely than women to enter computer work from other technical fields. Men were more likely to exit computer work for related lines of work, whereas women were more likely to leave the labor force entirely. When relevant factors were controlled, men were less likely to leave computer work than were women. Thus the mid-career attrition of men did not contribute to the feminization of computer work; on the contrary, women were more likely to leave computer work than men with similar characteristics.

Moreover, the particular mechanisms held to be responsible for men leaving computer work do not account for the variation in male exit rates. The variation in men's earnings relative to their peers in the labor force was not a reliable predictor of men's attrition. This finding is inconsistent with the prediction that declines in earnings are responsible for male flight from feminizing occupations. Nor did feminization per se provoke male flight. In those specialties where women's entry was most pronounced, male exits were not statistically different from other specialties.

The disproportionate attrition of women from computer work is paralleled by a decline in the proportion of women pursuing bachelor's degrees in fields leading to careers in computer work. The proportions of women receiving bachelor's degrees in computer and information science, computer engineering, and electrical engineering have been declining since the mid-1980s. The proportions of all college graduates in these majors have been falling for both men and women, but the decline has been steeper among women. Women's representation among computer and information science degree recipients grew from 14% in 1971 to 37% in 1984, and then fell back to 29% in 1991.[18]

For both men and women, much of the low level of interest in computer science has been ascribed to inadequate steering and marketing early in the educational pipeline (Committee on Women in Science and Engineering, 1991; Steering Committee on Human Resources in Computer Science and Technology, 1993; Rochester, 1988). Jacobs (1994) finds that the decline in women's share of computer science degrees is not the by-product of their greater attraction to alternative male-dominated fields, such as business or engineering. Factors inhibiting women's interest may include the avoidance of math in high school, a lack of role models, hostile work environments, and frequent unplanned overtime in computer work that conflicts with family responsibilities (Leveson, 1989; Pearl et al., 1990).

Although recipients of college degrees in computer fields are not the only possible entrants into computer work (Carey, 1991), they nevertheless comprise a major pool that can be readily identified. The college-degree data do not indicate disproportionate male flight on the part of prospective entrants. Indeed, just the reverse is true: Men have been less likely than women to desert computer majors in college. If the computer field is perceived as less attractive by prospective entrants, it appears that women, rather than men, are more likely to have been affected. The presence of women among computer professionals does not seem to generate male flight among new entrants or among those currently employed.

Computer work does not appear likely to become resegregated, that is, to become a low-wage female-dominated occupation, in light of the declining proportions of women among new college graduates receiving computer science and engineering degrees. However, ghettoization is also not an accurate characterization of computer work, given the narrowing gender gap in earnings and the increasing dispersion of women across specialties. We conclude that during the 1980s computer work was in the process of integrating by gender. Based on the data at hand, however, we cannot say whether this process will continue until complete gender integration is achieved.

There are a number of reasons for being cautious about generalizing from these results to the process of resegregation in other occupations. First, despite the fact that we have analyzed the careers of over 6,000 computer professionals, our research represents only a single case study. Moreover, the case of computer work may not be an ideal test case of what happens when women enter an occupation, because earnings did not decline prior to feminization, as is presumed by the perspective from which we drew our hypotheses. Third, the time intervals examined may be too short to induce the anticipated response. Fourth, perhaps the resegregation process operates only at some "tipping" point, and computer work, which was 36% female in 1991, is not close enough to that point to produce the expected male flight.

Finally, computer work is a relatively new field, and as a result stereotypes about the appropriate gender of its occupants may not have had the time to take root. On the other hand, computer science is a close cousin to electrical engineering, a field rather inhospitable to women (McIlwee & Robinson, 1992). The masculine connotations of technical and scientific work have been borrowed by computer science (Frenkel, 1990). In that sense, gender stereotypes in computer work are not new, but rather are newly applied versions of longer-standing images. In the end, however, only further research can determine whether other test cases of the process of resegregation will confirm the results obtained here for computer work.

In this study we present no data on perceptions. We think it would be useful for future studies to gather such data, in concert with the kind of exit and entrance data we analyze here. Women's perceptions of barriers to opportunities, men's perceptions of changes in the status of their occupations, and attitudinal data on men's resistance to women's entry would help us better understand changes in the gender composition of occupations.

In our analysis, we took several steps to maximize the connection between our tests and the resegregation/ghettoization hypotheses we developed. We considered both narrow and general interpretations of the basic hypothesis. We considered two occupational specialties to increase our chances of finding a group whose experiences conformed to our predictions. If any computer specialty had "tipped," we thought, it would be computer programming—the lowest-status, most female-dominated specialty. Yet we found less support in this case than for computer work as a whole. Similarly, we focused on the case of systems analysts to reanalyze one of Reskin and Roos's case studies. Again, the results were even weaker for systems analysts than they were for all of computer work.

Studies of other occupations that have experienced resegregation, such as school teachers, bank tellers, and telephone operators, corroborate certain elements of the resegregation perspective (Cohn, 1985; Davies, 1982; Strober, 1984). Additional contrary evidence, however, has been offered by Jacobs (1989b), who examined the extent of internal segregation in medicine and law in response to dramatic increases in women's representation in these high-status fields. In both cases, he found that women's entry coincided with declines in the extent of sex segregation across fields within these professions. In another study, Jacobs (1992) maintained that while women's representation in management positions over the last 20 years has more than doubled (women were 18% of managers in 1970 and 40% in 1988), the earnings gap between male and female managers has narrowed, whereas a gender gap in authority has remained little changed. In medicine, law, management, and now computer work, a dramatic rise in the numbers of female participants has not resulted in a decline in the status of the occupation or in increasing differentiation within the field.

Although more studies of particular cases are undoubtedly needed, our findings pose the question, "Are integrated occupations possible?" Computer work is an occupation with gradually increasing numbers of women, in which men are not fleeing in response to women's entry. Imagine neighborhoods in which African Americans entered and whites did not leave: At least for a time, there would be movement toward integration.

We do not claim that computer work is perfectly egalitarian in gender terms or that there is no discrimination against women in the profession. We simply suggest that, if this case is a reliable guide, women's entry into an occupation does not necessarily follow or provoke a sustained flight of men, and women's entry does not necessarily cause or increase the ghettoization of women in the least desirable specialties within that occupation.

Appendix A

Mean Values of Logistic Regression Variables: Computer Workers From the SSE, 1984

	Men (N = 2,449)	Women (N = 799)	Men and Women (N = 3,248)
DEPENDENT VARIABLES[a]			
Exits from computer work	.272	.230	.262
Exits from the labor force	.018	.035	.022
Exits to a career switch	.149	.083	.133
Exits to management	.096	.089	.094
Stay in computer work	.728	.770	.739
INDEPENDENT VARIABLES[b]			
Male	1.000	.000	.754
BACKGROUND			
Race			
[White][c]	.831	.830	.831
Black	.043	.055	.046
Asian	.099	.081	.095
Other	.027	.034	.028
Marital Status			
Married	.821	.640	.776
[Not married][c]	.179	.360	.224
Children at Home			
Yes, under age 6	.266	.237	.259
[No, under age 6][c]	.734	.763	.741
Yes, ages 6-17	.443	.225	.389
[No, ages 6-17][c]	.557	.775	.611
Age	41.0	36.2	39.8
Years of experience	16.7	12.1	15.6
EDUCATION			
Degree			
None	.053	.073	.058
Associate	.032	.015	.028
[Bachelor's][c]	.454	.502	.466
Master's	.301	.287	.298
M.B.A.	.073	.086	.076
Professional/Ph.D.	.088	.040	.076
Major			
[Computer science][c]	.172	.242	.189
Business	.162	.141	.157
Engineering	.297	.074	.242
Math sciences	.143	.228	.164
Other technical	.148	.176	.155
Nontechnical	.078	.139	.093

(Continued)

Appendix A (Continued)

	Men (N = 2,449)	Women (N = 799)	Men and Women (N = 3,248)
PERIOD			
1982–1984	.000	.000	.000
1984–1986	1.000	1.000	1.000
[1986–1989][c]	.000	.000	.000
SPECIALTY			
Computer programmer	.103	.159	.117
Computer systems analyst	.344	.409	.360
Other systems analyst	.025	.020	.024
Computer scientist	.178	.069	.151
Computer engineer	.051	.046	.050
Systems engineer	.110	.045	.094
[Other computer specialist][c]	.189	.252	.204
INDUSTRY			
Manufacturing	.455	.339	.426
Professional services	.057	.103	.068
Finance/insurance	.189	.252	.204
Utilities	.053	.078	.059
Education	.030	.059	.037
Government	.077	.104	.083
[Other industry][c]	.208	.238	.216
RELATIVE FAVORABILITY[d]			
Earnings ratio[e]			
Labor force	1.79[f]	1.49f	1.72
Technical worker	.99	.83	.95
Computer worker	1.00	.83	.96
Computer specialty	1.00	.85	.96
Industry	.98	.82	.95
Earnings to education ratio[e]			
Labor force	1.33[f]	1.13[f]	1.28
Technical worker	.98	.83	.94
Computer worker	.98	.83	.95
Computer specialty	.98	.85	.95
Industry	.94	.81	.91

Appendix A *(Continued)*

	Men (N = 2,449)	Women (N = 799)	Men and Women (N = 3,248)
Female-to-male earnings ratio			
Computer specialty	.85	.85	.85
Industry	.78	.78	.78
Absolute earnings			
Earnings	40,618[f]	33,789[f]	38,938
Earnings trajectory	1.25	1.30	1.26
Percentage female			
Computer specialty	21.8	25.0	22.6
Industry	13.9	15.6	14.4

a. Dependent variable values reflect exits in the interval following the survey year, 1984 to 1986. Shown are the exit proportions that correspond to Table 12.3. Per Allison (personal communication with Rosemary Wright, June 5, 1992), omitted in the regressions were respondents exiting to other destinations and respondents not meeting the criteria in note 13.

b. Independent variable values reflect values in the survey year, 1984, with the exception of earnings trajectory, which is earnings in the survey year, 1984, divided by those in the previous survey year, 1982.

c. Variables in brackets indicate omitted categories.

d. Ratios were entered in regressions as percentages to see small coefficient values, but are shown as proportions for comparison to Table 12.1.

e. Shown are the ratio values with average earnings from male reference groups in the same interval. As described in the text, identical analyses were performed with earnings from sex-specific reference groups in the same interval, male reference groups from the previous interval, and sex-specific reference groups from the previous interval.

f. 1984 values for earnings are lower than those used in Table 12.1 because regressions include part-time workers per the argument in note 10.

Notes

1. These indices reflect the relative size of each occupation and are not size standardized. For a summary of segregation research, see Reskin (1993).

2. The 11 occupations include book editors, pharmacists, public relations specialists, bank managers, systems analysts, insurance sales occupations, real estate salespersons, insurance adjusters and examiners, bartenders, bakers, and typesetters and compositors. Reskin and Roos (1990) also draw on case studies of accountants and auditors, broadcast and print reporters, and bus drivers.

3. The SSE sample was stratified into 10 occupational groups, two of which were computer specialists and engineers. The survey also oversampled women and minorities.

NSF's "labor reserve" includes people not currently in the labor force who were employed in the last 5 years in a scientific, engineering, or related occupation (National Science Foundation, 1984).

4. Supporting our view of computer work as a single occupation are similarities in self-reported work activities (see note 16) between computer engineers and other computer professionals. We also found high rates of mobility among seven computer specialties, including computer and systems engineering, which suggest significant overlap between these fields.

5. We operationalized our definition of computer worker to include those SSE occupational titles for which at least one third of the workers in each survey year gave "computer applications" or "development" as their primary work activity; we excluded individuals with Ph.D.s whose primary work activity was teaching or research in an academic setting. Under this definition, there were six computer occupations on the SSE in 1982, seven (listed in the text above) in 1984 and 1986, and nine in 1989. For consistency, the six in 1982 were expanded to seven by estimating the number of computer engineers in 1982 from 1984 data. (All electrical engineers in 1982 who were computer engineers in 1984 and whose job data did not change from 1982 to 1984 were classified as computer engineers in 1982.) "Systems analysts, except computer systems or data processing" were included as "other systems analysts," their name notwithstanding, because they met our functional criteria and had high rates of mobility to and from the other six specialties. Unfortunately, the SSE retained only four of the seven titles in 1989, which limits our full use of the data.

6. The self-reported specialty data were solicited by providing respondents with a list of titles from which to choose. Because respondents chose their own labels, coding errors undoubtedly inflated our estimates of mobility. However, we have no reason to believe that gender differences in coding errors occurred.

7. In our multivariate analyses we include both age and experience. Despite the relatively high correlation between these measures, this is not a problem. Highly correlated independent variables used for control purposes only should both be included to make the specification as correct as possible. As long as one doesn't interpret the coefficients, there is no reason to be concerned about their multicollinearity (Hanushek & Jackson 1977, p. 88).

8. "Other" includes self-identified Hispanics, regardless of race; American Indians or Alaskan natives; and self-identified "other." White, African American, and Asian are residual categories constructed after the removal of the "other" group.

9. As described in note 5, 1984 and 1986 were the only two SSE survey years with consistent computer occupations. Appendix A presents data for 1984 to facilitate the interpretation of the results.

10. Reskin and Roos (1990) theorize about both full- and part-time workers, but calculate deterioration based on full-time workers. We've followed their approach. Part-time work is rare among computer workers for at least two reasons—required skills are constantly changing and such work is a "kiss of death" in moves to management (Wright, 1991). In 1982, 1984, and 1986, respectively, part-time workers made up .4%, .9%, and 1.2% of the SSE men and 6.6%, 9.0%, and 10.1% of the women.

11. The year-to-year and male-to-female patterns in Table 12.1 pertain for six of the seven specialties. The exception is other systems analysts (see note 5), a specialty declining in numbers during this period for both men and women.

12. These figures are obtained from the U.S. Bureau of Labor Statistics (1976-1992) and do not include engineers. When computer workers and electrical engineers are considered

jointly, the increases are 2.6, 1.6 and 1.6, percentage points for the three time intervals, respectively.

13. To test for period effects (as suggested by Paul Allison (in a personal communication to Rosemary Wright, June 5, 1992), regressions were run on a file of separate records for computer workers in 1982, computer workers in 1982 who stayed through 1984, and computer workers in 1982 who stayed through 1984 and 1986.

14. We tested a number of interaction terms to determine if the effects of earnings on exits in Tables 12.4 and 12.5 differed by gender. These terms were not significant when control variables were included in the analysis. We also tested whether the marital status effect differed by gender. With the exception of exits from the labor force, where married women were more likely to leave than married men, the gender interaction term was not significant, once other variables in the model were controlled. We also looked for different engineering effects by gender, given engineering's overwhelmingly male representation. We ran models with interaction terms between engineering majors and gender, and again between gender and the two engineering specialties (computer engineers and systems engineers). These interaction terms were not significant for any exit type, when all control variables were included, with the exception that male systems engineers were more likely to move into management and therefore also to exit computer work.

15. Figure 12.1 was generated from annual average occupational figures obtained from data published in *Employment and Earnings* (U.S. Bureau of Labor Statistics 1976-1992) and from unpublished U.S. Bureau of Labor Statistics data for 1971-1974. The percent female for engineers in computer work was assumed to be the same as for electrical and electronic engineers. From 1971 to 1982, percent female was available for computer specialists (including computer programmers, computer systems analysts, and others not listed), operations systems researchers and analysts, and electrical and electronic engineers. From 1983 to 1991, percent female was available for mathematical and computer scientists (including computer systems analysts and scientists, operations systems researchers and analysts, and others not listed), computer programmers, and electrical and electronic engineers. The transition between the 1970 and 1980 Census categories was made by forming a new category of computer systems analysts and other specialists, calculating its percent female in 1971 to 1982 from the difference between computer specialists and computer programmers, and in 1983 to 1991 from the difference between mathematical and computer scientists and operations systems researchers and analysts.

16. Listed in order of numbers of workers in 1984, the primary work activities applicable to SSE computer workers were: computer applications; product, process, and technical development; management or administration of other than research and development; consulting; management or administration of research and development; design of equipment, processes, and models; operations—production, maintenance, construction, installation; applied research; report and technical writing; quality control, testing, evaluation, or inspection; teaching and training; distribution and sales; statistical work; basic research; and other.

17. During the 4 survey years, the index of dissimilarity (D) across the seven industry groups decreased from 13.3 to 15.6 to 10.7 to 9.4; across the 15 work activities, D declined from 18.1 to 16.8 to 16.8 to 16.3.

18. This analysis is based on Tables 6-38, 7-5, 7-15, and 7-16 in Vetter (1991) and Table 7-11 in Vetter (1992), supplemented by data from the U.S. Department of Education (1992 and unpublished data for 1991).

References

Abbott, A. (1988). *The system of professions: An essay on the division of expert labor.* Chicago: University of Chicago.

Arnold, C. L. (1988). *Salary and occupation by gender among community college computer science graduates.* Ph.D. dissertation, Graduate School of Education, Stanford University, Stanford, CA.

Carey, M. L. (1989). Characteristics of occupational entrants. *Occupational Outlook Quarterly, 33*(2), 9-17.

Carey, M. L. (1991). Occupational advancement from within. *Occupational Outlook Quarterly, 35*(4), 19-25.

Cohn, S. (1985). *The process of occupational sex typing.* Philadelphia: Temple University Press.

Committee on Women in Science and Engineering. (1991). *Women in science and engineering: Increasing their numbers in the 1990s.* Washington, DC: National Academy Press.

Davies, M. (1982). *Woman's place is at the typewriter: Office work and office workers, 1870-1930.* Philadelphia: Temple University Press.

Debons, A., King, D. W., Mansfield, U., & Shirey, D. L. (1981). *The information professional—survey of an emerging field.* New York: Marcel Dekker.

Denning, P. (1991). The scope and directions of computer science: Computing applications, and computational science. *Communications of the ACM, 34*(10), 129-131.

Donato, K. M. (1990). Programming for change? The growing demand for women systems analysts. In B. Reskin & P. Roos (Eds.), *Job queues, gender queues: Explaining women's inroads into male occupations* (pp. 167-182). Philadelphia: Temple University Press.

Donato, K. M., & Roos, P. A. (1987). Gender and earnings inequality among computer specialists. In B. D. Wright et al. (Eds.), *Women, work and technology: Transformations* (pp. 291-317). Ann Arbor: University of Michigan.

England, P. (1992). *Comparable worth: Theories and evidence.* Hawthorne, NY: Aldine de Gruyter.

Eskow, D. (1990, August 27). It takes a scorecard to tell who's who in PC management game. *PC Week,* pp. 127-128.

Frenkel, K. A. (1990). Women and computing. *Communications of the ACM, 33*(11), 34-46.

Glenn, E. N., & Tolbert, C. M., II. (1987). Technology and emerging patterns of stratification for women of color: Race and gender segregation in computer occupations. In B. D. Wright et al. (Eds.), *Women, work and technology: Transformations* (pp. 318-331). Ann Arbor: University of Michigan.

Greenbaum, J. M. (1979). *In the name of efficiency: Management theory and shopfloor practice in data processing work.* Philadelphia: Temple University Press.

Hanushek, E. A., & Jackson, J. E. (1977). *Statistical methods in the social sciences.* New York: Academic Press.

Haver Analytics: *US-ECON* [on-line database]. New York: Haver Analytics. (Accessed in October 1992).

Hughes, Everett C. (1971). The study of occupations. In *The sociological eye: Selected papers on work, self and the study of society, book two* (pp. 283-297). Chicago: Aldine Atherton.

Institute for Women's Policy Research. (1993). *The wage gap: Women's and men's earnings* (Briefing Paper). Washington, DC: Author.

Jacobs, J. A. (1989a). Long term trends in occupational segregation by sex. *American Journal of Sociology, 95,* 160-173.

Jacobs, J. A. (1989b). *Revolving doors: Sex segregation and women's careers.* Stanford, CA: Stanford University.

Jacobs, J. A. (1992). Women's entry into management: Trends in earnings, authority, and values among salaried managers. *Administrative Science Quarterly, 37,* 282-301.

Jacobs, J. A. (1994, August). *The sex typing of academic specialties: Trends among college and graduate degree recipients during the 1980s.* Paper presented at the annual meeting of the American Sociological Association, Los Angeles.

Jacobs, J. A., & Steinberg, R. J. (1990). Compensating differentials and the male-female wage gap: Evidence from the New York state pay equity study. *Social Forces, 69,* 439-468.

Jacobsen, J. P. (1994). Trends in workforce sex segregation, 1960-1990. *Social Science Quarterly, 75*(1), 204-211.

Kraft, P. (1977). *Programmers and managers: The routinization of programming in the United States.* New York: Springer-Verlag.

Kraft, P., & Dubnoff, S. (1983, November 14). Software workers survey. *Computerworld,* pp. 1-13.

Kuhn, S. (1989). The limits to industrialization: Computer software development in a large commercial bank. In S. Wood (Ed.), *The transformation of work? skill, flexibility and the labour process* (pp. 266-278). London, England: Unwin Hyman.

Leveson, N. (1989). *Women in computer science: A report for the NSF-CISE Cross-Directorate Activities Advisory Committee.* Washington, DC: National Science Foundation.

Massey, D. S., & Denton, N. A. (1993). *American apartheid: Segregation and the making of the underclass.* Cambridge, MA: Harvard University Press.

McIlwee, J. S., & Robinson, J. G. (1992). *Women in engineering: Gender, power and workplace culture.* Albany: State University of New York.

National Science Foundation. (1984). *The 1982 postcensal survey of scientists and engineers* (NSF 84-330). Washington, DC: National Science Foundation.

National Science Foundation. (1988). *Profiles—computer sciences: Human resources and funding* (NSF 88-324). Washington, DC: National Science Foundation.

Orlikowski, Wanda J. (1988). The data processing occupation: Professionalization or proletarianization? *Research in the Sociology of Work, 4,* 95-124.

Pearl, A., Pollack, M., Riskin, E., Thomas, B., Wolf, E., & Wu, A. (1990). Becoming a computer scientist: A report by the ACM Committee on the Status of Women in Computing Science. *Communications of the ACM, 33*(11), 48-57.

Reskin, B. F. (1993). Sex segregation in the workplace. *Annual Review of Sociology, 19,* 241-270.

Reskin, B. F., & Roos, P. A. (1990). *Job queues, gender queues: Explaining women's inroads into male occupations.* Philadelphia: Temple University Press.

Reskin, B. F., & Ross, C. E. (1992). Jobs, authority, and earnings among managers: The continuing significance of sex. *Work and Occupations, 9,* 342-365.

Rochester, J. B. (1988, January/February). The crisis in computer education. *Computer Update,* pp. 18-21.

Silvestri, G. T., & Lukasiewicz, J. M. (1992). Occupational employment projections. In *Outlook 1990-2005* (BLS Bulletin 2402) (pp. 62-92). Washington, DC: U.S. Government Printing Office.

Steering Committee on Human Resources in Computer Science and Technology. (1993). *Computing professionals: Changing needs for the 1990s.* Washington, DC: National Academy.

Strober, M. H. (1984). Toward a general theory of occupational sex segregation: The case of public school teaching. In B. Reskin (Ed.), *Sex segregation in the workplace: Trends, explanations, remedies* (pp. 144-156). Washington, DC: National Academy.

Strober, M. H., & Arnold, C. L. (1987). Integrated circuits/segregated labor: Women in computer-related occupations and high-tech industries. In H. L. Hartmann (Ed.), *Computer chips and paper clips: Technology and women's employment. Case studies and policy perspectives* (Vol. 2, pp. 136-182). Washington, DC: National Academy.

Tang, J. (1991). *The career mobility of Asian American engineers: Earnings, career status, promotion and attrition.* Ph.D. dissertation, Department of Sociology, University of Pennsylvania, Philadelphia.

Tarallo, B. M. (1987). *The production of information: An examination of the employment relations of software engineers and computer programmers.* Ph.D. dissertation, Department of Sociology, University of California, Davis.

U.S. Bureau of the Census. (1991a). *Computer use in the United States: 1989* (Current Population Reports Special Studies, Series P-23, No. 171). Washington, DC: U.S. Government Printing Office.

U.S. Bureau of the Census. (1991b). *Survey of natural and social scientists and engineers (SSE), 1989* (ICPSR 9504). Ann Arbor, MI: Inter-University Consortium for Political and Social Research.

U.S. Bureau of Labor Statistics, Department of Labor. (1976–1992, January). *Employment and earnings.* Washington, DC: U.S. Government Printing Office.

U.S. Department of Education. (1992). *Digest of educational statistics.* Washington, DC: U.S. Government Printing Office.

Vetter, B. M. (1991). *Professional women and minorities: A manpower data resource service* (9th ed.). Washington, DC: Commission of Professionals in Science and Technology.

Vetter, B. M. (1992). *Professional women and minorities: A manpower data resource service* (10th ed.). Washington, DC: Commission of Professionals in Science and Technology.

Wright, R. (1990, August). *Gendered promotion tracks within and from computer work.* Paper presented at the annual meeting of the American Sociological Association, Washington, DC.

Wright, R. (1991, April). *Gender differences in computer careers.* Paper presented at the annual meeting of the Eastern Sociological Society, Providence, RI.

Wright, R. (1992, April). *What do the careers of computer workers tell us about technical work?* Paper presented at the annual meeting of the Eastern Sociological Society, Arlington, VA.

13

Gender and the Formation of a Women's Profession

The Case of Public School Teaching

JO ANNE PRESTON

Despite the burgeoning literature on gender and occupations, little attention has been given to the influence of gender in the formation of professions. For almost half a century sociologists have recognized differences between predominantly female professions and predominantly male professions, but most theoretical and empirical considerations of the professionalization process have failed to account for the development of these differences. Without examining the influence of gender in the formation of professions, sociologists have difficulty explaining how inferior status and wages have become associated with female professions. Employing historical data, this chapter seeks to demonstrate how gender affects professionalization of teaching. Evidence from 19th century school records reveals that the development of gender distinctions in wages, in authority, and in cultural representation was an essential part of professionalization of teaching.

Carr-Saunders and Wilson (1933) first identified common characteristics of predominantly female professions when they developed the category *semiprofessions* to include all major women's professions. Following Carr-Saunders and Wilson's conceptualization, Simpson and Simpson (1969) recognized that women's professions have been governed by more extensive bureaucratic structures than men's professions. Working within a functionalist framework, they proposed that women workers needed greater bureaucratic control due to their lesser commitment to work. Simpson and Simpson also postulated that a woman's concern for her duties outside the workplace induced her to submit more readily to authority. Gender, in this formulation, has an impact on professionalization by calling forth extensive bureaucratic structures. Although correctly identifying bureaucracy as characteristic of many women's professions, Simpson and Simpson failed to recognize another gender dimension of this development: Men control and often completely make up the bureaucratic structures that govern female professionals.

More recent theoretical considerations of professionalization, eschewing simple ahistorical trait-based views, stress the importance of locating professionalization within its historical period and in reference to external processes. Most, however, do not accord gender much significance. Johnson (1967) conceptualizes professionalization as a process transformed by the growth of the state but ignores the influence of gender in this transformation. He defines professionalization as a process that results in control over an occupation without examining how gender affects that control. Larson (1977), arguing that professions developed as part of the evolution of late-18th-century and 19th-century capitalism, emphasizes the historically bound character of professions as they are locked into broader structural and historical processes. Although she discusses how a category of supervisors was created as a result of the bureaucratization of teaching, she fails to recognize that most of these newly created supervisory positions were filled by men whereas women remained the vast majority of classroom teachers. These gender distinctions, with their attendant wage and power differences, constituted an integral part of the professionalization of teaching.

Abbott (1988) calls for an ecological perspective, viewing professions as a system of continuous, historically located struggles over jurisdictions. In his historical analysis, he concludes that gender had limited significance in the formation of professions. He considers that in cases of occupational transformation gender acts only as a following variable. Like Larson, he discusses the emergence of school supervisors with professionalization without recognizing the importance of the growing number of female teachers to the creation of supervisory positions. The increase in female teachers may not have followed bureaucratization as he suggests; rather, bureaucratic structures may have arisen during and after the increased employment of female teachers. Historical evidence shows that the development of male-dominated bureaucratic structures in New England teaching occurred during the feminization of teaching.

Not all contemporary considerations of professionalization have ignored or minimized the importance of gender. In the last decade two English sociologists, Hearn and Witz, independently proposed models to explain the relationship of gender and professionalization. Hearn (1982) formulated a model for gendered professionalization that places the process within a patriarchal society. Based both on a stage theory of professionalization and the conception of female professions as semiprofessions, his model proposes that occupations achieve full professionalization only when they are completely dominated by men; that is, so long as women make up the rank and file in teaching, nursing, social work, and public librarianship, these occupations will be denied many of the benefits accruing to male professions. As men increase their participation in semiprofessions, Hearn forecasts that they will gain more control until, when men compose the entire workforce, a semiprofession becomes a full profession. In his model, the process of professionalization is equated with process of achieving male hegemony. His analysis, however, conflates patriarchal power and professional power, denying women the possibility of achieving professional power. More problematic is his view of semiprofessions as on a continuum with full professions and eventually becoming entirely composed of men. The historical studies of women's professions, such as nursing (Melosh, 1982) and public librarianship (Garrison, 1979), reveal no such trend. In teaching, the labor force has remained predominantly female since 1880 (Oppenheimer, 1970).

In contrast, Witz (1990, 1992) views professionalization as a process that is profoundly altered by the dynamics of gender relations. Using a neo-Weberian framework, she argues for a model of gendered closure strategies in which men as a dominant social collectivity seek to exclude or to control women who, in turn, respond either by challenging the male monopoly of an occupation or by creating a related, exclusively female occupation. Closure practices—exclusionary, inclusionary, demarcationary, and dual—have gendered dimensions. Gendered agents choose specific closure strategies and bring gender-determined differential power to bear upon specific professionalization projects. Male doctors, for example, choose to exclude women from medicine by employing their greater power over credentialing institutions and the state. Female nurses and midwives, on the other hand, engage in a dual closure strategy which contains both usurpationary and exclusionary activities; they resist domination from male doctors and, at the same time, restrict entry to their own professions. Gendered agents, therefore, can construct women's professions through dual closure strategies. Although Witz's model may explain the development of medical professions, it is less revealing in the case of school teaching, in which state officials have always prevailed and teachers have had little success in influencing the social construction of their profession.

Borrowing from Witz's conception of gendered agents, however, this chapter considers the actions of those gendered agents who influenced the professionalization of teaching, chiefly school reformers Horace Mann and Henry Bernard. In addition to considering the influence of these gendered agents and rather than simply confining their influence to closure strategies, it recognizes that gender "is present in the processes, practices, images and ideologies, and distributions of power" (Acker, 1992, p. 567). According to Acker, gender is "the patterning of difference and domination through distinctions between men and women that is integral to many social processes" (p. 565). I argue, therefore, that gender is integral to the process of professionalization. Thus gender, as a part of the process of professionalization, affects both the dynamics and the outcome of the process in a variety of ways. This study employs this broader conceptualization of gender.

The definition of professions and professionalization is more problematic, with little consensus among sociologists. Abbott (1988) defines professions as "exclusive occupational groups applying somewhat abstract knowledge to particular cases" (p. 8). He explains that he arrives at this conceptualization because of its relevance to answering his theoretical questions on how professions control skill and knowledge in relation to one another. The process of professional development of any occupation, he demonstrates, is influenced by jurisdictional conflicts. Abbott proposes that professionalization theory should focus on work rather than the structure of occupations. This study focuses on how gender influences the development, structural as well as ideological, of one profession; my conceptualization of professionalization follows from those theoretical formulations that concentrate more extensively on these changes within an occupation. This chapter considers professionalization as a process that can result in the development of bureaucracy (Larson, 1977), in the evolution of cultural legitimation (Bledstein, 1976), in the establishment of formal training and credentialing with the related raise in material rewards (Wilensky, 1964), and in changes in workers' autonomy and control over their occupation (Johnson, 1967).

Using these formulations, this study examines the case of the professionalization of teaching in 19th-century Massachusetts. In the United States, school teaching became professionalized first in Massachusetts, which later served as the model for other states. Over the course of the 19th century, driven by the same social and economic forces that professionalized law and medicine (Larson, 1979; Starr, 1982), it evolved from an undesirable occupation to a more highly regarded profession, experiencing all the changes enumerated above. At the beginning of the century, teaching was a low-status, low-paid occupation demanding little expertise or training. By the end of the century, it was a higher-paid, higher-status profession governed by bureaucratic structures and requiring education in teacher-training colleges and additional formal credentials. Each of these changes was affected by another important transformation in teaching, feminization. As teaching became increasing female through the first half of the century, the changes wrought by professionalization were shaped by the increasing presence of women in the classroom. In the second half of the century, when women composed the vast majority of teachers, gender had even a more powerful impact on workers' control over the profession and workers' autonomy.

I have analyzed the causes of feminization of teaching in New England extensively elsewhere and will not discuss them here at length. My empirical work has demonstrated that the transformation of teaching from a male occupation to a female occupation was a process that took more than 200 years and was finally completed in the 19th century with structural and ideological changes in teaching, both driven by the school reform movement (Preston, 1982, 1989, 1993). The new hierarchical job segregation by sex, increased supervision, and a female representation of the ideal teacher all reduced the prejudice against female teachers, the greatest impediment to feminization. Strober and Landford (1986), analyzing 19th-century quantitative school data in six states for the years 1850–1880, also found that feminization was associated with structural changes in teaching. Specifically, they found higher percentages of female teachers in counties where teaching was formalized, where it was calculated by length of the school year and teachers per school, and where women's earning were a small fraction of men's. These changes were also developments in the professionalization of teaching and as such were, in turn, extensively transformed by the increase in female teachers. In related work, Strober and Tyack (1980) identified the development of sex-segregated, male-dominated bureaucratic structures in schooling. Empirical evidence from the history of teaching cited below demonstrates that these sex-segregated bureaucratic structures arose with professionalization and increased the gender gap in absolute wages.

In the following sections, the chapter presents some empirical evidence from the history of teaching demonstrating the impact of gender on professionalization. The evidence reveals that professionalization, rather than being a gender neutral process, was profoundly influenced by gender. The first section explores changes in teachers' autonomy. Freidson (1986), who considers an increase in autonomy critical to professonalization, defines autonomy as "the right to use discretion and judgment in the performance of their work" (p. 184). Similarly, Jaffe (1989) measured autonomy by "the extent to which employees exercise self-direction and discretion over the execution of their jobs" (p. 381). Others define autonomy as the absence of supervision imposed on the worker. For example, Forsyth and Danisiewicz (1985) conceptualize professional autonomy as a phenomenon "manifested by freedom from the client and employing organizations" (p. 61). To explore the various dimensions of autonomy, this section employs these definitions to examine 19th-century changes in teachers' capacity for self-direction and the degree to which they have control over their work.

The second section presents historical data on the changes in teachers' control over their occupation during professionalization. Johnson (1972) defined a profession as "not an occupation but a way to control an occupation" (p. 45). In contrast, as teaching evolved from a male occupation to a female profession, male administrators assumed more control over recruitment, licensing, and training. Despite the efforts of male and female teachers and prominent female educators, the male leaders of the school reform movement gradually transferred teacher training from female academies to state-dominated normal schools and successfully lobbied for greater state control over credentialing teachers.

The third section of this chapter discusses changes in wages during professionalization. During professionalization wages rose for both men and women teachers. Although not extensively discussed in the work and occupations literature, professionalization customarily elevates financial rewards by creating an elite occupation. Despite feminization, which is associated with declining wages (Reskin & Roos, 1990), professionalization caused teachers' wages to rise. More significantly, the gender difference in absolute wages of teachers also increased, with men benefiting more economically from professionalization than did women. The causes of the gender gap in wages are not well-explained by neoclassical economic theories; the problems with these approaches are extensively discussed elsewhere (Marini, 1989; Stevenson, 1988), and they will not be reviewed here. In spite of the failure of various theoretical approaches to fully account for the gender gap in wages, empirical studies have found a relationship between the gender gap in wages and job segregation by sex (Bielby & Baron, 1984; Treiman & Hartmann, 1981). Data presented in this section suggest that the increase in the gender gap in teachers' wages was caused, in part, by the creation of sex-segregated bureaucratic structures.

Gender, however, was not expressed solely by structures. A specific cultural representation of the female schoolteacher evolved during professionalization of school teaching, and this representation had a direct effect upon the process. Professions acquire sex-specific ideologies, like all occupations, as they are socially constructed, and these constructions are informed by gender ideology—that is, a set of ideas that consider either men or women better suited to do the work required of an occupation because of their supposed innate qualities. Milkman (1987) identifies these ideas as the "idiom" of an occupation. Although the idiom of every female profession prescribes that women are best suited for that type of work, the content of each idiom is idiosyncratic and not necessarily related to women's domestic roles (Crompton, 1987; Milkman, 1987); neither is it always shared by the professional workers themselves (Preston, 1989, 1993). The construction of the idiom may well be part of image building during the professionalization process and may act to limit the aspirations of the female professionals (Forsyth & Danisiewicz, 1985; Hearn, 1982). Ideology is crucial to the professionalization of occupations because professions need cultural legitimation (Bledstein, 1976). As part of that legitimation process, the public must be convinced that the service rendered is "essential, exclusive, and complex" (Forsyth & Danisiewicz, 1985, p. 64). They must view the professional worker as competent to perform the professional service. Section four examines the evolution of a gendered professional image of the school teacher.

The final section of this chapter discusses the findings of limited autonomy and control over the occupation, gendered bureaucratic structures, increased gender gap in wages, and sex-typed ideology. It then speculates on the implication of these findings in light of current understandings of professions and professionalization.

Autonomy in the Teaching Profession

The autonomy of the teacher, whether measured by capacity for self-direction or by degree of control over the work process, declined over the course of the 19th century. In the 18th century, when the occupation was predominantly male, little supervision was exercised over Massachusetts teachers. Teachers' diaries and correspondence reveal that teachers could open and close their schools as their needs dictated. Thomas Robbins, teaching in Torringford in 1798, felt entitled to close his school when he had a pain in his jaw (Tarbox, 1886-1887). After he heard of a disturbance in Cambridge in 1775, Scituate schoolmaster Paul Litchfield (1881-1882) closed his school for two and one half days to check on his rooms at Harvard. Earlier in the same week he chose to miss one morning of school because of "rainey weather." Likewise, female teachers had some control over their schedules. Elizabeth Bancroft, a teacher in Groton, freely dismissed her school for funerals and barn raisings during her 1773 summer session (Bancroft, 1793-99). In these accounts, use of the term *schoolkeeping* rather than *school teaching* indicates the control 18th-century teachers had over their workplace.

From the second decade of the 19th century, when feminization of the winter session began, changes in schooling increased the supervision of teachers. Towns had traditionally reserved the winter sessions, usually equivalent to the summer sessions in length and content, for male teachers while appointing only women to summer session schools. As towns began to hire women for winter session positions, they directed male supervisors to assume more control over schoolteachers' work, curtailing their freedom to execute their job as they chose. The timing of the increase in supervision, coincident with the feminization of the winter sessions, suggests that the state and towns perceived a need to assume more control over an increasingly female workforce. The frequency and character of the selectmen's visits changed in the 1820s with the passage of state legislation granting more powers to the selectmen and requiring more stringent supervision of teachers. The Massachusetts acts of 1826 and 1827 conferred on local school committees, which comprised male leaders of the community, powers to appoint and certify teachers, to visit and inspect the classroom work of the teacher, to direct and supervise the teacher's work, and to select textbooks. Authority to certify and appoint gave the committee the power to decide what personal qualifications and training made an applicant an acceptable teacher. Selection of textbooks allowed the committee to influence the curriculum but not yet the course of study or teaching methods, changes which were to come later (Suzzallo, 1906). More importantly, the school committee now had general charge and "superintendence" over the teachers' work. To assure that the school committeemen carried out their new function, the 1826 and 1827 acts stipulated that they visit the classroom once a month without advance notice to observe the teacher and question the students. Superintendence of the teacher, therefore, increased the control of the administrators, all men, over the standards of teaching and, consequently, diminished teachers' autonomy.

The new superintendence of the teachers is well described by a Massachusetts teacher writing home in 1826:

Dear Achsah,
. . . I am almost tired to death. . . . I have engaged a school. . . . Oh I have been brought under the most rigid laws this season than I ever was in New York State. The Legislature of this state has adopted a new system in regard to public schools. This is that each town choose a committee of five or more to superintend the schools in town . . . that is to process the teacher, select the books and direct the studies and everything concerning the schools. No teacher in entitled to their pay unless they are examined by the committee. . . . They also visit the school the first or second week after commencement and give the teacher notice before coming after that once a month without previous notice to the teacher until the last week when they are there to let them know they are coming . . . I have been under their contract since the first of may when i went befor them for inspection since then they have visited my school six times—sometimes one at a time sometimes two or more just as they choose but thank fortune I am almost done with them a week from monday comes my exam on tuesday I close my school and I think I shall rejoice if I ever did [school] has almost worn me out . . . It has made my fat checks look rather hollow. (Brammer, 1826)

In addition to reporting the changes in Massachusetts school laws, Electa Snow's account also illustrates the resentment generated by the selectmen's expanded authority over teachers' work.

By the 1830s, Massachusetts towns hired male teachers in the winter to supervise female teachers, thereby seeking to lessen their residents' resistance to hiring female teachers for the exclusively male-taught winter session. Towns, for example, often consolidated two district schools during the winter session, assigned the younger students to a female teacher and the older students to a male teacher, and placed "the whole school" under the male teacher (Massachusetts school reports, 1833–

1834). These districts often referred to the man as teacher and the woman as assistant teacher. The town of Sunderland, for example, reported that it incorporated two female teachers into the winter session schools as follows:

> District No. 3 and 4 lying near each other unite and in winter have a central school attended by the scholars in each district over ten years of age. This school is taught by a man. Those under ten attend schools in each district taught by a woman. (Massachusetts School Reports, 1833–1834)

Sunderland then granted the male teacher authority over the female teachers. Restructuring schooling along gender lines thus maintained male dominance of the winter sessions.

The subsequent proliferation of managerial positions, which accompanied professionalization, further constrained teachers' autonomy. Towns evolved a structure of control and supervision that included a school committee, a superintendent, and one or more principals, all of whom were male, with the exception of principals of female high schools. The most developed of these systems were the fully bureaucratized school systems of cities and large towns. In the bureaucratizing urban school systems that developed with professionalization, full-time administrators, all male, supervised teachers, who were primarily female. In addition, grammar masters began to supervise female assistant teachers.

As shown in Table 13.1, Boston in 1852 hired 37 male grammar schoolmasters and submasters to supervise 138 female "assistants." In 1866, the Boston School Committee also extended the powers of the grammar masters to include overseeing the primary mistresses in their respective districts. In 1875, new legislation abolished the school committee, created a school board of 24 members, added six new supervisors, and formed a board of supervisors to be chaired by the superintendent (Katz, 1987)—actions that definitively placed most of the power in the superintendent's office. Table 13.2 shows the new configuration of hierarchy in the Boston schools. Female and male teachers were segregated not only by job title but also increasingly by the degree of autonomy conferred by the title. By 1876, 48 men held administrative posts as principals whereas one woman occupied the recently created position of assistant principal of the normal school, an institution attended by a majority of female students. Other female positions in the primary, grammar, and high schools had been divided into first, second, third, and fourth assistants. Boston now gave all women the rank of assistant—

Table 13.1 Hierarchy and Annual Wages of Boston Teaching Positions by Sex, 1852

Position	Number	Wages
Male (N = 82)		
Supervisory		
Superintendent	1	$2,500
High School		
Masters	2	$2,400
Submasters	3	$1,500
Ushers	5	$800–$1,200
Grammar Schools		
Grammar masters	23	$1,500
Writing masters	5	$1,500
Submasters	9	$1,000
Ushers	13	$ 800
Female (N = 315)		
Grammar Schools		
Head assistants	3	$ 400
Assistants	135	$250–$300
Primary Schools		
Primary mistresses	177	$ 300

SOURCE: Report on the Boston Schools, 1852; Massachusetts State School Returns, 1851-1852.

assistant principal; first, second, and third assistant in the high schools; normal school assistant; first, second, and third assistant in the grammar schools; and fourth assistant in the primary schools. Gone were the female positions that implied some independence, such as head assistant or primary mistress. All of these changes in job titles accompanied the increase in supervision and the resulting decline in autonomy experienced by teachers. Significantly, the erosion of autonomy was greater among female teachers.

In these bureaucratized school systems, the resident principal and various members of the school committee made frequent, unannounced visits to each classroom to assess the progress of the teacher by examining the students. These evaluations were more extensive than those of the 1820s. In her diary, Lynn, Massachusetts, school teacher Mary Mudge (1854) described one visit as follows:

Table 13.2 Hierarchy and Annual Wages of Boston Teaching Positions by Sex, 1876

Position	Number	Wages
Male (*N* = 124)		
Supervisory		
Superintendent	1	$4,500
Supervisor	6	$4,000
Principal	48[a]	(wages for teaching rank)
High schools		
Master	40	$1,700–$4,000
Submaster		
Usher		
Grammar schools		
Master	87	$1,700–$3,200
Submaster		
Usher		
Female (*N* = 962)		
High schools		
Assistant principal; first, second, and third assistant; normal school assistant	46	$1,000–$2,000
Grammar schools		
First, second, and third assistant	493	$600–$1,200
Primary schools		
Fourth assistant	423	$600–$800

SOURCE: City of Boston Abstract of Semi-Annual Returns, January 31, 1876.

a. Principals are also enumerated in high school and grammar schoolmaster categories.

Dr. Callaupe and Mr. Ambler into the school this P.M. . . . Heard the 1st class read . . . asked many questions not in their lesson. Harriet Brown got confused and could not spell Alcohol. 2nd class read "The Father" . . . did very well in reading and spelling. 1st class in Colburns recited on division of mixed numbers . . . 1st Class in Geography did well but could not tell what year Greenland was discovered. Dr. [Callaupe] made a few remarks; . . . said he had been well pleased . . . they did well in Geography and Arithmetic and would be excellent readers if they kept their voices up at the comma.

Although female teachers privately lamented the encroachment on their work by the extended, intrusive classroom visits of supervisors, the historical record reveals no direct opposition. Finding no meaningful means of protest, female and male teachers' most common recourse was to seek alternative employment. Men sought and gained employment in the emerging exclusively male professions of law and medicine. Women, more limited in their options, moved from teaching job to teaching job in search of more suitable employment. For example, in the mid-19th century, Massachusetts school teacher Aurelia Smith, constantly dissatisfied with her work, taught in five towns during her 6-year teaching career. Work biographies of 19th-century Mount Holyoke graduates show that female teachers continually moved from one teaching position to another (Preston, 1982).

Even more central to workers' autonomy is the capacity to determine how the work is done. In 18th-century Massachusetts, pedagogy, the method of teaching, remained primitive. Teachers developed what teaching methods they had idiosyncratically. Although they frequently followed a series of texts, teachers could choose the lessons or recitation exercises. Supervisors rarely imposed a method of teaching. Most 18th-century teachers taught alone in one-room schoolhouses; supervision consisted of occasional visits by one or more town selectmen. Because the average selectman had less education than the teacher, he usually concerned himself only with decorum and the physical appearance of the classroom (Suzzallo, 1906). Teachers had control over how teaching was done and over other conditions of their work.

Nineteenth-century male administrators, at more elevated positions, began to assume responsibility for developing teaching methods. The science of pedagogy was almost nonexistent in Massachusetts until the first decades of the 19th century, when Horace Mann and other leaders of school reform began to advocate teaching methods. Mann's second annual report (1838) included a treatise on methods of instruction. But even before Mann published his directives, Samuel Hall (1829), founder of the first teacher-training institution in America, published his *Lectures on Schoolkeeping*. In his lectures, he spelled out the teacher's appropriate presentation of lessons, the proper curriculum to be taught in each type of school, and the correct relationship between the teacher and the student. Such instructions, when followed, may have improved teachers' performance in the classroom. From the standpoint of the autonomy of the worker, however, teaching methods imposed by managers reduced teachers' control over the work process. Later developments in curriculum reform further restricted teachers' decision making in the formulation of the content and methods of teaching (Apple, 1986). Consequently, the mid- to late-19th-century teacher became less autonomous as a result of the professionalization of teaching.

Thus changes in the structure and content of teaching during the professionalization of the occupation curtailed the professional workers' control over their work. Significantly, I argue, the professional workers were increasingly women. Because 19th-century women's low social status and subordination to men in all other aspects of their lives allowed school reformers to create male-dominated bureaucratic structures to control female teachers and because women's limited employment opportunities curtailed their options, teaching evolved as a profession that was structured by a sex-segregated system of hierarchical control and supervision. This hierarchical restructuring of teaching permitted reformers to achieve their goal of making schooling a more influential social institution without granting power to the growing number of female teachers. Gender, then, rather than having an influence after the fact, determined important and enduring characteristics of the teaching profession. These changes are in contrast to those occurring in the 19th century male occupations of law and medicine. The professionalization of these occupations resulted in greater power for the individual worker and for the profession in general (Larson, 1977; Starr, 1982). The much more limited autonomy of the teachers resembled that experienced by workers in other female professions. For example, the development of managerial positions primarily held by men can also be found in the professionalization of librarianship (Garrison, 1979). Although nursing did not develop a male-dominated managerial structure, control was exercised by a related male profession—that of medicine (Hearn, 1982; Witz, 1990).

Control Over the Teaching Profession

Teachers never achieved control over the development of their emerging profession. During the course of professionalization, the state took over the responsibility of training teachers, denying teachers authority over the training of the new members of their profession. This further constraint on female teachers' autonomy came about as state-financed and state-controlled normal schools replaced the female academies as the educators of teachers. Normal schools, first established in the late 1830s, became the primary institution for teacher training by the end of the Civil War. The state legislature also mandated criteria for certification and employment (Woody, 1929).

Female academies were first established in New England in the 18th century and proliferated during the antebellum period. Most academies were not specifically aimed at training women to become teachers; rather, they were devoted to educating young women in liberal arts, science, and religion. Many academy founders explicitly saw themselves as committed to improving the situation of women, who were barred from studying at men's colleges (Woody, 1929). Some academies even conferred explicitly female degrees. The Springfield Female Collegiate Institute, for example, awarded an M.E.L., or Mistress of English Literature, an L.B.A., or Lady Baccalaureate, and an M.L.A., or Mistress of Liberal Arts (Springfield Female Collegiate Institute, 1860-1861).

Less concerned with intellectual development, the curriculum at normal schools prescribed methods of teaching developed by male administrators. When the first normal school was established in 1839, female academies were the main educators of female teachers. By 1860, with the founding in Massachusetts of five more normal schools, school committees—with the encouragement of the state legislature—hired normal school graduates over female academy graduates (Magnum, 1928). Increasingly, more teachers prepared for their work at normal schools with their state-mandated course of study rather than at female academies. Because normal schools emphasized methods and most female academies taught only subject matter, leaving choice of method to the prospective teacher, the transition from female academies to normal schools gave the state control over the training of new workers.

The state also usurped any power teachers may have possessed over recruitment and standards of the profession. By passing legislation requiring training in state-run normal schools and setting criteria for certification, the state, rather than a professional organization, assumed control of entry to the profession. Town school committees still retained the power to hire teachers; these committees, however, were directly influenced by the voters—not by teachers' associations. How voters conceived of the proper role of the teacher in any particular historical period can further dictate what the school committee sets as professional standards (Freidson, 1986).

Teachers made repeated unavailing efforts to influence the development of teaching. In 1830, 45 men met in Topsfield to form the Essex County Teachers' Association, whose express purpose was "the improvement of teachers and the system of education generally." By the 1850s, the organization allowed women to attend their lectures but reserved all policy making to male members. In its first 3 decades, the organization sponsored lectures on timely educational issues, petitioned Congress for federal support of education, and established a fund to aid disabled teachers. It expressed its dissatisfaction with the current system of supervising teachers through published essays in *The Massachusetts Teacher.* Unfortunately, the association's recommendations on this issue and other matters were spurned by state officials. Norfolk County also formed an all-male teachers' association in 1830 for "mutual improvement, with reference to professional duties." It too failed to shape the profession. Later teachers' organizations, such as the American Institute for Instruction, an organization also dominated by men, suffered a similar fate (Messerli, 1972).

Promoters of female education were also enthusiastic supporters of the professionalization of teaching, perceiving it as a way of increasing the status and wages of female teachers and ultimately elevating them to a position equal to that of male professionals. Prominent educators Catherine Beecher and Emma Willard advocated professional status for female teachers (Lutz, 1964; Sklar, 1973). Catherine Beecher (1851), for example, argued for upgrading teaching to a "profession for women, as honorable and lucrative for her as the legal, medical, and theological professions are for men" (p. 79). Rather than establishing separate teacher-training schools run by the state, Beecher recommended adding teaching departments to already existing female academies (Beecher, 1835). Correspondence of female teachers describes similar aspirations for their new profession (Preston, 1989). These women, however, lacked the power to control the development of the profession. It was the school reformers and the state legislatures with their greater political power who ultimately determined its shape and content. Teachers became the objects of school reform: Having found no effective means of gaining political influence, they were excluded from active participation.

Furthermore, with the development of bureaucratic structures during professionalization, male administrators directly oversaw the implementation of state- or local-mandated educational policy. As managers, they had decision-making power over the formulation of classroom instruction. Frequent supervision of classroom instruction ensured that certain pedagogical techniques were followed. Formal and impromptu oral examinations of students, as in the case cited in Mary Mudge's diary, guaranteed that teachers adhered to certain curricular directives. By

1880, the very content of teaching became determined and enforced by male administrators, not teachers, the vast majority of whom were now women.

Professionalization and the Gender Gap in Wages

Massachusetts teachers' wages rose from 1840 until the end of the century. Yet many studies of feminized occupations find that wages decline (Reskin & Roos, 1990). Thus, in teaching, the effects of professionalization must have outweighed those of feminization. When broken down by sex, however, the data show that men benefited more from professionalization than did women. The average monthly wages of Massachusetts teachers from 1840 to 1870, inclusive of board, are presented in Table 13.3. Men's wages rose from $33.08 in 1840 to $74.24 in 1870, whereas women's wages rose from $12.75 in 1840 to only $30.24 in 1870. The gender difference in absolute wages grew from $20.33 to $44. Relative wages, however, remained nearly the same; women continued to make approximately 40% of what male teachers earned.

Towns exploited the gender gap in pay to contain the cost of the wage bill. By hiring female teachers, they could raise teachers' wages without significantly increasing the school budget. If, for example, a town hired three male teachers and one female teacher in 1840 at the respective average wages, the cost of wages would be $111.99. By hiring one female to replace one male teacher in 1850, at the average wages paid for that year, the town expense for teachers' wages would be only $98.62. In 1860, if the same town replaced one more male teacher with a female teacher, paying the higher average wage, the cost to the town would be $110.50, less than the 1840 figure. Thus feminization contained or even lowered the total cost of wages to the towns, even as professionalization increased the wages of both male and female teachers.

Even with the gender gap in wages, 19th century women sought teaching positions. Although female teachers continued to earn less than male teachers, increasingly they earned more than other categories of female workers. In 1840, textile corporations in Massachusetts paid female operatives approximately the same wages as Massachusetts towns paid female teachers. After 1840, female teachers' wages rose while female textile workers' wages plummeted; by 1860 female teachers earned twice the wages of millgirls (Gitelman, 1967). Other women's occupations, such as shoe binder, seamstress, tailoress, and domestic

Table 13.3 Average Monthly Wages (Inclusive of Board) of
Massachusetts Teachers, by Sex, 1840–1880

Year	1839–40	1849–50	1859–60	1869–70
Males	$33.08	$34.89	$50.56	$74.24
Females	$12.75	$14.42	$19.98	$30.24
Female wages as percent of male wages	39%	41%	40%	41%

SOURCE: Massachusetts Board of Education, 1839-1870.

service, paid even less than factory work (Abbott, 1910). In comparison to other forms of employment available to women, school teaching, despite the gender gap in pay, represented a remunerative opportunity (Carter, 1986).

Although women schoolteachers were relatively well paid, the gendered wage differential still denied women the full advantages of professionalization. Towns that were willing to pay higher wages for professional workers paid more to male teachers. Data from local school reports indicate that the greater gender gap may be related to the establishment of hierarchical structures during professionalization. In bureaucratized school systems, where qualifications for teachers were the most stringent, school committees hired men as supervisors of female teachers. Men not only held different jobs from female teachers but ones that were regarded as clearly superior and that paid higher wages. The wage structure in the Boston school system in 1852, for example, indicates a clear relationship between hierarchical structure and the gender gap in earnings: Men hold all the higher-paying, supervisory positions and women predominate in the lower-paying teaching positions (see Table 13.1). With the increased number of supervisory positions, all filled by men, and the greater preponderance of female teachers in lower-level teaching positions in 1876, the gender gap widened. In 1852, the average male wage was $1,134 and the average female wage, $290. In 1876, the average male wage rose to $2,654 while the average female wage increased to only $840 (see Table 13.2).

Even in those towns that did not report by job title a special supervisory role for men, male teachers may have acted as supervisors to female assistant teachers, a practice discussed earlier and a rationale for differential pay. To further complicate matters, some towns routinely included the wages of their male principals and superintendents in their calculations of the average male teacher wage, thus inflating the wage of regular male teachers (Preston, 1982). Much of the gender gap in wages, therefore, may be accounted for by the assignment of supervisory tasks to male teachers, a practice which became widespread during professionalization.

The wage differential was not wholly due to men's supervisory positions in teaching, however. Evidence from antebellum Massachusetts shows that where the professionalization and feminization of teaching had yet to have much impact, male teachers, segregated from female teachers only by the season in which they taught, earned higher wages. Table 13.4 shows that in 10 towns that continued under the district system, male teachers, all of whom taught in the winter season, earned on average higher wages than did female teachers—almost all of whom taught in the summer session. Because most towns did not hire female teachers for the winter session and because each male teacher taught alone in a one-room district school, the male teachers could not have been supervisors. Female teachers who taught in the winter session made on average more than females teaching in the summer but less than their male counterparts. The higher wage for female teachers may have been due to their participation in the winter session, which was considered "men's work."

Prevailing attitudes toward women workers may also have contributed to women's lower wages. Many state and local school officials announced in their annual reports their intention of paying female teachers, yet to be hired, lower wages than male teachers. School reformer Henry Bernard, for example, argued that "a female teacher could be hired for twelve weeks for the same price as hiring a male teacher for five weeks" (Rhode Island Board of Education, 1846, p. 144). Massachusetts town school reports are replete with remarks on the economic advantages of hiring female teachers. Gardner reported "Females may be procured for sixteen dollars per month . . . males [for] . . . twenty dollars a month" (Massachusetts Board of Education, 1845, p. 128). Northbridge stated that "A female might be employed . . . at an expense of nearly one half a male" (Massachusetts Board of Education, 1845, p. 150). The savings realized by paying female teachers less than males for the winter session, Ashburnham calculated, "would hire a competent man for six months" (Massachusetts Board of Education, 1840-1841, p. 85). Significantly, the wage was determined by the gender of the worker, because no other

Table 13.4 Average Monthly Wage (Including Board) of Summer and Winter Session Teachers, by Sex, in 10 Selected Massachusetts Towns, 1833–34

Town	Summer Session Female	Winter Session Female	Winter Session Male
Dalton	$5.58 (4)	$8.00 (1)	$12.80 (5)
Granby	4.53 (6)	5.50 (2)	10.17 (4)
Greater Barrington	4.59 (14)	7.33 (3)	12.78 (11)
Middlefield	4.00 (10)	5.00 (1)	11.78 (9)
Montague	4.54 (8)	6.06 (2)	12.25 (6)
Russell	4.60 (5)	5.00 (1)	10.75 (4)
Rutland	9.10 (10)	9.44 (2)	18.29 (8)
Shelburne	4.67 (9)	8.00 (3)	13.17 (6)
Tolland	4.00 (5)	5.00 (3)	10.00 (2)
Westfield	3.75 (4)	6.00 (1)	11.75 (4)

SOURCE: Massachusetts School Reports, 1833-1834.
NOTE: Number of teachers is in parentheses.

differences between the two workers were known to the school committeemen. This evidence suggests that women's work was devalued independent of its structural position in the occupation. Moreover, it shows that jobs became female jobs as women were hired for them; that is, a teaching job acquired a woman's wage as women were hired.

The absolute wage gap between male and female teachers increased over the 19th century. As shown in Table 13.3, male teachers earned on average $21.33 a month more than female teachers in 1840 and by 1870, male teachers earned on average $44.00 a month more than female teachers. Many of the male workers in this category were administrators, and by 1870 their numbers had increased, a possible cause for the widening the gender gap in absolute wages. The further development of hierarchical structures in teaching, then, may have been the cause of the change in absolute wages.

Centralized, bureaucratic school systems also created the conditions for collective action. In the Lynn school system, female teachers organized to improve their wages. In 1854, Lynn schoolteacher Mary Mudge recorded the following in her diary: "about 8 1/2 o'clock Miss Row, Miss Nickerson, Cook, and Dodge called to get me to sign a petition to have the Female Teachers' salaries raised. Called with them on Misses Newhall, Neal and Anna. They all signed." Their campaign was unsuccessful. Lynn schools records report no increase in female wages in the next year (Lynn [MA] School Committee, 1855). An examination of the writings of 92 female teachers' writings revealed no other collective endeavor to improve wages (Preston, 1993). As discussed above, most female teachers strove to improve their situation by seeking alternative employment.

Undeterred by female teachers' complaints or brief tenure, school committees continued to appoint male supervisors at superior wages. Thus, the material gains from the professionalization of teaching continued to affect male and female workers differently. Higher-paying supervisory positions for men amplified the existing gender gap in wages caused by sex segregation by season and by discriminatory attitudes. These attitudes were strengthened by the association of gender ideology with the newly constructed jobs within teaching, a development that also influenced the creation of a gendered image of the professional teacher.

Professionalization and the Cultural Representation of the Female Schoolteacher

During the professionalization of school teaching, Horace Mann, Henry Bernard, and other school reformers created a representation of the ideal professional teacher to persuade towns to increase the wages and status of female teachers. Like other aspects of the professionalization process, this cultural representation was gendered; the conception of the professional teacher as female constituted an integral part of the social construction of the profession. The reformers argued that women possessed gender-specific characteristics that enabled them to do the work required of professional teachers: that the characteristics attributed to women in the 19th century, qualities of nurturance and moral rectitude, gave women a special expertise in teaching.

The school reformers, all men, actively created and propagated a new cultural representation of the female teacher that later became firmly implanted in the educational and popular literature of the second half of the 19th century. The ideology of woman's domestic sphere, ideas that emerged with the advent of industrial capitalism, furnished the basis for this new representation. Both reformers and female advocates of women's education—Catherine Beecher, Mary Lyons, and Emma Willard— borrowed selectively from this dominant ideology to argue that the ideal teacher must be a woman. Catherine Beecher strove for 40 years to advance the cause of women by advocating that women's domestic duties necessitated improving female education and hiring women as public school teachers (Sklar, 1973). Because women lacked access to political power, especially within the male-dominated state administration, the view of the female teacher promoted by Beecher and other female educators, one that stressed a capacity for intellectual achievement and merited high wages, failed to predominate. Instead, the representation provided by the reformers, which attributed to women a lack of interest in wages and little intellectual ability, became the 19th-century cultural image of the female schoolteacher.

The school reformers had one primary goal: They sought to create a school system that would socialize students to the changing requirements of work in industrial society by instilling habits of obedience and respect for authority (Bowles & Gintis, 1976; Katz, 1971). Whether school reform created an appropriate workforce for New England factories, or more generally quelled social disorder by producing more obedient citizens, the school reformers' rhetoric leaves no doubt that they perceived a new school system as critical to the smooth transition from an agricultural to an industrial society. In achieving this goal, the reformers concluded that professional female teachers were essential. To promote public acceptance of women as professional teachers and to encourage school committees to hire them, the school reformers created a new conception of the female teacher, which they propagated by using lectures, essays, and reports widely disseminated throughout New England (Preston, 1989, 1993).

Four supposedly innate qualities of 19th-century women made them the appropriate teachers for the new school system: high moral character, disregard for material gain, limited intellectual capacity, and a natural love of children. The first quality, high moral character, was congruent with their mission to instill in children appropriate values. Horace Mann, the most eminent of the school reformers, argued in his numerous essays and lectures that female teachers were more qualified to teach because "by nature" they possessed purer morals (Massachusetts Board of Education, 1841). Another school reformer, Henry Bernard, proclaimed that women were ideal teachers because, among "their peculiar talents," were "purer morals" (in Rhode Island Board of Education, 1845, p. 11). Drawing on this supposed natural quality of women, the reformers hoped to reduce the use of corporal punishment in the schools, substituting instead moral control. They advocated that "moral influence should be substituted, as far as possible, in place of mere coercion" and that "it must follow that women are, in most respects, preeminently qualified to administer such a discipline" (Bernard in Rhode Island Board of Education, 1852, p. 6). School reformers, then, sought to persuade the 19th-century public that purer morals, an assumed characteristic of women, uniquely qualified them to assume professional positions in the new school systems.

School reformers also ascribed to 19th century women a lack of ambition, especially for financial gain. Mann first proposed this self-serving belief in the 1841 school report: "As a class, they [women] never look forward as young men invariably do, . . . to build up a fortune for themselves; and hence the sphere of hope and of effort is narrower, . . . and the whole forces of the mind are more readily concentrated upon present duties." He cited this as one of the characteristics that make "females incomparably better teachers for young children than males" (Massachusetts Board of Education, 1841, p. 45). Although this quality is consistent with moral purity, it contradicts the notion of the monetary value of expert labor. Here one must consider that the development of professional ideology, as a part of the professionalization process, is gendered: Among the emerging 19th-century professions, the desire for financial remuneration consistent with the value of their expert knowledge is acceptable for male professionals in law and medicine, but not for female professionals in teaching and nursing. As part of the professionalization of teaching, school reformers represented female teachers as morally pure, self-sacrificing professional workers. Accordingly, towns could pay female teachers low wages and still regard them as professionals.

Third, school reformers argued that female teachers, like all women, had limited capacity and interest in intellectual endeavors. Since the colonial period, the predominant view was that women had little intellectual capacity. Contrary to popular thinking, the reformers asserted that women did have enough mental ability to teach school, but they did not go so far as to claim that women's intellect was equal to men's. Women, "although deficient in natural brilliance and literary attainments," could acquire enough knowledge to teach children (Rust in New Hampshire Board of Education, 1848, p. 8). Their lack of intelligence was compensated for by other qualities. In the "female character there is always a preponderance of affection over intellect," which, reasoned Mann, "made the female . . . the guide and guardian of young children" (Massachusetts Board of Education, 1842, p. 9). The limited intellectual abilities ascribed to female schoolteachers were sufficient for teaching. Their claim to expert knowledge, however, lay not in their intellect but in their unique relationship to children.

Women's "natural" association with children proved the most compelling reason for school committees to consider women the ideal teachers. Transformations in 19th-century gender ideology prescribed a more intense relationship between mother and child. Elaborating on this new conception of motherhood, school reformers extolled the special ability of women to teach children: "Women's stronger parental impulse makes the society of children delightful [for them], and turns duty into pleasure" (Mann in Massachusetts Board of Education, 1841, p. 45); "The influence of the mother on the young mind is far greater than even the father" (Cembe in Rhode Island Board of Education, 1853, p. 87); "Heaven has plainly appointed females as the natural instructors of young children, and endowed them with those qualities of mind and disposition . . . a greater measure of the gentleness so winning and grateful to the feelings of a child, and of . . . patient forbearance" (Bernard in Connecticut Board of Education, 1840, p. 6). This special relationship extended to the ability to control children "by the silken cord of affection, [which has] led many a stubborn will, and wild ungovernable impulse into habits of obedience and study" (Bernard in Connecticut Board of Education, 1840, p. 7). Drawing on the dominant gender ideology of the mid-19th century, the school reformers portrayed female teachers as possessing unique talents enabling them to become superior teachers. These talents were not acquired through rigorous professional training; they were bestowed on women "by nature."

My examination of 92 female teachers' correspondence found that these 19th-century women held different self-conceptions (Preston, 1993). Their correspondence is replete with discussions of wages. Instead of eschewing the material rewards of teaching as claimed by Mann, Massachusetts women constantly bargained for better wages and, if the school committee was unyielding, sought better-paying teaching positions. Female teachers, rather than limiting their intellectual goals, read poetry, studied foreign languages, attended public lectures, and wrote compositions. Although the woman concerned themselves with moral questions, especially as related to religious doctrine, they did not conceive of moral behavior as a means of managing unruly children. Spurning "moral suasion," female teachers maintained discipline by employing various forms of corporal punishment. Although some demonstrated affection and concern for their students, many others, shocked by their first contact with the bedraggled and underfed children who populated 19th-century public schools, expressed disapproval and disdain.

In spite of female teachers' self-conceptions, the four qualities of the ideal 19th-century schoolteacher—moral rectitude, limited intellectual ambition, disregard for material gains, and a natural love of children—constituted the popular cultural representation. All were derived from the prevailing mid-19th-century gender ideology, which postulated separate spheres for men and women. Because this ideology consigned male and female qualities to mutually exclusive categories, only women could fulfill the social ideal of the professional teacher. The evolution of this social ideal of the professional worker was, therefore, necessarily a gendered process.

Once in place, the cultural representation of the ideal worker is difficult to modify and hence acts as a conservative force upon an occupation (Milkman, 1987). In the present case, it principally affects the actions and attitudes of the employers and the public, although, as stated before, not the female schoolteachers themselves (Preston, 1989). This incorporation of a certain conception of the female teacher in the social construction of the teaching profession offers a compelling explanation for the persistence of sex-typing in teaching. Moreover, it may account for why certain negative characteristics of teaching—low wages, limited intellectual content, restricted upward mobility—are so resistant to change.

Conclusions

Gender influenced historically specific changes in teaching during the process of its professionalization, including sex-segregated structures of supervision and bureaucratic control. These structures allowed male administrators and state legislatures to curtail the autonomy of female teachers and limit their collective control over the teaching profession. By examining changes in wage levels, one finds that whereas professionalization raised the wages of both male and female workers, men benefited more from the increase. The gender gap in teachers' pay was associated with sex-segregated hierarchical structures and job location, and with discriminatory attitudes. Finally, the chapter identifies and discusses four qualities of the ideal professional schoolteacher and shows how the evolution of this ideal, based on 19th-century gender ideology, specified that women would make the best professional teachers.

The evidence presented shows that men came to dominate teaching during professionalization—a finding that confirms the models proposed by both Hearn and Witz. Other findings of this investigation are not accounted for in either model. Witz (1992) ignores the influence of gender ideology. Hearn (1982), although acknowledging the importance of gender ideology, limits its power to persuading women to enter a women's profession—a contention that has been contradicted by empirical studies (Preston, 1989, 1993). Moreover, Hearn attributes the content of gender ideology to women's domestic roles, an assertion disputed by Milkman's study of the electrical and automobile industries (1987). Both ignore the gendered effect professionalization has on wages. Witz accords women's actions the power of usurping a portion of a profession from men while, through closure, also denying entry to other workers. Hearn disregards the agency of women in professionalization. In 19th-century Massachusetts, women attempted to shape teaching so it would be a profession equal to men's; their efforts, however, were overpowered by those of male state officials. A complete model of gendered professionalization should therefore consider how gender affects wages, professional ideology, and actions of agents.

Even without a comprehensive model, the empirical findings of this investigation support the proposition that professionalization is a gendered process: that occupations in the process of becoming female professions undergo unique changes that in time may differentiate them from male professions. The transformations occurring in the teaching occupation during professionalization included formation of male-dominated bureaucratic structures restricting autonomy, wage restructuring leading to greater gender differences in absolute wages while increasing wages overall, and the creation of a cultural representation of the female teacher. The evidence suggests that female professions may not be occupations in a state of arrested development, stalled on the road to full professionalization, as the category semiprofessions implies; rather, they may be in many respects qualitatively different from male professions, acquiring these differences during the process of professionalization.

The generality of this interpretation will remain unclear until the results of investigations on the influence of gender on professionalization of other occupations can be assessed. Furthermore, comparative data based on historical studies will enable sociologists to determine if the social construction of all female professions differs from that of male professions. Such findings would have important theoretical implications for the sociology of the professions because they would indicate that current conceptions of a profession and of the professionalization should be revised to consider gender as constitutive of the process.

References

Abbott, A. (1988). *The system of professions.* Chicago: The University of Chicago Press.

Abbott, E. (1910). *Women in industry: A study in American economic history.* New York: Appleton.

Acker, J. (1992). From sex roles to gendered institutions. *Contemporary Sociology, 21*(5), 565-569.

Apple, M. W. (1986). *Teachers and texts: A political economy of class and gender relations in education.* New York: Routledge and Kegan Paul.

Bancroft, E. (1793-1799). Diary. Boston: Massachusetts Historical Society.

Beecher, C. (1835). *Essay on the education of female teachers.* New York: Van Nostrand & Dwight.

Beecher, C. (1851). *True remedies for the wrongs of women.* Boston: Phillips, Sampson.

Bielby, W. T., & Baron, J. N. (1984). A woman's place is with other women: Sex segregation within firms. In B. F. Reskin (Ed.), *Sex segregation in the workplace: Trends, explanations, remedies* (pp. 27-55). Washington, DC: National Academy Press.

Bledstein, B. J. (1976). *The culture of professionalism.* New York: W. W. Norton.

Bowles, S., & Gintis, H. (1976). *Schooling in capitalist America: Educational reform and the contradictions of economic life.* New York: Basic Books.

Brammer, E. S. (1826). *Correspondence, 1818-1838.* Berkeley: Bancroft Library, University of California.

Carr-Saunders, A. M., & Wilson, P. A. (1933). *The professions.* Oxford: Oxford University Press.

Carter, S. B. (1986). Occupational segregation, teachers' wages and American economic growth. *Journal of Economic History, 46*(2), 373-383.

Connecticut Board of Education. 1837-1860. *Connecticut school reports.* Hartford: Author.

Crompton, R. (1987). Gender, status, and professionalism. *Sociology, 21*(3), 413-428.

Essex County Teachers' Association. (1830). Journal, 1830-1888. Salem, MA: James Duncan Phillips Library, Peabody and Essex Institute.

Forsyth, P. B., & Danisiewicz, T. J. (1985). Toward a theory of professionalization. *Work and Occupations, 12*(5), 59-76.

Freidson, E. (1986). *Professional powers: A study of the institutionalization of formal knowledge.* Chicago: University of Chicago Press.

Garrison, D. (1979). *Apostles of culture: The public librarian and American society, 1876-1920.* New York: Free Press.

Gitelman, H. M. (1967). The Waltham system and the coming of the Irish. *Labor History, 8,* 227-253.

Hall, S. R. (1829). *Lectures on schoolkeeping.* Unpublished manuscript, Boston.

Hearn, J. (1982). Notes on patriarchy, professionalization and the semi-professions. *Sociology, 16*(2), 184-202.

Jaffe, D. (1989). Gender inequality in the workplace autonomy and authority. *Social Science Quarterly, 70*(2), 375-390.

Johnson, T. J. (1972). *Professions and power.* London: Macmillan.

Kanter, R. (1976). The impact of hierarchical structures on the work behavior of women and men. *Social Problems, 23,* 415-430.

Katz, M. B. (1971). *Class, bureaucracy and schools: The illusion of educational change in America.* New York: Praeger.

Katz, M. B. (1987). *Reconstructing American education.* Cambridge, MA: Harvard University Press.

Larson, M. S. (1977). *The rise of professionalism.* Berkeley: University of California Press.

Litchfield, P. (1881-1882). Diary July 1 to March 23, 1775, Massachusetts Historical Society. *Proceedings of the Massachusetts Historical Society, 19,* 376-379.

Lutz, A. (1964). *Emma Willard: Pioneer educator of American women.* Boston: Beacon.

Lynn [MA] School Committee. (1855). *City of Lynn school report.* Lynn, MA: Author.

Magnum, U. L. (1928). *The American normal school: Its rise and development in Massachusetts.* Baltimore: Warweek & York.

Marini, M. M. (1989). Sex differences in earnings in the United States. *Annual Review of Sociology, 15,* 343-380.

Massachusetts Board of Education. (1839-1880). *Massachusetts school reports.* Boston: Author.

Massachusetts school reports. (1833-1834). Manuscripts, 1830-39. Boston: Massachusetts State Library, Special Collections.

Melosh, B. (1982). *The physicians' hand.* Philadelphia: Temple University Press.

Messerli, J. (1972). *Horace Mann: A biography.* New York: Knopf.

Milkman, R. (1987). *Gender at work: The dynamics of job segregation by sex during World War II.* Urbana: University of Illinois Press.

Mudge, M. (1854). Diary. Cambridge, MA: Schlesinger Library, Radcliffe College.

New Hampshire Board of Education. (1848-1867). *New Hampshire School Reports.* Concord: Author.

Oppenheimer, V. K. (1970). *The female labor force in the United States* (Population Monograph Series No. 5). Berkeley: University of California Press.

Preston, J. A. (1982). *Feminization of an occupation: Teaching becomes women's work in nineteenth-century New England.* Unpublished doctoral dissertation, Brandeis University.

Preston, J. A. (1989). Female aspiration and male ideology: Schoolteaching in nineteenth-century New England. In A. Angerman (Ed.), *Current issues in women's history* (pp. 171-182). London: Routledge.

Preston, J. A. (1993, December). Domestic ideology, school reformers, and female teachers: Teaching becomes women's work in nineteenth-century New England. *New England Quarterly,* pp. 531-561.

Reskin, B., & Roos, P. (1990). *Job queues and gender queues: Explaining women's inroads into male occupations.* Philadelphia: Temple University Press.

Rhode Island Board of Education. (1845–1860). *Rhode Island school reports.* Providence: Author.

Simpson, R. L., & Simpson, I. H. (1969). Women and bureaucracy in the semi-professions. In A. Etzioni (Ed.), *The semi-professions and their organization: Teachers, nurses, social workers* (pp. 196-265). New York: Free Press.

Sklar, K. K. (1973). *Catherine Beecher: A study in American domesticity.* New York: W. W. Norton.

Springfield Female Collegiate Institute. (1860-1861). Catalogue. Cambridge, MA: Special collections, Gutman Library, Harvard University.

Starr, P. (1982). The social transformation of medicine. New York: Basic Books.

Stevenson, M. H. (1988). Some economic approaches to the persistence of wage differences between men and women. In A. H. Stromberg & S. Harkness (Eds.), Women working: Theories and facts in perspective (pp. 87-100). Mountain View, CA: Mayfield.

Strober, M., & Tyack, D. (1980). Why do women teach and men manage? A report on research on schools. Signs: Journal of Women in Culture and Society, 5(3), 494-503.

Strober, M. H., & Landford, A. G. (1986). The feminization of public school teaching: Cross-sectional analysis, 1850-1880. Signs, 11(2), 212- 235.

Suzzallo, H. (1906). The rise of local school supervision in Massachusetts. New York: Columbia University Press.

Tarbox, I. N. (Ed.). (1886-1887). Diary of Thomas Robbins. Boston: Connecticut Historical Society.

Treiman, D., & Hartmann, H. (Eds.). (1981). Women, work, and wages: Equal pay for jobs of equal value. Washington, DC: National Academy of Sciences.

Wilensky, H. L. (1964). The professionalization of everyone? American Journal of Sociology, 70, 137-158.

Witz, A. (1990). Patriarchy and professions: The gendered politics of occupational closure. Sociology, 24(4), 675-690.

Witz, A. (1992). Professions and patriarchy. London: Routledge.

Woody, T. (1929). Women's education in the United States. New York: Octagon Press.

14

Assessing Gender at Work

Evidence and Issues

PAMELA STONE

After almost two decades of sustained research, the centrality of sex segregation in the creation and maintenance of gender inequality in the workplace has been well established. This is no small accomplishment, given the politically volatile nature of the subject and the sometimes fractious nature of the academic debate surrounding it. Segregation not only depresses the wages of women, it circumscribes their goals, aspirations, and options. As the chapters in this volume make clear, its effects are pervasive and insidious, playing themselves out in every aspect, and throughout the course, of women's work lives.

As a focus of inquiry, sex segregation has wrested center stage from earnings per se in recent years. This shift of focus has, not coincidentally, also shifted the terms of discourse—from a preoccupation among sociologists (at least in most empirical work) with challenging the insistently individual-level account of neoclassical economics to efforts to develop and test our own more sociological explanations, some of which seek to synthesize sociological and economic theories or to explicitly reconcile their apparent contradictions (e.g., Jacobs, 1989; Reskin & Roos, 1990). The fruits of these efforts—and the fruitfulness of these approaches—are demonstrated by the chapters in this volume.

Summary and Highlights

The link between segregation and the wage gap has been well-documented, with most estimates to date attributing about one quarter to one third of the gap to differences in jobs held by men and women. Tomaskovic-Devey (Chapter 2, this volume) challenges this estimate, showing that when properly specified, using features of jobs rather than occupations to characterize work, as much as 75% of the gap is due to segregation. Use of occupational measures, which entail more error than their job-level counterparts, not only results in underestimates of the impact of sex segregation, and hence of discrimination, it also results in overestimates of the influence of better-measured variables derived from human capital explanations, thereby giving them more credence than they deserve. Thus, in light of Tomaskovic-Devey's results, reliance on occupational estimates appears to overstate women's progress in the workplace on two fronts: the extent to which they have entered nontraditional jobs and the degree to which wage discrimination has been eroded.

Tomaskovic-Devey makes a useful distinction between the "dual processes of segregation": *allocative,* by which women are channelled into less desirable jobs, and *valuative,* by which women's jobs and the skills and responsibilities they entail are socially devalued. In Chapter 3 (this volume), Steinberg explores an important institutional mechanism of this devaluation in her analysis of a widely used system of job evaluation. Devaluation of women's jobs comes about as a result of two factors: (a) the system's managerial bias, which places a premium on fiscal and supervisory reponsibilities, and (b) the historical circumstances of its development in the postwar period and subsequent failure to keep up with changes in the nature and organization of work. Continued use of this system thus perpetuates the devaluation of women's work under the gender-neutral guise of rationalization by overlooking or minimizing the contribution of factors commonly found in female-dominated jobs. That the same evaluation plan or variants of it can still result in identifying significant underpayment of women's jobs in the context of comparable worth studies suggests that they are even more biased in implementation than design (e.g., Evans & Nelson, 1989).

In Chapter 4 (this volume), Jacobs and Steinberg extend their earlier work (1990) on the role of compensating differentials (whereby jobs offer a wage premium to offset dangerous or unpleasant working conditions) in explaining the earnings gap. Even considering curvilinear effects and extreme working conditions, this analysis leaves unchallenged their earlier conclusion that such differentials do not account for the gap. Although they find some evidence of a premium to attract workers to extremely undesirable jobs, the positive effect is small and more than offset by the penalty assessed due to sex. Thus, these results undermine even more conclusively a major explanation by neoclassical economics for the wage gap.

Some of women's most visible successes have occurred with their movement into the managerial ranks. As both Jacobs (Chapter 6) and Boyd, Mulvihill, and Myles (Chapter 7) report in this volume, the increasing representation of women in management accounts for one fourth of the decline in occupational segregation since 1970. But, given the slipperiness of the slope to the top—and the slipperiness of managerial titles—nagging questions remain as to the meaning of this trend. The question is raised "Is this progress real or illusory?" In Chapter 5 (this volume), Reskin and Ross offer a pessimistic assessment. Employing a broader definition of manager than that used by the U.S. Bureau of the Census, they find that despite women's increasing qualifications, the predictions of the meritocratic human capital and status attainment approaches do not prevail: Net of qualifications, women managers are lower in the chain of command, have limited decision-making powers, and tend to supervise other women. They attribute women's position in the "managerial ghetto" to efforts by male managers to maintain their own power, which they do via institutional mechanisms such as the creation of internal labor markets and via attitudinal methods such as stereotyping.

Boyd, Mulvihill, and Myles ask what are the implications for gender inequality of the structural transformation occurring as industrialized economies make the transition to postindustrialism. Features of the postindustrial economy would seem to favor the erosion of a sexual division of labor and the fostering of equality (for example, the sheer numbers of women in the labor force and the more egalitarian nature of increasingly prominent public-sector employment). The same line of reasoning is invoked in modernization theory to explain and predict changes in women's status in the earlier transition to industrialism.

Boyd, Mulvihill, and Myles concur with Reskin and Ross in finding that women are in managerial ghettos, concentrated in lower-skill, lower-pay sectors of the economy where they exercise less true power and authority. Thus, in the service sector of the economy, where women are concentrated, women managers supervise other women, resulting in a bigger sex gap in authority than in the industrial sector. Moreover, it is in the sectors most identified with postindustrialism—female-dominated service industries—that authority relations take the form of men supervising women, whereas in traditionally male-dominated industrial sectors, men supervise men. Boyd et al. find no evidence of an improvement in women's access to power and authority and conclude that postindustrialism carries over the gendered inequality of the industrial era. They suggest a law of "anti-matriarchy" to explain the particular configuration of authority relations that finds men rarely if ever subordinate to women.

Jacobs (Chapter 6) addresses the same question as Reskin and Ross and comes to a somewhat different conclusion, but this may be due to his more stringent definition of manager, as well as to his assessment of progress as changes in women's status over time relative to their initial starting point and relative to men. Thus he finds a narrowing of compensation differentials between male and female managers, although the gap is still larger for managers than for the labor force as a whole. He concludes that women's entry into management is real, and not the result of title inflation or reclassification. At the same time, his results concur with Reskin and Ross's in finding that although the titles may be real, male managers exercise far more decision-making authority than do their female counterparts, with no narrowing of this "authority gap over time." While Reskin and Ross conclude on a note of pessimism, Jacobs is optimistic, arguing that "strength in numbers" accounts for women's gains as managers and augurs well for their continued progress.

The next section of the book examines underlying career processes and trends in segregation. In Chapter 8, Bielby and Bielby's account of women's inroads into the (still) male-dominated world of television writing demonstrates that a model of continuous rather than cumulative disadvantage better explains the earnings gap in this occupation. In results similar to Jacobs's (1989) finding for women's careers generally, they characterize women's earnings attainment process as reflecting uniform as opposed to increasingly consequential disadvantage.

Their discussion of how this process of disadvantage is created and maintained by the particular features of the labor market of network television is especially insightful and compelling, for it makes clear that even this glamorous, high-stakes world is not immune to forces seen in the prosaic world of the large corporation or government bureaucracy. In fact, the very absence of structure and predictability in network television, coupled with the lack of objective, a priori measures of success and diffused authority, actually heighten the tendency of almost exclusively white male executives to play it safe by relying on gender stereotypes in assigning work. Thus women's inroads appear due in no small measure to the eclipse of "male" action/adventure dramas by the more "female" family situation comedies. This last fact highlights the vulnerability of women's gains to date, for if audience tastes change, so too may executives' preferences for the "women's point of view." Further contributing to the precariousness of women's status, the same labor market features that lead to reliance on sexist stereotyping also impede the straightforward application of equal employment remedies that could benefit women.

Structural features of the organization of work play such an important role in understanding women's status in television writing in part because the ephemeral nature of popular culture means the basis of evaluation and reward in this occupation is extraordinarily short-term and the operative question is: "What have you done lately?" Consequently, in this context, longer-term human capital investments, such as experience and seniority, central to the neoclassical view, are less important. Neoclassical explanations necessarily figure more prominently in Rosenfeld and Spenner's study of the work histories of individual women (Chapter 9, this volume). Addressing the paradox of the "aggregate stability [of occupational segregation] and individual mobility [throughout work careers]" (Jacobs, 1989, p. 3), they replicate Jacobs's findings and extend them by showing that the determinants and rate of movement across jobs of different sex types vary depending on the type of move being made. Consistent with neoclassical predictions, higher work commitment and greater job rewards appear to slow movement across all types of moves. However, contrary to the neoclassical approach, family considerations do not slow movement to "male" occupations nor speed moves to "female" ones.

Invoking Jacobs's (1989, p. 168) image of occupational mobility across gender-type boundaries as "revolving doors" powered by processes of access and attrition, Rosenfeld and Spenner conclude that "the doors spin at different speeds and send women in different directions depending on the type of move." Their finding that women tend to leave male-dominated jobs involuntarily implies, they suggest, that men may be actively hastening the attrition process.

The significance of women's considerable movement across occupations of different sex types has been questioned in light of the high degree of *job* segregation within integrated *occupations*. Baron (1990), for example, asks whether such mobility represents "little or no change in a person's actual line of work and rewards available" (p. 348). Rosenfeld and Spenner's analysis presents an equivocal answer to this question. On the one hand, moving to a male-dominated job is not statistically significantly associated with increased pay, although pay is higher in a move to a male-dominated job. In addition, their detailed examination of a small subset of work histories with at least one move from a predominately female to male job (or vice versa) reveals three patterns, only one of which can be considered a move to a male career line. On the other hand, despite objective evidence to the contrary, women who had moved to a male-dominated job perceived that doing so resulted in a "better job or promotion," implying greater levels of satisfaction in that job.

In Chapter 10 (this volume), Jacobs and Lim explore cross-national trends over a 20-year period to see whether the relatively recent decline in sex segregation in the United States has occurred elsewhere. Using conventional and size-standardized measures of segregation that control for differences in the size of occupations, Jacobs and Lim arrive at mixed results, although the size-standardized results are more consistent. On balance, most countries did experience decreased segregation, contrary to the predictions of Marxist and world-systems theory.

As we saw in Chapter 6, modernization theory was of limited utility in predicting trends in segregation in the shift to a postindustrial economy. In this application, the theory, although correct in predicting the direction of change, nonetheless failed to explain its causes. Declines in segregation, for example, were not associated with changes in fertility or women's education. Jacobs and Lim interpret the decline as modest evidence that the status of women is not deteriorating with the onset of industrialization. The skeptical reader may question this conclusion in light of the heterogeneity of jobs within occupations, more potentially problematic in economies as diverse as those studied. The authors acknowledge this problem; their analysis of trends at different levels of aggregation supports the notion, however, of what they term "parallel lines," that is, that such trends run in the same, not counter, direction.

Issues surrounding the differentiation of occupations by jobs—as well as by firms and industries—and the implications of this differentiation for women's status and progress in the workplace are addressed in Section 4, with case studies of sociologists, computer programmers, and teachers. Reskin and Roos (1990) have provided the most extensive documentation of pervasive gender stratification within recently integrating occupations. Their case studies reveal that women are ghettoized in lower-status and lower-paying specialties rather than broadly represented across the occupation's full spectrum. Moreover, they suggest that ghettoization may be a stage in a process of resegregation, whereby a formerly male-dominated occupation becomes predominantly female, redefined as to gender-type and devalued as a result of its feminization.

Using a queueing perspective developed in Reskin and Roos (1990), which emphasizes the interplay of employer and employee preferences (features of demand and supply, respectively) in creating gendered job and labor queues, Roos and Jones (Chapter 11, this volume) chronicle efforts by the discipline's founding fathers to keep women out of sociology. They attribute the growing presence of women in the discipline to several factors. Declines in fellowship and research funding prompted male flight as men sought better opportunities in business and professional schools. Women were attracted to the discipline by its attention to their concerns. Simultaneously, women already in the field successfully championed the admission of women, their efforts facilitated by equal employment laws. Roos and Jones focus primarily on access to training, specifically doctorate production, but they note several indications that women in sociology are ghettoized: Women are less likely to be employed in academic departments, they have lower rates of tenure and promotion in these positions, and they cluster in less prestigious subspecialties. The authors cite sociology's attention to feminist issues as a reason for women's increased entry, raising an important question as to whether their ghettoization in such specialties as gender and family results from women's preferences rather than structural discrimination or lack of access to more prestigious specialties.

In Chapter 12 (this volume), Wright and Jacobs study a set of feminizing occupations in computer programming. Like sociology, a relatively new line of work requiring considerable training and special expertise, computer programming differs from it in two notable respects: (a) it has, throughout its short history, enjoyed high rates of growth and, correspondingly, a tight labor market; and (b) it must continually adapt to rapid technological change. Under these conditions, and employing a multidimensional operationalization of ghettoization that focuses on relative progress over time (rather than on an absolute standard of integration as parity with men), Wright and Jacobs find no evidence of male flight or ghettoization, concluding that programming is moving toward true occupational integration. Certainly computer programming's profile is one that Reskin and Roos (1990) found to be most conducive to women's entry into nontraditional occupations. Although Donato's (1990) study of programmers in the Reskin and Roos volume was more pessimistic about women's status in this occupation, the very different methodology employed by Wright and Jacobs and their focus on relative progress over time probably account for their different conclusion. Although it is too early to predict whether feminization will ultimately lead to resegregation in sociology or computer programming, Preston's account (Chapter 13, this volume) of teachers offers an unequivocal example of resegregation. Similar to Roos and Jones's account of sociology, Preston makes clear that teaching was gendered from its inception. Through institutional mechanisms which undermined autonomy and controlled professionalization, male administrators effectively devalued the occupation, prompting men to leave it or, in a pattern characteristic of the female semiprofessions, ascend to supervisory positions within it. In addition, men ensured feminization by promulgating a cultural representation of teaching that emphasized skills and aptitudes stereotypically associated with the feminine ideal of the time. Women offered little well-organized resistance to these developments (not surprising in the context of the times), evincing their displeasure in the privacy of letters and diaries and in movement from school to school. Despite the unrelenting nature of male efforts to feminize teaching, its complete resegregation was a long, slow process, taking over 200 years.

Discussion

Theoretical Considerations

This collection displays the recent theoretical advances that have been made in explaining sex segregation and its consequences, especially in efforts to specify the meaning and mechanisms of structure. It also continues to challenge human capital theory and undermines it in some important respects (see, for example, chapters by Tomaskovic-Devey and Steinberg and Jacobs).

Jacobs's (1989) theory of social control and Reskin and Roos's (1990) theory of queues are the predominant perspectives in the volume. Jacobs (1989) posits that sex segregation "is maintained by a lifelong system of social control [which begins with sex-role socialization and] . . . is continually reinforced and recreated" (p. 48) by institutional mechanisms. Because these mechanisms of control are not all-powerful, and values and circumstances change throughout the life course, individual women can make nontraditional job choices while overall levels of segregation remain high.

Reskin and Roos (1990) develop a dual-queueing theory by which segregation results from the intersection of labor queues, which "order groups of workers in terms of their attractiveness to employers," and job queues, which "rank jobs in terms of their attractiveness to workers" (p. 29). With regard to job queues, men and women have similar preferences; however, for a variety of reasons largely rooted in stereotype and custom, employers prefer male workers over women, even though they can pay women less. Thus labor queues are effectively gender queues, and segregation is the result. Occupations change their sex type in response to forces which change the job rankings of workers for particular jobs or make it no longer possible for employers to maintain their preference for hiring men.

Although emphasizing different mechanisms of operation (Jacobs, for example, gives greater weight to the role of socialization in sex-typing women's job preferences), the two theories have in common their attention to both supply (workers) and demand (employers), their recognition of the gendered nature of control, and their accommodation of selected features of human capital theory. Both theories, however, dispute the neoclassical requirement of perfectly competitive markets and its model of lifetime decision making.

Social control and queueing theories represent enormous achievements in their breadth and synthesis. Despite the centrality of gender in both, however, these accounts explain how gender works rather than why gender is such a major force in the organization of work. Specifically, they assume rather than take as problematic that men are superior, women subordinate. Almost 20 years ago, Hartmann (1976) advanced a theory of patriarchy to explain segregation. Accumulating evidence, as exemplified in these chapters and elsewhere, suggests that she was right, and that it is patriarchy (or perhaps, as Boyd and coauthors provocatively suggest, "anti-matriarchy") that is the engine of sex segregation. Chapter after chapter in this volume offers examples of men's concerted and often conscious efforts to

1. prevent women's entry into an occupation (e.g., Roos and Jones, writing about sociology),
2. push out women who gain entry (e.g., Rosenfeld and Spenner's analysis of women's exits from male-dominated jobs),

3. flee from occupations where women have entered (e.g., Preston's study of the resegregation of teaching),

4. ghettoize them (Bielby and Bielby's account of TV writing),

5. devalue them (Steinberg), or

6. deprive them of authority (Reskin and Ross, Jacobs, and Boyd et al.'s studies of managers).

What one recognizes from this litany is that in the processes of segregation, men are always proactive, women reactive. Whether an occupation integrates or resegregates is fundamentally determined by men's responses, with women trailing in their wake. Male reactions—whether as employers or employees—mediate almost entirely other forces of change (technology, competitive pressures, etc.) in determining whether women will gain access to an occupation. Because the best theories evolve from the interplay of theory and evidence, my reading of the evidence suggests that sociological theories such as social control and queueing would be strengthened by more explicit attention to patriarchy or to the gendered process approach being developed by Acker (1988, 1989, 1990). Acker's work is, in fact, cited several times by authors in this volume, which gives me hope that the field is moving in the direction I advocate.

Feminist approaches also provide promising avenues for future research. One would hope that hypotheses derived from them will be tested with the same vigor (and rigor) that has been shown in testing explanations drawn from neoclassical economics and the so-called new structuralism in sociology.

The Future of Occupation

Amid a growing concern about whether the use of occupation obscures more than it illuminates in the study of segregation, Tomaskovic-Devey's research might be taken as sounding occupation's death knell. For practical reasons, of course, we will continue to use occupational characteristics such as those available from *The Dictionary of Occupational Titles* and census reports. There are other reasons, as well. Occupation represents an abstract conceptualization of a task in the larger division of labor and *job* its concrete manifestation in a firm or industry (Cain & Treiman, 1981). As such, occupation represents an ideal type, job a specific operationalization. This distinction, I would argue, can increase our understanding of segregation. For example, Tomaskovic-Devey (1993) describes two processes involved in segregation. The *status closure* process allocates women to less desirable jobs, and the *status composition* process attaches value to work such that jobs associated with women become devalued. Status closure processes can be seen as taking place at the level of job with the act of hiring. Status composition or valuative processes occur at the larger occupational level, reflecting norms about the status, prestige, and appropriate level of remuneration of a particular type of work. Similarly, Reskin and Roos's (1990) distinction between the institutional and attitudinal factors that perpetuate segregation can also be understood as reflecting a distinction between forces at work at the job and occupational levels, respectively. Institutional considerations such as internal labor markets come into play for jobs, whereas attitudinal forces such as stereotyping are established at the level of occupation.

With this distinction in mind, Preston's study of teachers can be seen as an illustration of the way in which male bureaucrats skillfully promoted the broad cultural representation of teaching as congruent with womanly virtues in order to encourage the *occupation's* feminization by attracting only women to teaching *jobs*. Steinberg's (Chapter 3, this volume) depiction of a widely used compensation system can be construed as exemplifying the application of *occupational* values to maintain a salary advantage for predominantly male *jobs*. Through their control of the ideal, men act as gatekeepers of the norms surrounding an occupation, such as its status and gender type. Through their control over jobs, they enforce adherence to these norms and, moreover, as the nature of work changes, are able to maintain their dominance in the jobs that best typify characteristics of the ideal. Thus men's possession of the defining power of occupation and their implementing power at the level of job together ensure segregation of occupations and jobs.

Another reason to continue to work at the occupational level is that notwithstanding Tomaskovic-Devey's results in this volume, his emphasis on differences between occupational- and job-based results tends to obscure their similarities. For example, on the critical question of the impact of sex composition on earnings (taken as the measure of discrimination), results based on jobs estimate this as accounting for 46% of the gender gap, whereas in occupational models the comparable figure is 33%. We expect the finer-grained analysis of jobs to reveal stronger effects, but what is important too is that the results are in the same direction, revealing the same basic trends.

Similarly, as Jacobs and Lim demonstrate in Chapter 10, at different levels of occupational aggregation, similar trends prevail. Their notion of "parallel lines" between trends at the job and occupational level is further supported by Tomaskovic-Devey's comparison of his findings with Bielby and Baron's (1984) earlier job-level analysis. He finds a drop in job segregation over the last 2 decades that mirrors quite closely the levels and rate of decrease of occupational segregation. This accumulating evidence of convergence between job and occupational trends gives us confidence that use of occupation will not fundamentally obscure the nature and direction of segregation trends. As Tomaskovic-Devey's work reminds us, however, we have to be aware of occupation's limitations in describing levels and magnitude. And, as Reskin and Roos (1990) illustrate in the context of segregation, the considerable diversity of jobs within occupations means women sometimes occupy an occupation's less desirable niches or enclaves. As yet, it appears that this phenomenon does not represent a serious countervailing trend that would preclude the continued use of occupation, but its existence sensitizes us to the need for continued caution in doing so in empirical work.

Progress—Illusory or Real?

The women's and civil rights movements advance an absolute standard of equality as their goal. With regard to segregation, this has resulted in policies to enhance and guarantee access, such as equal employment laws and affirmative action programs, as well as a variety of efforts to recruit women into nontraditional jobs. With regard to segregation's link to pay, it has resulted in pay equity policies such as comparable worth, the goal of which is to close the wage gap by paying women's jobs the same as men's jobs requiring similar skill, effort, and responsibility. More broadly framed in sociological terms, the goal is a meritocratic one, to overcome barriers to achievement based on gender.

The chapters in this volume illustrate, and grapple with, the difficulty of assessing progress toward this goal. At some level, we all know there *is* progress. Two women on the U.S. Supreme Court, for example, are not merely tokens, but emblematic of real change in women's roles and status in society. After decades unchanged, the wage gap at last began to show closure in the 1980s, narrowing from approximately 59% to 69% among all full-time workers, and even more among younger workers. However, assessing the extent and meaning of changes in segregation is more complicated. Several factors make it so.

One has to do with the unit and level of analysis. There has been long-standing recognition that the extent of segregation among jobs is much greater than among occupations (Bielby & Baron, 1984). The degree to which the use of occupation underestimates both the extent of segregation and its impact on wages is made clear by Tomaskovic-Devey, and the results are disheartening in their implications for women's gains.

Assessing progress is made difficult, too, by the use of different yard-sticks: one that adheres to the absolute standard of equality and another that measures progress in more relative terms, such as improvements over time. By relative measures, women do appear to be making progress in terms of their inroads into male-dominated occupations and the narrowing of the wage gap. However, there is one notable exception to this pattern: All the chapters in Section 2, including Jacobs's, generally more optimistic assessment, show that women managers exercise much less authority than men. The existence of this authority gap, along with the continuing existence of a high level of segregation and of a sizable wage gap, means that progress toward equality has far to go. Moreover, as several chapters in this volume demonstrate (for example, the case studies of television writers, sociologists, and teachers, as well as Steinberg's of compensation practices), even amid relative gains, processes governing access to jobs and their rewards remain highly—and seemingly unrelentingly—gendered.

A third factor complicating the assessment of progress is the long-term nature of the changes involved in the sex-typing of jobs. Does feminization measured over one period in time represent equal access and portend true integration, or does it augur the occupation's eventual resegregation? No one pretends to have a crystal ball, but some analysts see women's increasing numbers as a basis for optimism or as an explanation for women's progress to date (Roos & Jones, Wright & Jacobs, and Jacobs in this volume). However, judging the eventual outcome of feminization is tricky, because women's entry to an occupation affects men's exit. Research on school integration and residential segregation, often cited as processes analogous to occupational segregation, suggests the existence of a tipping point, past which the rate of white flight accelerates. If a similar phenomenon operates in occupational segregation, the tipping point can occur anywhere in the course of an occupation's feminization prior to complete resegregation. Because women's inroads into many occupations are fairly recent, it is too early in many cases to capture this process, but we need to be alert to it. The existence of a tipping point would suggest that women's strength in an occupation is not a straightforward linear function of their numbers, and it would cast doubt on an explanation that figures prominently in the literature on women and work since being proposed by Kanter (1977).

Finally, the use of different units of analysis and different measures of status outcomes, as well as the use of a variety of data sets and methods, makes it more difficult to discern clear-cut trends.

With these considerations in mind, what conclusions can be drawn from the evidence presented in this volume about the nature of women's progress? Despite some favorable overall trends, the majority of authors in this volume take the position that women's gains are, if not illusory, certainly compromised, falling far short of meeting policy goals of true integration and parity. Women *are* doing better, but too often they are not doing well enough when compared to men. Traditional gender/status hierarchies are maintained by strongly gendered processes, which appear to operate as effectively in the newly emerging postindustrial as the industrial economy. The picture emerges that women's entry into nontraditional jobs is linked to male flight and ghettoization, short tenure, high turnover, less autonomy and decision-making authority, and low pay. Although women enter male-dominated jobs over the course of their work careers, "revolving doors" spin them in and out, but not necessarily upward. More troubling, perhaps, many women do not move at all, and these women especially tend to be mired in traditional female-dominated jobs.

Interpretation of results is more art than science and vulnerable to the "half-full/half-empty" problem of perception; thus it should be noted that the chapters in this volume offer some offsetting evidence to the foregoing gloomy depiction. In Chapter 9, for example, Rosenfeld and Spenner show that high levels of attrition from male-dominated jobs are accompanied by high rates of entry to such jobs. Women keep coming back, asserting their presence. They do so, moreover, because male-dominated jobs are attractive to them, representing in the wording of the questionnaire a "better job or promotion." Even ghettoization in a male-dominated occupation may represent increased opportunity over remaining in a female-dominated one. The evidence on this is mixed, but a common way of gauging progress, looking at wage increases, may be especially unreliable given the myriad influences to which they are subject. Perhaps we need to focus, as well, on less tangible but no less real benefits such as enhanced self-esteem.

We can more charitably assess progress, too, by putting it in its larger context. In occupations to which women have recently gained access they are, of course, new entrants, handicapped by their lack of seniority, firm-specific tenure, and other aspects of experience—human capital that we know is relevant to earnings growth, promotion, and assumption of authority. Thus, by focusing on occupations in transition (understandably interesting), we nonetheless perhaps run the risk of exaggerating the "downside" prognosis for women in general, simply by virtue of focusing on recent entrants, any occupation's most vulnerable and disadvantaged group. In other words, characterizing it in its most extreme form, we mistake a cohort for a gender effect. Although I would not argue that there is no gender effect, my point is simply that the cohort effect is at its strongest in the occupations to which women have recently gained entry, which are the focus of many of the chapters in this volume.

Unfortunately, not even historical studies of feminized occupations can provide much guidance as to the extent of the cohort effect for occupations that are currently feminizing, because the circumstances on both the supply and demand sides of the equation are so different now from then. Women are working in much greater numbers, for longer periods of time across the life course, in a greater (although still limited) set of jobs than in the past. The American economy is in the midst of a truly epochal transformation, the contours and implications of which are still emerging, making it difficult, for example, to extrapolate the effect of technology from one historical period to the next. The answer is unfolding before our eyes, but for now we can still entertain the prospect that women may yet be able to enjoy access not only to male-dominated jobs but also to the full array of rewards they offer.

Computer programmers provide perhaps the most successful example of women's advancement in a nontraditional job, for their entry was accompanied neither by male flight nor ghettoization (Wright & Jacobs). Programming enjoys a set of circumstances that Reskin and Roos (1990), among others, have found to be among the most important in fostering integration: It is an emerging occupation without the baggage of historical convention as to its sex-typicality, it has very high rates of growth, and it is characterized by rapid technological change requiring high levels of education, training, and expertise. The experience of computer programmers suggests that successful integration may require an especially propitious confluence of job and labor market features. Judging from the studies in this volume and others, such a confluence appears relatively uncommon, but we need to carefully identify these facilitating conditions to ensure their continuation and wider emulation. What is it about this occupation that makes it successful? Is new technology gender-free? Does the entrepreneurial nature of the field make it gender blind? Does a severe shortage of highly specialized skills give workers the power of unique expertise? Ultimately, women's status in the labor market relative to men's depends on the answers to these questions and the mix of different factors at play. Too often, based on evidence to date, women's entry into male-dominated jobs has seemed a pyrrhic victory; the challenge ahead is to make it a real one.

References

Acker, J. (1988). Gender, class and the relations of distribution. *Signs, 13,* 473-497.

Acker, J. (1989). The problem with patriarchy. *Sociology, 23,* 235-240.

Acker, J. (1990). Hierarchies, jobs, bodies: A theory of gendered organization. *Gender and Society, 4,* 139-158.

Baron, J. (1990). Are the doors revolving or still locked shut? *Contemporary Sociology, 19,* 347-349.

Bielby, W., & Baron, J. (1984). A woman's place is with other women: Sex segregation within organizations. In B. Reskin (Ed.), *Sex segregation in the workplace: Trends, explanations, remedies* (pp. 27-55). Washington, DC: National Academy Press.

Cain, P., & Treiman, D. (1981). The *Dictionary of Occupational Titles* as a source of occupational data. *American Sociological Review, 46,* 253-278.

Donato, K. (1990). Programming for change? The growing demand for women systems analysts. In B. Reskin & P. Roos (Eds.), *Job queues, gender queues: Explaining women's inroads into male occupations* (pp. 167-182). Philadelphia: Temple University Press.

Evans, S., & Nelson, B. (1989). *Wage justice: Comparable worth and the paradox of technocratic reform.* Chicago: University of Chicago Press.

Hartmann, H. (1976). Capitalism, patriarchy, and job segregation by sex. *Signs, 1,* 137-170.

Jacobs, J. (1989). *Revolving doors: Sex segregation and women's careers.* Stanford, CA: Stanford University Press.

Jacobs, J., & Steinberg, R. (1990). Compensating differentials and the male-female wage gap: Evidence from the New York State Pay Equity Study. *Social Forces, 69,* 439-468.

Kanter, R. (1977). *Men and women of the corporation.* New York: Basic Books.

Reskin, B., & Roos, P. (1990). *Job queues, gender queues: Explaining women's inroads into male occupations.* Philadelphia: Temple University Press.

Index

Abbott, A., 17, 380, 382
Abbott, E., 301
Academic sociology. *See* Sociology, academic
Acker, J., 75, 76, 78, 85, 87, 88n, 89n, 96, 118, 156, 199, 382, 417
Addams, J., 302
Affirmative action, 154, 255, 299, 315-316, 322. *See also* Barriers to advancement; Comparable worth; Discrimination; Government regulation
African Americans, 6, 7, 15, 17, 28, 51n, 52n, 157, 163, 166, 167, 339, 349. *See also* Race and ethnicity
Afshar, H., 265
Age, 13, 14, 30, 34, 216, 217, 221-225, 229n, 255n, 349. *See also* Earnings; Career mobility; Cumulative disadvantage; Earnings; Human capital; Internal labor markets; Labor market experience
Allen, M., 1
Allison, P., 375n

Ambiguity, and workers' performance. *See* Performance
Ambition, 401. *See also* Career aspirations; Values
American Institute for Instruction, 394
American Sociological Association, 297, 302, 309, 315, 322, 325n, 326n, 327n
Anderson, A. B., 214, 219
Anthropology, gender inequality and, 3, 261
Anti-matriarchy, 200, 411. *See also* Authority; Barriers to advancement; Patriarchy
Armstrong, P., 200n
Arnold, C. L., 345
Asian Americans, 359. *See also* Race and ethnicity
Aspirations, career. *See* Career aspirations
Authority, 1, 2, 4, 11-12, 410, 415, 421
  access to, 128, 129, 135
  among teachers, 380, 403
  artificial reclassification, 147, 154
  budgets and spending, 137-139
  decision making, 131, 136, 145, 410-411

About the Contributors

Denise D. Bielby is Professor of Sociology at the University of California, Santa Barbara. Her research interests are in the areas of gender, work, and popular culture. Her current research examines the coproduction of meaning between viewers and producers of television series. Her forthcoming book with Lee Harrington is on the subculture of soap opera fans.

William T. Bielby is Professor of Sociology and Department Chair at the University of California, Santa Barbara. His research interests include organizations, popular culture, gender, and quantitative methods. His current research examines social networks and careers in the television industry.

Monica Boyd is the Mildred and Claude Pepper Distinguished Professor of Sociology and a Research Associate, Center for the Study of Population, Florida State University. She writes on topics such as the changing family, gender inequality, international migration, social stratification, and ethnic stratification. A past president of the Canadian Population Society and a previous member of the Canadian Advisory Council on the Status of Women (federal cabinet appointment), she is currently preparing a book on immigrant women.

Jerry A. Jacobs is Associate Professor and Chair of the Graduate Program in Sociology at the University of Pennsylvania. He has written extensively in the areas of gender and labor markets and is the author of *Revolving Doors: Sex Segregation and Women's Careers*. His current projects include a study of part-time employment in the United States and a 10-country study of women in public sector employment.

Katharine W. Jones is a doctoral candidate in sociology at Rutgers University. She received her bachelor's degree from Oxford University in philosophy, politics, and economics, and an M.A. in sociology and certificate in women's studies from Rutgers University. Her research interests include gender, race, and identity. She is currently working on a project examining national symbolism among British immigrants.

Suet T. Lim received her Ph.D. in demography at the University of Pennsylvania. Her papers include an investigation of African American marriage patterns in the United States and a study of the intersection of race and gender in employment patterns in Malaysia. Her research interests center on gender, race, and development, especially in Southeast Asia.

Mary Ann Mulvihill completed her M.A. degree in sociology at Carleton University, in Ottawa Canada. She currently works at Interpares in Ottawa.

John Myles is Professor of Sociology and Director, Pepper Institute on Aging and Public Policy, Florida State University. He is currently conducting research on the changing distribution of earnings, family incomes, and the structure of the economic life course. His most recent book is *Relations of Ruling: Class and Gender in Postindustrial Societies* (with Wallace Clement).

Jo Anne Preston is an Assistant Professor in Sociology at Brandeis University. She is currently completing a book on the feminization of school teaching. Her previous publications address the relationship of millgirl narratives to collective identity and labor activism, the conflict between female apprentices and merchant-tailors in the early industrial period, and the discrepancy between female teachers' self-conceptions and 19th-century gender ideology.

Barbara F. Reskin is Professor of Sociology at Ohio State University. She has authored four books related to women and men in the workplace, including *Women's Work, Men's Work* with Heidi Hartmann, *Job Queues, Gender Queues* with Patricia Roos, and *Women and Men at Work* with Irene Padavic. Themes in her research include sex differentiation; occupational segregation by sex, race, and ethnicity; and the effects of sex and race on workers' access to promotions, authority, and other job outcomes.

Patricia A. Roos is Professor and Chair of the Department of Sociology at Rutgers University. Her current research includes an ongoing interest in the feminization of typesetting/composition, work with Barbara Reskin on a quantitative analysis of the determinants of changing occupational sex composition using 1970-1990 census data, and work with Joan Manley on the feminization of human resources work.

Rachel A. Rosenfeld is the Lara G. Hoggard Professor of Sociology at the University of North Carolina at Chapel Hill and a Fellow of the Carolina Population Center there. Her recent research interests include work-family linkages in advanced industrialized societies, the life course of older undergraduates, and manifestations of the contemporary U.S. women's movement.

Catherine E. Ross is Professor of Sociology at the Ohio State University. She studies the effect of work and family on women's and men's sense of control and psychological well-being. With John Mirowsky, she wrote a book on this research, *The Social Causes of Psychological Distress.* She and Mirowsky are currently studying the links between aging; economic, employment, and family status; and the sense of control. Their recent article on this topic appeared in the *Journal of Health and Social Behavior.*

Kenneth I. Spenner is Professor of Sociology at Duke University. He also directs an interdisciplinary certificate program in Markets and Management Studies. His current research deals with the career dynamics of men and women, the effects of technology on the quality and quantity of work, and organizational survival and adaptation of Bulgarian state-owned enterprises during market reform.

Ronnie J. Steinberg is Associate Professor of Sociology at Temple University. She is author of *Wages and Hours: Labor and Reform in Twentieth Century America* and editor of *Equal Employment Policy for Women* and *Job Training for Women* (with Sharon Harlan). She edits a book series entitled *Women in the Political Economy*. Her current research involves the design of gender-neutral compensation systems and the politics by which feminist reforms are contained.

Pamela Stone (formerly Cain) is Associate Professor and Chair of the Department of Sociology, Hunter College of the City University of New York (CUNY). At CUNY, she also holds an appointment at the Graduate School and University Center. Her research interests lie in the areas of work and occupations and gender stratification. She is currently engaged in a study of pay equity.

Donald Tomaskovic-Devey is Professor of Sociology at North Carolina State University. He is the author of *Gender and Racial Inequality at Work: The Sources and Consequences of Job Segregation* and *Race*. In addition to studies of earnings inequality, he is exploring the role of race and class politics in local economic development and methodological issues in organizational sampling.

Rosemary Wright is a Ph.D. candidate at the University of Pennsylvania and Instructor of Sociology at Fairleigh Dickinson University. She previously worked as a computer professional, manager, and consultant. Her dissertation analyzes gender differences in computer careers in the 1980s using the NSF Survey of Natural and Social Scientists and Engineers.